The Quantum Theory of Atoms, Molecules, and Photons

Consulting Editor
P. Sykes, M.Sc., Ph.D.
Fellow of Christ's College
University of Cambridge

The Quantum Theory of Atoms, Molecules, and Photons

John Avery
Lecturer, Department of Chemistry, Imperial College of
Science and Technology, University of London

London · New York · St. Louis · San Francisco · Düsseldorf
Johannesburg · Kuala Lumpur · Mexico · Montreal · New Delhi
Panama · Rio de Janeiro · Singapore · Sydney · Toronto

Published by
McGRAW-HILL Book Company (UK) Limited
MAIDENHEAD · BERKSHIRE · ENGLAND

---

07 094178 5

PRINTED AND BOUND IN GREAT BRITAIN

To my parents

Preface

The quantum theory of atoms, molecules, and photons is a subject which lies halfway between physics and chemistry, and it can be approached from either side. It is intrinsically a mathematical subject. Some authors, writing for chemists, have tried to avoid the use of advanced mathematics. This book takes an alternative course and uses advanced mathematical techniques freely when they are needed, but it does not assume a prior knowledge of these techniques on the part of the reader. In other words, the book attempts to be mathematically self-contained. It includes a review of the necessary background in differential and integral calculus, calculus of variations, partial differential equations, tensor analysis, group theory, classical mechanics, relativity theory, and electrodynamics. I hope that the historical and biographical material which has been included in the review sections will make them interesting even to those readers who are already familiar with the scientific material.

Almost all of chapter 3 is devoted to a treatment of the properties of eigenfunctions of Hermitian operators, (i.e., to Hilbert space), since this branch of mathematics forms such a central part of the theory of atomic and molecular orbitals. The discussion of molecular orbital theory in chapter 5 includes a treatment of configuration interaction, as well as a review of some current semi-empirical approximations.

Since spectroscopy is such an important tool in the investigation of atomic and molecular structure, I have included a discussion of both classical electrodynamics and quantum electrodynamics. The Maxwell-Lorentz equations in vacuum are approached from the standpoint of special relativity, an approach which makes the symmetry and simplicity of the equations more apparent. Boson creation and annihilation operators are introduced in chapter 7 in connection with molecular vibrations. Together with Fermion creation and annihilation operators, they are used in chapter 8 to sketch an introduction to quantum electrodynamics. The Fermion creation and annihilation operators are also used in chapter 9 to discuss the Russel-Saunders coupling scheme, as well as seniority, spin-orbit coupling, and crystal field theory.

Preface

I certainly have enjoyed writing this book, and I hope that you will enjoy reading it. One of the things which made the writing so enjoyable was the advice and encouragement of a number of distinguished scientists. It is a great pleasure to thank them here for their help (although they should not be blamed for the shortcomings of this book). Among those to whom thanks are also due are Professor Albert Szent-Györgyi, Dr Z. Bay, Professor R. Mason, Dr J. Wood, Dr M. Gerlach, Mr R. S. Milner, Dr J. C. Packer, Dr A. E. Hansen, Dr J. Ladik, Mrs E. Ottonello, Mr S. Josephs, and Miss K. Baxter. I would also like to thank Professor N. Kemmer, FRS, Professor G. Wilkinson, FRS, and Professor C. J. Ballhausen for the hospitality of their laboratories. I am grateful to the Royal Society for a European Programme Fellowship spent at the University of Copenhagen, and to Kemisk Laboratorium IV of the H. C. Ørsted Institute for an additional year spent in Copenhagen. Last, but by no means least, I would like to thank Professor J. P. Dahl for contributing so generously his time and his mathematical insight.

John Avery

Contents

Contents

Contents

Contents

1. The development of mechanics

Newton's law of gravitation

1684 was an important year in the history of mechanics. In that year three men were gathered in a London public house discussing the motion of the planets. One of them was the brilliant but irritable Robert Hooke, author of *Micrographia*, and professor of geometry at Gresham College. Hooke maintained that each planet is attracted to the sun by a force which is inversely proportional to the radius of its orbit. Listening to him were Sir Christopher Wren and the astronomer Edmond Halley (after whom Halley's comet is named). Wren offered to present Hooke with a book costing 40 shillings if he could prove by mathematics the validity of his $1/r^2$ hypothesis. Hooke tried for two months but he was unable to win Wren's reward. At the end of this time Halley suggested a journey to the University of Cambridge to discuss the question with Isaac Newton (who was rumoured to know much more about these matters than he had revealed in his published papers). In August 1684, Halley finally confronted Newton and asked him what form the planetary orbits would take if the sun's attraction followed a $1/r^2$ law. Newton replied immediately that the orbits would be ellipses. 'How do you know?' asked Halley. 'Why' replied Newton, 'I have calculated it'. He had mislaid the calculations, but pressed by Halley, he reconstructed them. He also wrote and sent to Halley a small book on the principles of mechanics based on his Cambridge lectures.

With much tact and patience Halley persuaded Newton to develop his ideas into a book and paid the costs of publication. The result was Newton's *Principia*, one of the greatest unifying works in the history of science. The philosophical implications of the *Principia* caused a revolution in the outlook of the seventeenth and eighteenth centuries in much the same way that Darwin's *Origin of Species* has affected the outlook of the nineteenth and twentieth centuries. Newton's contemporary, Alexander Pope (1688–1744), wrote:

> Nature and nature's law lay hid in night,
> God said 'Let Newton be' and all was light.

1

This couplet in praise of Newton was so popular during the 'Age of Reason' that it was set to music and sung in the taverns. Why was Newton's work such a revelation that it created the philosophy of an age? He considered the motion of a set of point masses under the influence of their mutual gravitational interaction. Given a knowledge of the initial position and momentum of each particle, the whole evolution of the system can be determined by an integration of Newton's equations of motion; not only the future, but also the past. The nature of the universe seemed suddenly clear. It was like an enormous clock which had to run on in a predictable way once it was wound up. The prediction of all future events was possible in principle, although in practice one lacked both information and labour. Of course, at that time, only gravitational forces were understood, but Newton's contemporaries had no doubt that the other force-laws could be discovered. He himself correctly believed that chemical bonds between atoms would someday be understood in terms of electrical forces, and he expressed this belief in a note at the end of the second edition of his *Principia*. Newton's great work *Philosophiae Naturalis Principia Mathematica* (*Mathematical Principles of Natural Philosophy*) is divided into three sections. The first book sets down the general principles of mechanics together with the elements of differential and integral calculus. The second book applies these methods to the motion of systems of particles and to hydrodynamics. The third is entitled *The System of the World*. In it Newton sets out to derive the entire astronomical behaviour of the solar system from his three laws of mechanics and from the assumption of an inverse square law for gravitational attraction. He discusses not only the elliptical orbits and periods of the planets and their moons but also details such as the flattened non-spherical shape of the earth and the slow precession of its axis of rotation about a fixed axis in space.

The *Principia* was immediately recognized as the synthesis which unified the work of Newton's great predecessors: Copernicus, Kepler, Galileo, Descartes, Fermat, Huygens, and Hooke. To bring together such a vast number of phenomena and to explain them with so few assumptions was a magnificent and unprecedented achievement. Inspired by this brilliant success Newton's followers went all the way and saw the universe as an enormous self-solving set of differential equations (the phrase is due to the mathematician Airy). The generalization was a very bold one—it is doubtful whether the 'natural philosophers' of the seventeenth and eighteenth centuries realized how bold it was. It is one thing to talk about the mechanics of a falling apple and to predict correctly the motion of its centre of mass. It is quite another thing to try to unravel the inner workings of the apple and to understand its chemical and biological behaviour on the basis of a few general mathematical principles. Today, in the middle of the twentieth century, not only biology and chemistry but also physics and mathematics seem vastly more complicated than they did in the seventeenth century. We can see now how far we are from the ideal of deducing the entire range of natural phenomena from a few simple mathematical principles. Nevertheless, quantum chemistry is today a well-established discipline whose aim is to derive all of the chemical properties of matter from a handful of mathematical equations.

Analytic geometry and differential calculus

Let us return to the seventeenth century and follow the history of mechanics, until it joins with chemistry in the twentieth century to form quantum chemistry. Until the night of 10 November 1619, the two mathematical disciplines of geometry and algebra were quite separate. That autumn evening the troops of the Elector of Bavaria were celebrating the Feast of St Martin in the little village of Newberg in Bohemia. Among them was the young French philosopher, René Descartes, who had enlisted in the army of the Elector in order to get away from his rowdy friends in Paris. That night Descartes had a series of dreams which, as he said later, filled him with enthusiasm, converted him to a life of philosophy, and put him in possession of a wonderful key to unlock the secrets of nature. That key was the invention of algebraic geometry. In the hands of Fermat (1601–1665), Newton (1642–1727), and Leibniz (1646–1716) algebraic geometry developed into the differential and integral calculus. In order to understand how this development came about, let us consider an example: Let y be some algebraic function of x—for example we might consider the function

$$y = f(x) = x^2 \tag{1.1}$$

We can make a graph of the values of y which correspond to various values of x as shown in Fig. 1.1. Obviously the infinite variety of geometrical figures which can be generated in this way forms a very much richer field for investigation than the rather limited repertory of classical Greek geometry. One of the problems of classical geometry was the construction of tangents. Fermat gave the following general prescription for the algebraic determination of the slope of the tangent of a given curve $y = f(x)$ at a particular point x:

Compute

$$\Delta y \equiv f(x + \Delta x) - f(x) \tag{1.2}$$

divide by Δx and let Δx tend to zero. Then

$$\tan \theta = \lim_{\Delta x \to 0} \left(\frac{\Delta y}{\Delta x} \right) = \lim_{\Delta x \to 0} \left\{ \frac{f(x + \Delta x) - f(x)}{\Delta x} \right\} \tag{1.3}$$

The geometrical meaning of this process can be seen from Fig. 1.2.

3

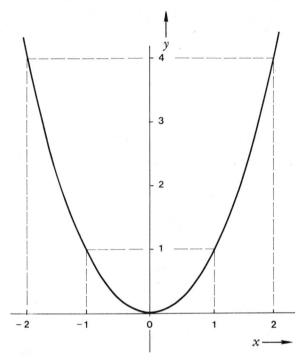

Figure 1.1 shows the curve, (a parabola), generated by the equation $y = x^2$.

As Δx approaches zero the angle θ' at the corner of the small right triangle with perpendicular sides Δy and Δx approaches the angle θ between the tangent line and the x-axis. In our example, where $f(x) = x^2$ we have

$$
\begin{aligned}
\tan \theta &= \lim_{\Delta x \to 0} \left\{ \frac{(x + \Delta x)^2 - x^2}{\Delta x} \right\} \\
&= \lim_{\Delta x \to 0} \left\{ \frac{x^2 + 2x(\Delta x) + (\Delta x)^2 - x^2}{\Delta x} \right\} \\
&= \lim_{\Delta x \to 0} \{2x + \Delta x\} = 2x
\end{aligned}
\tag{1.4}
$$

Newton, following Fermat and Isaac Barrow (the Cambridge mathematician who resigned his chair as Lucasian Professor so that Newton could succeed him) developed the differential calculus into a workable tool. He considered first the case where

$$
f(x) = x^n
\tag{1.5}
$$

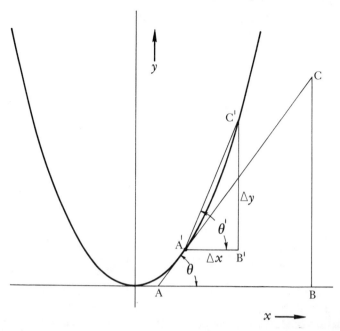

Figure 1.2 A line has been drawn tangent to the curve at the point A′. In the limit $\Delta x \to 0$, the small right triangle A′B′C′ becomes similar to the large right triangle ABC, so that $\theta' \to \theta$ and $\tan \theta \to \Delta y / \Delta x$.

Then

$$f(x + \Delta x) = (x + \Delta x)^n$$
$$= \underbrace{(x + \Delta x)(x + \Delta x) \ldots (x + \Delta x)}_{n \text{ factors}} \qquad (1.6)$$

Newton collected together the powers of Δx in his famous binomial expansion formula

$$(x + \Delta x)^n = x^n + nx^{n-1}\Delta x + \frac{n(n-1)}{2!} x^{n-2}(\Delta x)^2$$
$$+ \cdots + \frac{n(n-1)(n-2)\ldots 2}{(n-1)!} x(\Delta x)^{n-1} + (\Delta x)^n$$
$$(1.7)$$

where n is an integer. This formula can be proved by induction. If you assume that it is true for some value of n, then multiplication by $(x + \Delta x)$ shows that it is true for $n + 1$. But Eq. (1.7) is certainly true for $n = 1$ and

5

therefore holds for all positive integers. Applying Fermat's prescription for finding the slope of the curve

$$y = f(x) = x^n \qquad (1.8)$$

Newton obtained

$$\frac{dy}{dx} = \lim_{\Delta x \to 0} \left\{ \frac{f(x + \Delta x) - f(x)}{\Delta x} \right\}$$

$$= \lim_{\Delta x \to 0} \left\{ \frac{(x^n + nx^{n-1}\Delta x + \cdots) - x^n}{\Delta x} \right\}$$

$$= \lim_{\Delta x \to 0} \left\{ nx^{n-1} + \frac{n(n-1)}{2!} x^{n-2}\Delta x + \cdots \right\}$$

$$= nx^{n-1} \qquad (1.9)$$

The notation

$$\frac{dy}{dx} = \lim_{\Delta x \to 0} \left(\frac{\Delta y}{\Delta x} \right) = \left\{ \frac{f(x + \Delta x) - f(x)}{\Delta x} \right\} \qquad \mathbf{(1.10)}$$

is due to Leibniz who developed the calculus independently a few years after Newton (precipitating a bitter quarrel over priority). By continued application of Eq. (1.10) one obtains the relationships listed in Table 1.1. The quantities dy/dx which we call 'the first' derivative of y with respect to x were called 'fluxions' by Newton because he thought of them as 'flowing quantities'. It may be that he associated them in his mind with the water-clock which he made as a boy. If y represents the amount of water in the tank of the clock and t represents time, then $-dy/dt$ represents the rate at which the water is flowing out.

Integral calculus

The process of starting with some function $y(x)$ and finding dy/dx is called differentiation. Newton also introduced what he called 'inverse fluxions' (we call them integrals). *Integration is the reverse of differentiation. It is the process of starting with dy/dx and finding y,* that is, of starting with the derivative of a function and finding the function. If we have made a sufficiently extensive table like Table 1.1 then integration can be performed by finding dy/dx in the right-hand column and then looking in the left-hand column to see to what function y corresponds. For example, suppose that we know that

$$\frac{dy}{dx} = nx^{n-1} \qquad (1.11)$$

then we can look in Table 1.1 and see that

$$y = x^n + C \qquad (1.11a)$$

Table 1.1

$y = u + v + w + \cdots$ u, v, w = functions of x	$\dfrac{\mathrm{d}y}{\mathrm{d}x} = \dfrac{\mathrm{d}u}{\mathrm{d}x} + \dfrac{\mathrm{d}v}{\mathrm{d}x} + \dfrac{\mathrm{d}w}{\mathrm{d}x} + \cdots$
$y = au$ a independent of x	$\dfrac{\mathrm{d}y}{\mathrm{d}x} = a\dfrac{\mathrm{d}u}{\mathrm{d}x}$
$y = uv$	$\dfrac{\mathrm{d}y}{\mathrm{d}x} = u\dfrac{\mathrm{d}v}{\mathrm{d}x} + v\dfrac{\mathrm{d}u}{\mathrm{d}x}$
$y = u^n$	$\dfrac{\mathrm{d}y}{\mathrm{d}x} = nu^{n-1}\dfrac{\mathrm{d}u}{\mathrm{d}x}$
$y = f(u)$	$\dfrac{\mathrm{d}y}{\mathrm{d}x} = \dfrac{\mathrm{d}f}{\mathrm{d}u}\dfrac{\mathrm{d}u}{\mathrm{d}x}$
$y = \log_e x = \ln x$ $(\mathrm{e}^y = x)$ $\mathrm{e} \equiv \lim\limits_{\varepsilon \to 0}\left(1 + \dfrac{1}{\varepsilon}\right)^{1/\varepsilon}$ $\quad = 2 \cdot 71828 \ldots$	$\dfrac{\mathrm{d}y}{\mathrm{d}x} = \dfrac{1}{x}$
$y = \mathrm{e}^x$	$\dfrac{\mathrm{d}y}{\mathrm{d}x} = \mathrm{e}^x$
$y = \sin x$ $\equiv \dfrac{1}{2i}(\mathrm{e}^{ix} - \cdot \mathrm{e}^{-ix})$ $i = \sqrt{-1}$	$\dfrac{\mathrm{d}y}{\mathrm{d}x} = \cos x$ $\equiv \tfrac{1}{2}(\mathrm{e}^{ix} + \mathrm{e}^{-ix})$
$y = \sinh x$ $\equiv \tfrac{1}{2}(\mathrm{e}^x - \mathrm{e}^{-x})$	$\dfrac{\mathrm{d}y}{\mathrm{d}x} = \cosh x$ $\equiv \tfrac{1}{2}(\mathrm{e}^x + \mathrm{e}^{-x})$
$y = \cosh x$	$\dfrac{\mathrm{d}y}{\mathrm{d}x} = \sinh x$
$y = \sin^{-1} x$ $(\sin y = x)$	$\dfrac{\mathrm{d}y}{\mathrm{d}x} = \dfrac{1}{\sqrt{(1 - x^2)}}$
$y = \cos^{-1} x$	$\dfrac{\mathrm{d}y}{\mathrm{d}x} = \dfrac{-1}{\sqrt{(1 - x^2)}}$

Table 1.1 *(continued)*

$y = \tan^{-1} x$	$\dfrac{dy}{dx} = \dfrac{1}{1 + x^2}$
$y = \cot^{-1} x$	$\dfrac{dy}{dx} = \dfrac{-1}{1 + x^2}$
$y = \sinh^{-1} x$	$\dfrac{dy}{dx} = \dfrac{1}{\sqrt{(1 + x^2)}}$
$y = \tanh^{-1} x$	$\dfrac{dy}{dx} = \dfrac{1}{1 - x^2}$

where C is an arbitrary constant, called the 'constant of integration'. In this way one can construct a table of integrals such as Table 1.2.

The symbol for integration is an old-fashioned S standing for *summa*, the latin equivalent of 'sum'. One writes

$$y = \int dy = \int \frac{dy}{dx} dx \qquad (1.12)$$

For example, the relationship (1.11)–(1.12) is written

$$x^n + C = \int nx^{n-1} dx \qquad (1.13)$$

If dy/dx is plotted as a function of x then the increment $\Delta y = (dy/dx)\Delta x$ can be thought of as the area of a narrow strip of width Δx and height dy/dx underneath the curve, as illustrated in Fig. 1.3. If x_1 and x_2 are two points on the x-axis then $y(x_2) - y(x_1)$ is approximately equal to the sum of the increments Δy shown in Fig. 1.3. Each of the increments Δy corresponds to the area of one of the small strips shown in the right-hand side of Fig. 1.3, so that in the limit where the width of the strips tends to zero and their number tends to infinity, $y(x_2) - y(x_1)$ corresponds to the area under the curve dy/dx between the vertical lines at x_1 and x_2. Thus the trapezoidal area covered by strips in Fig. 1.3 is given by

$$y(x_2) - y(x_1) = \int_{x_1}^{x_2} \frac{dy}{dx} dx = \int_{x_1}^{x_2} 2x \, dx$$

$$= x_2^2 - x_1^2 = (x_2 - x_1)\left(\frac{2x_1 + 2x_2}{2}\right) \qquad (1.14)$$

This is just the answer which is given by elementary geometry. The area of a trapezoid is equal to the base multiplied by the height at the centre.

Table 1.2

$$\int a \, dx = ax + C$$

where a and C are constants

$$\int x^n \, dx = \frac{x^{n+1}}{n+1} + C$$

$$\int \left(\frac{du}{dx} + \frac{dv}{dx} + \frac{dw}{dx} + \cdots \right) dx = u + v + w + \cdots + C$$

where u, v, w, etc., are functions of x

$$\int \left(u \frac{dv}{dx} + v \frac{du}{dx} \right) dx = uv + C$$

$$\int \left(\frac{v \dfrac{du}{dx} - u \dfrac{dv}{dx}}{v^2} \right) dx = \frac{u}{v} + C$$

$$\int u^n \frac{du}{dx} \, dx = \frac{u^{n+1}}{n+1} + C$$

$$\int \frac{dx}{x} = \ln x + C$$

$$\int e^x \, dx = e^x + C$$

$$\int \cos x \, dx = \sin x + C$$

$$\int \sin x \, dx = -\cos x + C$$

$$\int \sinh x \, dx = \cosh x + C$$

$$\int \cosh x \, dx = \sinh x + C$$

$$\int \frac{dx}{\sqrt{(1 - x^2)}} = \begin{cases} \sin^{-1} x + C \\ \cos^{-1} x + C \end{cases}$$

$$\int \frac{dx}{1 + x^2} = \begin{cases} \tan^{-1} x + C \\ -\cot^{-1} x + C \end{cases}$$

Table 1.2 *(continued)*

$$\int \frac{dx}{\sqrt{(1 + x^2)}} = \sinh^{-1} x + C$$

$$\int \frac{dx}{1 - x^2} = \begin{cases} \tanh^{-1} x + C \\ \coth^{-1} x + C \end{cases}$$

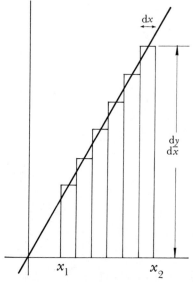

Figure 1.3 shows the slope of the parabola $y = x^2$ plotted as a function of x. The slope is found by differentiation and turns out to be $dy/dx = 2x$. The area under the line $dy/dx = 2x$ is approximated by the sum of a large number of rectangular strips, each with area $(dy/dx)dx = dy$.

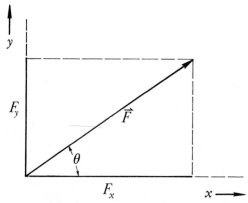

Figure 1.4 shows a vector $\vec{F}$ resolved into its components along the x- and y-axes: $F_x = F \sin \theta$ and $F_y = F \cos \theta$.

Problem (1.1) Use Tables 1.1 and 1.2 to show that the area of a circle is equal to πr^2. Also show that the volume of a sphere is given by $\frac{4}{3}\pi r^3$.

Newton's law of motion

Newton applied his calculus of 'flowing quantities' to the mechanics of point masses. If the position of a point-mass is given by the values of three coordinates x, y, and z and if the components of the force acting on the particle in the x, y, and z directions are given respectively by F_x, F_y, and F_z, then Newton's equations of motion state that

$$F_x = m \frac{d^2x}{dt^2}$$

$$F_y = m \frac{d^2y}{dt^2}$$

$$F_z = m \frac{d^2z}{dt^2} \tag{1.15}$$

In Eq. (1.15), m is the mass of the particle and d^2x/dt^2, the 'second derivative of x with respect to t' is just the rate of change of the first derivative.

$$\frac{d^2x}{dt^2} \equiv \frac{d}{dt}\left(\frac{dx}{dt}\right) \tag{1.16}$$

dx/dt represents the velocity of the particle and d^2x/dt^2 its acceleration. In vector notation, Eq. (1.15) can be written

$$\vec{F} = m \frac{d^2\vec{x}}{dt^2} \tag{1.17}$$

i.e., *force equals mass times acceleration.* To say that force and acceleration are vector quantities is just to say that they have a direction as well as a magnitude. The components of a vector are its projections onto the directions of the coordinate axes as shown in Fig. 1.4. To say that two vectors are equal implies that the components of one vector are equal respectively to the components of the other. Thus Eq. (1.17) is a shorthand statement which is identical in meaning to Eq. (1.15). As an example of Newton's equations of motion, consider a mass m dropped from a height z_0. The gravitational force is proportional to the mass m and at the earth's surface it has a magnitude such that it produces a constant acceleration of 32 feet per second per second.

$$F_z = -mg, \quad g = 32 \text{ ft/sec}^2 \tag{1.18}$$

Then

$$m \frac{d^2 z}{dt^2} = -mg \qquad (1.19)$$

$$\frac{dz}{dt} = \int dt \frac{d^2 z}{dt^2} = \int dt(-g) = -gt \qquad (1.20)$$

$$z = \int dt \frac{dz}{dt} = \int dt(-gt) = z_0 - \tfrac{1}{2}gt^2 \qquad (1.21)$$

Equation (1.21) means, for example, that neglecting air resistance, an apple dropped from the height of 16 feet will strike the ground in one second. Dropped from 64 feet it will take 2 seconds, and so on. The constants of integration in the two integrations Eq. (1.20) and Eq. (1.21) are determined by the initial conditions. There is no initial velocity, but the initial height z_0 must appear as a constant of integration in order for z to have the right value at $t = 0$. If the mass is thrown horizontally instead of being dropped, then there can be an initial velocity v_0 in the x direction. Since the gravitational force acts downwards, there is no component of force in the horizontal direction

$$F_x = m \frac{d^2 x}{dt^2} = 0 \qquad (1.22)$$

$$\frac{dx}{dt} = \int dt \frac{d^2 x}{dt^2} = \int dt(0) = v_0 = \text{constant} \qquad (1.23)$$

$$x = \int dt \frac{dx}{dt} = \int dt\, v_0 = v_0 t \qquad (1.24)$$

Then the trajectory of the body is given by eliminating time from Eq. (1.21) and Eq. (1.24)

$$z - z_0 = -\tfrac{1}{2}g \left(\frac{x}{v_0} \right)^2 \qquad (1.25)$$

Thus the trajectory is a parabola, as shown in Fig. 1.5.

It is interesting to think of the moon as a projectile thrown to the side with a certain velocity v_0 and at the same time, falling towards the earth. Figure 1.6 shows the orbit of the moon (assumed circular) drawn together with the parabolic trajectory of Fig. 1.5 in such a way that near the top of the parabola, where x is very small, the two curves coincide. By comparing the equation of the parabola Eq. (1.25)

$$z - z_0 = z - R = \frac{g}{2} \left(\frac{x}{v_0} \right)^2 \qquad (1.26)$$

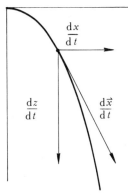

Figure 1.5 shows the trajectory of a particle moving under the influence of gravity with a constant horizontal velocity $dx/dt = v_0$. Because of the influence of gravity, the vertical component of its velocity increases steadily with time: $dz/dt = -gt$. Integrating these equations of motion we obtain the parabolic trajectory, $z = -\frac{1}{2}g(x/v_0)^2$.

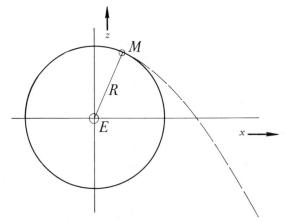

Figure 1.6 shows an enlarged view of the parabola $z - R = -\frac{1}{2}g(x/v_0)^2$ as a dotted line. For small values of x, the parabola coincides with the circle $x^2 + y^2 = R^2$ if $R = v_0^2/g$. In this figure, M represents the moon and E represents the earth.

with the approximate equation of the circle, valid for small x,

$$z - R = \sqrt{R^2 - x^2} - R \cong R - \frac{1}{2}\frac{x^2}{R} - R = -\frac{1}{2}\frac{x^2}{R} \quad (1.27)$$

we can make the identification

$$\frac{g}{v_0^2} = \frac{1}{R} \quad (1.28)$$

13

The velocity v_0 can be calculated because we know that the moon takes 28 days or $2\cdot42 \times 10^6$ seconds to travel a distance $2\pi R$ where R, the radius of the lunar orbit, is approximately 240 000 miles or $1\cdot27 \times 10^9$ feet. From this we can calculate that

$$v_0 = \frac{2\pi R}{\tau} = 3320 \text{ ft/sec} \tag{1.29}$$

and

$$g = \frac{v_0^2}{R} = 0\cdot0086 \text{ ft/sec}^2 \tag{1.30}$$

If we compare the acceleration, Eq. (1.30), with the gravitational accelera-tion at the earth's surface, Eq. (1.18), we see that their ratio is the same as the square of the ratio between the radius of the earth and the radius of the lunar orbit,

$$\frac{0\cdot0086}{32} \cong \left(\frac{4000}{240\ 000}\right)^2 \tag{1.31}$$

Newton made this calculation during the years 1665 and 1666 when an outbreak of plague forced Cambridge University to close. During this time he returned to his family's home at Woolsthorpe Manor in Lincoln-shire. Cared for by his mother, the twenty-three year old philosopher devoted himself to intense solitary thought on physical and mathematical problems. The initial ideas which he later developed in the *Principia* came during those years. Writing later about this period in his life Newton says 'I invented the method of series and fluxions in 1665 and improved them in 1666'. Newton's famous experiments in optics also date from this period or soon afterwards, since he writes '. . . in the beginning of the year 1666 (at which time I applied myself to the grinding of optic glasses of other figures than spherical) I procured a triangular prism to try there-with the celebrated phenomena of colours'. Also it seems probable that during the time at Woolsthorpe, Newton had already formulated his law of motion, Eq. (1.17), and guessed at an inverse square law of gravitational attraction, since he writes 'I thereby compared the force requisite to keep the Moon in her orb with the force of gravity at the Earth's surface and found them to answer pretty nearly', and 'All this was in the plague years of 1665 and 1666, for in those days I was in the prime of my age for invention, and minded mathematics and philosophy more than at any time since'. However, Newton did not publish most of his discoveries until much later. The delay may have been partly due to his inability to show that if every particle of matter in the universe attracts every other with a force directly proportional to the product of their masses and inversely proportional to the square of their separation, then a spherical body like the earth attracts bodies outside itself just as though all its mass were concentrated in its centre. He finally was able to demonstrate this theorem by means of the integral calculus which he had invented. Part of Newton's reluctance to publish may also have been due to the savage manner in which his first published paper on optics was attacked by various critics among whom was a Belgian named Linus. Newton wrote 'I see I have made myself a slave to philosophy, but if I get free of Mr Linus's business I will resolutely bid adieu to it eternally, excepting what I do for my private satisfaction or leave to come out after me; for I see that either a man must be resolved to put out nothing new, or become a slave to defend it'. Newton's reluctance to publish may also have been connected with his introverted and secretive personality. He may have wished to exploit as fully as possible the powerful secret tool which he had constructed before making it public property. At any rate, he showed his work on the calculus only to a few of his close associates, and did not publish it for almost thirty years.

Problem (1.2) A golf ball is struck from the tee at an angle of 45° with the horizon, and it just barely clears the top of a tree 64 feet high. Show that, neglecting air resistance, it will travel 256 feet.

Leibniz and the Bernoulli family

Meanwhile, on the Continent, Gottfried Wilhelm Leibniz (1646–1716) had developed the calculus independently. Leibniz was a man of universal and spectacular talent. He was a lawyer, diplomat, historian, philosopher, and mathematician to whose credit also belong the doctrine of balance of power, an attempt to unify the Catholic and Protestant Churches, the founding of the Academies of Science of Berlin and St Petersburg, the invention of combinatorial analysis and the theory that 'this is the best of all possible worlds'. Leibniz learned his mathematics from Christian Huygens whom he met during his travels as an emissary of the Elector of Mainz. During the period between the death of Descartes and the publication of Newton's *Principia*, Huygens was the most famous natural philosopher (i.e., scientist) in Europe. Since he was himself a man with a very wide range of interests and accomplishments Huygens found the versatile Leibniz congenial and gladly agreed to give him lessons. Leibniz continued to send Huygens letters about his mathematical research and to receive encouragement from him, until the end of the older man's life.

Among the followers of Leibniz was an extraordinary family of mathematicians called Bernoulli. They were descended from a wealthy merchant family of Basle, Switzerland. The head of the family, Nicolas Bernoulli the Elder, tried to force his three sons, James (1654–1705), Nicolas II (1662–1716), and John (1667–1748) to follow him in carrying on the family business. But the eldest son, James, had taught himself Leibnizian calculus and instead became professor of mathematics at the University of Basle. His motto was 'Against my father's will, I study the stars'— 'Invicto patre sidera verso'. Nicolas II and John soon caught their brother's enthusiasm and learned the calculus from him. John became the professor of mathematics at Groningen and Nicolas II joined the faculty of the newly formed Academy of St Petersburg. John had three sons who also became mathematicians. In fact the family of Nicolas Bernoulli the Elder produced a total of nine famous mathematicians in three generations. John Bernoulli had three sons, Nicolas III (1695–1726), Daniel (1700–1782), and John II (1710–1790) all of whom made notable contributions to mathematics and physics. Daniel Bernoulli's brilliance made him stand out even among the other members of his gifted family. He became professor of mathematics at the Academy of Sciences in St Petersburg when he was twenty-five. After eight Russian winters, however, he returned to his native Basle. Since the chair in mathematics was at that time already occupied by his father he was given a vacant chair first in anatomy, then in botany, and finally in physics. In spite of the variety of his titles, however Daniel's main work was in applied mathematics and he has been called the father of mathematical physics. One of the good friends of Daniel Bernoulli and his brothers was a young man named Léonard Euler (1707–1783). He came to their house once a week to take private lessons from their father, John Bernoulli. Euler was destined to become the most prolific mathematician in history and the Bernoullis were quick to recognize his great ability. They persuaded Euler's father not to force him into a theological career but instead to allow him to go with Nicolas III and Daniel to work at the Academy in St Petersburg. Euler remained there for most of his life. In those days (under Empress Anna Ivanovna) Russia was going through a period of savage political repression and it was dangerous to say very much. Instead, Euler married the daughter of a French painter and settled down to a life of quiet work producing a large family and an unparalleled output of papers. In the eighteenth century it was customary for the French Academy of Sciences to propose a mathematical topic each year and to award a prize for the best paper dealing with the problem. Léonard Euler and Daniel Bernoulli each won the Paris prize more than ten times and they share the distinction of being the only men to do so. John Bernoulli is said once to have thrown his son out of the house for winning the Paris prize in a year when he himself had competed for it.

Point masses joined by weightless springs

The Bernoullis and Euler did more than anyone else to develop the Leibnizian form of calculus into a workable tool and to spread it throughout Europe. They applied it to a great variety of problems from the shape of ships sails to the kinetic theory of gases. An example of the sort of problem which they considered, is that of a vibrating string. Daniel Bernoulli first developed a set of difference equations by considering the string to be made up of a set of point masses elastically joined together, as shown in Fig. 1.7.

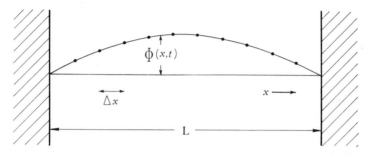

Figure 1.7 shows a vibrating string approximated by point masses elastically joined together. The string's displacement Φ from its equilibrium position is a function of the coordinate x and the time t. The string is fixed at its endpoints, so that $\Phi(x = 0, t) = 0$ and $\Phi(x = L, t) = 0$.

According to Newton's laws of motion, the acceleration of the jth point mass is proportional to the net force applied to it

$$F(j) = m \frac{\partial^2 \Phi(j)}{\partial t^2} \tag{1.32}$$

For small displacements and neglecting gravitation this restoring force will be perpendicular to the string and will result from the slight difference in the direction of the tension force pulling the point mass to the right, and the opposing tension force pulling it to the left as shown in Fig. 1.8.

If the magnitude of the tension in the string is T, the vertical component of the restoring force will be given approximately by

$$F(j) = T \left\{ \frac{\Phi(j) - \Phi(j - 1)}{\Delta x} + \frac{\Phi(j) - \Phi(j + 1)}{\Delta x} \right\} \tag{1.33}$$

as shown in the force diagram, Fig. 1.9. The horizontal components of the force cancel one another.

17

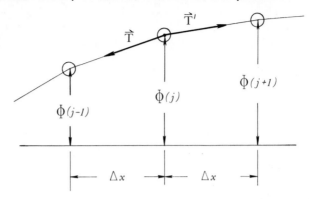

Figure 1.8 shows the forces $\vec{T}$ and $\vec{T}'$ acting on the jth point mass. The two forces are equal in magnitude, but, (because of the curvature of the string), they are not quite opposite in direction. Thus they yield a resultant force which tends to restore the jth point mass to its equilibrium position.

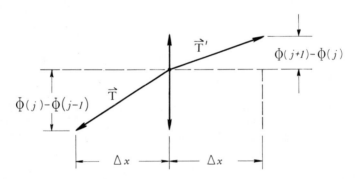

Figure 1.9 shows in more detail the forces acting on the jth point mass. If $\Phi(j) - \Phi(j-1)$ is small compared with Δx, then the vertical component of $\vec{T}$ is given approximately by $T\{\Phi(j) - \Phi(j-1)\}/\Delta x$ while the vertical component of $\vec{T}'$ is given approximately by $T\{\Phi(j) - \Phi(j+1)\}/\Delta x$. The resulting force is given by Eq. (1.33).

The equation of motion of a uniform vibrating string; partial differentiation

If we introduce the coordinate

$$x = j\Delta x \tag{1.34}$$

to denote the horizontal position of the jth mass on the string and let both Δx and m become infinitesimally small in such a way that the mass per unit length, μ, remains constant

$$\frac{m}{\Delta x} \equiv \mu = \text{constant} \tag{1.35}$$

18

then the set of equations (1.32) and (1.33) for all values of j can be written in the form:

$$\frac{m}{\Delta x} \frac{\partial^2 \Phi}{\partial t^2} = \mu \frac{\partial^2 \Phi}{\partial t^2}$$

$$= T \lim_{\Delta x \to 0} \left\{ \frac{\Phi(x - \Delta x) - 2\Phi(x) + \Phi(x + \Delta x)}{(\Delta x)^2} \right\}$$

$$\equiv T \frac{\partial^2 \Phi}{\partial x^2} \tag{1.36}$$

or

$$\frac{\partial^2 \Phi}{\partial x^2} - \frac{1}{c^2} \frac{\partial^2 \Phi}{\partial t^2} = 0 \tag{1.37}$$

where

$$c \equiv \sqrt{\frac{T}{\mu}} \tag{1.38}$$

Equation (1.37) must hold for all values of x as well as for all values of t. Since the smoothed-out displacement $\Phi(x, t)$ is *a function of two variables*, we have introduced a special notation for the derivatives. Thus

$$\frac{\partial \Phi}{\partial x} \equiv \lim_{\Delta x \to 0} \left\{ \frac{\Phi(x + \Delta x) - \Phi(x)}{\Delta x} \right\} \tag{1.39}$$

'*The partial derivative of Φ with respect to x*' means that in the evaluation of the derivative, t is to be treated as a constant. *Similarly, in taking the partial derivative of Φ with respect to time*

$$\frac{\partial \Phi}{\partial t} \equiv \lim_{\Delta t \to 0} \left\{ \frac{\Phi(t + \Delta t) - \Phi(t)}{\Delta t} \right\} \tag{1.40}$$

x is held constant. In Eq. (1.36) we have used the relationship

$$\frac{\partial^2 \Phi}{\partial x^2} \equiv \lim_{\Delta x \to 0} \left\{ \frac{\left.\dfrac{\partial \Phi}{\partial x}\right]_{x + \Delta x} - \left.\dfrac{\partial \Phi}{\partial x}\right]_x}{\Delta x} \right\}$$

$$= \lim_{\Delta x \to 0} \left[\left\{ \frac{\Phi(x + 2\Delta x) - \Phi(x + \Delta x)}{(\Delta x)^2} \right\} - \left\{ \frac{\Phi(x + \Delta x) - \Phi(x)}{(\Delta x)^2} \right\} \right]$$

$$= \lim_{\Delta x \to 0} \left\{ \frac{\Phi(x) - 2\Phi(x + \Delta x) + \Phi(x + 2\Delta x)}{(\Delta x)^2} \right\} \tag{1.41}$$

19

Since Δx is infinitesimally small, there is no difference between the last expression in Eq. (1.41) and the corresponding term in Eq. (1.36). (Incidentally, it can be seen from Figs 1.7, 1.8, and 1.9 that the second derivative of a function is a measure of the curvature of its graph.)

Daniel Bernoulli's superposition principle

In 1727, John Bernoulli in Basle corresponding with his son Daniel in St Petersburg solved the problem of the vibrating string approximated by point masses, Eqs. (1.32) and (1.33). Then Daniel boldly passed over to the continuum and wrote down the partial differential equation, Eq. (1.37), the 'wave equation'. He showed that the time-dependence of the displacement, $\Phi(x, t)$, could be separated out by writing

$$\Phi(x, t) = \phi(x) \cos(\omega t + \theta) \tag{1.42}$$

Then, since

$$\frac{\partial^2}{\partial t^2} \cos(\omega t + \theta) = -\omega^2 \cos(\omega t + \theta) \tag{1.43}$$

as shown in Table 1.1, the space-dependent part of the wave function obeys the equation

$$\frac{\partial^2 \phi(x)}{\partial x^2} + \left(\frac{\omega}{c}\right)^2 \phi(x) = 0 \tag{1.44}$$

It can be seen (again from Table 1.1) that Eq. (1.44) is satisfied by the function

$$\phi(x) = \sin(kx) \tag{1.45}$$

where $k \equiv \pm\omega/c$. Since the string is fixed at its end points, $x = 0$ and $x = L$, *a valid solution also must obey the 'boundary conditions'*

$$\phi(0) = \phi(L) = 0 \tag{1.46}$$

The boundary conditions impose a restriction on the allowed values of k. If we require that

$$\phi(L) = \sin(kL) = 0 \tag{1.47}$$

then we must have

$$k = \frac{n\pi}{L}, \quad n = 1, 2, 3, \ldots \tag{1.48}$$

For each integral value of n we get a solution of the wave equation, Eq. (1.37):

$$\Phi_n(x, t) = \sin\left(\frac{n\pi x}{L}\right) \cos\left(\omega t + \theta\right) \qquad (1.49)$$

Daniel Bernoulli asserted that if *two or more of the solutions, Eq. (1.49), are added together in no matter what proportion, then the resulting function will still be a solution of the wave equation.* This is his famous 'superposition principle'. It is easy to see that it is true. Suppose that the function $\Psi(x, t)$ is a superposition of the solutions multiplied by a set of arbitrary constant coefficients a_n

$$\Psi(x, t) = a_1\Phi_1 + a_2\Phi_2 + \cdots$$
$$= \sum_{n=1}^{\infty} a_n\Phi_n \qquad (1.50)$$

Then if we apply the operator $\partial^2/\partial x^2 - 1/c^2(\partial^2/\partial t^2)$ to Ψ we will have

$$\left(\frac{\partial^2}{\partial x^2} - \frac{1}{c^2}\frac{\partial^2}{\partial t^2}\right)\Psi = \left(\frac{\partial^2}{\partial x^2} - \frac{1}{c^2}\frac{\partial^2}{\partial t^2}\right)\sum_n a_n\Phi_n$$
$$= \sum_n a_n\left(\frac{\partial^2}{\partial x^2} - \frac{1}{c^2}\frac{\partial^2}{\partial t^2}\right)\Phi_n \qquad (1.51)$$

Since Φ_n is a solution of the wave equation we have

$$\left(\frac{\partial^2}{\partial x^2} - \frac{1}{c^2}\frac{\partial^2}{\partial t^2}\right)\Phi_n = 0 \qquad (1.52)$$

and therefore, from (1.51) and (1.52)

$$\left(\frac{\partial^2}{\partial x^2} - \frac{1}{c^2}\frac{\partial^2}{\partial t^2}\right)\Psi = 0 \qquad (1.53)$$

no matter what arbitrary values are chosen for the constants a_n. Now suppose that initially, at the time $t = 0$, the displacement of the string from its initial position is represented by some function $f(x)$. If $\Psi(x, t)$ is to represent the actual motion of the string, then the constants a_n have to be chosen in such a way that they will satisfy the initial condition

$$f(x) = \Psi(x, 0)$$
$$= \sum_n a_n\Phi_n(x, 0)$$
$$= \sum_n a_n \sin\left(\frac{n\pi x}{L}\right) \qquad (1.54)$$

For example, suppose that the initial displacement of the string is

$$f(x) = \alpha \sin\left(\frac{\pi x}{L}\right) + \beta \sin\left(\frac{2\pi x}{L}\right) \tag{1.55}$$

Then

$$a_1 = \alpha, \qquad a_2 = \beta, \qquad a_3 = 0, \qquad a_4 = 0, \ldots \tag{1.56}$$

and the time-dependent displacement is

$$\Psi(x, t) = \alpha \sin\left(\frac{\pi x}{L}\right)\cos\left(\frac{\pi}{L}ct\right) + \beta \sin\left(\frac{2\pi}{L}x\right)\cos\left(\frac{2\pi}{L}ct\right) \tag{1.57}$$

This was Daniel Bernoulli's solution to the problem of the vibrating string.

The argument between Euler and Bernoulli

Meanwhile Léonard Euler and a French mathematician named d'Alembert had discovered that the wave equation (Eq. (1.37)), could be satisfied by any well-behaved function of the variable $x + ct$ or of $x - ct$.

$$\Psi(x, t) = f(x + ct) + g(x - ct) \tag{1.58}$$

For example, suppose that

$$f(x + ct) = (x + ct)^2 \tag{1.59}$$

Then from Table 1.1

$$\frac{\partial^2 f}{\partial x^2} = \frac{\partial}{\partial x}\{2(x + ct)\} = 2 \tag{1.60}$$

and

$$\frac{1}{c^2}\frac{\partial^2 f}{\partial t^2} = \frac{1}{c^2}\frac{\partial}{\partial t}\{2c(x + ct)\} = 2 \tag{1.61}$$

so that

$$\left(\frac{\partial^2}{\partial x^2} - \frac{1}{c^2}\frac{\partial^2}{\partial t^2}\right)f = 0 \tag{1.62}$$

The boundary conditions, of course, impose some restrictions on f and g: the left-travelling wave f and the right-travelling wave g must cancel each other to give zero at the end-points. But apart from this restriction

22

the functions can be completely arbitrary. This result started a long scientific controversy. If the solution of Daniel Bernoulli was as general as that of Euler and d'Alembert, then it must follow that *an arbitrary function can be represented as a superposition of sine functions*. In fact if Daniel Bernoulli had really found the complete solution this must be true because from (1.54)

$$f(x) = \sum_n a_n \sin\left(\frac{n\pi x}{L}\right) \tag{1.63}$$

The initial displacement of the string, $f(x)$, can be a completely arbitrary function, *except that it must be single-valued and continuous and obey the boundary conditions*.

Fourier analysis

Euler refused to believe that an arbitrary function can be represented by such a series, and the controversy was still raging when Jean-Baptiste Fourier (1768–1830) came onto the scene. Fourier, the orphaned son of a tailor, grew up to become professor of mathematics at Napoleon's École Normale and a friend of the emperor. He accompanied Napoleon on his expedition to conquer Egypt and to bring to the Egyptians 'the benefits of European civilization'. When the Egyptians proved less than grateful and began to cut the throats of the French troops, Napoleon hurried back to France leaving Fourier to set up the Egyptian Institute. Later as Prefect of the district of France around Grenoble, Fourier found that the citizens resented the archeological work that he had done in Egypt. The dates which he had estimated for the ancient monuments were earlier than the date of creation calculated from the Book of Genesis. Fourier overcame this hostility by pointing out to the citizens of Grenoble that his great-uncle was a saint, the Blessed Pierre Fourier, founder of a religious order. He went on to become an excellent and enlightened administrator draining the swamps and eliminating malaria from his district. It was while he was in Grenoble that Fourier composed his monumental *Mémoire sur la Chaleur*, a treatise on heat conduction in which he expounds the mathematical method now known as 'fourier analysis'. This method is based on the fact that

$$\frac{2}{L}\int_0^L \sin\left(\frac{n\pi x}{L}\right) \sin\left(\frac{m\pi x}{L}\right) dx = \begin{cases} 0 & \text{if } m \neq n \\ 1 & \text{if } m = n \end{cases} \tag{1.64}$$

where m and n are integers. (It is an interesting exercise to verify Eq. (1.64) using the relations of Tables 1.1 and 1.2.) Equation (1.64) gives us a method

23

for evaluating the coefficients a_n which appear in Eq. (1.63). If we multiply both sides of Eq. (1.63) by $\sin(m\pi x/L)$ and integrate we obtain

$$\int_0^L dx \sin\left(\frac{m\pi x}{L}\right) f(x)$$

$$= \sum_{n=1}^\infty a_n \int_0^L dx \sin\left(\frac{m\pi x}{L}\right) \sin\left(\frac{n\pi x}{L}\right)$$

$$= \frac{L}{2} a_m \tag{1.65}$$

so that if we wish to expand a function $f(x)$ as a series of sine functions, valid in the interval $0 < x < L$

$$f(x) = \sum_{n=1}^\infty a_n \sin\left(\frac{n\pi x}{L}\right) \tag{1.66}$$

then

$$a_n = \frac{2}{L} \int_0^L dx' \sin\left(\frac{n\pi x'}{L}\right) f(x') \tag{1.67}$$

A series of this type is called a fourier series. For example, suppose that we would like to expand the function $f(x)$ shown in Fig. 1.10 as a fourier series

$$f(x) = \begin{cases} 1 & 0 < x < \dfrac{L}{2} \\ 0 & \dfrac{L}{2} < x < L \end{cases}$$

$$= \sum_{n=1}^\infty a_n \sin\left(\frac{n\pi x}{L}\right) \tag{1.68}$$

Then the coefficients in the series (1.68) are given by

$$a_n = \frac{2}{L} \int_0^L dx' \sin\left(\frac{n\pi x'}{L}\right) f(x')$$

$$= \frac{2}{L} \int_0^{L/2} dx' \sin\left(\frac{n\pi x'}{L}\right)$$

$$= \frac{2}{L} \frac{L}{n\pi} \left[-\cos\left(\frac{n\pi x'}{2}\right) \right]_0^L$$

$$= \frac{2}{n\pi} \left\{ 1 - \cos\left(\frac{n\pi}{2}\right) \right\} \tag{1.69}$$

Since all of the terms $a_n \sin(n\pi x/L)$ in a fourier sine series repeat themselves with the period L, and since they all are equal to zero at the end-

24

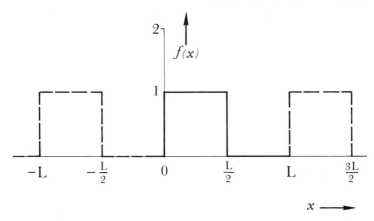

Figure 1.10 shows the function $F(x)$ which is defined as being equal to 1 in the range $0 < x < L/2$ and 0 in the range $L/2 < x < L$. The Fourier series for this function is $F(x) = \sum_{n=1}^{\infty} (2/n\pi) (1 - \cos n\pi/2) \sin n\pi x/L$. You can test your 'hi-fi' system by seeing whether it will pass a square wave of this kind without distortion. If the high frequencies are not passed, the corners of the output wave will not be sharp.

points $x = 0$ and $x = L$, the function $f(x)$ represented by the series must have the same properties: it must have the periodicity

$$f(x + L) = f(x) \tag{1.70}$$

and it must vanish at the end points

$$f(0) = f(L) = 0 \tag{1.71}$$

If a fourier series is used to represent a function which does not obey these boundary conditions, then the series will be valid only in the range $0 < x < L$. Fourier analysis is an enormously powerful mathematical tool. In fact (as we shall see), a generalized form of fourier analysis is one of the cornerstones of quantum chemistry. Perhaps future generations will decide that Jean-Baptiste Fourier was as great a saint as his uncle Pierre. However, when he submitted his memoir on heat conduction to the Paris Academy of Sciences it was severely criticized and failed to win the annual prize of the Academy. The jury consisted of three of the most eminent mathematicians of the time, Joseph-Louis Lagrange (1736–1813), Pierre-Simon Laplace (1749–1827), and Adrien-Marie Legendre (1752–1833). They objected that although Fourier's method worked extremely well in practice, it was unsatisfactory as a mathematical theory because Fourier had not really overcome Euler's objection. He had not demonstrated that an *arbitrary* function of x which obeys the boundary conditions can be

25

expanded as an infinite series of sine functions. This property is called the 'completeness' of the set of functions,

$$\phi_n = \sin\left(\frac{n\pi x}{L}\right), \quad n = 1, 2, 3, \ldots \tag{1.72}$$

The set ϕ_n is complete in the sense that no other functions are needed to represent an arbitrary function obeying the same boundary conditions. The proof of the completeness property is somewhat difficult and was not carried out until much later. However, Fourier disregarded the criticisms of the Paris Academy and published his book without any changes. Both parties were right. Fourier was right in believing that the set of sine functions was complete, and Lagrange, Laplace, and Legendre were right in pointing out that he had not proved it.

Problem (1.3) Use the relation

$$\int x \sin(Ax)\, dx = \frac{1}{A^2} \sin(Ax) - \frac{x}{A} \cos(Ax)$$

together with Eqs. (1.66)–(1.67) to establish the identity

$$x = \sum_{n=1}^{\infty} \frac{(-1)^{n+1} 2L}{n\pi} \sin\left(\frac{n\pi x}{L}\right), \quad 0 < x \le L$$

Variational calculus; the Euler–Lagrange equations

Now that Lagrange has entered the story it may be the right time to describe some of his contributions. Together with Euler and the Bernoullis he is chiefly responsible for the development of the calculus of variations and its application to mechanics. In a typical problem of the calculus of variations one considers an integral of the form

$$S = \int L\left(x^1, x^2, \ldots, x^N, \frac{dx^1}{dt}, \frac{dx^2}{dt}, \ldots, \frac{dx^N}{dt}\right) dt = \text{extremum} \tag{1.73}$$

L is some function of the coordinates $x^1, \ldots, x^N$ and their t-derivatives

$$\frac{dx^1}{dt}, \frac{dx^2}{dt}, \ldots, \frac{dx^N}{dt}$$

The problem is to find the coordinates as functions of t which will give a minimum or maximum value to the integral S. For example the principle of Pierre Fermat (1601–1665) states that *in geometrical optics, the actual path of a ray of light is the one which takes the least time.* The infinitesimal time dt required for the light signal to move an infinitesimal distance dl along its path is given by

$$c \, dt = n(\bar{x}) \, dl \tag{1.74}$$

where $n(x)$ is the index of refraction. By the Pythagorean Theorem we have

$$dl = \sqrt{dx^2 + dy^2 + dz^2} = \sqrt{d\bar{x} \cdot d\bar{x}}$$

$$= \sqrt{\frac{d\bar{x}}{dl} \cdot \frac{d\bar{x}}{dl}} \, dl = \frac{d\bar{x}}{dl} \cdot \frac{d\bar{x}}{dl} \, dl \tag{1.75}$$

(In Eq. (1.75) we have used a dot to denote the 'scalar product' of two vectors. If the three components of the vector $\vec{A}$ are A_1, A_2, and A_3 and those of $\vec{B}$ are B_1, B_2, and B_3, then the scalar product of $\vec{A}$ and $\vec{B}$ is defined as $A_1 B_1 + A_2 B_2 + A_3 B_3$ and it is written $\vec{A} \cdot \vec{B}$.) From Eqs. (1.74) and (1.75) it follows that *we can write Fermat's principle in the form*

$$S = \int dt$$

$$= \int L\left(x, y, z, \frac{dx}{dl}, \frac{dy}{dl}, \frac{dz}{dl}\right) dl = \text{minimum} \tag{1.76}$$

where

$$L = n(\bar{x}) \frac{d\bar{x}}{dl} \cdot \frac{d\bar{x}}{dl} \tag{1.77}$$

A similar principle was discovered by the great Irish mathematician Sir William Rowan Hamilton (1805–1865). In 1835 he showed that *for a system of particles whose state in Newtonian mechanics is specified at a given time t by the N coordinates $x^1, \ldots, x^N$ and the N velocities $dx^1/dt, \ldots, dx^N/dt$ the integral*

$$S = \int L \, dt = \int (T - V) \, dt \tag{1.78}$$

is an extremum where T is the kinetic energy of the system

$$T = \frac{1}{2} \sum_i m_i \frac{d\bar{x}_i}{dt} \cdot \frac{d\bar{x}_i}{dt} \tag{1.79}$$

and $V(x_1, x_2, \ldots)$ is the potential energy. The potential energy V is related to the force by

$$F_i \equiv -\frac{\partial V}{\partial x^i} \tag{1.80}$$

F_i, the ith component of the force vector is the partial derivative of the potential V with respect to x^i. Euler and Lagrange showed that *if the coordinates obey the differential equations*

$$\frac{d}{dt}\frac{\partial L}{\partial\left(\dfrac{dx^\mu}{dt}\right)} - \frac{\partial L}{\partial x^\mu} = 0, \quad \mu = 1, 2, 3, \ldots, N \qquad (1.81)$$

then integral $S = \int L \, dt$ *will be an extremum, and vice versa.* The simultaneous differential equations (1.81) are called the Euler–Lagrange equations. Let us try to show that they follow from Eq. (1.73). Suppose that we have found the true path x^μ for which $S = \int L \, dt$ is an extremum. Now consider what happens to S when we wander very slightly away from the true path. The situation is analogous to calculating the change of a function as we move slightly away from one of its maxima or minima. If we are at the top of a mountain or at the bottom of a valley, then taking a very slight step in any direction will not change our altitude, since at that point the ground is level. In the same way if we alter the path by an amount δx^μ the resulting alteration in $\int L \, dt$ will be zero

$$\delta \int L \, dt = \int \delta L \, dt = 0 \qquad (1.82)$$

The variation of the Lagrangian function L resulting directly from the variation of the coordinates, or indirectly through the consequent variation of the velocities is

$$\delta L = \sum_{\mu=1}^{N} \left\{ \frac{\partial L}{\partial x^\mu} \delta x^\mu + \frac{\partial L}{\partial\left(\dfrac{dx^\mu}{dt}\right)} \frac{d}{dt}(\delta x^\mu) \right\} \qquad (1.83)$$

Using the relationship

$$\int_a^b u \, dv = [uv]_a^b - \int_a^b v \, du \qquad (1.84)$$

from Table 1.2 we can write

$$\int_a^b \sum_{\mu=1}^{N} \frac{\partial L}{\partial\left(\dfrac{dx^\mu}{dt}\right)} \frac{d}{dt}(\delta x^\mu) \, dt$$

$$= \left[\sum_{\mu=1}^{N} \frac{\partial L}{\partial\left(\dfrac{dx^\mu}{dt}\right)} \delta x^\mu \right]_a^b$$

$$- \int_a^b \sum_{\mu=1}^{N} \frac{d}{dt} \frac{\partial L}{\partial\left(\dfrac{dx^\mu}{dt}\right)} \delta x^\mu \, dt \qquad (1.85)$$

Since the slightly altered path must still reach the end points a and b, the variation from the true path, δx^μ, must vanish at those points and therefore

$$\left[\sum_{\mu=1}^{N} \frac{\partial L}{\partial \left(\dfrac{dx^\mu}{dt} \right)} \delta x^\mu \right]_a^b = 0 \tag{1.86}$$

Using Eqs. (1.83), (1.85), and (1.86) we can write

$$\int_a^b \delta L \, dt = \int_a^b \sum_{\mu=1}^{N} \left\{ -\frac{d}{dt} \frac{\partial L}{\partial \left(\dfrac{dx^\mu}{dt} \right)} + \frac{\partial L}{\partial x^\mu} \right\} \delta x^\mu \, dt = 0 \tag{1.87}$$

To ensure that the integral (1.87) will vanish for an arbitrary slight variation of path, δx^μ, it is necessary that

$$\frac{d}{dt} \frac{\partial L}{\partial \left(\dfrac{dx^\mu}{dt} \right)} - \frac{\partial L}{\partial x^\mu} = 0, \quad \mu = 1, 2, \ldots, N \tag{1.88}$$

Therefore the Euler–Lagrange equations (1.81) are a consequence of Eq. (1.73). According to Hamilton's principle, the Lagrangian function for a single point mass m moving in the potential $V(x)$ is given by

$$L = \frac{1}{2} m \frac{d\bar{x}}{dt} \cdot \frac{d\bar{x}}{dt} - V(\bar{x}) \tag{1.89}$$

The Euler–Lagrange equations corresponding to the Lagrangian (1.89) are

$$m \frac{d^2 x}{dt^2} = -\frac{\partial V}{\partial x} = F_x$$

$$m \frac{d^2 y}{dt^2} = -\frac{\partial V}{\partial y} = F_y \tag{1.90}$$

$$m \frac{d^2 z}{dt^2} = -\frac{\partial V}{\partial z} = F_z$$

These are just Newton's equations of motion.

Problem (1.4)   Show that Fermat's principle (Eqs. (1.76)–(1.77)), leads to Snell's law,

$$n_1 \sin \theta_1 = n_2 \sin \theta_2$$

when it is applied to refraction at a plane boundary between two media of refractive indices n_1 and n_2.

The Lagrangian of a point mass expressed in spherical polar coordinates

The advantage of the Lagrangian formulation of classical mechanics is that it allows us to introduce generalized coordinates which are often more convenient than the original cartesian coordinates of the system. For example, if we think of a particle moving in a spherically symmetric potential $V(r)$, then it is convenient to write the Lagrangian in terms of the spherical polar coordinates r, θ, and φ, shown in Fig. 1.11. r can be

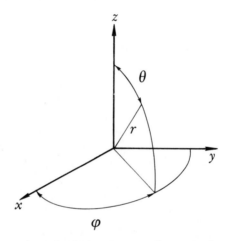

Figure 1.11 shows the spherical polar coordinates r, θ, and φ, which are related to the cartesian coordinates x, y, and z, by Eq. (1.91). If we think of r as the radius of a globe, then θ corresponds to latitude, while φ corresponds to longitude.

thought of as the radius of a sphere centred on the origin. θ represents the degrees of latitude on the sphere, and φ the degrees of longitude. The spherical polar coordinates r, θ, and φ are related to the cartesian coordinates x, y, and z by

$$x = r \sin \theta \cos \varphi$$
$$y = r \sin \theta \sin \varphi \qquad (1.91)$$
$$z = r \cos \theta$$

In cartesian coordinates the element of length dl is given by the Pythagorean rule

$$dl^2 = dx^2 + dy^2 + dz^2 \qquad (1.92)$$

It is easy to show from the relationship (1.91) that in terms of spherical polar coordinates the element of length is

$$dl^2 = dr^2 + r^2 \, d\theta^2 + r^2 \sin^2\theta \, d\varphi^2 \qquad (1.93)$$

This allows us to write L in terms of r, θ, and φ

$$
\begin{aligned}
L &= \frac{1}{2} m \left\{ \left(\frac{dx}{dt}\right)^2 + \left(\frac{dy}{dt}\right)^2 + \left(\frac{dz}{dt}\right)^2 \right\} - V \\
&= \frac{1}{2} m \left(\frac{dl}{dt}\right)^2 - V \\
&= \frac{1}{2} m \left\{ \left(\frac{dr}{dt}\right)^2 + r^2 \left(\frac{d\theta}{dt}\right)^2 + r^2 \sin^2\theta \left(\frac{d\varphi}{dt}\right)^2 \right\} - V(r) \quad (1.94)
\end{aligned}
$$

The Euler–Lagrange equations (1.88) which follow from (1.94) are

$$\frac{d}{dt} \left\{ \frac{\partial L}{\partial \left(\frac{dr}{dt}\right)} \right\} = \frac{\partial L}{\partial r} = m \frac{d^2 r}{dt^2} = -\frac{\partial V}{\partial r} \qquad (1.95)$$

$$\frac{d}{dt} \left\{ \frac{\partial L}{\partial \left(\frac{d\theta}{dt}\right)} \right\} = \frac{\partial L}{\partial \theta} = \frac{d}{dt} \left(mr^2 \frac{d\theta}{dt} \right) = 0 \qquad (1.96)$$

$$\frac{d}{dt} \left\{ \frac{\partial L}{\partial \left(\frac{d\varphi}{dt}\right)} \right\} = \frac{\partial L}{\partial \varphi} = \frac{d}{dt} \left(mr^2 \sin^2\theta \frac{d\varphi}{dt} \right) = 0 \qquad (1.97)$$

Equation (1.96), for example gives us immediately one of Kepler's three laws

$$r^2 \frac{d\theta}{dt} = \text{constant} \qquad (1.98)$$

that is, 'A line from the sun to one of the planets sweeps out equal areas during equal intervals of time'. The quantity $mr^2(d\theta/dt)$ is called 'angular momentum' and it is, according to (1.98), a constant of the motion. One says that for a particle moving in a spherically symmetric potential 'angular momentum is conserved'. It is a general rule that if the Lagrangian of a mechanical system is independent of some generalized coordinate, i.e., if

$$\frac{\partial L}{\partial x^\mu} = 0 \qquad (1.99)$$

then an associated dynamical variable is conserved

$$\frac{d}{dt}\left\{\frac{\partial L}{\partial\left(\dfrac{dx^{\mu}}{dt}\right)}\right\} = \frac{\partial L}{\partial x^{\mu}} = 0 \tag{1.100}$$

and

$$p_{\mu} \equiv \frac{\partial L}{\partial\left(\dfrac{dx^{\mu}}{dt}\right)} = \text{constant} \tag{1.101}$$

The quantity p_{μ}, defined as the partial derivative of L with respect to dx^{μ}/dt, is called the 'momentum' associated with the generalized co-ordinate x^{μ}.

Centre of mass coordinates

As a second example think of two particles with masses m_1 and m_2, interacting with each other through a potential V which is a function of the distance between them. In terms of the cartesian coordinates $\vec{x}_1$ and $\vec{x}_2$ which represent the positions of the two particles, the Lagrangian of the system is given by

$$L = \frac{1}{2}m_1\frac{d\vec{x}_1}{dt}\cdot\frac{d\vec{x}_1}{dt} + \frac{1}{2}m_2\frac{d\vec{x}_2}{dt}\cdot\frac{d\vec{x}_2}{dt} - V(\vec{x}_1 - \vec{x}_2) \tag{1.102}$$

The Lagrangian formulation allows us to introduce a new set of co-ordinates which are much more convenient. Let

$$\vec{X}_{\text{c.m.}} \equiv \frac{m_1\vec{x}_1 + m_2\vec{x}_2}{m_1 + m_2} \tag{1.103}$$

and

$$\vec{X}_{12} \equiv \vec{x}_1 - \vec{x}_2 \tag{1.104}$$

In terms of the centre-of-mass coordinates $\vec{X}_{\text{c.m.}}$ and the relative position coordinates $\vec{X}_{12}$, the Lagrangian of the system becomes

$$L = \frac{1}{2}(m_1 + m_2)\frac{d\vec{X}_{\text{c.m.}}}{dt}\cdot\frac{d\vec{X}_{\text{c.m.}}}{dt}$$
$$+ \frac{1}{2}\left(\frac{m_1 m_2}{m_1 + m_2}\right)\frac{d\vec{X}_{12}}{dt}\cdot\frac{d\vec{X}_{12}}{dt} + V(\vec{X}_{12}) \tag{1.105}$$

Since the Lagrangian is independent of $\vec{X}_{\text{c.m.}}$ the momentum associated with the centre-of-mass coordinate is conserved

32

$$\frac{\mathrm{d}}{\mathrm{d}t}(\vec{p}_{\text{c.m.}}) = \frac{\mathrm{d}}{\mathrm{d}t}\left\{\frac{\partial L}{\partial\left(\frac{\mathrm{d}\vec{X}_{\text{c.m.}}}{\mathrm{d}t}\right)}\right\}$$

$$= \frac{\mathrm{d}}{\mathrm{d}t}\left\{(m_1 + m_2)\frac{\mathrm{d}\vec{X}_{\text{c.m.}}}{\mathrm{d}t}\right\} = 0 \qquad (1.106)$$

In the absence of external forces, V cannot depend on the orientation of $\vec{X}_{12}$ but only on its magnitude. Therefore following the procedure of Eqs. (1.91)–(1.98), one can show that the angular momentum associated with the angle of the relative position vector $\vec{X}_{12}$ is also conserved.

A final example is given in Appendix I, where the Lagrangian formalism is applied to the problem of calculating the small vibrations of a complicated system about its equilibrium state. It turns out that in this problem, a new set of coordinates can be introduced in such a way that the Lagrangian of the system separates into a sum of terms each of which involves only one of the new coordinates.

Lagrange's life was quiet in spite of the unsettled times in which he lived. As a young man he became famous among the mathematicians of Europe for his work on the calculus of variations, and at the age of thirty he was appointed director of the physico-mathematical division of the Berlin Academy of Sciences under Frederick the Great. Frederick was very fond of the courtly and enlightened Lagrange whom he much preferred to the sanctimonious Euler. After the death of Frederick, Lagrange took refuge in Paris. But Paris in the aftermath of the French revolution soon became far from safe. Lagrange witnessed the execution of his friend Lavoisier and remarked 'It took them only a moment to cut off his head, and a hundred years perhaps will not suffice to produce its like'. Lagrange's tact, modesty, and usefulness kept him alive during the 'Terror' and finally he became the Professor of Mathematics in Napoleon's École Polytechnique. He died at the age of seventy-six, loved by all who knew him. Fourier said of him 'Lagrange was no less a philosopher than he was a great mathematician. By his whole life he proved this: by the moderation of his desires, his immovable attachment to the general interests of humanity, by the noble simplicity of his manners and the elevation of his character, and finally, by the accuracy and depth of his scientific work'.

Hamilton's unified formulation of classical mechanics and geometrical optics

After Lagrange, the next great figure who enters the history of mechanics is Sir William Rowan Hamilton (1805–1865). Hamilton was a spectacular child prodigy. At thirteen he had mastered as many languages as he had years of age. Among these, besides the classical and modern European languages were included Persian, Arabic, Sanskrit, and even Malay. His early interest in languages was due to the influence of his uncle to whom he had been given to be educated. In those days Hamilton slept with a string tied to the back of his night-shirt. The string went through a hole in the wall to his uncle's room. When it was time to get up and work, his uncle pulled the string. Fortunately this orgy of linguistics was not continued and Hamilton became interested in mathematics. At eighteen he submitted to the Royal Irish Academy a memoir on systems of rays which caused the Astronomer Royal of Ireland to exclaim 'This young man I do not say *will be* but *is* the first mathematician of his age'. At twenty-two Hamilton was appointed Professor of Astronomy at Dublin University, and settled down to work at the observatory nearby. He married a clergy-man's daughter and they had three children, but she could not stand the strain of living with him and returned to her parents. Hamilton was a close friend of Wordsworth, Southey, and Coleridge, and his life had a profligate, poetic quality. He drank a great deal and the heaps of papers in his study were always in a state of extreme disorder. Towards the end of his life, Hamilton was alone and often ill, cared for by the housekeeper of the observatory. He had few regular meals but from time to time the housekeeper would thrust a mutton-chop into his study which he would accept without a word and without looking up from his work. After his death, dozens of partly-eaten mutton chops were found sandwiched among the mountains of papers in his study.

Hamilton's work contains some remarkably modern insights, foreshadowing quantum mechanics and relativity. In his first paper, on systems of rays in geometrical optics, he considers the rays of light coming from a point source which flashes on at a certain instant of time, as shown in Fig. 1.12. In this illustration the light passes from a medium of low density (where it travels rapidly) into a dense medium (where it travels slowly). For example, Fig. 1.12 might represent the rays and wave fronts of a flash of light originating at a point in the air in front of a flat piece of glass. The circles represent the positions of the wave front at successive instants of time. The rays are the lines perpendicular to the wave fronts, and they represent the direction of propagation of the wave. As long as the wave remains in the air, where the velocity of propagation is constant, the wave fronts are circular and the rays are straight lines. When the wave reaches the glass, the front is distorted, and the rays are bent. Figure 1.12 is like the map that the commander of an expedition might make sitting in his camp a little distance from the edge of a desert. He might draw a series of closed curves to represent the maximum distance that his men could travel from the camp in one day's march, two day's march, etc. In

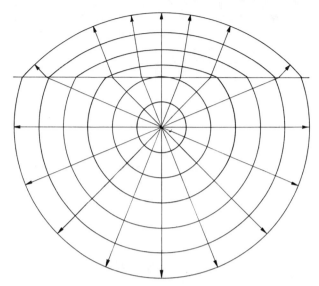

Figure 1.12 shows the system of rays and wave fronts from a point source of light as they enter a glass plate. While the wave fronts travel through the air, they are spherical surfaces to which the rays are perpendicular. When the waves enter the glass plate, they are slowed, and the distance between crests is diminished, so that the rays are bent.

the desert (the glass) where progress is slower, the distance covered in a day (the distance between two wave fronts) is less. If the men marched shoulder to shoulder forming a 'thin red line' (a front) and if each man marched in a direction perpendicular to the front, their progress would be quite similar to that of a light wave.

The integral

$$S = \int dt = \frac{1}{c} \int n(\vec{x}) \, dl \qquad (1.107)$$

taken along the path of a ray of light gives the time needed for the wave front to reach a particular point. Hamilton considered the value of this integral at various points in space always starting at the origin of the light flash and integrating along the paths of the rays. The value of S is then a function of the space-coordinates. For example, in a uniform medium where the index of refraction is constant and the rays are straight lines,

$$S(\vec{x}) = \frac{n_0}{c} \int dl = \frac{n_0}{c} \sqrt{x^2 + y^2 + z^2} \equiv \frac{n_0}{c} r \qquad (1.108)$$

The surfaces of constant phase shown in Fig. 1.12 are given by the equation

$$S(\vec{x}) - t = 0 \qquad (1.109)$$

35

The surfaces corresponding to various values of t show the position of the wave front at various instants of time. Hamilton called the function $S(\bar{x})$ the 'eikonal function', a name which he took from the Greek word for 'image'. He showed that the eikonal function satisfies the differential equation

$$\frac{1}{\{2n(\bar{x})\}^2} \left\{ \left(\frac{\partial S}{\partial x}\right)^2 + \left(\frac{\partial S}{\partial y}\right)^2 + \left(\frac{\partial S}{\partial z}\right)^2 \right\} = 1 \qquad (1.110)$$

where $n(\bar{x})$ is the index of refraction. Equation (1.110) follows from Fermat's principle, Eqs. (1.74)–(1.77), which states that the actual path of a ray of light is the one which requires the least time.

$$S = \int dt = \int L \, dl = \int n(\bar{x}) \frac{d\bar{x}}{dl} \cdot \frac{d\bar{x}}{dl} = \text{minimum} \qquad (1.111)$$

The Euler–Lagrange equations, applied to Eq. (1.111), require that

$$\frac{d}{dl} \left\{ \frac{\partial L}{\partial \left(\frac{dx^\mu}{dl}\right)} \right\} - \frac{\partial L}{\partial x^\mu} = 0 \qquad (1.112)$$

so that

$$\frac{\partial S}{\partial x^\mu} = \int \frac{\partial L}{\partial x^\mu} \, dl = \int \frac{d}{dl} \left\{ \frac{\partial L}{\partial \left(\frac{dx^\mu}{dl}\right)} \right\} dl \qquad (1.113)$$

From the definition of dl as the element of length (Eq. (1.75)) it follows that

$$\frac{d\bar{x}}{dl} \cdot \frac{d\bar{x}}{dl} = 1 \qquad (1.114)$$

Equations (1.114) and (1.113) combine to give Hamilton's eikonal equation (1.110).

With remarkable intuition Hamilton saw the analogy between the rays of geometrical optics and the trajectories of point masses in classical mechanics. His next step was to put mechanics on the same footing as optics by defining what he called the 'characteristic function' for a system of trajectories.

For example, think of the fragments from an exploding skyrocket, as shown in Fig. 1.13. If all of the fragments leave the point of the explosion with equal velocity, then their trajectories will form the sort of system

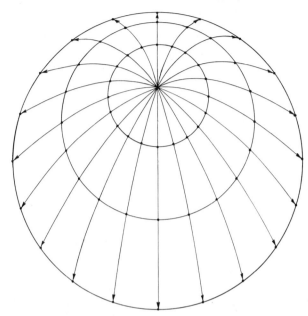

Figure 1.13a shows a system of parabolic trajectories spreading out from the initial position of an exploding skyrocket. All of the fragments shown here start with the same initial velocity, but because of gravity, the upward-moving fragments are decelerated while the downward-moving ones are accelerated. The positions of the fragments at three successive instants of time after the explosion lie on the three spheres drawn around the falling centre of mass of the system.

which Hamilton studied. He defined the characteristic function of the system as the integral

$$S(\bar{x}) = \int_{\bar{x}_0}^{\bar{x}} L \, dt \qquad (1.115)$$

taken along the possible paths of motion. Here L is the Lagrangian of the system. Since the integration in equation (1.115) is taken along trajectories which satisfy the Euler–Lagrange equations it follows that

$$\frac{\partial S}{\partial x^\mu} = \int \frac{\partial L}{\partial x^\mu} \, dt$$

$$= \int \frac{d}{dt} \left\{ \frac{\partial L}{\partial \left(\dfrac{dx^\mu}{dt} \right)} \right\} \, dt = \frac{\partial L}{\partial \left(\dfrac{dx^\mu}{dt} \right)} = p_\mu \qquad \textbf{(1.116)}$$

37

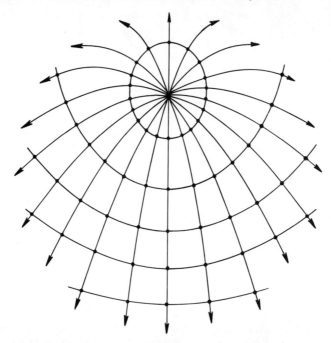

Figure 1.13b shows the same system of parabolic trajectories with Hamilton's surfaces of constant phase cutting the trajectories everywhere at right angles.

Hamilton used the relationship (1.116) to show that his characteristic function satisfies a differential equation similar to his eikonal equation (1.110). He first defined the total energy function (we call it the 'Hamiltonian') of a mechanical system as

$$H = \sum_{\mu} p_{\mu} \frac{\mathrm{d}x^{\mu}}{\mathrm{d}t} - L \tag{1.117}$$

It follows from (1.117) and from the Euler–Lagrange equations, that

$$\frac{\mathrm{d}p_{\mu}}{\mathrm{d}t} \equiv \frac{\mathrm{d}}{\mathrm{d}t} \left\{ \frac{\partial L}{\partial \left(\dfrac{\mathrm{d}x^{\mu}}{\mathrm{d}t} \right)} \right\} = \frac{\partial L}{\partial x^{\mu}} = -\frac{\partial H}{\partial x^{\mu}} \tag{1.118}$$

Also from the definition (1.117),

$$\frac{\partial H}{\partial p_{\mu}} = \frac{\mathrm{d}x^{\mu}}{\mathrm{d}t} \tag{1.119}$$

Equations (1.118) and (1.119) are called Hamilton's equations of motion. From these equations it follows that for systems where the potential

38

energy V is independent of time and where there are no velocity-dependent forces, the Hamiltonian function (1.117) is a constant of the motion. For such 'conservative' systems,

$$\frac{dH}{dt} = \frac{\partial H}{\partial t} + \sum_{\mu} \left\{ \frac{\partial H}{\partial p_{\mu}} \frac{dp_{\mu}}{dt} + \frac{\partial H}{\partial x^{\mu}} \frac{dx^{\mu}}{dt} \right\}$$

$$\sum_{\mu} \left\{ \frac{\partial H}{\partial p_{\mu}} \left(-\frac{\partial H}{\partial x^{\mu}} \right) + \frac{\partial H}{\partial x^{\mu}} \left(\frac{\partial H}{\partial p_{\mu}} \right) \right\} = 0 \qquad (1.120)$$

so that for 'conservative systems' the Hamiltonian function H is a constant of the motion which we will call E. Hamilton expressed his total energy function H in terms of p_{μ} (eliminating the velocities dx^{μ}/dt) and then substituted $\partial S/\partial x^{\mu}$ for p_{μ} to obtain the 'Hamilton–Jacobi equation' for the function S.

$$H(x^{\mu}, p_{\mu}) = H\left(x^{\mu}, \frac{\partial S}{\partial x^{\mu}} \right) = E \qquad \textbf{(1.121)}$$

For example, in the case where the mechanical system is a single point mass moving in a potential $V(\bar{x})$, the Hamiltonian of the system is

$$H = \frac{m}{2} \frac{d\bar{x}}{dt} \cdot \frac{d\bar{x}}{dt} + V(\bar{x}) = \frac{1}{2m} \bar{p} \cdot \bar{p} + V(\bar{x}) \qquad (1.122)$$

and the Hamilton–Jacobi equation is

$$\frac{1}{2m} \left\{ \left(\frac{\partial S}{\partial x} \right)^2 + \left(\frac{\partial S}{\partial y} \right)^2 + \left(\frac{\partial S}{\partial z} \right)^2 \right\} + V(\bar{x}) = E \qquad (1.123)$$

which is analogous to equation (1.110).

Huygens' principle for wave propagation; interference and diffraction of waves

But what is the meaning of S, and why was such a brilliant man as Hamilton preoccupied with it? In the case of a light wave, S is a surface of constant phase defining the position of the crest of the wave at a given instant of time. In the 1830's when Hamilton was working on this problem there was no reason to think that a particle was anything but a tiny billiard ball. What could Hamilton have been thinking of to give it a wavelike property—a surface of constant phase? It is interesting, from the historical point of view, to notice that Newton and Huygens had opposite opinions on the question of whether *light* consisted of particles or waves. Huygens believed that a hot body like a candle flame set up waves in the surrounding medium and that these light waves propagated more or less in the same way as sound except that their wave length was very much shorter and their velocity very much greater. (Huygens knew the velocity of light fairly accurately from the work of Roemer (1644–1710) who observed the moons of Jupiter from the near and far sides of the earth's orbit.) Newton objected that if Huygens' wave theory of light were correct then light would be able to bend around corners in the same way that sound does. Huygens had put forward a principle for calculating the surfaces of constant phase for wave motion. His principle states that *if we know the surface which defines the wave front at the time t, then in order to construct the new front corresponding to the time t + Δt we must draw a large number of small spheres of radius cΔt/n($\vec{x}$) whose centres lie on the old wave front. The new wave front is the envelope of this family of spheres*, as shown in Fig. 1.14. It is easy to understand Huygens' principle by thinking again of an expedition commander who makes a map showing how far his men can move in a day's march. This time the men are not localized in a camp, Fig. 1.12, but spread out along a front. The commander wants

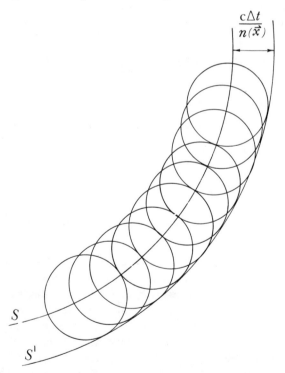

Figure 1.14 illustrates Huygens' principle for constructing wave fronts: A large number of small spheres of radius $c\Delta t/n(\vec{x})$ are constructed with their centres on the old wave front S. After an interval Δt, the wave front will form the surface S' which is the envelope of the small spheres.

to know how far his men can hope to move in a day. They can walk at a rate $c/n(\bar{x})$, a velocity which depends on the terrain. If they do this for a time Δt in a direction perpendicular to the old front they will finally form a new front given by the envelope of the family of circles of radius $c\Delta t/n(\bar{x})$ drawn around their old positions. Huygens thought of each point on a wave crest as a source of wavelets which add together to form the new wave crest an instant later. We can see from his method of constructing wave fronts how it is possible for a wave to bend around a corner. Figure 1.15 shows wave at successive instants of time. Beyond the barrier, the

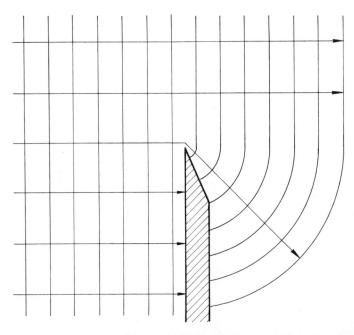

Figure 1.15   A train of light waves passing a knife edge is diffracted into the shadow region. You can observe this effect yourself, looking at the light from a distant street lamp: The lamp remains visible even after it is geometrically obscured by the knife edge. The wave fronts, constructed according to Huygens' principle, resemble a train of ocean waves passing the breakwater of a harbour.

new wave fronts, constructed according to Huygens' principle, bend into the shadow region. This is why Newton refused to believe that light is wavelike. If we are standing on the other side of a high brick wall from another person, we may be able to hear him talking, but we cannot see him. Also, if we shoot at him with a gun we will not hit him. According to Newton we can hear our friend talking behind the wall but we cannot see him or hit him with a bullet because sound is wavelike but light and matter are not. As it turned out he was wrong on both counts. Both light and matter have wave-like properties! It is strange that Newton opposed Huygens' wave theory of light because he himself had discovered an effect which ought to have given him a clue to light's wavelength properties. He found that if he placed a curved lens on a flat piece of glass and pressed the two together a series of bright and dark rings appeared around the point of contact. Newton's rings are caused by interference between waves reflected from the top and bottom of the air film between the two pieces of glass, Fig. 1.16. When twice the thickness of the film is a multiple of the wave

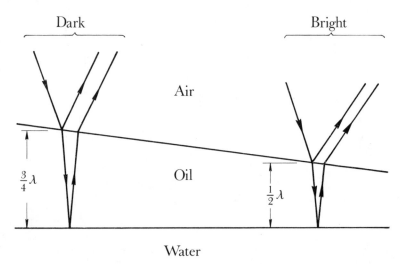

Figure 1.16 shows Newton's rings in a film of oil floating on water. When the film thickness is $\frac{1}{2}\lambda$, the wave reflected from the air-oil interface is in phase with the wave reflected from the oil-water interface (constructive interference) and a bright ring is observed. When the film thickness is $\frac{3}{4}\lambda$, the two waves are out of phase (destructive interference) and a dark ring is observed. The rings are coloured because the wave-length λ is different for different frequencies. It is strange that having studied these rings, Newton still opposed the wave theory of light.

length of the light the two reflected waves add together constructively and the light is strongly reflected. When twice the film thickness is half the wave length or one and half times the wave length, etc., the two waves cancel each other because their phases are opposite, and the reflected wave is destroyed. The rings are coloured because the wave length and hence the film thickness corresponding to efficient reflection, is different for the different colours. You can see Newton's rings in many kinds of thin films. The beautiful colours of oil films floating on water, butterfly wings, iridescent oxide films on metals, the colours of mother of pearl and soap bubbles are all caused by this effect. Another way to see the wavelike nature of light is to look at a distant street light through a narrow slit between your fingers. As you make the gap between your fingers narrower, the distant point-like source of light will appear to spread into a series of bands. If the slit is narrow enough you can see the light even though a part of your hand has blocked the direct line between the pupil of your eye and the lamp. This is because a small part of the wave can spread into the shadow region as shown in Fig. 1.17. The amplitude of the part of the wave that

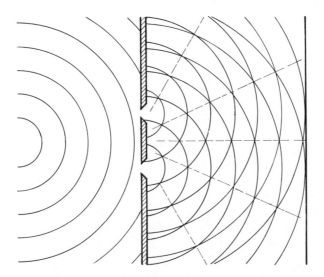

Figure 1.17 shows the wave fronts in Young's diffraction experiment. When waves from the point source at the left arrive at the two slits, each slit acts as a source of a new train of wavelets. In the directions indicated by the dotted lines, the crests of the two wave trains are superimposed so that they add together to produce a net wave of larger amplitude (constructive interference). At intermediate angles, the crest of one wave is superimposed on the trough of the other so that they cancel (destructive interference).

is turned or 'diffracted' into the shadow region is very small and you have to look quite carefully to see the effect. You can understand in a rough way why the amplitude is small in the shadow region by noticing that relatively few of the rays constructed perpendicular to the surfaces of constant phase lead into the shadow (Fig. 1.17). The light bands of the diffraction pattern correspond to angles of observation for which the wavelets from the different parts of the slit add together constructively— the dark bands correspond to destructive interference. Once you have learned to recognize the bands of a diffraction pattern you will begin to see these patterns everywhere. For example, if you wear glasses on a rainy night, the light from a distant street lamp hitting a drop of water on the surface of your glasses will make a tiny point source of light. As the spherical waves from this point source enter the pupil of your eye diffraction and interference effects will occur, producing in the image on your retina, a series of bright and dark rings. Presumably Newton never wore glasses on a rainy night or if he did, he failed to see the clues that might have converted him to Huygens' point of view.

Young's experiment

Because of Newton's great prestige, the wave theory of light was neglected for a hundred years until it was taken up again by Fresnel and Young. Young performed a crucial experiment. Between a point source of light and a ground-glass screen he placed an opaque screen containing two narrow, closely spaced parallel slits as shown in Fig. 1.17. Each of the slits acted as a source of wavelets which added together to produce a pattern of illumination on the ground glass screen. If the angle θ in Young's experiment (Fig. 1.18) is such that the wavelets from the two slits arrive 'in phase' they add together constructively and make a bright band on the screen. At other angles θ the crest of a wavelet from one slit arrives at the same time as the trough of the wavelet from the other slit and the two waves destroy each other making a dark band. In Young's experiment the bright bands are formed at angles θ which satisfy the condition

$$\sin \theta \cong n\frac{\lambda}{d}, \quad n = 1, 2, 3, \ldots \qquad (1.124)$$

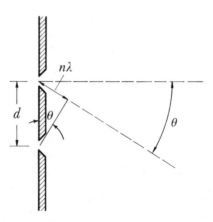

Figure 1.18 shows the geometrical relationship in Young's diffraction experiment. If d is the distance between the slits, and if λ is the wave length of the light, then constructive interference will occur at angles θ which satisfy the relationship $d \sin \theta = n\lambda$, where n is an integer. In the electron diffraction experiments of Davisson, Germer, and G. P. Thomson, constructive interference was observed at angles which fulfilled a similar criterion, d being the distance between two atoms in the crystal.

This is easy to understand if λ represents the wave length of the light and d represents the distance between the slits. From the geometry of the situation (Fig. 1.18), you can see that if Eq. (1.124) is fulfilled, then the crest of the wavelet from one slit will arrive at the 'starting line' at just the moment when a crest leaves the other slit.

Young's experiment showed elegantly and conclusively that in optics, the surfaces of constant phase, constructed according to Huygens' principle have a physical reality and that interference effects depend on the relative phase of two wave trains. If this is so, then we might also ask whether the surface of constant phase which Hamilton introduced into mechanics has any reality. Can we observe interference effects in mechanics? For example, suppose we tried to do an experiment analogous to Young's experiment but with a 'beam' of material particles instead of a beam of light. Could we observe an interference pattern on the screen? This experiment had to wait for the discovery of the electron because as it turns out, the wave length associated with a particle is inversely proportional to its momentum. Heavy particles have such a small wave length that they are not suitable for diffraction experiments. However, at the turn of the century, Sir J. J. Thomson at the Cavendish Laboratory in Cambridge discovered the electron, and twenty years later, Davisson, Germer, and Sir G. P. Thomson (J. J.'s son) used beams of electrons to perform the analogue of Young's experiment. They directed a monoenergetic electron beam at a crystal lattice and observed that at certain preferred angles the beam was strongly scattered. This effect could only be explained by assuming that the motion of the electron obeys some sort of wave equation and that Hamilton's characteristic function S really does correspond to a wave front. According to the modern point of view, both light and matter obey wave equations. However, classical mechanics and geometrical optics become valid when the wave length is very small compared with the dimensions of the system. For example the wave effect of interference in thin films is most important when the film thickness is comparable with the wave length of visible light. For large thicknesses the phase relationships become incoherent and the effect is lost. In the limit of very small wave lengths wave mechanics reduces to classical mechanics and wave optics reduces to geometrical optics. The rays of geometrical optics are analogous to the trajectories of classical mechanics. From the point of view of wave optics and wave mechanics, they are just lines drawn perpendicular to the wave fronts.

Foundations of relativity; the meaning of Hamilton's characteristic function

It is also interesting to see the connection of the characteristic function S with the modern ideas of general relativity. These ideas had their origin in the work of the great German mathematician Carl Friederich Gauss (1777–1855) and his tragically short-lived young protegé, Bernhard Riemann (1826–1866). Riemann's doctoral dissertation at the University of Göttingen was submitted to Gauss in 1851. The dissertation, entitled *Foundations for a general theory of functions of a complex variable* had excited the enthusiasm and admiration of Gauss. Two years later, Riemann had to give a trial lecture in order to obtain the post of 'Privatdozent' (a lecturer paid by his students rather than by the University). He submitted three titles for the lecture, hoping that, in accordance with tradition one of the first two would be chosen. Gauss was anxious to see what such a brilliant young man would do with a really difficult subject, and so, to Riemann's dismay he chose the third topic: 'On the hypotheses which lie at the foundations of geometry'. This was a subject with which Gauss himself had struggled for many years, and so his curiosity was understandable. Riemann had not prepared himself at all on this topic. He procrastinated, worried, became ill, finally recovered, and spent seven weeks preparing the lecture. Gauss was ill too, but he dragged himself up to hear Riemann's classic lecture—a lecture which fully confirmed Gauss' hopes and which laid the foundations of modern non-Euclidean geometry. Riemann considered the distance between two points in space. According to the Pythagorean theorem, Eq. (1.75), the infinitesimal distance ds between two very closely neighbouring points in two-dimensional space is given by

$$ds^2 = dx^2 + dy^2 \qquad (1.125)$$

where dx and dy are respectively the difference in the x, and y coordinates of the two points. Riemann generalized this formula so that it could be applied to curved surfaces. For example, we might wonder how to find the distance between two closely neighbouring points on the surface of a sphere. This two-dimensional curved surface is embedded in our ordinary flat three-dimensional space. If we write the element of length in the ordinary Euclidean three-dimensional space in terms of spherical polar coordinates, Eq. (1.93),

$$ds^2 = dr^2 + r^2 \, d\theta^2 + r^2 \sin^2 \theta \, d\varphi^2 \qquad (1.126)$$

and then add the constraint $dr = 0$, we have the element of length on the spherical surface

$$ds^2 = r^2 \, d\theta^2 + r^2 \sin^2 \theta \, d\varphi^2 \qquad (1.127)$$

If we let

$$x^1 \equiv \theta, \qquad x^2 \equiv \varphi \qquad (1.128)$$

and

$$g_{\mu\nu} = \begin{pmatrix} r^2 & 0 \\ 0 & r^2 \sin^2\theta \end{pmatrix} \tag{1.129}$$

then Eq. (1.127) can be rewritten in the form

$$ds^2 = \sum_{\mu=1}^{2} \sum_{\nu=1}^{2} g_{\mu\nu}\, dx^\mu\, dx^\nu \tag{1.130}$$

If we introduce the convention of summing over repeated indices we can drop the summation signs in Eq. (1.130) and write simply

$$ds^2 = g_{\mu\nu}\, dx^\mu\, dx^\nu \tag{1.131}$$

(The set of coefficients $g_{\mu\nu}$ is called the 'covariant metric tensor'.) This is Riemann's generalization of the Pythagorean rule. The coordinates x^μ, Eq. (1.128), are no longer simply the Cartesian coordinates of Euclidean geometry, but can be general curvilinear coordinates—i.e., non-linear functions of the Cartesian coordinates. The space itself may have an intrinsic curvature. For example, it is impossible to make a sphere out of a flat sheet of paper even by cutting and pasting it because the paper is intrinsically flat whereas the sphere is intrinsically curved. Curved spaces can be produced (as in our example) by starting with a space of higher dimension, expressing the element of length in terms of curvilinear coordinates and constraining the variation of one or more of these coordinates to be zero. For example, we could think of a four-dimensional curved space embedded in a Euclidean space of a higher dimension, just as our two-dimensional sphere was embedded in three-dimensional Euclidean space. If we are dealing with a curved space (sometimes called a Riemannian manifold) most of traditional Euclidean geometry has to be thrown overboard and replaced by something else. The sum of the angles of a triangle drawn on the surface of a sphere fails to add up to 180°, parallel lines cross one another, and so on. (The axioms of Euclidean geometry were first challenged by the Russian mathematician Nicholas Ivanovitch Lobatchevski, 1793–1856.) In a curved space we are not even allowed to say that a straight line is the shortest distance between two points. What ought we to say instead? Here the variational calculus of Euler, Lagrange, and the Bernoullis will help us. The shortest path between two points is the line which minimizes the integral

$$\begin{aligned} s &= \int ds = \int \sqrt{g_{\mu\nu}\frac{dx^\mu}{ds}\frac{dx^\nu}{ds}}\, ds \\ &= \int g_{\mu\nu}\frac{dx^\mu}{ds}\frac{dx^\nu}{ds}\, ds \\ &= 2\int L\, ds \end{aligned} \tag{1.132}$$

The quantum theory of atoms, molecules, and photons

where

$$L \equiv \frac{1}{2} g_{\mu\nu} \frac{dx^\mu}{ds} \frac{dx^\nu}{ds} \qquad (1.133)$$

The Euler–Lagrange equations (1.86) with t replaced by s give us a set of differential equations for $x^\mu(s)$, $\mu = 1, \ldots, N$

$$\frac{d}{ds} \left\{ \frac{\partial L}{\partial \left(\dfrac{dx^\rho}{ds} \right)} \right\} - \frac{\partial L}{\partial x^\rho} = 0, \quad \rho = 1, \ldots, N \qquad (1.134)$$

where L is given by Eq. (1.133) and N is the dimension of the space. The shortest path between two points in a curved space is called a 'geodesic'. It is easy to see by comparing Eqs. (1.74)–(1.77) with Eqs. (1.132)–(1.134) that the problem of finding the path of light rays in geometrical optics is identical with the problem of finding the geodesic lines in a space whose 'metric tensor' is given by

$$g_{\mu\nu} = n(x)\, \delta_{\mu\nu}, \quad \mu = 1, 2, 3, \ldots \qquad (1.135)$$

where $n(x)$ is the index of refraction and $\delta_{\mu\nu}$, the 'Kronecker δ-function', is defined by

$$\delta_{\mu\nu} = \begin{cases} 0 & \mu \neq \nu \\ 1 & \mu = \nu \end{cases} \qquad (1.136)$$

Hamilton's eikonal function S, Eqs. (1.108)–(1.114), is just the distance from the source point along the geodesic paths in this curved space. Can we do the same thing with classical mechanics; that is, can we show that the problem of finding classical trajectories is identical with the problem of finding geodesics in some sort of curved space, and can we identify the distance with Hamilton's characteristic function S? (see Eq. (1.115)). In order to do this we would have to express the Lagrangian of a system in classical mechanics, Eq. (1.78), in the form of Eq. (1.133). The kinetic energy term, Eq. (1.79), already has the right form, but what about the potential energy? For the sake of concreteness, let us think of a single particle moving in a potential $V(x)$, so that the Lagrangian of the system is given by Eq. (1.89). Suppose that we introduce a four-dimensional curved space in which the element of length is given by

$$ds^2 = d\bar{x}.d\bar{x} + \left(1 + \frac{2V(x)}{mc^2} \right) dx^4\, dx^4 \qquad (1.137)$$

where

$$\left. \begin{array}{l} dx^4 = ic\, dt \\ i = \sqrt{-1}, \quad c = \text{velocity of light} \end{array} \right\} \qquad (1.138)$$

48

Then in the limit where

$$\frac{V(x)}{mc^2} \ll 1 \tag{1.139}$$

the equations which determine a geodesic in this curved space-time continuum are identical with the equations for the classical trajectory of the particle. In the case of a many-particle system, a curved space of higher dimensionality is needed. If it is possible to express the Lagrangian of a classical system of point masses in the form of Eq. (1.133), then perhaps something similar can be done with the Hamiltonian. The momentum p_μ associated with the coordinate x^μ is defined (Eq. (1.101)) as the partial derivative of the Lagrangian with respect to dx^μ/dt. With t replaced by s we have

$$p_\mu \equiv \frac{\partial L}{\partial \left(\dfrac{dx^\mu}{ds}\right)} \tag{1.140}$$

If L has the form of Eq. (1.133) then

$$p_\mu = g_{\mu\nu} \frac{dx^\nu}{ds} \tag{1.141}$$

We can also write a reciprocal relationship

$$\frac{dx^\mu}{ds} = g^{\mu\nu} p_\nu \tag{1.142}$$

where the matrix of coefficients, $g^{\mu\nu}$, is defined in such a way that it forms the reciprocal of the covariant metric tensor $g_{\mu\nu}$.

$$g^{\mu\nu} g_{\nu\rho} \equiv \delta^\mu_\rho = \begin{cases} 0 & \mu = \rho \\ 1 & \mu \neq \rho \end{cases} \tag{1.143}$$

This set of coefficients is called the 'contravariant metric tensor'. The Hamiltonian H in classical mechanics is related to the Lagrangian L by Eq. (1.117) so that if L is given by Eq. (1.133) then

$$\begin{aligned}
H &= p_\mu \frac{dx^\mu}{ds} - L \\
&= \frac{1}{2} g_{\mu\nu} \frac{dx^\mu}{ds} \frac{dx^\nu}{ds} \\
&= \frac{1}{2} p_\mu \frac{dx^\mu}{ds} = \frac{1}{2} g^{\mu\nu} p_\mu p_\nu
\end{aligned} \tag{1.144}$$

and the Hamilton–Jacobi equation, Eq. (1.123), becomes

$$g^{\mu\nu} \frac{\partial s}{\partial x^\mu} \frac{\partial s}{\partial x^\nu} = 1 \tag{1.145}$$

Thus, from the modern point of view, *Hamilton's characteristic function S has a double significance. It corresponds to a surface of constant phase associated with the wavelike properties of matter. At the same time it represents the distance from a source point in a curved space-time continuum. The two roles are related, because the crest of a wave propagating outward from a central source defines a spherelike many-dimensional surface all the points on which are equidistant from the centre.* Such ideas, of course, did not enter mechanics until they were introduced by Einstein, Minkowski, de Broglie, Schrödinger and others in the twentieth century. Nevertheless, it is remarkable to see the intuition shown by Hamilton, Gauss, and Riemann in laying the foundations of the modern viewpoint.

Classical electrodynamics from the standpoint of special relativity; experimental background; the requirement of Lorentz-invariance

Gauss and Riemann lived at a time when the connection between electricity and magnetism had just been discovered and they both did important work in developing the mathematical theory of electromagnetic forces. The greatest experimental worker in the field of electromagnetism was Michael Faraday (1791–1867). In fact, because of his important contributions both to physics and to chemistry, Faraday certainly ranks as one of the greatest experimental scientists in history. His scientific career is closely connected with the Royal Institution in Albemarle Street, London, which had been founded by Count Rumford to 'develop the applications of science'. At that time the head of the laboratory at the Royal Institution was the brilliant young chemist, Sir Humphry Davy (1778–1829), among whose many discoveries were the metals sodium, potassium, magnesium, calcium, strontium, and barium. Davy had shown that an electric current could be used to decompose chemical compounds and he had isolated the metals from their salts by this method. He was considered to be the foremost chemist of his time. Meanwhile, Faraday, the son of a poor blacksmith, had been taken from school at the age of thirteen and apprenticed to a London bookbinder. Nevertheless, Faraday succeeded in educating himself in his spare time. When he was twenty-one, a friend gave him tickets to attend four of Davy's lectures at the Royal Institution. The lectures struck a chord in Faraday's mind. He wrote them out into a beautiful set of notes which he bound himself and presented to Davy, asking to be taken as an assistant in the laboratory. He said that he wanted to devote himself to science because of the detachment from petty motives and the unselfishness of natural philosophers. Davy told him to reserve judgment on that point until he had met a few natural philosophers, but he took Faraday as his assistant. The modest, honest, and devoted Faraday finally rose to outshine Davy and to become his successor as head of the Royal Institution. Prince Albert often attended his lectures there and when Faraday retired, Queen Victoria gave him a house in Hampton Court. Together with Volta, Coulomb, Cavendish, Ørsted, Ohm, Ampere, and Henry, he established experimentally the relationships between electricity and magnetism. Faraday had no mathematical training but a strong intuition. He visualized 'lines of force' filling the space around charged and magnetized bodies. He suspected that light waves are transmitted by means of these lines of force. On the other hand, German mathe-maticians (of whom Gauss and Riemann were the most prominent) had noticed immediately the similarity between Coulomb's law describing the forces between charged bodies and the Newtonian law of gravitational attraction. Coulomb's law states that the force between two charged particles is proportional to the product of the charges and inversely pro-portional to the square of the distance between them. The close similarity with Newton's $1/r^2$ law for gravitational attraction allowed the German mathematicians to take over most of the methods which had been developed in celestial mechanics. Faraday, however, did not like the German 'action at a distance' school of thought because it was contradictory to his in-tuitive picture of lines of force. He expressed this opinion to the young Scottish mathematician James Clerk Maxwell (1831–1879). Maxwell achieved a magnificent synthesis by showing, first of all, that when Faraday's lines of force were described in mathematical language, the resulting theory complemented rather than contradicted the ideas of the German mathematicians. Secondly, Maxwell showed that the relations which Faraday could demonstrate in the laboratory between electrical currents, magnets, and charged bodies led to a set of equations from which the existence of electromagnetic waves could be predicted. Maxwell's equations could therefore explain light waves as an electromagnetic effect. He developed his ideas into a book which is a scientific classic almost on a par with Newton's *Principia*. Maxwell's contemporaries found almost as much difficulty in reading it too, but it was clear that he had achieved a remarkable synthesis when Heinrich Hertz (1857–1894) was able to produce and detect Maxwell's electromagnetic waves. This experiment of Hertz was in fact the precursor of radio, television, and radar transmission. Maxwell still thought of his waves as analogous to sound waves—that is to say, he thought of the electromagnetic waves as propagating through a medium which existed everywhere, even in interstellar space. The properties of this medium were somewhat puzzling since although it carried light waves, it had to be 'ethereal' in the sense of offering no resistance to the motion of material bodies. At the end of the nineteenth century there was a great deal of discussion of the properties of this so-called 'luminiferous ether'. It seemed that it ought to be possible to measure the motion of the earth relative to the ether by detecting an 'ether wind'. This idea was based on the analogy with sound waves. If an observer is moving in the same direction as a sound wave the velocity of the wave seems to him to be less. If he is moving in the opposite direction, the apparent velocity of the sound wave is increased. At the turn of the century Michaelson and Morley performed an extremely accurate experiment which ought to have measured the 'ether wind' but their results were completely negative. They repeated the experiment half a year later when the earth was at the opposite side of its orbit but their results again were negative. Even if, by some coincidence, the earth had been stationary with respect to the ether on one side of its orbit, the precise experiments of Michaelson and Morley ought to have been able to detect an 'ether wind' on the other side. But there was none. The observed velocity of light was completely constant, independent of the motion of the observer. This startling result was the basis of Einstein's special theory of relativity, one of the principles of which is that the fundamental laws of nature are the same for an observer moving uniformly in a straight line as they are for an observer at rest. In other words, velocity is not absolute, but only relative. This is an extension of Galileo's principle of relativity which states that position is not absolute but only relative. According to Galileo, there is no experiment that we can do which will tell us our absolute position in the universe, and according to Einstein there is no experiment which will tell us our absolute velocity: hence the negative result of the Michaelson–Morley experiment.

The coordinates which are appropriate for a moving observer are related to those of an observer at rest by a 'Lorentz transformation'. Let us imagine a four-dimensional space-time continuum called Minkowski space in which the element of length is given by

$$\mathrm{d}s^2 = -\mathrm{d}\vec{x}.\mathrm{d}\vec{x} + c^2\,\mathrm{d}t^2$$
$$= g_{\mu\nu}\,\mathrm{d}x^\mu\,\mathrm{d}x^\nu, \quad \mu = 1, \ldots, 4 \qquad (1.146)$$

where

$$g_{\mu\nu} = -\delta_{\mu\nu} = \begin{cases} 0 & \mu \neq \nu \\ -1 & \mu = \nu \end{cases}$$
$$x^4 = ict, \quad c = \text{velocity of light} = 3 \times 10^{10}\ \text{cm/sec} \qquad (1.147)$$

A Lorentz transformation is a rotation of the space–time axes. For example, the Lorentz transformation relating the coordinates of an observer at rest to those of an observer moving in the z direction is

$$\left.\begin{array}{l} x^{1'} = x^1 \\[4pt] x^{2'} = x^2 \\[4pt] x^{3'} = x^3 \cos \gamma - x^4 \sin \gamma \\[4pt] x^{4'} = x^3 \sin \gamma + x^4 \cos \gamma \end{array}\right\} \tag{1.148}$$

We said above that one of the principles of Einstein's special theory of relativity is that no experiment can be devised to measure absolute velocity. Another way of expressing this principle is to say that *the fundamental laws of nature must be unchanged by a Lorentz transformation.* Maxwell's electromagnetic equations are sufficiently fundamental to exhibit this symmetry, whereas the equation of motion of a sound wave is a secondary consequence of underlying fundamental laws and therefore need not be Lorentz-invariant. If an equation is to be Lorentz-invariant, the space and time coordinates must enter it on an equal footing.

Coulomb's law and Poisson's equation fail to meet the requirement

From the point of view of Lorentz-invariance, Coulomb's law of electrostatic attraction by itself is unsatisfactory. Coulomb's law states that if an electric charge e_1 is placed at the point $\bar{x}_1$ and a second charge e_2 is placed at the point $\bar{x}_2$, then the potential energy of the two charges is given by

$$V = \frac{e_1 e_2}{|\bar{x}_1 - \bar{x}_2|} \tag{1.149}$$

where $|\bar{x}_1 - \bar{x}_2|$ is the distance between the two points

$$|\bar{x}_1 - \bar{x}_2| = \sqrt{(x_2 - x_2)^2 + (y_1 - y_2)^2 + (z_1 - z_2)^2} \tag{1.150}$$

From this it follows that the potential energy of a test charge e placed at the point $\bar{x}$ in the presence of a large number of other charges e_1, e_2, $e_3, \ldots$, etc., at the positions $\bar{x}_1, \bar{x}_2, \bar{x}_3, \ldots$, etc., is given by

$$V = \sum_n \frac{e\, e_n}{|\bar{x} - \bar{x}_n|} = e\, \phi(\bar{x}) \tag{1.151}$$

where

$$\phi(\bar{x}) \equiv \sum_n \frac{e_n}{|\bar{x} - \bar{x}_n|} \tag{1.152}$$

53

If the point charges are replaced by a continuous distribution of charge whose density is given by $\rho(x)$ then the sum in Eq. (1.152) must be replaced by an integral

$$\phi(\bar{x}) = \int d^3x' \frac{\rho(\bar{x}')}{|\bar{x} - \bar{x}'|} \tag{1.153}$$

ϕ is called the electrostatic potential. It can be shown that if ϕ and ρ are related by Eq. (1.153) then

$$\nabla^2 \phi(x) = -4\pi \rho(x) \tag{1.154}$$

where ∇^2 is the Laplacian operator defined by

$$\nabla^2 = \frac{\partial^2}{\partial x^2} + \frac{\partial^2}{\partial y^2} + \frac{\partial^2}{\partial z^2} \tag{1.155}$$

Equation (1.154) is called Poisson's equation. We can see at once that it does not fulfil the criterion of Lorentz-invariance, since the space and time coordinates do not enter on an equal footing.

The Lorentz-invariant generalization of Poisson's equation

We can modify Poisson's equation and make it Lorentz-invariant by replacing the Laplacian operator ∇^2 with an operator called the 'd'Alembertian' in which the space and time coordinates enter symmetrically. The d'Alembertian operator is represented by the symbol $\Box^2$ and defined by

$$\begin{aligned}\Box^2 &\equiv \frac{\partial^2}{\partial x^2} + \frac{\partial^2}{\partial y^2} + \frac{\partial^2}{\partial z^2} - \frac{1}{c^2}\frac{\partial^2}{\partial t^2} \\ &= \delta_{\mu\nu}\frac{\partial^2}{\partial x^\mu \partial x^\nu}, \quad \mu, \nu = 1, \dots, 4\end{aligned} \tag{1.156}$$

The modified version of Eq. (1.154) becomes

$$\Box^2 \phi(\bar{x}, x^4) = -4\pi\rho(\bar{x}, x^4) \tag{1.157}$$

The potential ϕ and the charge density ρ are now allowed to depend on the time-coordinate $x^4 = ict$. Since Eq. (1.157) reduces to Eq. (1.154) in the limit where ϕ and ρ are independent of time, Poisson's equation is valid for static problems. Equation (1.157) by itself is still not completely satisfactory from the standpoint of special relativity. Suppose that we view a charge distribution ρ from a moving frame of reference. It will appear to us to be a current. According to relativity both points of view are equally valid. Therefore *charge and current must form part of the same physical entity*. This relationship between the charge density ρ and the current density which we shall call $\bar{j}$ can be expressed mathematically by incorporating them into a four-dimensional vector

$$j_\mu = \{j_1, j_2, j_3, j_4\} \tag{1.158}$$

The first three components of this '4-current' are the components of the ordinary electrical current vector, while the fourth component is given by

$$j_4 = ic\rho \tag{1.159}$$

The law of conservation of charge, written in terms of j_μ, becomes

$$\frac{\partial j_1}{\partial x^1} + \frac{\partial j_2}{\partial x^2} + \frac{\partial j_3}{\partial x^3} + \frac{\partial j_4}{\partial x^4} \equiv \frac{\partial j_\mu}{\partial x^\mu} = 0 \tag{1.160}$$

Equation (1.160) certainly fulfils the relativistic requirement that the space and time coordinates should enter on an equal footing. However it is now clear that Eq. (1.157) cannot stand by itself. If we view the charge-density ρ from a moving frame of reference it will appear as a current. How will the scalar potential appear in a moving frame? Since $ic\rho$ is the time-component of the four-dimensional current vector j_μ, symmetry requires us to introduce another 4-vector of which $i\phi$ is the time-component. Let

$$A_\mu \equiv \{A_1, A_2, A_3, A_4\} \tag{1.161}$$

where

$$A_4 = i\phi \tag{1.162}$$

We shall see later that the first three components of the four-dimensional potential vector A_μ are related to the magnetic field. The complete relationship which must stand in place of Eq. (1.157) now becomes

$$\Box^2 A_\mu = -\frac{4\pi}{c} j_\mu, \quad \mu = 1, 2, 3, 4 \tag{1.163}$$

Since A_μ is related to j_μ by Eq. (1.163) and since j_μ obeys the conservation law, Eq. (1.160), we can add the requirement

$$\frac{\partial A_\mu}{\partial x^\mu} = 0 \tag{1.164}$$

without contradicting Eq. (1.163).

The Lorentz-invariant Lagrangian of a charged particle

According to Newtonian mechanics, the Lagrangian function which determines the motion of a charged particle in the electrostatic potential ϕ is given by

$$L = \frac{m}{2} \frac{d\bar{x}}{dt} \cdot \frac{d\bar{x}}{dt} - e\phi \tag{1.165}$$

This expression is certainly not Lorentz-invariant because the time and space do not enter it in a symmetrical way and because only the time-component of the electromagnetic potential A_μ appears. We need a Lorentz-invariant expression to replace Eq. (1.165). It turns out that the equations of motion which follow from the Lorentz-invariant Lagrangian

$$L = \frac{1}{2} \delta_{\mu\nu} \frac{dx^\mu}{ds} \frac{dx^\nu}{ds} + \frac{e}{mc^2} A_\nu \frac{dx^\nu}{ds} \tag{1.166}$$

are in agreement with experiment. The Euler–Lagrange equations which follow from Eq. (1.166) are

$$\frac{d}{ds}\left(\delta_{\mu\nu} \frac{dx^\nu}{ds} + \frac{e}{mc^2} A_\mu \right) = \frac{e}{mc^2} \frac{\partial A_\nu}{\partial x^\mu} \frac{dx^\nu}{ds} \tag{1.167}$$

where ds is the element of length in the four-dimensional space–time continuum given by Eq. (1.146). If we make use of the identity

$$\frac{dA_\mu}{ds} \equiv \frac{\partial A_\mu}{\partial x^\nu} \frac{dx^\nu}{ds} \tag{1.168}$$

then we can write Eq. (1.167) in the form

$$\delta_{\mu\nu} \frac{d^2 x^\nu}{ds^2} = \frac{e}{mc^2} F_{\mu\nu} \frac{dx^\nu}{ds} \tag{1.169}$$

where $F_{\mu\nu}$ is defined by

$$F_{\mu\nu} \equiv \frac{\partial A_\nu}{\partial x^\mu} - \frac{\partial A_\mu}{\partial x^\nu} \tag{1.170}$$

The quantity $F_{\mu\nu}$ defined by Eq. (1.170) is called the 'electromagnetic field strength tensor'. The components of $F_{\mu\nu}$ are the familiar three-dimensional vectors $\vec{E}$ and $\vec{H}$ which represent the strength of the electric and magnetic fields.

$$F_{\mu\nu} = \begin{pmatrix} 0 & H_3 & -H_2 & -iE_1 \\ -H_3 & 0 & H_1 & -iE_2 \\ H_2 & -H_1 & 0 & -iE_3 \\ iE_1 & iE_2 & iE_3 & 0 \end{pmatrix} \tag{1.171}$$

Equations (1.163), (1.164), (1.169), and (1.170) are the fundamental Maxwell–Lorentz equations written in a modern notation which makes their space–time symmetry apparent. Equations (1.163) and (1.164) tell us how to find the electromagnetic potential A_μ produced by a given charge and current distribution j_μ. Equations (1.169) and (1.170) tell us how this potential affects the motion of another charged particle. The whole system of equations tells us how charged particles affect one another when they are moving in empty space. The equations need to be modified if polarizable, conducting, or magnetizable media are introduced into the problem and these effects will be discussed in a later section.

Problem (1.5) Show that in the non-relativistic limit, the equations of motion of a charged particle in an electromagnetic field, Eq. (1.169), reduce to

$$\frac{dx^1}{dt} = \frac{e}{m_0} E_1 + \frac{e}{m_0 c} \left(\frac{dx^2}{dt} H_3 - \frac{dx^3}{dt} H_2 \right)$$

$$\frac{dx^2}{dt} = \frac{e}{m_0} E_2 + \frac{e}{m_0 c} \left(\frac{dx^3}{dt} H_1 - \frac{dx^1}{dt} H_3 \right)$$

$$\frac{dx^3}{dt} = \frac{e}{m_0} E_3 + \frac{e}{m_0 c} \left(\frac{dx^1}{dt} H_2 - \frac{dx^2}{dt} H_1 \right)$$

Motion in a uniform magnetic field; the relativistic increase in mass

As an example of the Einstein–Lorentz equations of motion, Eq. (1.169), think of a particle with charge e and mass m_0 moving in a constant external magnetic field $\vec{H}$. Suppose that the magnetic field is pointed in the z direction so that all of the components of the electromagnetic field strength tensor, Eq. (1.171), are zero except

$$F_{12} = -F_{21} = H \tag{1.172}$$

Then the set of equations (1.169) becomes

$$\left.\begin{array}{c} \dfrac{d^2 x^1}{ds^2} = \dfrac{eH}{m_0 c^2} \dfrac{dx^2}{ds} \\[2ex] \dfrac{d^2 x^2}{ds^2} = \dfrac{eH}{m_0 c^2} \dfrac{dx^1}{ds} \\[2ex] \dfrac{d^2 x^3}{ds^2} = 0 \\[2ex] \dfrac{d^2 x^4}{ds^2} = 0 \end{array}\right\} \tag{1.173}$$

We can use Eq. (1.146) to eliminate the parameter s from the equations of motion. Dividing Eq. (1.146) by $c^2 dt^2$ we have

$$\frac{ds^2}{c\,dt} = -\frac{1}{c^2} \frac{d\bar{x}}{dt} \cdot \frac{d\bar{x}}{dt} + 1 \tag{1.174}$$

so that

$$\frac{c\,dt}{ds} = \frac{1}{\sqrt{1 - \left(\dfrac{v}{c}\right)^2}} \tag{1.175}$$

where

$$v = \left|\frac{d\bar{x}}{dt}\right| \tag{1.176}$$

Substituting Eq. (1.175) in Eq. (1.173), letting x^1, x^2, and x^3 be the usual Cartesian coordinates x, y, and z we have

$$\left.\begin{array}{l} \dfrac{d^2x}{dt^2} = \dfrac{eH}{mc}\dfrac{dy}{dt} \\[2ex] \dfrac{d^2y}{dt^2} = -\dfrac{eH}{mc}\dfrac{dx}{dt} \\[2ex] \dfrac{d^2z}{dt^2} = 0 \end{array}\right\} \tag{1.177}$$

where

$$m \equiv \frac{m_0}{\sqrt{1 - \left(\dfrac{v}{c}\right)^2}} \tag{1.178}$$

(It is interesting to see that the mass m appears to become larger and larger as the velocity of the particle approaches the velocity of light. This striking relativistic effect has been amply verified by experiment.) As a solution of the set of equations (1.177) we can try the helical path

$$\left.\begin{array}{l} x = r_0 \sin \omega t \\[1ex] y = r_0 \cos \omega t \\[1ex] z = v_{\parallel} t \end{array}\right\} \tag{1.179}$$

This will satisfy Eq. (1.177) provided that

$$\omega_0 = \frac{eH}{mc} \tag{1.180}$$

ω_0 (the cyclotron frequency) is independent of the radius of the helical trajectory r_0. ω_0 is determined by the velocity of the charged particle, since from Eq. (1.179)

$$\left(\frac{dx^2}{dt}\right) + \left(\frac{dy^2}{dt}\right) \equiv v_\perp^2$$

$$= (\cos^2 \omega_0 t + \sin^2 \omega_0 t)(r_0 \omega_0)^2$$

$$= (r_0 \omega_0)^2 \qquad (1.181)$$

It follows that

$$r_0 = \frac{v_\perp}{\omega_0} = \frac{mc\, v_\perp}{eH} \qquad (1.182)$$

Problem (1.6) A cyclotron whose radius is 1·35 metres operates at a frequency of 2×10^8 cycles/sec. What is the maximum velocity to which it can accelerate an electron?

Radiation from a time-dependent current

Knowing the trajectory of the charged particle and hence its current j_μ, we could go on to calculate the electromagnetic potential A_μ which results from its motion by solving the partial differential equation (1.163). The problem is somewhat simplified if the current (and hence also the potential) depend sinusoidally on time. If (for $\mu = 1, 2, 3$)

$$j_\mu = \mathrm{Re}\{j_\mu(\bar{x})\, e^{-ikct}\} \qquad \textbf{(1.183)}$$

so that

$$A_\mu = \mathrm{Re}\{A_\mu(\bar{x})\, e^{-ikct}\} \qquad (1.184)$$

where 'Re' means 'real part of', then

$$\Box^2 A_\mu = (\nabla^2 + k^2)A_\mu = 4\pi j_\mu \qquad (1.185)$$

It can be shown that Eq. (1.185) has the solution

$$A_\mu(x^1, \ldots, x^4) = \mathrm{Re}\left\{\frac{e^{-ikct}}{c} \int d^3x' \frac{j_\mu(\bar{x}')\, e^{ik|\bar{x}-\bar{x}'|}}{|\bar{x}-\bar{x}'|}\right\} \qquad \textbf{(1.186)}$$

Now suppose that the current j_μ is localized in a small region of space near $\bar{x}' = \bar{x}_0$. At very large distances from this region the integral of Eq. (1.186) can be approximated by factoring out the slowly-varying term and we can write

$$A_\mu(x^1, \ldots, x^4) = \mathrm{Re}\left\{\frac{e^{ik(|\bar{x}-\bar{x}_0| - \omega t)}}{c|\bar{x}-\bar{x}_0|}\right\} \int d^3x'\, j_\mu(\bar{x}') \quad (1.187)$$

This solution corresponds to an outward-travelling wave whose amplitude falls off inversely as the separation between the point of observation $\bar{x}$

and the centre of the region in which the current is confined, $\vec{x}_0$. The wave of electromagnetic radiation produced by an accelerated charged particle carries energy into the distant parts of space where it is absorbed. This is the way that Huygens pictured the light from a candle flame. The violent agitation of particles in the flame, according to Huygens, produces waves which carry energy into distant parts of space. We can also see from Eq. (1.187) that an oscillating current in a loop of wire will produce electromagnetic waves and this is the way that radio waves are produced. The wave length λ of radio waves in common use is about a metre or so and therefore the corresponding frequency is of the order of magnitude

$$ v = \frac{\omega}{2\pi} = \frac{kc}{2\pi} = \frac{c}{\lambda} = 3 \times 10^8 \text{ cycles/sec} \qquad (1.188) $$

Microwave radiation such as 'radar' has a wave length in the centimetre range. Infrared radiation is intermediate between microwave frequencies and visible light. The visible range of light corresponds to a wave length of approximately 4000–7000 Å or 4–7 $\times$ 10^{-5} cm. (An 'angstrom unit' is defined as 10^{-8} cm and abbreviated by the symbol Å.) The frequencies associated with visible light thus have the general order of magnitude 10^{15} cycles/sec. Beyond the visible range lie first, the ultraviolet range, then X-rays, and finally 'gamma rays' which are produced in nuclear processes and which can have frequencies as high as 10^{20} cycles/sec. The higher the frequency of the wave the shorter the wave length and the more closely the approximations of geometrical optics become valid. At low frequencies, diffraction and interference effects are easy to observe. At high frequencies an electromagnetic wave behaves almost like a particle. For example, the path of a gamma ray can leave a track in a photographic emulsion. The production of such a track can, however, be shown to follow from the underlying wave equations (see, for example, L. I. Schiff *Quantum Mechanics*, McGraw-Hill, 2nd edition (1955), pp. 209–213).

The paradox of Rutherford's atomic model; why is it stable?

The Maxwell–Lorentz equations were brilliantly successful in correlating a vast range of experimental data and in predicting new phenomena. However, there were signs that something was seriously wrong. For example, the structure of the atom presented a paradox. Sir J. J. Thomson (1856–1940) (who occupied Maxwell's former position as head of the Cavendish Laboratory at Cambridge University) studied the 'cathode rays' which were observed at the negative electrode when an electric current was passed through a rarefied gas. He was able to show that the 'cathode rays' were actually charged particles whose mass was very much less than that of an atom. He called these small particles electrons. Thomson guessed that the electrons might be a constituent of atoms knocked out by impact when the ions of the discharge tube collided with the negative electrode. Meanwhile Bequerel and the Curies had discovered radioactivity. The 'alpha particles' which were produced in the decay of radium were in fact helium ions moving with a high velocity. These provided a handy kind of artillery for bombarding atoms. Ernest Rutherford (later Lord Rutherford, 1871–1937), a young New Zealander working in J. J. Thomson's laboratory, measured the amount by which the alpha particles were deflected when they collided with atoms. He found that when he bombarded a thin film, many of the alpha particles were actually scattered back towards the source. Writing of this discovery later he said 'It was quite the most incredible event that ever happened to me in my life. It was almost as incredible as if you fired a fifteen-inch shell at a piece of tissue paper and it came back and hit you'. Shortly afterwards Rutherford announced to his co-workers 'I know what an atom looks like'. In order to explain the results of his scattering experiments Rutherford had to assume that nearly all of the mass of an atom is concentrated in an extremely tiny nucleus at its centre around which the electrons move in orbits like planets moving around the sun. Rutherford's model of the atom accounted very well for the wide-angle scattering of alpha particles. On the other hand, Maxwell's equations predicted that an accelerated charged particle ought to produce electromagnetic radiation. The orbiting electrons in Rutherford's model of the atom were continually accelerated towards the nucleus at the centre. Therefore they ought to continually radiate away their kinetic energy, finally lose it all, and spiral in to the nucleus. The classical theory not only offered no explanation of why Rutherford's atom did not collapse—it also did not begin to explain the fact that only certain frequencies of radiation can be absorbed and emitted by an atom. The complicated line spectra of the elements had been measured with great accuracy and constituted a jungle of experimental information in which theory was entirely lost. There was still more hand-writing on the wall—the unexplained photoelectric effect; anomalies in specific heats; and the 'ultraviolet catastrophe' (a failure of thermo-dynamics as applied to radiation). The mechanics of Newton and Einstein (incorporating the electromagnetic equations of Maxwell and Lorentz) formed the classical system. It was an elegant system of laws which was in most respects highly successful, but in the early years of this century it became clear that the classical system had broken down. Hence the sequel to Pope's couplet in praise of Newton:

> Ah well! It could not last! The Devil, shouting 'Ho!
> Let Einstein be!', restored the status quo.

The quantum theory of atoms, molecules, and photons

However, after twenty-five years of struggle, of which Planck, Einstein, Bohr, Sommerfeld, Born, de Broglie, Schrödinger, Heisenberg, Dirac, and Pauli are the chief heros, a new form of mechanics emerged in 1926 which was as complete and satisfactory as classical mechanics once had seemed. *What was needed was a wave equation for material particles—a wave equation which would be related to classical mechanics in the same way that Maxwell's electromagnetic wave equations are related to geometrical optics.*

2. A wave equation for matter

Bohr's atomic model

According to the model of the atom which Ernest Rutherford proposed in 1910, nearly all of the mass is concentrated in a tiny nucleus at the centre whose diameter is less than 10^{-12} cm. Rutherford thought of the electrons as circling around the nucleus in orbits, just as the planets circle around the sun. But Maxwell's equations predict that the accelerated electrons must lose their energy in electromagnetic radiation. The system ought to collapse almost immediately instead of lasting for billions of years. Something was certainly wrong with the model. At that time a young Dane named Niels Bohr came to Cambridge to work in the laboratory of the famous J. J. Thomson, discoverer of the electron. He brought with him a paper which he had written on the electron theory of metals and something which he thought would be especially interesting to Thomson—a list of mistakes in the latter's own papers. Although Thomson treated Bohr with the utmost kindness and courtesy he was probably not as enthusiastic about this method of introduction as the innocent young Dane had expected, and Bohr's paper on the theory of metals remained unread by Thomson. Meanwhile Rutherford (by that time famous for his model of the atom) passed through Cambridge on his way to Manchester where he was setting up a laboratory. After hearing him describe his revolutionary experiments, Bohr knew instantly that he wanted to work with Rutherford, and he soon left Cambridge for Manchester. The contrast between Bohr and Rutherford was a striking one. Rutherford was a hearty, energetic, and earthy New Zealander. Bohr was a dreamer, soft-spoken, unworldly, and philosophical. Nevertheless a strong friendship developed between them and they began a lifelong scientific collaboration. Bohr soon realized that the stability of the atom could be explained only by making a very radical departure from classical mechanics. Several years earlier, in 1901, Max Planck had studied the radiation coming from a small hole in an oven. In order to explain the frequency distribution of the radiation as a function of the oven temperature, Planck had been forced to introduce arbitrarily the idea that the

63

energy of electromagnetic radiation can be absorbed and emitted only in amounts E which are multiples of the frequency v of the radiation, so that

$$E = \hbar\omega = hv \qquad (2.1)$$

(We can express the frequency as v cycles/second or alternatively as ω radians/second.) Planck called these little packages of energy 'quanta'. The constant of proportionality is called Planck's constant and it has the value

$$\hbar = \frac{h}{2\pi} = 6\cdot58 \times 10^{-16} \text{ (electron-volt)-sec} \qquad (2.2)$$

In 1905 Einstein had used Planck's quantum hypothesis to explain the photoelectric effect. (When a beam of light knocks an electron out of a metal it always transmits to the electron an amount of energy $hv = \hbar\omega$ regardless of the intensity of the illuminating beam.) Bohr took over some of Planck's quantum ideas and applied them to Rutherford's model of the atom. In Bohr's model, only certain orbits were allowed. Bohr postulated that for an allowed circular orbit the angular momentum must be an integral multiple of Planck's constant

$$p_\phi \equiv mr^2\omega = n\hbar, \quad n = 1, 2, 3, \ldots \qquad (2.3)$$

He then used a theorem from classical mechanics called the 'Virial Theorem' which states that for circular orbits in an attractive Coulomb potential where $V = -Ze^2/r$ the kinetic energy is minus one-half the potential energy. Since the kinetic energy of a particle in a circular orbit is given by $\frac{1}{2}mr^2\omega^2$, this gave Bohr a second equation for the angular velocity $\omega = d\varphi/dt$:

$$\frac{1}{2}mr^2\omega^2 = \frac{1}{2}\frac{Ze^2}{r} \qquad (2.4)$$

where Ze is the charge on the atomic nucleus. Solving Eq. (2.3) for ω and substituting into Eq. (2.4) Bohr found a condition for the radius of the allowed orbits,

$$r = \frac{n^2\hbar^2}{Ze^2m_0}, \quad n = 1, 2, 3, \ldots \qquad (2.5)$$

The magnitude of the charge e on an electron, the electron mass, m_0, and Planck's constant $\hbar$ is such that

$$\frac{\hbar^2}{e^2m_0} \equiv a_0 = 0.529 \times 10^{-8} \text{ cm}$$

$$\equiv 0.529 \text{ Å} \qquad (2.6)$$

The 'Bohr radius' a_0 corresponding to $n = 1$ and $Z = 1$ is the radius of the smallest allowed orbit in Bohr's picture of the hydrogen atom. The next larger allowed orbit of hydrogen would have four times this radius, and so on. Bohr also postulated that an electron can jump from one allowed orbit to another and that when it makes such a transition it absorbs or emits an amount of energy equal to the energy difference between the two orbits. The energy of an allowed orbit can be found by using the Virial theorem, Eq. (2.4). The total energy E is equal to the sum of the kinetic energy and the potential energy

$$E = \tfrac{1}{2}mr^2\omega^2 - \frac{Ze^2}{r} \qquad (2.7)$$

Combining Eqs. (2.7), (2.4), and (2.5) we have

$$E = -\frac{1}{2}\frac{Ze^2}{r} = -\frac{1}{2}\frac{(Ze^2)^2 m_0}{n^2\hbar^2}$$

$$= -\frac{1}{2}\left(\frac{Z}{n}\frac{e^2}{\hbar c}\right)^2 m_0 c^2 \qquad (2.8)$$

The quantity $e^2/\hbar c$ is dimensionless and has the value

$$\frac{e^2}{\hbar c} = \frac{1}{137} \qquad \textbf{(2.9)}$$

$m_0 c^2$ has the dimension of energy and a magnitude such that

$$\frac{m_0 c^2}{(137)^2} = 27{\cdot}1 \text{ electron volts} \qquad \textbf{(2.10)}$$

This means that according to Eq. (2.8) the amount of energy needed to remove an electron from the smallest allowed orbit of hydrogen is about 13·5 electron volts and this agrees well with experiment. In this way Bohr could calculate the amount of energy given up when an electron jumps from an allowed orbit corresponding to the integer n_1 to another orbit corresponding to a smaller integer n_2. The energy difference E is given by

$$E = -\frac{1}{2}\left(\frac{Z}{137}\right)^2 m_0 c^2 \left(\frac{1}{n_1^2} - \frac{1}{n_2^2}\right) \qquad \textbf{(2.11)}$$

and the frequency of the radiation, according to Planck's relationship, Eq. (2.1) is $E/\hbar$.

Bohr's 'number juggling' caused a great outcry among conservative scientists. They felt that he had not justified his postulate that angular momentum must come in units of $\hbar$ or his picture of 'quantum jumps'. Nevertheless, no one could deny that his theory was spectacularly successful in explaining many of the mysterious features of the atom. In the first place, provided that one was willing to accept Bohr's postulates, there was no longer any problem in explaining why the atom does not collapse. An electron in the smallest allowed orbit cannot go into a smaller one. Secondly, the energy required to ionize hydrogen agreed exactly with the amount predicted by Bohr. Thirdly, Bohr's theory unravelled the mystery of the absorption and emission spectra of atoms. These had been extensively studied but were totally unexplained. It was known that the lines of the hydrogen spectrum could be arranged in series. The low-frequency lines of a spectral series were widely spaced. At higher frequencies, near to the 'series limit' the lines became more and more closely spaced and finally merged into a continuum. Prior to Bohr's theory, the Swedish spectroscopist Rydberg had proposed a formula for the frequencies of the hydrogen spectrum exactly similar to Eq. (2.11) except that the constant of proportionality was empirical. In Bohr's theory, the integers n_1 and n_2 of Eq. (2.11) represented the 'quantum numbers' of the initial and final states of the system. A series in the emission spectrum corresponded to transitions from a series of 'excited states' labelled by various values of n_1 to a particular final state labelled by n_2 as shown in Fig. 2.1. It was the custom to name the series after spectroscopists. The series with $n_2 = 1$ is called the 'Lyman series'. The 'Balmer series' has $n_2 = 2$. In the 'Paschen series' $n_2 = 3$; in the 'Bracket series' $n_2 = 4$. There is even a 'Pfund series' with $n_2 = 5$. That makes a good question for after-dinner guessing games. Who was Pfund? At any rate, whoever he was, he has become one of the patron saints of spectroscopy: Lyman, Balmer, Paschen, Bracket, and Pfund. If it were possible to arrange the spectroscopists in order of merit one could honour all of them in this way since there are an infinite number of such series in the hydrogen spectrum.

The periodic table

Bohr's theory also explained many features of the X-ray spectra of the elements. X-rays are electromagnetic radiation of a very high frequency (see Fig. 2.1). They are produced when an electron is knocked out of an inner orbit of a heavy atom and another electron falls down from a higher orbit to take its place. Using Bohr's model, Moseley was able to arrange the elements in order of increasing nuclear charge Z on the basis of their X-ray spectra. He showed that the nuclear charge increases in steps of e where e is the unit charge, negative for an electron and positive for the particles which form the atomic nucleus. When Moseley arranged the elements in order of increasing Z the order was the same as an arrangement on the basis of increasing atomic mass. The nuclear mass does not increase in quite such a regular way as the nuclear charge Ze. For the lighter elements, the nuclear mass is more or less (but not exactly) an

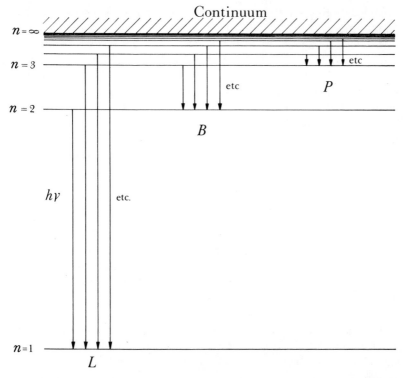

Figure 2.1 shows the energy levels of a hydrogen atom and the first three series in the hydrogen emission spectrum. The allowed energy levels lie below the ionization limit by an amount proportional to $1/n^2$, where n is the principal quantum number. As n increases, the levels become more and more closely spaced, until finally they merge into a continuum. When light is absorbed or emitted, the electron changes from one energy level to another, and the frequency of the light must satisfy the Einstein relationship, $\Delta E = h\nu$.

integral multiple of the mass of the hydrogen nucleus. For example, helium, with $Z = 2$ has a nuclear mass which is approximately four times that of hydrogen. This fact caused Rutherford to postulate that an atomic nucleus is made up of two types of heavy particles: a charged particle which he called a 'proton' and an equally massive neutral particle which he called a 'neutron'. Rutherford, Chadwick, and Ellis were later able to produce beams of free neutrons by bombarding beryllium with alpha particles (helium nuclei) from disintegrating radium. It was of course apparent that the forces which held the nucleus together could not be either electromagnetic or gravitational. In fact, the problem of adequately describing this third kind of force occupies most of the effort of physics at the present time. However, if one assumed the existence of very strong forces to hold the nucleus together, the 'mass defect' of the heavy elements could be

67

explained by Einstein's relationship $E = mc^2$ equating it with the nuclear binding energy.

Moseley's arrangement of the elements in order of increasing nuclear charge showed the periodicity of chemical behavior which had first been pointed out by Mendeleev. However, after Moseley's work, the gaps in the periodic tables were apparent since only a few integral values of Z were missing. After the First World War, during the course of which Moseley was killed, Bohr received the Nobel prize, and he was able to announce at the presentation ceremony that he and his co-workers in Copenhagen had discovered a new element, which they called hafnium after the ancient name of Copenhagen. Bohr felt that his allowed electron orbits were somehow involved in the explanation of the periodic table. If two electrons could fit into the smallest orbit of a many-electron atom, eight into the second orbit, and eighteen into the third, etc., then a correspondence could be established with the periodic table. The elements whose largest filled orbit were completely full corresponded to chemically inert elements. Those elements with one or two extra electrons in the outer orbit (or 'shell') corresponded to chemically active metals. Elements with one or two missing electrons in the outer shell corresponded to active non-metals. But here the weakness of Bohr's theory began to show. It offered no explanation of the fact that the nth atomic orbit could contain just $2n^2$ electrons. It could not give a quantitative description of chemical binding forces. It offered no way of calculating the relative intensities of spectral lines.

de Broglie waves; the Schrödinger equation

Suddenly, in 1925, two different theories were simultaneously proposed both of which completely solved the problem. A French aristocrat, Prince Louis de Broglie, writing his doctoral dissertation at the Sorbonne, had proposed that in order to overcome the difficulties in Bohr's atomic theory it might be necessary to write down a wave equation for matter analogous to Maxwell's equations for light. This thesis came to the attention of Erwin Schrödinger, who was a powerful mathematician. Taking de Broglie's suggestion, he wrote down his famous wave equation for matter. Although the name of Schrödinger is perhaps not exactly a household word, it is nevertheless immortal in the scientific community. Schrödinger was well acquainted with relativity and in fact the first equation which he tried was a relativistically invariant one

$$\left[\nabla^2 - \frac{1}{c^2} \frac{\partial^2}{\partial t^2} - k_0^2 \right] \psi = 0 \qquad (2.12)$$

where k_0 was a quantity with the dimension of reciprocal length made up of the electron mass m_0, the velocity of light c, and Planck's constant $\hbar$,

$$k_0 = \frac{m_0 c}{\hbar} \equiv \frac{1}{\lambda_0} \tag{2.13}$$

where

$$\lambda_0 = \frac{\hbar}{m_0 c} = 3 \cdot 86 \times 10^{-11} \text{ cm} \tag{2.14}$$

λ_0 is called the 'Compton wave length' and is related to the first Bohr radius a_0 of Eq. (2.6) by

$$\lambda_0 = \frac{e^2}{\hbar c} a_0 = \frac{a_0}{137} \tag{2.15}$$

Because of some difficulties in knowing how to insert electromagnetic potential and because of troubles with the interpretation of the wave function ψ, Schrödinger abandoned the search for a relativistically invariant wave equation. (This objective was achieved two years later in 1927 by P. A. M. Dirac who later occupied Newton's former chair at Cambridge.) Schrödinger next tried to find an equation which would be valid in the non-relativistic limit. It can be seen that Eq. (2.12) can be derived by making the substitutions

$$\vec{p} = \frac{\hbar}{i} \frac{\partial}{\partial \vec{x}} \tag{2.16}$$

and

$$E = \frac{-\hbar}{i} \frac{\partial}{\partial t} \tag{2.17}$$

in the relativistic expression

$$-p^2 c^2 + E^2 - m_0^2 c^4 = 0 \tag{2.18}$$

and letting the resulting operator act on the wave function ψ. The non-relativistic limit is the limit where

$$pc \ll m_0 c^2 \tag{2.19}$$

In that limit we can write

$$\begin{aligned} E &= \sqrt{(pc)^2 + (m_0 c^2)^2} \\ &\cong m_0 c^2 + \frac{1}{2} \frac{(pc)^2}{m_0 c^2} \\ &= m_0 c^2 + \frac{p^2}{2m_0} \end{aligned} \tag{2.20}$$

69

The quantum theory of atoms, molecules, and photons

If we measure the energy from a zero taken at the value m_0c^2 and if we also take into account the potential energy V, we have the usual non-relativistic expression

$$-E + \frac{p^2}{2m_0} + V = 0 \tag{2.21}$$

Schrödinger made the substitutions of Eq. (2.16) and Eq. (2.17) into Eq. (2.21) and let the resulting operator act on the wave function ψ. The outcome was his famous non-relativistic wave equation

$$i\hbar \frac{\partial \psi}{\partial t} = \left(\frac{-\hbar^2}{2m_0} \nabla^2 + V \right) \psi \tag{2.22}$$

The hydrogen atom; spherical harmonics; angular dependence of the wave function

The next step was to try to apply the equation to the case of the hydrogen atom where

$$V = \frac{-Ze^2}{r} \tag{2.23}$$

In that case it is convenient to write the Laplacian operator ∇^2 in terms of spherical polar coordinates (see Appendix II).

$$\nabla^2 = \frac{1}{r^2} \frac{\partial}{\partial r} r^2 \frac{\partial}{\partial r} + \frac{1}{r^2 \sin \theta} \frac{\partial}{\partial \theta} \sin \theta \frac{\partial}{\partial \theta} + \frac{1}{r^2 \sin^2 \theta} \frac{\partial^2}{\partial \varphi^2} \tag{2.24}$$

It is also convenient to make use of the spherical harmonics $Y_{l,m}(\theta, \varphi)$. These are a family of functions which have the following properties

$$\left(\frac{1}{\sin \theta} \frac{\partial}{\partial \theta} \sin \theta \frac{\partial}{\partial \theta} + \frac{1}{\sin^2 \theta} \frac{\partial^2}{\partial \varphi^2} \right) Y_{l,m}(\theta, \varphi) = -l(l+1) Y_{l,m}(\theta, \varphi)$$

$$= 0, 1, 2, 3, \ldots \tag{2.25}$$

$$\frac{1}{i} \frac{\partial}{\partial \varphi} Y_{l,m}(\theta, \varphi) = m Y_{l,m}(\theta, \varphi), \quad m = l, l-1, l-2, \ldots, -l \tag{2.26}$$

and

$$\int_0^{2\pi} d\varphi \int_0^{\pi} \sin \theta \, d\theta \, Y_{l',m'}^*(\theta, \varphi) Y_{l,m}(\theta, \varphi)$$

$$= \delta_{l',l} \delta_{m',m} \equiv \begin{cases} 0 & \text{if } l' \neq l \text{ or } m' \neq m \\ 1 & \text{if } l' = l \text{ and } m' = m \end{cases} \tag{2.27}$$

The asterisk in Eq. (2.27) means 'complex conjugate'. The first few spherical harmonics are listed in Table 2.1

Table 2.1

$l = 0, \quad 2l + 1 = 1$

$$Y_{0,0} = \frac{1}{\sqrt{4\pi}}$$

$l = 1, \quad 2l + 1 = 3$

$$Y_{1,1} = -\sqrt{\frac{3}{8\pi}} \sin\theta \, e^{i\varphi}$$

$$Y_{1,0} = \sqrt{\frac{3}{4\pi}} \cos\theta$$

$$Y_{1,-1} = \sqrt{\frac{3}{8\pi}} \sin\theta \, e^{-i\varphi}$$

$l = 2, \quad 2l + 1 = 5$

$$Y_{2,2} = \sqrt{\frac{15}{32\pi}} \sin^2\theta \, e^{2i\varphi}$$

$$Y_{2,1} = -\sqrt{\frac{15}{8\pi}} \sin\theta \cos\theta \, e^{i\varphi}$$

$$Y_{2,0} = \sqrt{\frac{5}{16\pi}} (3\cos^2\theta - 1)$$

$$Y_{2,-1} = \sqrt{\frac{15}{8\pi}} \sin\theta \cos\theta \, e^{-i\varphi}$$

$$Y_{2,-2} = \sqrt{\frac{15}{32\pi}} \sin^2\theta \, e^{-2i\varphi}$$

$l = 3, \quad 2l + 1 = 7$

$$Y_{3,3} = -\sqrt{\frac{35}{64\pi}} \sin^3\theta \, e^{3i\varphi}$$

$$Y_{3,2} = \sqrt{\frac{105}{32\pi}} \sin^2\theta \cos\theta \, e^{2i\varphi}$$

$$Y_{3,1} = -\sqrt{\frac{21}{64\pi}} (5\cos^2\theta - 1) \sin\theta \, e^{i\varphi}$$

$$Y_{3,0} = \sqrt{\frac{63}{16\pi}} (\tfrac{5}{3}\cos^3\theta - \cos\theta)$$

$$Y_{3,-1} = \sqrt{\frac{21}{64\pi}} (5\cos^2\theta - 1) \sin\theta \, e^{-i\varphi}$$

$$Y_{3,-2} = \sqrt{\frac{105}{32\pi}} \sin^2\theta \cos\theta \, e^{-2i\varphi}$$

$$Y_{3,-3} = \sqrt{\frac{35}{64\pi}} \sin^3\theta \, e^{-3i\varphi}$$

(It should be noticed that the spherical harmonics with positive odd values of m are given a negative sign. The majority of authors who deal with ligand field theory adhere to this choice of phases. It is important to be consistent about the phase convention when discussing the Condon–Shortley coefficients, Table 9.4.)

It is a good exercise to try a few examples and verify that the spherical harmonics listed in Table 2.1 have the properties of Eqs. (2.25)–(2.27). It can be seen that they arrange themselves in sets labelled by a particular value of the index l. For each value of l there are $2l + 1$ values of m, starting with l and running in steps of 1 down to $-l$. Apart from a normalizing constant $Y_{l,l}$ is always given by

$$Y_{l,l} \sim \sin^l \theta \, e^{il\varphi} \tag{2.28}$$

The spherical harmonics corresponding to lower values of m are found by successive application of the 'lowering operator'

$$e^{-i\varphi} \left(\frac{\partial}{\partial \theta} - i \cot \theta \, \frac{\partial}{\partial \varphi} \right) \tag{2.29}$$

so that apart from a normalizing factor

$$Y_{l,m} \sim \left\{ e^{-i\varphi} \left(\frac{\partial}{\partial \theta} - i \cot \theta \, \frac{\partial}{\partial \varphi} \right) \right\}^{l-m} \sin^l \theta \, e^{il\varphi} \tag{2.30}$$

With a certain amount of labour one can show by direct substitution that Eq. (2.25) and Eq. (2.26) are satisfied by the function given in Eq. (2.30). In fact, the partial differential equations Eq. (2.25) and Eq. (2.26) can be satisfied by a function of the form shown in Eq. (2.30) even for non-integral values of l. However, if we add the 'boundary condition' that $Y_{l,m}(\theta, \varphi)$ must be a single-valued function of the angles θ and φ, then l and m are restricted to integral values. The reason why Eq. (2.27) holds will be discussed later. In fact, for the moment, we do not really need to know about this last property of the spherical harmonics which is called 'orthonormality'.

It is easy to see that the spherical harmonics will be very helpful in finding a solution of Schrödinger's equation for the electron in a hydrogen atom. We can try to find solutions of the form

$$\psi = R(r) Y_{l,m}(\theta, \varphi) e^{-i(Et/\hbar)} \tag{2.31}$$

If ψ has the form of Eq. (2.31) then

$$i\hbar \frac{\partial \psi}{\partial t} = E\psi \tag{2.32}$$

Substituting Eqs. (2.31), (2.32), and (2.24) in Eq. (2.22) we have

$$\left[\frac{-\hbar^2}{2m_0}\left\{\frac{1}{r^2}\frac{\partial}{\partial r}r^2\frac{\partial}{\partial r} + \frac{1}{r^2}\left(\frac{1}{\sin\theta}\frac{\partial}{\partial\theta}\sin\theta\frac{\partial}{\partial\theta} + \frac{1}{\sin^2\theta}\frac{\partial^2}{\partial\varphi^2}\right)\right\} - E - \frac{Ze^2}{r}\right]$$

$$\times\ R(r)Y_{l,m}(\theta,\varphi) = 0 \quad (2.33)$$

Problem (2.1) (a) Show by direct integration that Eq. (2.27) holds for the spherical harmonics with $l = 0$ and $l = 1$.

(b) Show that $Y_{l,l} \sim \sin^l\theta\ e^{il\phi}$ satisfies Eq. (2.25).

(c) Use Eq. (2.30) to generate the spherical harmonics with $l = 2$.

The radial dependence of hydrogen-like atomic orbitals

Making use of Eq. (2.25) and dividing by $Y_{l,m}(\theta,\varphi)$ we have an equation for the radial part of the wave function:

$$\left[\frac{1}{r^2}\frac{d}{dr}r^2\frac{d}{dr} + k^2\right]R(r) = 0 \quad (2.34)$$

where

$$k^2 = \frac{2m_0}{\hbar^2}(E - U) \quad (2.35)$$

and U is an effective potential composed of the Coulomb attraction and a term which corresponds to the centrifugal repulsion.

$$U(r) = \frac{-Ze^2}{r} + \frac{\hbar^2 l(l+1)}{2m_0 r^2} \quad (2.36)$$

The effective potential $U(r)$ is shown in Fig. 2.2 for various values of l.

In order to solve the radial equation, Eq. (2.34), it is convenient to make use of the 'confluent hypergeometric function', so-called because it is a generalized type of geometric series. The confluent hypergeometric function $F(a|b|x)$ is defined as the series

$$F(a|b|x) \equiv 1 + \frac{a}{b}x + \frac{a(a+1)x^2}{b(b+1)2!} + \frac{a(a+1)(a+2)\,x^3}{b(b+1)(b+2)\,3!} + \cdots, \text{etc.}$$

$$(2.37)$$

Both this type of function and the spherical harmonics had been invented and studied long before the advent of quantum theory. In fact, the hypergeometric functions had been introduced by Gauss in the nineteenth

73

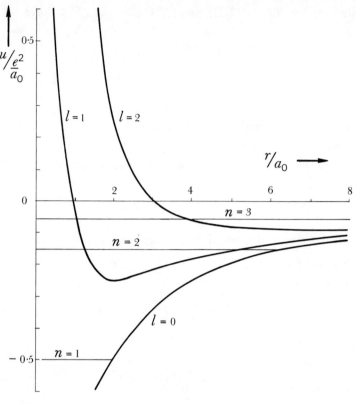

Figure 2.2 shows the effective potential experienced by an electron in a hydrogen atom: $U = (e^2/a_0)(-1/\rho + l(l + 1)/2\rho^2)$, where $\rho = r/a_0$, $a_0 = 0.529$ Å and $e^2/a_0 = 27.09$ eV. The higher the angular momentum quantum number l, the greater the centrifugal potential which tends to keep the electron away from the nucleus. The minimum of the potential U occurs at $r = l(l + 1)a_0$ and at that radius U has the value $-(e^2/2a_0)l(l + 1)$. Comparing this value with the hydrogen atom energy eigenvalues $E = -e^2/2a_0n^2$, we can see that we must have $l \leq n - 1$ if the energy levels are not to fall below the minimum of U.

century. One can show by laborious but direct substitution that the function

$$R_{n,l}(\rho) \sim \rho^l e^{-\rho/n} F\left(l + 1 - n \,\middle|\, 2l + 2 \,\middle|\, \frac{2\rho}{n}\right)$$

$$= \rho^l e^{-\rho/n} \left\{ 1 + \frac{(l + 1 - n)}{(2l + 2)} \frac{2\rho}{n} \right.$$

$$\left. + \frac{(l + 1 - n)(l + 2 - n)}{(2l + 2)(2l + 3)} \frac{(2\rho/n)^2}{2!} + \cdots \right\} \tag{2.38}$$

74

where

$$\rho \equiv \frac{Zr}{a_0} \equiv \frac{Zm_0e^2r}{\hbar^2} \tag{2.39}$$

and

$$n^2 \equiv \frac{-(Ze)^2}{2a_0E} \tag{2.40}$$

is a solution of Eq. (2.34). From a physical standpoint it is plausible to add the boundary condition that the wave function ψ must not become larger and larger as $r \to \infty$. This catastrophe will occur unless the series of Eq. (2.38) terminates. In order for the series to terminate, n must be a positive integer. This brings us back again to Bohr's formula since from Eq. (2.40) we have

$$E = \frac{-(Ze)^2}{2a_0n^2} = \cdot -\frac{1}{2}\left(\frac{Z}{137n}\right)^2 m_0c^2, \quad n = 1, 2, 3, \ldots \tag{2.41}$$

Schrödinger thus was able to derive Bohr's important results from an entirely different point of view. His wave equation showed the meaning of the quantum numbers which had been introduced in an arbitrary way into the older theory. They were like indices labelling the harmonics of an organ pipe. To be more exact, the allowed wave functions for an electron in a hydrogen atom were analogous to the harmonics of an oriental flute with a spherical resonating cavity; the higher the quantum numbers, the greater the number of nodes in the harmonic. Apart from a normalizing constant which is chosen so that

$$\int_0^\infty r^2 \, dr\{R_{n,l}(r)\}^2 = 1 \tag{2.42}$$

the radial part of the wave function is given by Eq. (2.38). The first few of the allowed wave functions $R_{n,l}$ are shown in Table 2.2 in terms of the dimensionless parameter $\rho = Zr/a_0$.

The complete space-dependent part of the electron wave functions for hydrogen are now easily found by combining Tables 2.1 and 2.2 according to Eq. (2.31). These functions are called 'hydrogen-like atomic orbitals'. The first few of them are listed in Table 2.3 and illustrated in Fig. 2.3. Except where $m = 0$, the orbitals $\chi_{n,l,m}$ and $\chi_{n,l,-m}$ have been combined to give the two corresponding real solutions which are more easily visualized. We can do this because a linear combination of two solutions belonging to the same energy is also a solution.

Table 2.2

The radial wave functions $R_{n,l}$ with $\rho = Zr/a_0$. The normalizing factor,

$$\frac{2^{l+1}}{n^{l+2}(2l+1)!}\sqrt{\frac{(n+l)!}{(n-l-1)!}}\left(\frac{Z}{a_0}\right)^{3/2}$$

is chosen so that Eq. (2.42) will be fulfilled.

$$R_{1,0} = 2\left(\frac{Z}{a_0}\right)^{3/2} e^{-\rho}$$

$$R_{2,0} = \frac{1}{\sqrt{2}}\left(\frac{Z}{a_0}\right)^{3/2} e^{-\rho/2}\left(1 - \frac{\rho}{2}\right)$$

$$R_{2,1} = \frac{1}{2\sqrt{6}}\left(\frac{Z}{a_0}\right)^{3/2} e^{-\rho/2}\rho$$

$$R_{3,0} = \frac{2}{3\sqrt{3}}\left(\frac{Z}{a_0}\right)^{3/2} e^{-\rho/3}\left(1 - \frac{2\rho}{3} + \frac{2\rho^2}{27}\right)$$

$$R_{3,1} = \frac{8}{27\sqrt{6}}\left(\frac{Z}{a_0}\right)^{3/2} e^{-\rho/3}\left(\rho - \frac{\rho^2}{6}\right)$$

$$R_{3,2} = \frac{4}{81\sqrt{30}}\left(\frac{Z}{a_0}\right)^{3/2} e^{-\rho/3}\rho^2$$

$$R_{4,0} = \frac{1}{4}\left(\frac{Z}{a_0}\right)^{3/2} e^{-\rho/4}\left(1 - \frac{3\rho}{4} + \frac{\rho^2}{8} - \frac{\rho^3}{192}\right)$$

$$R_{4,1} = \frac{1}{16}\sqrt{\frac{5}{3}}\left(\frac{Z}{a_0}\right)^{3/2} e^{-\rho/4}\left(\rho - \frac{\rho^2}{4} + \frac{\rho^3}{80}\right)$$

$$R_{4,2} = \frac{1}{64\sqrt{5}}\left(\frac{Z}{a_0}\right)^{3/2} e^{-\rho/4}\left(\rho^2 - \frac{\rho^3}{12}\right)$$

$$R_{4,3} = \frac{1}{768\sqrt{35}}\left(\frac{Z}{a_0}\right)^{3/2} e^{-\rho/4}\rho^3$$

Problem (2.2) (a) Show that with the substitution

$$R(r) = \chi(r)/r$$

Eq. (2.34) becomes

$$\left(\frac{d^2}{dr^2} + k^2\right)\chi(r) = 0$$

(b) According to the semiclassical approximation of Wentzel, Kramers, and Brillouin, this equation has the approximate solution,

$$\chi(r) \sim \frac{1}{\sqrt{k}} e^{\pm i\int k\,dr}$$

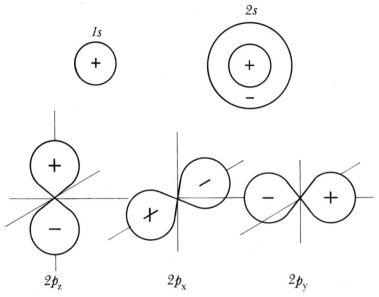

Figure 2.3 shows schematically the first few hydrogen-like wave functions listed in Table 2.3. The 1s and 2s functions are spherically symmetric. However, while the 1s function decreases exponentially from a maximum value at the nucleus, all of the $n = 2$ functions have a 'nodal surface' where they change sign. It is interesting to compare these functions with the harmonics of a vibrating string, a drum-head, and a spherical cavity. The last is, of course, the closest analogy, and in fact the harmonics of a spherical cavity have exactly the same angular dependence as the hydrogen-like wave functions.

At what values of r does the W.K.B. solution break down? Can you use it to evaluate the energy levels of hydrogen for $l = 0$? (Hint: Use the Bohr–Sommerfeld–Wilson quantum condition $\int k \, dr = n\pi$ with $\hbar k = \sqrt{2m(E - V)}$. The substitution $-Er/e^2 = \sin^2\eta$ is helpful in evaluating the integral.)

Degeneracy of the atomic orbitals

The interesting thing to notice about Table 2.3 is that there are exactly n^2 different linearly independent hydrogen wave functions corresponding to the energy level labelled by a particular value of n. (Several functions ϕ_k are linearly independent if the statement $\sum_k a_k \phi_k = 0$ implies that all of the constants a_k are zero). One says that the nth energy level has a 'degeneracy' equal to n^2, meaning that n^2 is the number of different solutions which correspond to that energy. The reason why the degree of degeneracy is exactly n^2 is that the possible values of the quantum number l run from 0 up to $n - 1$, while for each value of l there are $2l + 1$ values of

77

The quantum theory of atoms, molecules, and photons

Table 2.3

The hydrogen-like atomic orbitals $x_{n,l,m} = R_{n,l}(r)\, Y_{l,m}(\theta, \varphi)$ with $\rho = Zr/a_0$. The terminology $s, p, d, f, g, h, \ldots$, etc. for $l = 0, 1, 2, 3, 4, \ldots$, etc., is based on an old spectroscopic notation.

$$n = 1, \quad E_1 = -\frac{(Ze)^2}{2a_0}$$

$$\chi_{1s} \equiv \chi_{1,0,0} = \frac{1}{\sqrt{\pi}} \left(\frac{Z}{a_0}\right)^{3/2} e^{-\rho}$$

$$n = 2, \quad E_2 = -\frac{(Ze)^2}{8a_0}$$

$$\chi_{2s} \equiv \chi_{2,0,0} = \frac{1}{2\sqrt{2\pi}} \left(\frac{Z}{a_0}\right)^{3/2} e^{-\rho/2} \left(1 - \frac{\rho}{2}\right)$$

$$\chi_{2p_x} \equiv \frac{1}{\sqrt{2}} (\chi_{2,1,1} + \chi_{2,1,-1})$$

$$= \frac{1}{4\sqrt{2\pi}} \left(\frac{Z}{a_0}\right)^{3/2} e^{-\rho/2} \rho \sin\theta \cos\varphi$$

$$\chi_{2p_y} \equiv \frac{1}{\sqrt{2i}} (\chi_{2,1,1} - \chi_{2,1,-1})$$

$$= \frac{1}{4\sqrt{2\pi}} \left(\frac{Z}{a_0}\right)^{3/2} e^{-\rho/2} \rho \sin\theta \sin\varphi$$

$$\chi_{2p_z} \equiv \chi_{2,1,0} = \frac{1}{4\sqrt{2\pi}} \left(\frac{Z}{a_0}\right)^{3/2} e^{-\rho/2} \rho \cos\theta$$

$$n = 3, \quad E_3 = -\frac{(Ze)^2}{18a_0}$$

$$\chi_{3s} \equiv \chi_{3,0,0} = \frac{1}{3\sqrt{3\pi}} \left(\frac{Z}{a_0}\right)^{3/2} e^{-\rho/3} \left(1 - \frac{2\rho}{3} + \frac{2\rho^2}{27}\right)$$

$$\chi_{3p_x} \equiv \frac{1}{\sqrt{2}} (\chi_{3,1,1} + \chi_{3,1,-1})$$

$$\frac{2}{27} \sqrt{\frac{2}{\pi}} \left(\frac{Z}{a_0}\right)^{3/2} e^{-\rho/3} \left(\rho - \frac{\rho^2}{6}\right) \sin\theta \cos\varphi$$

$$\chi_{3p_y} \equiv \frac{1}{\sqrt{2i}} (\chi_{3,1,1} - \chi_{3,1,-1})$$

$$= \frac{2}{27} \sqrt{\frac{2}{\pi}} \left(\frac{Z}{a_0}\right)^{3/2} e^{-\rho/3} \left(\rho - \frac{\rho^2}{6}\right) \sin\theta \sin\varphi$$

$$\chi_{3p_z} \equiv \frac{2}{27} \sqrt{\frac{2}{\pi}} \left(\frac{Z}{a_0}\right)^{3/2} e^{-\rho/3} \left(\rho - \frac{\rho^2}{6}\right) \cos\theta$$

Table 2.3 (continued)

$$\chi_{3d_{xy}} \equiv \frac{1}{\sqrt{2}} (\chi_{3,2,2} + \chi_{3,2,-2})$$

$$= \frac{1}{81\sqrt{2\pi}} \left(\frac{Z}{a_0}\right)^{3/2} e^{-\rho/3} \rho^2 \sin^2 \theta \cos (2\varphi)$$

$$\chi_{3d_{x^2-y^2}} \equiv \frac{1}{\sqrt{2i}} (\chi_{3,2,2} - \chi_{3,2,-2})$$

$$= \frac{1}{81\sqrt{2\pi}} \left(\frac{Z}{a_0}\right)^{3/2} e^{-\rho/3} \rho^2 \sin^2 \theta \sin (2\varphi)$$

$$\chi_{3d_{xz}} \equiv \frac{1}{\sqrt{2}} (\chi_{3,2,1} + \chi_{3,2,-1})$$

$$= \frac{1}{81} \sqrt{\frac{2}{\pi}} \left(\frac{Z}{a_0}\right)^{3/2} e^{-\rho/3} \rho^2 \cos \theta \sin \theta \cos \varphi$$

$$\chi_{3d_{yz}} \equiv \frac{1}{\sqrt{2i}} (\chi_{3,2,1} - \chi_{3,2,-1})$$

$$= \frac{1}{81} \sqrt{\frac{2}{\pi}} \left(\frac{Z}{a_0}\right)^{3/2} e^{-\rho/3} \rho^2 \cos \theta \sin \theta \sin \varphi$$

$$\chi_{3d_{z^2}} \equiv \chi_{3,2,0} = \frac{1}{81\sqrt{6\pi}} \left(\frac{Z}{a_0}\right)^{3/2} e^{-\rho/3} \rho^2 (3 \cos^2 \theta - 1)$$

m. To compute the total number of different solutions corresponding to a particular value of energy we have to calculate the sum

$$\sum_{l=0}^{n-1} (2l + 1) = 2 \sum_{l=0}^{n-1} l + n \qquad (2.43)$$

If we think of a checker board with n squares along each edge, we can see that the sum $0 + 1 + 2 + \cdots + (n - 1)$ represents the number of squares below the diagonal, as shown in Fig. 2.4. Twice this sum plus the n diagonal squares will give us the total number of squares, that is, n^2. Comparing this with Eq. (2.43) we can see that

$$\sum_{l=0}^{n-1} (2l + 1) = n^2 \qquad (2.44)$$

The Pauli exclusion principle and the periodic table

This fact gave Wolfgang Pauli a clue to the explanation of the periodic table. He proposed his famous 'exclusion principle' which states that *the*

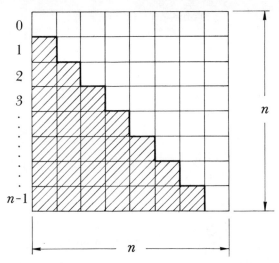

Figure 2.4 illustrates the method of C. F. Gauss for summing the series $1 + 2 + 3 + \cdots + (n - 1)$. We can see from the figure that the sum is equal to the number of squares below the diagonal. The total number of squares in the checker board is n^2. Taking away the diagonal and dividing by 2 gives us the shaded area, so that $1 + 2 + 3 + \cdots + (n - 1) = \frac{1}{2}(n^2 - n)$. Gauss invented this method independently when he was only nine years old (although it may have been known to others before him). His teacher was in the habit of asking the class to do problems like summing up all the integers from one to a hundred. One day, Gauss amazed the teacher by handing in the correct answer almost as soon as the problem had been written down!

wave function of a many-electron system must be antisymmetric with respect to the operation exchanging the coordinates of any two electrons. Pauli's exclusion principle is connected with the fact that the electrons are fundamental particles without any internal structure and it is impossible to tell two electrons apart. One feels that Mao Tse Tung would be delighted with quantum theory. Not only are the electrons all equal—they are so equal that it is impossible to identify them. This being so, the energy of a system ought not to be affected when two electrons trade places. Now consider a many-electron system such as a helium atom. In order to generalize the Schrödinger equation, Eq. (2.22), to a many-electron system we notice that Eq. (2.22) can be written in the form

$$i\hbar \frac{\partial \Psi}{\partial t} = H\Psi \qquad (2.45)$$

where H is the classical Hamiltonian function of the electron with the substitutions of Eq. (2.16). The Schrödinger equation for a many-electron system is formally identical with Eq. (2.45) but now H is the many-electron Hamiltonian with each electron momentum $\vec{p}_i$ replaced by $(\hbar/i)(\partial/\partial \vec{x}_i)$.

80

The wave function Ψ now involves the coordinates of all the electrons in the system. Thus, for example, the quantum mechanical Hamiltonian for the two electrons in a helium atom, with nuclear charge $Z = 2$ would be

$$H = \frac{-\hbar^2}{2m_0}(\nabla_1^2 + \nabla_2^2) - \frac{2e^2}{|\vec{x}_1|} - \frac{2e^2}{|\vec{x}_2|} + \frac{e^2}{|\vec{x}_1 - \vec{x}_2|} \tag{2.46}$$

Equation (2.46) involves three position coordinates for each electron, making a total of six. The symbols ∇_1^2 and ∇_2^2 in Eq. (2.46) mean the Laplacian operator in terms respectively of the coordinates $\vec{x}_1$ and $\vec{x}_2$. As in the case of the hydrogen atom we can look for solutions whose time-dependence is harmonic, so that

$$i\hbar \frac{\partial \Psi}{\partial t} = E\Psi = H\Psi \tag{2.47}$$

Now think of an operator P which exchanges the identity of the two electrons. The Hamiltonian of the system, Eq. (2.46) is unchanged if the two electrons trade places, and from this it follows that

$$PH\Psi = HP\Psi \tag{2.48}$$

Equation (2.48) shows that it is possible to find solutions to Eq. (2.47) which satisfy

$$P\Psi = \lambda\Psi \tag{2.49}$$

where λ is a constant. (You can check that if Eq. (2.48) did not hold, then Eq. (2.47) and Eq. (2.49) would be mutually contradictory.) Since applying the exchange operator P twice makes the electrons trade places and then trade back again, it does nothing at all and so we write

$$P^2\Psi = \lambda^2\Psi = \Psi \tag{2.50}$$

from which

$$\lambda = \pm 1 \tag{2.51}$$

It turns out that the states which one finds in nature for a two-electron system correspond to $\lambda = -1$; in other words, they are antisymmetric with respect to the exchange of the two electrons. For a many-electron system, the observed states are antisymmetric with respect to the exchange of any two electrons. We can try to write the time-independent part of an antisymmetric wave function for a two-electron system in the form

$$\Psi = \frac{1}{\sqrt{2}}\{\chi_a(1)\chi_b(2) - \chi_b(1)\chi_a(2)\} \tag{2.52}$$

If the two 'one-electron orbitals' χ_a and χ_b are exactly the same, then Ψ just disappears. That is why Pauli's principle is called the exclusion principle.

It implies that no two one-electron orbitals in a many-electron system can be exactly alike. In helium, we might try to construct a solution to Eq. (2.47) with H given by Eq. (2.46) using the hydrogen-like atomic orbitals of Table 2.3. If we neglect the interelectron repulsion $e^2/|\vec{x}_1 - \vec{x}_2|$ and let $\chi_a = \chi_{n,l,m}$ with $\chi_b = \chi_{n',l',m'}$ then the antisymmetric wave function Ψ of Eq. (2.52) will be a solution. According to Pauli's exclusion principle, χ_a and χ_b are not allowed to be exactly the same. On the other hand, as you may remember, when Bohr was trying to explain the periodic table on the basis of his orbits, he found that he could do it by assuming that two electrons can fit into the $n = 1$ energy level (or 'shell'), eight into the $n = 2$ shell, 18 into the $n = 3$ shell and so on. In other words, $2n^2$ electrons must fit into the nth shell. But we have just shown that there are n^2 hydrogen-like atomic orbitals corresponding to the nth shell.

The spin quantum number and spin magnetic moment

The discrepancy caused the Dutch physicists Uhlenbeck and Goud-schmidt[24] to postulate that another quantum number is needed which can take on two possible values. This quantum number seemed to be associated with an intrinsic angular momentum and magnetic moment of the electron —as though the electron were spinning—and so they called it 'spin'. In a magnetic field the spectral lines were split by an amount which could be explained if the electron had an intrinsic magnetic moment equal to

$$\frac{e\hbar}{2m_0c} = 0 \cdot 579 \times 10^{-9} \frac{\text{electron-volts}}{\text{gauss}} = \text{one Bohr magneton} \quad \textbf{(2.53)}$$

which could point either parallel to the magnetic field or else perpendicular to it. The associated angular momentum in the direction of the magnetic field seemed to be $\pm\frac{1}{2}\hbar$. For this reason, Uhlenbeck and Goudschmidt postulated that their spin quantum number m_s could take on the values $\frac{1}{2}$ and $-\frac{1}{2}$. When P.A.M. Dirac wrote down his relativistic wave equation for an electron moving in an electromagnetic field, he was able not only to derive the existence of the electron's spin angular momentum but also to show that its magnetic moment had to be equal to $e\hbar/2m_0c$. We shall discuss the Dirac equation later on and show how this happened.

The helium atom

Let us denote the 'spin part' of an electron wave function by α when $m_s = \frac{1}{2}$ and by β when $m_s = -\frac{1}{2}$. Then we can write down an approximate wave function for the two electrons in a helium atom neglecting the interelectron repulsion.

$$\Psi = \frac{1}{\sqrt{2}} \{\chi_a(1)\chi_b(2) - \chi_b(1)\chi_a(2)\} \tag{2.54}$$

$$\Psi = \frac{1}{\sqrt{2}} \Bigg[\{\chi_{1,0,0}(\vec{x}_1)\alpha(1)\} \{\chi_{1,0,0}(\vec{x}_2)\beta(2)\}$$

$$- \{\chi_{1,0,0}(\vec{x}_1)\beta(1)\} \{\chi_{1,0,0}(\vec{x}_2)\alpha(2)\} \Bigg]$$

$$= \frac{1}{\sqrt{2}} \left(\frac{Z}{a_0}\right)^3 e^{-(Z/a_0)\,(|\vec{x}_1| + |\vec{x}_2|)} \{\alpha(1)\beta(2) - \beta(1)\alpha(2)\} \tag{2.55}$$

In Eq. (2.55), $\alpha(1)\beta(2)$ means a state where the first electron has the spin quantum number $m_s = \frac{1}{2}$ and the second electron has $m_s = -\frac{1}{2}$; $\beta(1)\alpha(2)$ represents the opposite situation. Both of the electrons fit into the lowest atomic orbital because there are two available spin states. However, when one comes to lithium with nuclear charge $Z = 3$, there is no more room in that bed (so to speak) and the antisymmetrized 3-electron wave function has got to make use of an energetically much more expensive wave function with $n = 2$. One says colloquially that the third electron goes into the $n = 2$ shell but strictly speaking you cannot say which electron does this since they are all mixed together democratically in the wave function. The chemical activity of lithium derives from the fact that the third electron has to sit up in such an uncomfortable position. It would much rather be somewhere else. On the other hand, in helium the binding energy per electron is already so large that the system cannot get any benefit from association with other atoms. The principle of building up the elements by putting the electrons into the lowest available atomic orbitals is called the 'aufbau principle' after the German word for 'building up'.

Shells and subshells

We have been neglecting the interelectron repulsion term $e^2/|\vec{x}_1 - \vec{x}_2|$. If this is taken into account, then we must think of each electron as moving not only in the Coulomb field of the nucleus but also in the field of the other electrons. The resulting potential, although it is central, is not a Coulomb potential. In other words, it depends only on r but it does not fall off as $1/r$. For an electron moving in a central potential which is not quite a Coulomb potential the wave functions are similar to the hydrogen-like atomic orbitals of Table 2.3 but the degeneracy of the energy levels is partly removed, as shown schematically in Fig. 2.5. The energy of the orbital in such a potential depends not only on the quantum number n but also on the quantum number l. If, in addition, an externally produced, non-central electrostatic potential, is added, then the energy also depends on m. Finally, in the presence of a magnetic field, the energy also depends on the spin quantum number m_s, and the degeneracy is completely removed. In a many-electron atom when there are no externally applied fields, the energy associated with a one-electron orbital depends only on n and l. (Later we shall discuss some small terms in the Hamiltonian which we have so far neglected. These terms can give an m and s dependence to the energy of an atomic orbital.) The energy levels corresponding to different values of l but the same value of n are called the 'subshells' belonging to that shell. Subshells with $l = 0$ are denoted by the letter s, (not to be confused with the spin quantum number), those with $l = 1$, are denoted by p, $l = 2$ by d, $l = 3$ by f, $l = 4$ by g, $l = 5$ by h, and so on. The names s, p, d, and f derive from an old spectroscopic terminology 'sharp, principal, diffuse, and

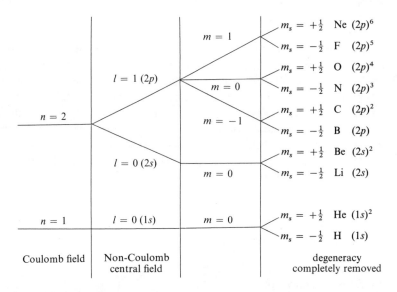

Figure 2.5a shows schematically the $2n^2 = 2$-fold degenerate $n = 1$ level and the $2n^2 = 8$-fold degenerate $n = 2$ level for electrons moving in a pure Coulomb field. In a many-electron atom, each electron feels not only the Coulomb field of the nucleus, but also a potential due to the other electrons which does not vary as $1/r$. In the resulting non-Coulomb central field, the levels belonging to different values of l are no longer degenerate. The $2(2l + 1) = 6$-fold degenerate $l = 1$ level splits away from the $2(2l + 1) = 2$-fold degenerate $l = 0$ level. However, the splitting here is small compared with the energy differences between the $n = 1$, $n = 2$, and $n = 3$ levels, so that the chemical properties of the first-row elements are not very much affected by it.

84

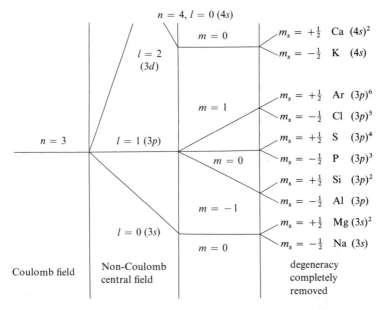

Figure 2.5b is similar to Fig. 2.5a, but shows the $n = 3$ levels. Here the splitting between the $l = 2$ level and the others is large compared with the energy difference between the $n = 3$ and the $n = 4$ levels. In fact, as one moves along the periodic table between argon, the next level to be filled is the $n = 4$, $l = 0$ ($4s$) level. One refers to the set of atomic orbitals or energy levels belonging to a particular value of n as a 'shell', and of these, the subset belonging to a particular value of l is called a 'subshell'. Thus we would say that as we move along the periodic table towards elements of increasing atomic number, adding more and more electrons and filling the lowest-lying atomic orbitals in accordance with the Pauli exclusion principle, the $4s$ subshell is filled before the $3d$ subshell.

fundamental'. Thus one speaks of the $1s$ subshell meaning the subshell with $n = 1$ and $l = 0$ or the $2p$ subshell meaning the subshell with $n = 2$ and $l = 1$. The common names of the atomic orbitals in Table 2.3 also follow this terminology.

Hund's rule

Because of an 'exchange effect' (see chapter 9) which tends to make the spins line up parallel to one another, the atomic orbitals with parallel spins within a particular subshell tend to be filled first as one progresses towards the heavier elements in the periodic table. This rule for the filling of the subshells is called 'Hund's rule'. For example, in Fig. 2.6 the electron configuration of nitrogen is shown in a schematic way. The number of available atomic orbitals in a given subshell is indicated by the number of circles on

85

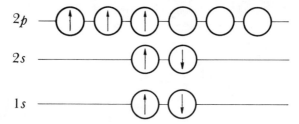

Figure 2.6 shows schematically the electron configuration of nitrogen, and helps to clarify the meaning of Figs. 2.5a and 2.5b. The circles stand for available atomic orbitals in a shell or subshell. When there is an upward-pointing arrow in a circle, it means an occupied 'spin-up' orbital, i.e., an occupied orbital with spin quantum number $m_s = \frac{1}{2}$. Similarly, a circle with a downward-pointing arrow indicates an occupied 'spin-down' orbital, and an empty circle indicates an unoccupied orbital. Notice that the orbitals within a subshell are degenerate. On the right-hand side of Figs. 2.5a and 2.5b, we show schematically the splitting of the levels in a strong magnetic field, which completely removes the degeneracy. However, in an unperturbed atom, the orbitals within a subshell are very nearly degenerate, and the order of filling is determined by an exchange effect (discussed in chapter 9). Because of this effect the atomic orbitals with parallel spins are filled first (Hund's rule). The electron configuration of nitrogen is written as $(1s)^2(2s)^2(2p)^3$, and in Fig. 2.5a it is abbreviated as $(2p)^3$, the superscript indicating the number of electrons in the subshell.

that line. When an orbital is used in the construction of the antisymmetrized many-electron wave function, an arrow is placed in the circle. An upward-pointing arrow indicates the $m_s = \frac{1}{2}$ spin state and a downward-pointing arrow indicates the $m_s = -\frac{1}{2}$ spin state. In order to represent the electron configuration of oxygen we would have to put a downward-pointing arrow in the next empty circle. We could not add another $m_s = \frac{1}{2}$ 'spin up' electron because the three remaining orbitals in the $2p$ subshell have the spin quantum number $m_s = -\frac{1}{2}$.

The electron configuration of the elements

As the value of the 'principal quantum number' n increases, the energy levels become more and more closely spaced, as shown in Fig. 2.1. For the higher values of n the shells overlap one another and the order of filling of the subshells depends on l as well as on n. For example, the $n = 3$ shell and the $n = 4$ shell are close enough together in energy so that the $4s$ subshell comes below the $3d$ subshell as shown schematically in Fig. 2.7. Next above the $3d$ subshell is $4p$, but where we would expect to find $4d$, we instead encounter the depressed $5s$ subshell. This l-dependence of the orbital energies, which is shown in Fig. 2.7, causes the regularity of the periodic table to break down. After the element argon with its completely filled $3p$ subshell, comes potassium, with a single $4s$ electron. Potassium is an active

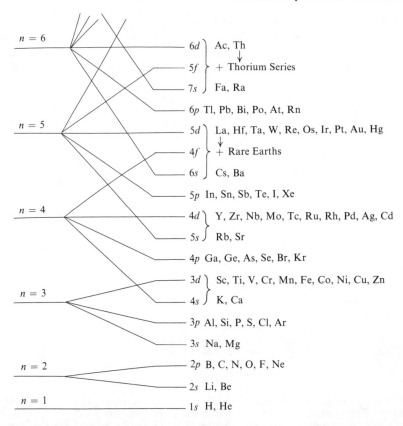

Figure 2.7 shows the electron configurations of the elements. The spacing of the energies is schematic rather than realistic. In reality, the shells become more closely spaced as n increases, and this accounts for the fact that for large values of n, the splitting of the subshells is greater than the spacing of the shells. The $4s$ and $3d$ subshells are bracketed together, indicating that they are so closely spaced that the order of filling is irregular (as shown in Fig. 2.8). Similarly, the $5s$ and $4d$ subshells are bracketed together, and fill irregularly, as do the sub-shells involved in the rare earth series and the thorium series.

monovalent metal although its nuclear charge Z does not follow the rule for monovalent metals, $Z = 2n^2 + 1$, a rule obeyed by hydrogen, lithium, and sodium. Chlorine is an active, monovalent non-metal although its nuclear charge does not follow the rule for monovalent non-metals, $Z = 2n^2 - 1$, a rule followed by hydrogen and fluorine. The negative valence of chlorine derives from a relatively large energy gap between the $3p$ and $4s$ subshells. Finally we come to gross irregularities such as the series of 'transition elements': scandium, titanium, vanadium, chromium, manganese, iron, cobalt, nickel, copper, and zinc, and the so-called 'rare earth elements'. Figure 2.8 shows the complete periodic table, and Table 2.4 shows the electron configurations of the various elements. One way of remembering the order of filling of the subshells is to memorize the following sad little story: 'Seven Shintu priests sadistically plot Saundra's death.

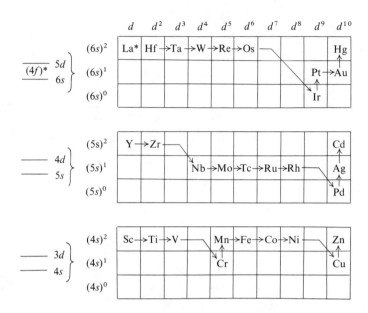

Figure 2.8 shows the irregular filling of shells in the three 'transition metal' series. Each arrow indicates a unit increase of atomic number Z, and an added electron. Vanadium, with atomic number $Z = 23$ has the ground-state electron configuration $(1s)^2(2s)^2(2p)^6(3s)^2(3p)^6(4s)^2(3d)^3$, which we can abbreviate as $(Ar)(4s)^2(3d)^3$. We would expect chromium, with atomic number $Z = 24$ to have the electron configuration $(Ar)(4s)^2(3d)^4$, but instead it has the configuration $(Ar)(4s)^1(3d)^5$. In the lanthanide or rare earth series (not shown here), the elements with atomic numbers between $Z = 57$ and $Z = 71$ have ground-state electron configurations of the form $(Xe)(4f)^{Z-56}(6s)^2$, or else $(Xe)(4f)^{Z-57}(6s)^2(5d)^1$. Since chemical properties are determined by the outer electrons, it is difficult to separate the rare earths from one another by chemical means.

Poor Saundra! Doesn't Peter sense (his) fiancée's danger? Peter seems fairly dumb'. From the first letters you can construct the sequence $s\,s\,p\,s\,p\,s\,d\,p\,s$ $d\,p\,s\,f\,d\,p\,s\,f\,d$. Every time you come to an s you know that you need a new value of n, and you also know that l cannot exceed $n - 1$. If you put in the values of n together with the degree of degeneracy of the subshells, $2(2l + 1)$, you will have the sequence $(1s)^2\ (2s)^2\ (2p)^6\ (3s)^2\ (3p)^6\ (4s)^2$ $(3d)^{10}\ (4p)^6\ (5s)^2\ (4d)^{10}\ (5p)^6\ (6s)^2\ (4f)^{14}\ (5d)^{10}\ (6p)^6\ (7s)^2\ (5f)^{14}\ (6d)^{10}$, which is to be compared with Fig. 2.7 and with Table 2.4.[30]

88

Table 2.4   Ground-state electron configuration of the elements

Z		name	configuration	I	E.A.
1	H	Hydrogen	$(1s)$	13·595	0·747
2	He	Helium	$(1s)^2$	24·581	0·19
3	Li	Lithium	$(He)(2s)$	5·390	0·82
4	Be	Beryllium	$(He)(2s)^2$	9.320	−0·19
5	B	Boron	$(He)(2s)^2(2p)$	8·296	0·33
6	C	Carbon	$(He)(2s)^2(2p)^2$	11·256	2·1
7	N	Nitrogen	$(He)(2s)^2(2p)^3$	14·53	0·05
8	O	Oxygen	$(He)(2s)^2(2p)^4$	13·614	1·46
9	F	Fluorine	$(He)(2s)^2(2p)^5$	17·418	3·6
10	Ne	Neon	$(He)(2s)^2(2p)^6$	21·559	−0·57
11	Na	Sodium	$(Ne)(3s)$	5·138	0·5
12	Mg	Magnesium	$(Ne)(3s)^2$	7·644	−0·32
13	Al	Aluminum	$(Ne)(3s)^2(2p)$	5·984	0·52
14	Si	Silicon	$(Ne)(3s)^2(2p)^2$	8·149	1·46
15	P	Phosphorus	$(Ne)(2s)^2(2p)^3$	10·484	0·77
16	S	Sulfur	$(Ne)(2s)^2(2p)^4$	10·357	2·2
17	Cl	Chlorine	$(Ne)(2s)^2(2p)^5$	13·01	3·8
18	Ar	Argon	$(Ne)(2s)^2(2p)^6$	15·755	
19	K	Potassium	$(Ar)(4s)^1$	4·339	0·8
20	Ca	Calcium	$(Ar)(4s)^2$	6·111	
21	Sc	Scandium	$(Ar)(4s)^2(3d)$	6·54	
22	Ti	Titanium	$(Ar)(4s)^2(3d)^2$	6·82	
23	V	Vanadium	$(Ar)(4s)^2(3d)^3$	6·74	
24	Cr	Chromium	$(Ar)(4s)(3d)^5$	6·764	
25	Mn	Manganese	$(Ar)(4s)^2(3d)^5$	7·432	
26	Fe	Iron	$(Ar)(4s)^2(3d)^6$	7·87	
27	Co	Cobalt	$(Ar)(4s)^2(3d)^7$	7·86	
28	Ni	Nickel	$(Ar)(4s)^2(3d)^8$	7·633	
29	Cu	Copper	$(Ar)(4s)(3d)^{10}$	7·724	
30	Zn	Zinc	$(Ar)(4s)^2(3d)^{10}$	9·391	
31	Ga	Gallium	$(Ar)(4s)^2(3d)^{10}(4p)$	6·00	
32	Ge	Germanium	$(Ar)(4s)^2(3d)^{10}(4p)^2$	7·88	
33	As	Arsenic	$(Ar)(4s)^2(3d)^{10}(4p)^3$	9·81	
34	Se	Selenium	$(Ar)(4s)^2(3d)^{10}(4p)^4$	9·75	
35	Br	Bromine	$(Ar)(4s)^2(3d)^{10}(4p)^5$	11·84	3·5
36	Kr	Krypton	$(Ar)(4s)^2(3d)^{10}(4p)^6$	13·996	
37	Rb	Rubidium	$(Kr)(5s)$	4·176	
38	Sr	Strontium	$(Kr)(5s)^2$	5·692	
39	Y	Yttrium	$(Kr)(5s)^2(4d)$	6·38	
40	Zr	Zirconium	$(Kr)(5s)^2(4d)^2$	6·84	
41	Nb	Niobium	$(Kr)(5s)(4d)^4$	6·88	
42	Mo	Molybdenum	$(Kr)(5s)(4d)^5$	7·10	
43	Tc	Technetium	$(Kr)(5s)(4d)^6$	7·28	

Table 2.4 (continued)

Z		name	configuration	I	E.A.
44	Ru	Ruthenium	$(Kr)(5s)(4d)^7$	7·346	
45	Rh	Rhodium	$(Kr)(5s)(4d)^8$	7·46	
46	Pd	Palladium	$(Kr)(4d)^{10}$	8·33	
47	Ag	Silver	$(Kr)(4d)^{10}(5s)$	7·574	
48	Cd	Cadmium	$(Kr)(4d)^{10}(5s)^2$	8·991	
49	In	Indium	$(Kr)(4d)^{10}(5s)^2(5p)$	5·785	
50	Sn	Tin	$(Kr)(4d)^{10}(5s)^2(5p)^2$	7·342	
51	Sb	Antimony	$(Kr)(4d)^{10}(5s)^2(5p)^3$	8·639	
52	Te	Tellurium	$(Kr)(4d)^{10}(5s)^2(5p)^4$	9·01	
53	I	Iodine	$(Kr)(4d)^{10}(5s)^2(5p)^5$	10·454	3·29
54	Xe	Xenon	$(Kr)(4d)^{10}(5s)^2(5p)^6$	12·127	
55	Cs	Cesium	$(Xe)(6s)$	3·893	
56	Ba	Barium	$(Xe)(6s)^2$	5·210	
57	La	Lanthanum	$(Xe)(6s)^2(5d)$	5·61	
58	Ce	Cerium	$(Xe)(6s)^2(4f)^2$	6·9	
59	Pr	Praseodymium	$(Xe)(6s)^2(4f)^3$	5·76	
60	Nd	Neodymium	$(Xe)(6s)^2(4f)^4$	6·3	
61	Pm	Promethium	$(Xe)(6s)^2(4f)^5$		
62	Sm	Samarium	$(Xe)(6s)^2(4f)^6$	5·6	
63	Eu	Europium	$(Xe)(6s)^2(4f)^7$	5·67	
64	Gd	Gadolinium	$(Xe)(6s)^2(4f)^7(5d)$	6·16	
65	Tb	Terbium	$(Xe)(6s)^2(4f)^9$	6·7	
66	Dy	Dysprosium	$(Xe)(6s)^2(4f)^{10}$	6·8	
67	Ho	Holmium	$(Xe)(6s)^2(4f)^{11}$		
68	Er	Erbium	$(Xe)(6s)^2(4f)^{12}$	6·1	
69	Tm	Thulium	$(Xe)(6s)^2(4f)^{13}$	6·1	
70	Yb	Ytterbium	$(Xe)(6s)^2(4f)^{14}$	6·2	
71	Lu	Lutetium	$(Xe)(6s)^2(4f)^{14}(5d)$	6·15	
72	Hf	Hafnium	$(Xe)(6s)^2(4f)^{14}(5d)^2$	7	
73	Ta	Tantalum	$(Xe)(6s)^2(4f)^{14}(5d)^3$	7·88	
74	W	Tungsten	$(Xe)(6s)^2(4f)^{14}(5d)^4$	7·98	
75	Re	Rhenium	$(Xe)(6s)^2(4f)^{14}(5d)^5$	7·87	
76	Os	Osmium	$(Xe)(6s)^2(4f)^{14}(5d)^6$	8·7	
77	Ir	Iridium	$(Xe)(4f)^{14}(5d)^9$	9	
78	Pt	Platinum	$(Xe)(4f)^{14}(6s)(5d)^9$	9·0	
79	Au	Gold	$(Xe)(4f)^{14}(5d)^{10}(6s)$	9·22	
80	Hg	Mercury	$(Xe)(4f)^{14}(5d)^{10}(6s)^2$	10·43	
81	Tl	Thallium	$(Xe)(4f)^{14}(5d)^{10}(6s)^2(6p)$	6·106	
82	Pb	Lead	$(Xe)(4f)^{14}(5d)^{10}(6s)^2(6p)^2$	7·415	
83	Bi	Bismuth	$(Xe)(4f)^{14}(5d)^{10}(6s)^2(6p)^3$	7·287	
84	Po	Polonium	$(Xe)(4f)^{14}(5d)^{10}(6s)^2(6p)^4$	8·43	
85	At	Astatine	$(Xe)(4f)^{14}(5d)^{10}(6s)^2(6p)^5$	9·2	
86	Rn	Radon	$(Xe)(4f)^{14}(5d)^{10}(6s)^2(6p)^6$	10·746	
87	Fa	Francium	$(Rn)(7s)$	4·0	
88	Ra	Radium	$(Rn)(7s)^2$	5·277	

Table 2.4   (continued)

Z		name	configuration	I	E.A.
89	Ac	Actinium	$(Rn)(7s)^2(6d)$	6·9	
90	Th	Thorium	$(Rn)(7s)^2(6d)^2$	6·9	
91	Pa	Protoactinium	$(Rn)(7s)^2(6d)(5f)^2$		
92	U	Uranium	$(Rn)(7s)^2(6d)(5f)^3$		
93	Np	Neptunium	$(Rn)(7s)^2(5f)^5$		
94	Pu	Plutonium	$(Rn)(7s)^2(5f)^6$		

I = ionization energy in electron volts
E.A. = electron affinity in electron volts

Data for this table was taken from *Advanced Inorganic Chemistry* by F. A. Cotton and G. Wilkinson, Interscience (1966) and *Bond Energies, Ionization Potentials and Electron Affinities*, by V. I. Vedeneyev *et al.*, Arnold, London (1965).

3. Hilbert space

The correspondence principle

When the news of Schrödinger's equation reached the Institute for Theoretical Physics which Niels Bohr had founded in Copenhagen, it caused tremendous excitement. Bohr immediately invited Schrödinger to lecture on his theory, and the meaning of the wave function ψ began to be debated. After many prolonged and heated sessions of discussion and calculation, Bohr and his co-workers arrived at what has come to be called the 'Copenhagen interpretation'. Bohr had previously evolved his 'correspondence principle' which states that in the limit of large quantum numbers or large values of momentum, quantum mechanics has to go over into classical mechanics. The substitutions of Eq. (2.16) and Eq. (2.17) serve to establish a correspondence between each function of the coordinates and momenta in classical mechanics and an associated operator in quantum mechanics. For example, we said that in classical mechanics, the energy of a particle moving in the potential V is given by the Hamiltonian function

$$H = \frac{p^2}{2m} + V$$

and that in quantum mechanics this goes over into the operator

$$H = \frac{-\hbar^2}{2m} \nabla^2 + V \tag{3.1}$$

In classical mechanics the angular momentum of a particle is a pseudovector whose components are defined by the relation

$$L_x = yp_z - zp_y$$
$$L_y = zp_x - xp_z$$
$$L_z = xp_y - yp_x \tag{3.2}$$

or in short-hand notation

$$\vec{L} = \vec{x} \wedge \vec{p} \tag{3.3}$$

The angular momentum pseudovector is said to be the 'cross-product' of the position vector $\vec{x}$ and the momentum vector $\vec{p}$. The operator corresponding to angular momentum in quantum mechanics is a pseudovector operator whose components are given by

$$L_x = \frac{\hbar}{i}\left(y\frac{\partial}{\partial z} - z\frac{\partial}{\partial y}\right)$$

$$L_y = \frac{\hbar}{i}\left(z\frac{\partial}{\partial x} - x\frac{\partial}{\partial z}\right)$$

$$L_z = \frac{\hbar}{i}\left(x\frac{\partial}{\partial y} - y\frac{\partial}{\partial x}\right) \tag{3.4}$$

or in shorthand notation

$$\vec{L} = \frac{\hbar}{i}\left(\vec{x} \wedge \frac{\partial}{\partial\vec{x}}\right) \tag{3.5}$$

In terms of the spherical polar coordinates, r, θ, and φ, the components of angular momentum become

$$L_x = \frac{\hbar}{i}\left(\sin\varphi\frac{\partial}{\partial\theta} + \cot\theta\cos\varphi\frac{\partial}{\partial\varphi}\right)$$

$$L_y = \frac{\hbar}{i}\left(\cos\varphi\frac{\partial}{\partial\theta} - \cot\theta\sin\varphi\frac{\partial}{\partial\varphi}\right)$$

$$L_z = \frac{\hbar}{i}\frac{\partial}{\partial\varphi} \tag{3.6}$$

The operator corresponding to the square of the angular momentum pseudovector can be calculated from Eq. (3.6) and turns out to be

$$L^2 \equiv L_x^2 + L_y^2 + L_z^2$$

$$L^2 = -\hbar^2\left(\frac{1}{\sin\theta}\frac{\partial}{\partial\theta}\sin\theta\frac{\partial}{\partial\theta} + \frac{1}{\sin^2\theta}\frac{\partial^2}{\partial\varphi^2}\right) \tag{3.7}$$

Equations (3.7) and (2.25) imply that when the operator corresponding to the square of the angular momentum acts on one of the hydrogen-like atomic orbitals listed in Table 2.3 it gives back the orbital multiplied by a constant factor:

$$L^2\chi_{n,l,m} = \hbar^2 l(l+1)\chi_{n,l,m} \tag{3.8}$$

According to Bohr's correspondence principle, in the limit of very large values of l, the number $\hbar^2 l(l+1)$ corresponds to the total classical angular

93

momentum of the electron in its orbit. We can also apply the operator L_z of Eq. (3.6) to a hydrogen-like orbital, and we find

$$L_z \chi_{n,l,m} = \hbar m \chi_{n,l,m} \qquad (3.9)$$

The number $\hbar m$ corresponds in the classical limit to the component of the angular momentum in the z direction. The largest possible value of $\hbar m$ is $\hbar l$ and this corresponds, in the classical limit, to the case where the angular momentum vector is pointing exactly in the z direction. The hydrogen-like atomic orbital with the largest value of total angular momentum for a given energy corresponds in the classical limit to a circular orbit. According to Eqs. (2.28), (2.38), and Table 2.3, the space-dependent part of such an orbital has the form:

$$\chi_{n,n-1,n-1} \sim \rho^{n-1} e^{-\rho/n} \sin^{n-1} \theta\, e^{i(n-1)\varphi} \qquad (3.10)$$

Let us try to imagine what the orbital of Eq. (3.10) looks like in the limit of very large values of n. The factor ρ^{n-1} increases sharply with increasing distance from the nucleus. However, at some radius the factor $e^{-\rho/n}$ will win out and the radial part of the wave function will have a maximum. The higher the value of n, the more sharply this maximum will be defined. Similarly, the function $\sin^{n-1} \theta$ will have a maximum at $\theta = \pi/2$ which is progressively more sharp the higher the value of n. Thus, the wave function of Eq. (3.10) really does correspond in the classical limit to a sharply-defined circular orbit.

Eigenfunctions and eigenvalues; the Copenhagen interpretation of the wave function

Equations (3.8) and (3.9) both have a similar form: an operator acting on a wave function gives back the same function multiplied by a constant. Thus we have an equation of the general form

$$\Omega \phi = \lambda \phi \qquad (3.11)$$

where Ω is an operator and λ is a constant. The possible solutions ϕ and the possible values of the constant λ are restricted by the boundary conditions on the problem, such as the condition that the wave function must be single-valued. In mathematical jargon, the solution ϕ in Eq. (3.11) is said to be an 'eigenfunction' of the operator Ω associated with the 'eigenvalue' λ. The name 'eigenfunction' comes from the German word meaning 'proper function'. It is proper in the sense that it satisfies a differential equation together with certain boundary conditions. According to the Copenhagen interpretation of quantum mechanics, the state of a system at a given instant of time is specified by the wave function ψ. The wave function evolves in time according to Schrödinger's equation

$$i\hbar \frac{\partial \psi}{\partial t} = H\psi \tag{3.12}$$

Each dynamical quantity in classical mechanics corresponds to some operator in quantum mechanics. If the wave function is an eigenfunction of the operator, then the result of a measurement of the corresponding dynamical quantity is certain to be the associated eigenvalue. On the other hand, suppose that the wave function is not an eigenfunction of the operator Ω but that it can be expanded in a series of these eigenfunctions

$$\psi = \sum_k a_k \phi_k \tag{3.13}$$

where

$$\Omega \phi_k = \lambda_k \phi_k \tag{3.14}$$

Then, according to the Copenhagen interpretation, *the probability that the measurement will result in the value λ_k is given by the expansion coefficient a_k multiplied by its complex conjugate:*

$$\text{probability} = a_k^* a_k \tag{3.15}$$

Bohr felt that this probabilistic interpretation was the ultimate reality. To others, notably to Einstein, it appeared to be an interim theory which can be accepted because it gives correct results but which may ultimately be replaced by something deeper.

Expectation values

In discussing Bohr's correspondence principle we talked only about the case where the wave function is an eigenfunction of the operator in question. In that case, (for example, in Eq. (3.8) and Eq. (3.9)), the associated eigenvalue reduces to the corresponding classical quantity in the limit of large quantum numbers. In the case where the wave function ψ is not an eigenfunction of the operator Ω, the Copenhagen interpretation postulated that it is the function

$$\langle \Omega \rangle = \int d\tau \psi^* \Omega \psi \tag{3.16}$$

which reduces to the corresponding dynamical quantity in the classical limit. In Eq. (3.16) ψ^* is the complex conjugate of the wave function and $\int d\tau$ means an integration over the coordinates of all the particles in the system. The quantity $\langle \Omega \rangle$ is called the 'expectation value' of the operator

95

The quantum theory of atoms, molecules, and photons

Ω. Ehrenfest was able to show that Newton's equations of motion hold for expectation values. For example, if we think of a single particle moving in a potential V, then

$$\frac{\partial}{\partial t} \langle \vec{p} \rangle = - \left\langle \frac{\partial V}{\partial x} \right\rangle \tag{3.17}$$

It is easy to see that Eq. (3.17) holds. Since the non-relativistic quantum mechanical Hamiltonian of the particle is given by

$$H = \frac{-\hbar^2}{2m} \nabla^2 + V \tag{3.18}$$

we have the identity

$$H \frac{\partial}{\partial \bar{x}} - \frac{\partial}{\partial \bar{x}} H = - \frac{\partial V}{\partial \bar{x}} \tag{3.19}$$

Then, using Eq. (3.19), the Schrödinger equation, Eq. (3.12), and the definition of the expectation value, Eq. (3.16), we have

$$\begin{aligned}
\frac{\partial}{\partial t} \langle \vec{p} \rangle &= \frac{\partial}{\partial t} \int d^3x \psi^* \frac{\hbar}{i} \frac{\partial}{\partial \bar{x}} \psi \\
&= \int d^3x \left(-i\hbar \frac{\partial \psi^*}{\partial t} \frac{\partial}{\partial \bar{x}} \psi - \psi^* \frac{\partial}{\partial \bar{x}} i\hbar \frac{\partial \psi}{\partial t} \right) \\
&= \int d^3x \psi^* \left(H \frac{\partial}{\partial \bar{x}} - \frac{\partial}{\partial \bar{x}} H \right) \psi \\
&= - \int d^3x \psi^* \frac{\partial V}{\partial x} \psi = - \left\langle \frac{\partial V}{\partial \bar{x}} \right\rangle
\end{aligned} \tag{3.20}$$

When people first become familiar with quantum theory they often have the feeling that it would be easier to learn if they only believed it. Certainly, some of the notions of wave mechanics seem contrary to common sense. As an antidote to this sort of scepticism it may be helpful to reflect that there is no reason at all for common sense to hold in the behaviour of very small particles. Common sense, after all is only a summary of common experience, and in our day-to-day living we encounter matter only in the enormous aggregates which our coarse senses are able to perceive. In order for quantum theory and common sense to coexist peacefully the only requirement is that the former should reduce to the latter when applied to the objects of our everyday experience, and from the preceding discussion we can see that this is the case.

We mentioned above a surprising aspect of the history of quantum mechanics: In 1925 two different theories appeared both of which worked beautifully. One of these was the theory based on Schrödinger's wave equation which we have been discussing; the other was Werner Heisenberg's 'matrix mechanics'. The two theories were soon shown to be equivalent, but when they first appeared they seemed to be completely independent. At the time when he developed his matrix mechanics, Heisenberg was a young researcher associated with Max Born at Göttingen in Germany. The University of Göttingen was distinguished in the nineteenth century by the presence of the great mathematician Carl Friedrich Gauss. From 1886 onwards, the former chair of Gauss was held by Felix Klein. Klein was not only an excellent mathematician, but also a very capable organizer and he gradually attracted to his institute a brilliant staff including Minkowski, (who did important work in relativity theory) and David Hilbert. Through the agency of the practical-minded Klein, Hilbert came into collision with physics, and is said to have remarked: 'This will never do! Physics is obviously much too difficult for physicists.' But the physicists who began to come to Göttingen were also men of great ability. The two chairs in physics were held by James Franck and Max Born. E. A. Hylleraas gives the following description of how he came from Norway to work for Max Born. Hylleraas had been eagerly following Born's work on crystal lattices, and expected to do more of the same in Göttingen. He writes:

'First of all, I was heartily disappointed when Max Born told me that he was no longer working in the field of crystal lattice theory. His new field of investigation bore the curious name "Matrix Mechanics", and, as I understood it, had been invented by himself, or rather by some bright fellows by the names of Werner Heisenberg and Pascaul Jordan. . . . Moreover, there was much talk of a curious sort of new waves called de Broglie waves. Obviously, they did not exist in the physical sense of the word, since they were running with super-light speed. Nevertheless, people persisted in talking about their wave length as something of particular importance, given by a simple formula reminding one of some sort of quantization. Non-existent waves in quantized form—quite a thrilling idea. Should I prefer them to my real crystals?

'One day in the institute's library, Dr E. H. Kennard from the United States was sitting and reading something which he told me was the Schrödinger wave equation, and he wondered why I was not doing the same, because that was just what people were doing now. . . . The shock which I had received from Max Born had not quite knocked me down, so I persisted for some time in working in the field of crystal optics.' (*Reviews of Modern Physics*, 1963, **35**, 421.)

Hermitian operators and orthonormal eigenfunctions

The matrix mechanics of Heisenberg, Born, and Jordan is discussed in Appendix III. Hilbert's mathematical work at Göttingen forms part of the background of matrix mechanics. The ideas which Hilbert helped to clarify are also important in the Schrödinger formulation, and so we shall treat them here at some length. Hilbert was interested in a generalized form of Fourier analysis see Eqs. (1.43)–(1.72) using solutions of equations like Eq. (3.11). We said that when an operator Ω, acting on a function ϕ, gives back the same functions multiplied by a constant λ, as in Eq. (3.11), then one says that ϕ is an eigenfunction of Ω associated with the eigenvalue λ. The possible eigenfunctions ϕ and the possible eigenvalues λ are limited by the boundary conditions of the problem. We can label the various allowed solutions by some index such as n in order to tell them apart. Now consider two different solutions ϕ_n and $\phi_{n'}$ which fulfil the equations

$$\Omega\phi_n = \lambda_n\phi_n \qquad (3.21)$$

and

$$\Omega\phi_{n'} = \lambda_{n'}\phi_{n'} \qquad (3.22)$$

The complex conjugate of Eq. (3.22) is

$$\Omega^*\phi_{n'}^* = \lambda_{n'}^*\phi_{n'}^* \qquad (3.23)$$

If we multiply Eq. (3.21) and Eq. (3.23) from the left with the functions $\phi_{n'}^*$ and ϕ_n respectively, integrate over all coordinates, and subtract, we obtain,

$$\int d\tau(\phi_{n'}^*\Omega\phi_n - \phi_n\Omega^*\phi_{n'}^*) = (\lambda_n - \lambda_{n'}^*)\int d\tau\phi_{n'}^*\phi_n \qquad (3.24)$$

If the operator Ω and the boundary conditions which ϕ_n and $\phi_{n'}$ must obey are such that

$$\int d\tau(\phi_{n'}^*\Omega\phi_n - \phi_n\Omega^*\phi_{n'}^*) = 0 \qquad \mathbf{(3.25)}$$

then Ω is said to be 'Hermitian'. If Ω is Hermitian, then

$$(\lambda_n - \lambda_{n'}^*)\int d\tau\,\phi_{n'}^*\phi_n = 0 \qquad (3.26)$$

When the product of two factors is zero, at least one of the factors must be zero also. Therefore if

$$(\lambda_n - \lambda_{n'}^*) \neq 0 \qquad (3.27)$$

then

$$\int d\tau \phi_{n'}^* \phi_n = 0 \tag{3.28}$$

When Eq. (3.28) holds, $\phi_{n'}^*$ and ϕ_n are said to be 'orthogonal'. With Hermiticity and orthogonality defined in this way, we can say from Eq. (3.27) and Eq. (3.28) that *eigenfunctions of Hermitian operators corresponding to different eigenvalues are orthogonal*. On the other hand, consider the case where ϕ_n and $\phi_{n'}$ are identical.

$$\phi_n = \phi_{n'} \tag{3.29}$$

Then, since $\phi_n^* \phi_n = \phi_n^* \phi_n$ which is everywhere positive we must have

$$\int d\tau \phi_{n'}^* \phi_n = \int d\tau \phi_n^* \phi_n \neq 0 \tag{3.30}$$

and

$$\lambda_n = \lambda_{n'}^* = \lambda_n^* \tag{3.31}$$

This shows that *Hermitian operators have real eigenvalues*. In fact, Hermiticity is to an operator what reality is to a number. We shall see later that just as any number can be decomposed into a real and an imaginary part, so any operator can be decomposed into an Hermitian and an anti-Hermitian part. We shall also show that the operators $\bar{x}$ and $(h/i)(\partial/\partial \bar{x})$ (together with the appropriate boundary conditions) are Hermitian. In fact all of the operators which we can construct to represent various dynamical quantities will be Hermitian. They must, of course, have this property if their eigenvalues are to represent quantities which can actually be measured.

Hermiticity of the operator $\partial^2/\partial x^2$

Another example of Hermiticity can be found in the harmonics of a vibrating string, Eqs. (1.37)–(1.72). After the time-dependence has been separated out, the wave equation, Eq. (1.37) can be written in the form

$$\frac{\partial^2}{\partial x^2} \phi = -k^2 \phi \tag{3.32}$$

The boundary conditions require that the function ϕ which represents the displacement of the string from its equilibrium position must vanish at the end points $x = 0$ and $x = L$.

$$\phi(0) = \phi(L) = 0 \tag{3.33}$$

99

Now let us try to see whether the operator

$$\Omega = \frac{\partial^2}{\partial x^2} \tag{3.34}$$

together with the boundary conditions of Eq. (3.33) satisfy the definition of Hermiticity, Eq. (3.25). In other words, we want to find out whether

$$\int_0^L dx \left(\phi_{n'}^* \frac{\partial^2}{\partial x^2} \phi_n - \phi_n \frac{\partial^2}{\partial x^2} \phi_{n'}^* \right) = 0 \tag{3.35}$$

where $\phi_{n'}^*$ and ϕ_n may be arbitrary functions of x provided only that

$$\phi_{n'}^*(0) = \phi_{n'}^*(L) = \phi_n(0) = \phi_n(L) = 0 \tag{3.36}$$

We can use the relation

$$\int u \, dv = [uv] - \int v \, du \tag{3.37}$$

of Table 1.2 with $u = \phi_{n'}^*$ and $dv = \partial^2 \phi_n / \partial x^2 \, dx$ to show that

$$\int_0^L dx \phi_{n'}^* \frac{\partial^2}{\partial x^2} \phi_n = \left[\phi_{n'}^* \frac{\partial \phi_n}{\partial x} \right]_0^L - \int_0^L dx \frac{\partial \phi_{n'}^*}{\partial x} \frac{\partial \phi_n}{\partial x} \tag{3.38}$$

and, similarly, that

$$\int_0^L dx \phi_n \frac{\partial^2}{\partial x^2} \phi_{n'}^* = \left[\phi_n \frac{\partial \phi_{n'}^*}{\partial x} \right]_0^L - \int_0^L dx \frac{\partial \phi_n}{\partial x} \frac{\partial \phi_{n'}^*}{\partial x} \tag{3.39}$$

Combining Eq. (3.38) and Eq. (3.39) and making use of the boundary conditions, Eq. (3.36) we have

$$\int_0^L dx \left(\phi_{n'}^* \frac{\partial^2}{\partial x^2} \phi_n - \phi_n \frac{\partial^2}{\partial x^2} \phi_{n'}^* \right)$$
$$= - \int_0^L dx \left(\frac{\partial \phi_{n'}^*}{\partial x} \frac{\partial \phi_n}{\partial x} - \frac{\partial \phi_n}{\partial x} \frac{\partial \phi_{n'}^*}{\partial x} \right) = 0 \tag{3.40}$$

so that the requirement for Hermiticity, Eq. (3.35), is satisfied. The solutions of the vibrating string problem, Eq. (3.32) and Eq. (3.33), are, of course, the set of sinusoidal harmonics

$$\phi_n = \sqrt{\frac{2}{L}} \sin \frac{n\pi}{L}, \quad n = 1, 2, 3, \ldots \infty \tag{3.41}$$

and Eq. (3.28) is the underlying reason for the relationship

$$\frac{2}{L} \int_0^L dx \sin \frac{n'\pi}{L} \sin \frac{n\pi}{L} = \delta_{n'n} \tag{3.42}$$

on which Fourier based his famous sine series, Eq. (1.67) and Eq. (1.68). We can see now, however, that the sine series is only a very special case of an enormously powerful and general concept. *The set of eigenfunctions of any Hermitian operator at all can form the basis for a generalized type of Fourier analysis, and there are infinitely many different Hermitian operators!* If we multiply the eigenfunctions by a normalizing constant so that

$$\int d\tau \phi_n^* \phi_n = 1 \tag{3.43}$$

then we can write the orthogonality relationship, Eq. (3.28), and the normalization condition, Eq. (3.43), simultaneously.

$$\int d\tau \phi_{n'}^* \phi_n = \delta_{n'n} \equiv \begin{cases} 0 & n' \neq n \\ 1 & n = n \end{cases} \tag{3.44}$$

The two words can also be combined. One speaks of the set of functions ϕ_n as 'orthonormal' meaning mutually orthogonal and normalized.

Completeness; the Dirac delta-function

Now suppose that we can expand some function as a series of the eigenfunctions ϕ_n

$$f(x) = \sum_n a_n \phi_n(x) \tag{3.45}$$

(For simplicity, we have assumed for the moment that f and ϕ_n are functions of only one variable.) We can use the orthonormality relationship, Eq. (3.44), to determine the set of constant coefficients a_n in Eq. (3.45)

$$\int dx \phi_{n'}^*(x) f(x) = \sum_n a_n \int dx \phi_{n'}^*(x) \phi_n(x) = \sum_n a_n \delta_{n'n} = a_{n'} \tag{3.46}$$

All this is precisely what one does in the case of a Fourier series: In practical examples the constants of the series Eq. (3.45) are easy to find. We only need to evaluate the integral

$$a_n = \int dx \phi_{n'}^*(x) f(x) \tag{3.47}$$

Substituting Eq. (3.47) in Eq. (3.45) gives an interesting identity:

$$f(x') = \sum_n a_n \phi_n(x') = \int dx f(x) \sum_n \phi_n^*(x) \phi_n(x') \tag{3.48}$$

A function $\delta(x - x')$ which has the property that

$$f(x') = \int dx f(x) \delta(x - x') \tag{3.49}$$

is called a Dirac δ-function. Comparing Eq. (3.48) and Eq. (3.49) we can see that the sum at the right-hand side of Eq. (3.48) must be a Dirac δ-function.

$$\sum_n \phi_n^*(x)\phi_n(x') = \delta(x - x') \tag{3.50}$$

From Eq. (3.49) we can see that a Dirac δ-function must be rather remarkable. However, it is not impossible to imagine a function which has this property. Think of a very tall, thin rectangle, like the one shown in Fig. 3.1,

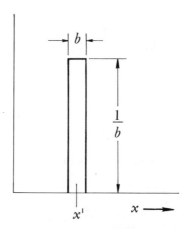

Figure 3.1 shows a very tall, thin rectangle centred on the point x'. If the width of the rectangle is b and the height $1/b$, then the area is unity. If we make b smaller and smaller, the height will increase while the width decreases, but the area will remain constant and equal to unity. In the limit $b \to 0$, this function becomes a representation of the Dirac δ-function.

with a width b and a height $1/b$, centred on the point $x = x'$. In the limit where $b \to 0$ the function will get taller and taller and thinner and thinner until finally it is quite dangerous-looking. If you now multiply the function of Fig. 3.1 by some function, $f(x)$, and integrate over x the only contribution to the integral comes from the small region around the point $x = x'$. The well-behaved function $f(x)$ changes very little as we pass from one side of this infinitesimal region to the other. It can be treated as a constant and factored out of the integral. The tall thin rectangle remains to be integrated but by definition it has a unit area. The effect of the integration is to punch out the value of $f(x)$ at the point $x = x'$ as in Eq. (3.49). This shows that in the limit where $b \to 0$, the tall thin rectangle of Fig. 3.1 is a Dirac δ-function. Equation (3.50) follows from the assumption of completeness. Completeness of the set of functions ϕ_n means that any arbitrary function obeying the same boundary conditions can be expanded in terms of them. If the set of eigenfunctions is complete then Eq. (3.50) holds. Conversely, if Eq.

(3.50) holds, then the set is complete. In fact, Eq. (3.50) can sometimes be used to establish the completeness of a set of orthonormal eigenfunctions.

Eigenfunctions of the momentum operator with periodic boundary conditions

For example, consider the set of eigenfunctions of the operator

$$\Omega = \frac{1}{i}\frac{\partial}{\partial x} \tag{3.51}$$

with the periodic boundary conditions

$$\phi\left(-\frac{L}{2}\right) = \phi\left(\frac{L}{2}\right) \tag{3.52}$$

(It is a good exercise to show that the operator Eq. (3.51) and the boundary conditions of Eq. (3.52) fulfil the conditions for the Hermiticity, Eq. (3.25).) The equation

$$\Omega\phi_n = \frac{1}{i}\frac{\partial}{\partial x}\phi_n = k_n\phi_n \tag{3.53}$$

has a set of solutions

$$\phi_n = \frac{1}{\sqrt{L}}e^{ik_n x} \tag{3.54}$$

where, to fulfil the periodic boundary conditions of Eq. (3.52), we must have

$$e^{-ik_n(L/2)} = e^{ik_n(L/2)} \tag{3.55}$$

which will be satisfied if

$$k_n = \frac{2\pi n}{L}, \quad n = 0, \pm 1, \pm 2, \pm 3, \ldots, \pm\infty \tag{3.56}$$

In this example, the orthonormality of the eigenfunctions is obvious, since

$$\int_{-L/2}^{L/2} dx\phi_{n'}^*\phi_n = \frac{1}{L}\int_{-L/2}^{L/2} dx\, e^{i(2\pi/L)(n-n')x}$$

$$= \begin{cases} \frac{1}{L}\int_{-L/2}^{L/2} dx = 1, & n = n' \\ \dfrac{e^{i\pi(n-n')} - e^{-i\pi(n-n')}}{i2\pi(n-n')} = 0, & n \neq n' \end{cases}$$

$$= \delta_{n'n} \tag{3.57}$$

103

Boundary conditions at infinity; continuous spectrum of eigenvalues; Fourier transforms

If we let $L \to \infty$, the allowed values of k will come closer and closer together and finally form a continuum. In that limit it is convenient to normalize eigenfunctions of Eq. (3.54) in a different way to prevent them from disappearing altogether. If we write

$$\phi_k = \frac{1}{\sqrt{2\pi}} e^{ikx} \tag{3.58}$$

then from the orthonormality relationship, Eq. (3.57), we can see that if we retain the periodic boundary conditions at $x = \pm L/2$, in the limit where $L \to \infty$ we will have

$$\lim_{L \to \infty} \int_{-L/2}^{L/2} dx \phi_{k'}^* \phi_k = \lim_{L \to \infty} \int_{-L/2}^{L/2} dx \frac{e^{i(k-k')x}}{2\pi}$$
$$= \begin{cases} 0 & k \neq k' \\ \infty & k = k' \end{cases} \tag{3.59}$$

Thus, in the limit where $L \to \infty$ the integral of Eq. (3.59), considered as a function of k and k', behaves very much like a Dirac δ-function: It is zero except where $k = k'$ and at that point, infinitely large. To be a Dirac δ-function it must also have a unit area; and in fact it does, although we shall not prove it here. Thus we can write the orthonormality relations for the continuum of eigenfunctions, Eq. (3.58), as

$$\frac{1}{2\pi} \int_{-\infty}^{\infty} dx\, e^{i(k-k')x} = \delta(k - k') \tag{3.60}$$

Interchanging the roles of k and x we have the relationship

$$\frac{1}{2\pi} \int_{-\infty}^{\infty} dk\, e^{i(x-x')k} = \delta(x - x') \tag{3.61}$$

Equation (3.61) is just the completeness relationship, Eq. (3.50), for the continuous set of eigenfunctions ϕ_k, with the sum over allowed quantum numbers replaced by an integration over the continuous range of k. Thus, in this case, we have proved the completeness of the set of eigenfunctions and solved the problem which so perplexed the Bernoullis, Euler, and Fourier. The orthonormality relation, Eq. (3.60), and the completeness relation, Eq. (3.61), allow us to express any well-behaved function of x as a superposition of the continuous set of eigenfunctions. *If*

$$f(x) = \frac{1}{\sqrt{2\pi}} \int_{-\infty}^{\infty} dk a(k) \, e^{ikx} \qquad (3.62)$$

then from Eq. (3.59)

$$a(k) = \frac{1}{\sqrt{2\pi}} \int_{-\infty}^{\infty} dx f(x) \, e^{-ikx} \qquad (3.63)$$

The function a(k) is called the 'Fourier transform' of f(x) and f(x) is called the 'inverse Fourier transform' of a(k). We shall use Fourier transforms in discussing Heisenberg's uncertainty principle, and also later, in connection with X-ray crystallography

The harmonics of a vibrating string with fixed end points gave us an example of a set of eigenfunctions with a discrete spectrum of eigenvalues. The Fourier transforms provided an example of a continuous spectrum. We will show later that the hydrogen-like wave functions of Table 2.3 are an example of a partly discrete and partly continuous spectrum. Above the bound states in energy lies a continuum of energy levels corresponding to states where the hydrogen atom has been ionized. If the continuum states are included, then the set of eigenfunctions of the Hamiltonian operator is complete in the sense that a superposition of the eigenfunctions can be used to represent any well-behaved function of x, y, and z. If the continuum states are left out, then the set is not complete.

Problem (3.1) (a) Use Eq. (3.63) to find the Fourier transform of the function,

$$f(x) = \begin{cases} 1 & -L/2 < x < L/2 \\ 0 & x \le -L/2, \ L/2 \le x \end{cases}$$

(b) What is the Fourier transform of the function, $f(x) = \delta(x - C)$?
(c) What is the Fourier transform of the function, $f(x) = 1$?

Functions of several variables; commuting operators; Three-dimensional Fourier transforms

The fact that the hydrogen-like atomic orbitals are functions of several coordinates raises the question of what happens when more than one coordinate is involved. In that case, it requires more than one index to label the eigenfunctions. For example, the hydrogen-like atomic orbitals (not including the spin part of the wave function) are labelled by three quantum numbers; n, l, and m, corresponding to the eigenvalues of three operators

The quantum theory of atoms, molecules, and photons

H, L^2, and L_z. It is interesting to ask under what conditions a function can be simultaneously an eigenfunction of several different operators. Suppose that we have two operators A and B and that the function ϕ is simultaneously an eigenfunction of both of them:

$$A\phi_{a,b} = \lambda_a \phi_{a,b} \qquad (3.64)$$

$$B\phi_{a,b} = \lambda_b \phi_{a,b} \qquad (3.65)$$

It follows that

$$(AB - BA)\phi_{a,b} = (\lambda_a \lambda_b - \lambda_b \lambda_a)\phi_{a,b} = 0 \qquad (3.66)$$

When the result of applying two operators to an arbitrary function is independent of the order in which they are applied, then the two operators are said to 'commute' with each other. We can see from Eqs. (3.64)–(3.66) that *when two operators commute with each other, it is possible to find functions which are simultaneously eigenfunctions of both of them.* It is an interesting exercise to try to show that the Hamiltonian operator H, the total angular momentum operator L^2, and the operator L_z representing the z component of angular momentum, all commute with one another, but that L_x, L_y, and L_z do not form a commuting set. The commutation relations between operators are so important that a special notation has been introduced for writing the expression $AB - BA$. By definition

$$AB - BA \equiv [A, B] \qquad \textbf{(3.67)}$$

This is called a 'commutator bracket'. Any algebraic function of an operator, of course, commutes with any other function of the same operator. For example,

$$[A^2, A] \equiv AAA - AAA = 0 \qquad (3.68)$$

Suppose that we find a set of operators $A, B, C, \ldots$ which are not functions of one another but which nevertheless form a commuting set so that

$$0 = [A, B] = [B, C] = [C, A] = \text{etc.} \qquad (3.69)$$

If this set is as large as it possibly can be in the space where we are working, then the set of operators is called a complete commuting set. We can find functions $\phi_{a,b,c,\ldots}$ which are simultaneously eigenfunctions of all the operators in the set. Provided that we remember that we are referring to the operators $A, B, C, \ldots$, the numbers $a, b, c, \ldots$ will completely specify the normalized eigenfunctions. We can carry through the expansion of an arbitrary function in just the same way as before except that now we have got more dimensions and more quantum numbers.

$$f(x^1, x^2, x^3, \ldots, x^n) = \sum_{a,b,c,\ldots} \alpha_{a,b,c,\ldots} \phi_{a,b,c,\ldots}(x^1, x^2, \ldots, x^n) \qquad (3.70)$$

The orthonormality relation

$$\int dx^1\, dx^2\, \ldots\, dx^N \phi^*_{a',\,b',\,c',\,\ldots}\, \phi_{a,\,b,\,c,\,\ldots} = \delta_{a'a}\delta_{b'b}\delta_{c'c}\, \ldots \qquad (3.71)$$

is used to obtain the constant coefficients $\alpha_{a,\,b,\,c,\,\ldots}$ in the expansion of Eq. (3.70)

$$\alpha_{a,\,b,\,c,\,\ldots} = \int dx^1\, \ldots\, dx^N \phi^*_{a,\,b,\,c,\,\ldots} \qquad (3.72)$$

Equation (3.72) combined with Eq. (3.70) gives us the completeness relation

$$\sum_{a,\,b,\,c,\,\ldots} \phi^*_{a,\,b,\,c,\,\ldots}(x^1, \ldots, x^N)\phi_{a,\,b,\,c,\,\ldots}(x^{1'}, \ldots, x^{N'})$$
$$= \delta(x^1 - x^{1'})\delta(x^2 - x^{2'}) \ldots \delta(x^N - x^{N'}) \quad (3.73)$$

For example, the three mutually commuting operators

$$A = \frac{\partial^2}{\partial x^2}$$

$$B = \frac{\partial^2}{\partial y^2}$$

and

$$C = \frac{\partial^2}{\partial z^2} \qquad (3.74)$$

together with the boundary conditions

$$\phi(x = 0) = \phi(x = L) = 0$$
$$\phi(y = 0) = \phi(y = L) = 0$$
$$\phi(z = 0) = \phi(z = L) = 0 \qquad (3.75)$$

satisfy the conditions for Hermiticity as shown in Eqs. (3.33)–(3.40). In the three-dimensional space of the coordinates x, y, and z, the three operators A, B, and C of Eq. (3.73) form a complete commuting set. The set of simultaneous eigenfunctions of A, B, and C,

$$\phi_{a,\,b,\,c} = \left(\frac{2}{L}\right)^{3/2} \sin\left(\frac{a\pi x}{L}\right) \sin\left(\frac{b\pi y}{L}\right) \sin\left(\frac{c\pi z}{L}\right), \quad a,\,b,\,c = 1,\,2,\,3\,\ldots\,\infty$$
$$(3.76)$$

form a sufficient basis for the expansion of any function of the coordinates x, y, and z obeying the boundary conditions of Eq. (3.75). Like an ordinary Fourier sine series, Eqs. (1.67)–(1.68), the expansion is periodic and will be valid only within a certain range of the coordinates unless the function f is also periodic.

Similarly, we can generalize the Fourier transforms of Eqs. (3.60)–(3.63) to three dimensions. The orthonormality and completeness relations become

$$\frac{1}{\sqrt{(2\pi)^3}} \int d^3x \, e^{i(\vec{k}-\vec{k}')\cdot\vec{x}}$$

$$= \delta(k_1 - k_1')\delta(k_2 - k_2')\delta(k_3 - k_3')$$

$$\equiv \delta^3(\vec{k} - \vec{k}') \tag{3.77}$$

and

$$\frac{1}{\sqrt{(2\pi)^3}} \int d^3k \, e^{i(\vec{x}-\vec{x}')\cdot\vec{k}}$$

$$= \delta(x^1 - x^{1\prime})\delta(x^2 - x^{2\prime})\delta(x^3 - x^{3\prime})$$

$$\equiv \delta^3(\vec{x} - \vec{x}') \tag{3.78}$$

from which it follows that a function of x can be represented as the integral

$$f(\vec{x}) = \frac{1}{\sqrt{(2\pi)^3}} \int d^3x \, e^{i\vec{k}\cdot\vec{x}} a(\vec{k}) \tag{3.79}$$

with

$$a(\vec{k}) = \frac{1}{\sqrt{(2\pi)^3}} \int d^3k \, e^{-i\vec{k}\cdot\vec{x}} f(\vec{x}) \tag{3.80}$$

Problem (3.2)   (a) Show that

$$[A, B^2] = [A, B]B + B[A, B]$$

Can you write a similar expression for $[A, B^N]$?
(b) Show that

$$[L_x, L^2] = [L_y, L^2] = [L_z, L^2] = 0$$

where L_x, L_y, L_z, and L^2 are the angular momentum operators defined by Eq. (3.4) and Eq. (3.7). Show that

$$[L_x, L_y] = i\hbar L_z$$

$$[L_y, L_z] = i\hbar L_x$$

and

$$[L_z, L_x] = i\hbar L_y$$

Is it possible to find simultaneous eigenfunctions of L_x and L_y?

108

The Dirac bras and kets

P. A. M. Dirac introduced a notation which makes equations involving eigenfunctions a little easier to write. Provided that we remember which complete set of commuting operators $A, B, C, \ldots$ is defining the set of eigenfunctions, all that we need to do to pick out a particular function $\phi_{a,b,c,\ldots}$ is to write down the numbers $a, b, c, \ldots$, etc. Dirac proposed the convention of letting the symbol $|a, b, c, \ldots\rangle$ which he called a 'ket' stand for the eigenfunction,

$$\phi_{a,b,c,\ldots}(x^1 \ldots x^N) \equiv |a, b, c, \ldots\rangle \qquad (3.81)$$

The conjugate function is represented by a symbol which he called a 'bra'.

$$\phi^*_{a,b,c,\ldots}(x^1 \ldots x^N) \equiv \langle a, b, c, \ldots| \qquad (3.82)$$

When you put the two together and integrate over all the coordinates you get what Dirac called a 'braket' (sometimes it is also called a 'scalar product' or 'inner product'). The scalar product is not a function of the coordinates, but just an ordinary number. In Dirac's notation, the orthonormality relation would be written as

$$\langle a', b', c', \ldots | a, b, c, \ldots\rangle = \delta_{a'a}\delta_{b'b}\delta_{c'c}, \qquad (3.83)$$

which means the same thing as Eq. (3.71), since integration over all the coordinates is implied when the bra and the ket are put together. In Dirac's notation an arbitrary function f, expanded in terms of the eigenfunctions $|a, b, c, \ldots\rangle$, would be written

$$|f\rangle = \sum_{a,b,c,\ldots} |a, b, c, \ldots\rangle \alpha_{a,b,c,\ldots} \qquad (3.84)$$

From the orthonormality relations we have

$$\alpha_{a,b,c,\ldots} = \langle a, b, c, \ldots | f\rangle \qquad (3.85)$$

Putting this back into Eq. (3.84) we have

$$|f\rangle = \sum_{a,b,c,\ldots} |a, b, c, \ldots\rangle\langle a, b, c, \ldots | f\rangle \qquad (3.86)$$

so that

$$\sum_{a,b,c,\ldots} |a, b, c, \ldots\rangle\langle a, b, c, \ldots| = 1 \qquad (3.87)$$

Equation (3.87) is the completeness relation written in the bra and ket notation, and it means exactly the same thing as Eq. (3.73). It seems a little surprising that in Dirac's notation one writes the δ-function as the unit

109

operator, but this is because integration over the coordinates is always implied. It would be correct to write

$$\int dx^{1'} \ldots dx^{N'} \delta(x^1 - x^{1'}) \ldots \delta(x^N - x^{N'}) = 1 \qquad (3.88)$$

The operation of multiplying some function f by the Dirac δ-function and integrating over all of the coordinates gives back f again completely unharmed, and it is equivalent to multiplying the function f by 1.

Matrix representations of operators

Having seen how to handle multi-dimensional examples, let us, (for the sake of simplicity) return to the one-dimensional case but let us retain the Dirac notation. Suppose that we have got a set of functions $|a\rangle$ which are eigenfunctions of the operator A

$$A|a\rangle = \lambda_a |a\rangle \qquad (3.89)$$

Now think of another operator B which does not necessarily commute with A. When B acts on $|a\rangle$ it produces some function or other, and if the set of eigenfunctions is complete, we can expand this new function in terms of them

$$B|a\rangle = \sum_{a'} |a'\rangle \langle a'|B|a\rangle \qquad \mathbf{(3.90)}$$

The set of constant coefficients $\langle a'|B|a\rangle$ in this expansion is called the 'matrix representation' of the operator B. In terms of our former notation we would write

$$\langle a'|B|a\rangle = \int dx \phi_{a'}^* B \phi_a \qquad (3.91)$$

For particular values of a' and a, $\langle a'|B|a\rangle$ is just a number. When we allow a' and a to run over all of their possible values, we obtain an array of such numbers (i.e., a matrix) with a' and a forming the indices of the rows and columns. The matrix representation of some other operator C can also be based on what it does to the set of functions $|a\rangle$

$$C|a\rangle = \sum_{a'} |a'\rangle \langle a'|C|a\rangle \qquad (3.92)$$

Let us apply B and C in succession to the function $|a\rangle$ and see what happens:

$$BC|a\rangle = \sum_{a'} B|a'\rangle \langle a'|C|a\rangle$$

$$= \sum_{a', a''} |a''\rangle \langle a''|B|a'\rangle \langle a'|C|a\rangle \qquad (3.93)$$

By definition the matrix which represents the operator BC is given by

$$BC|a\rangle = \sum_{a''} |a''\rangle\langle a''|BC|a\rangle \tag{3.94}$$

Comparing Eq. (3.93) and Eq. (3.94) we have

$$\langle a''|BC|a\rangle = \sum_{a'} \langle a''|B|a'\rangle\langle a'|C|a\rangle \tag{3.95}$$

which follows also from the completeness relation

$$\sum_{a'} |a'\rangle\langle a'| = 1 \tag{3.96}$$

If you are familiar with matrix algebra, you will recognize that the right-hand side of Eq. (3.95) is just the definition of matrix multiplication. Equation (3.95) says that *if we base the matrix representation of several operators on a set of eigenfunctions according to the prescription of Eq. (3.90) then the matrix which represents the product of two operators is the product of the two matrices which represent the operators separately.* If the operators follow a certain multiplication table, then the matrices which represent them will follow it also. For example, if two operators commute, then the corresponding matrices also will commute.

Unitary transformations from one orthonormal basis set to another

It is interesting to notice that the matrix representation of the operator A based on its own eigenfunction $|a\rangle$ is a diagonal matrix:

$$\langle a'|A|a\rangle = \langle a'|\lambda_a|a\rangle = \lambda_a\langle a'|a\rangle = \lambda_a\delta_{a'a} \tag{3.97}$$

Now suppose that we have another Hermitian operator B which does not commute with A

$$[B, A] \neq 0 \tag{3.98}$$

The operator B will also define a set of eigenfunctions

$$B|b\rangle = \lambda_b|b\rangle \tag{3.99}$$

In terms of the eigenfunctions $|b\rangle$, the matrix representation of B is diagonal but the representation of A is non-diagonal. We can go from one representation to the other in the following way: $|b\rangle$ is a function which can be expanded in terms of the eigenfunctions $|a\rangle$

$$|b\rangle = \sum_{a} |a\rangle\langle a|b\rangle \tag{3.100}$$

Similarly for the conjugate function $\langle b'|$, we have

$$\langle b'| = \sum_{a'} \langle b' \mid a'\rangle\langle a'| \tag{3.101}$$

Putting Eq. (3.100) and Eq. (3.101) together we have a transformation which takes us from the representation based on the set of functions $|a\rangle$ to a representation based on the set $|b\rangle$. Suppose that we know the representation of an operator C based on the set of functions $|a\rangle$. Then we can find a matrix representation of C based on the functions $|b\rangle$ by using the following prescription:

$$\langle b'|C|b\rangle = \sum_{a,a'} \langle b' \mid a'\rangle\langle a'|C|a\rangle\langle a \mid b\rangle \tag{3.102}$$

The transformation matrix $\langle a \mid b\rangle$ which takes us from one orthonormal set to another has the property that its conjugate transpose is equal to its inverse. We can see this by combining Eq. (3.101) and Eq. (3.102) with the orthonormality conditions of the sets $|b\rangle$ and $|a\rangle$

$$\langle b' \mid b\rangle = \sum_{a'a} \langle b' \mid a'\rangle\langle a' \mid a\rangle\langle a \mid b\rangle \sum_{a',a} \langle b' \mid a'\rangle\delta_{a'a}\langle a \mid b\rangle$$

$$= \sum_{a} \langle b' \mid a\rangle\langle a \mid b\rangle = \delta_{b'b} \tag{3.103}$$

Thus multiplication of the matrix $\langle a \mid b\rangle$ by its conjugate transpose $\langle b' \mid a\rangle$ gives the unit matrix. (The 'transpose' of a matrix is found by interchanging the rows and columns so that each element moves to a symmetrical position on the opposite side of the diagonal.)

$$\sum_{a} \langle b' \mid a\rangle\langle a \mid b\rangle = \delta_{b'b} \tag{3.104}$$

When the conjugate transpose of a matrix is equal to its inverse, then the matrix is said to be 'unitary'; i.e., Eq. (3.104) states that $\langle a \mid b\rangle$ is unitary. The transformation matrix relating two orthonormal sets of basis functions, (as in Eq. (3.100)), is always unitary. *When the conjugate transpose of a matrix is equal to the matrix itself, the matrix is said to be 'Hermitian', or 'self-adjoint'*. The representation of an Hermitian operator based on a set of orthonormal functions is always an Hermitian matrix.

Diagonalization of an Hermitian matrix by means of a unitary transformation; the secular equations and secular determinant

Unitary transformations have got a very important use: Suppose that we are trying to solve the differential equation, Eq. (3.99). We do not know the solutions $|b\rangle$ but we are trying somehow to find them. On the other hand we happen to know the complete set of solutions $|a\rangle$ of Eq. (3.89). If we write Eq. (3.99) in terms of the functions $|a\rangle$, the equation $B|b\rangle = \lambda_b|b\rangle$ becomes

$$0 = (B - \lambda_b)|b\rangle = \sum_a (B - \lambda_b)|a\rangle\langle a \,|\, b\rangle \tag{3.105}$$

Taking the scalar product of Eq. (3.105) with $\langle a'|$ gives the so-called 'secular equations'

$$\sum_a (\langle a'|B|a\rangle - \lambda_b \delta_{a'a})\langle a \,|\, b\rangle = 0 \tag{3.106}$$

Equation (3.106) is actually a set of simultaneous homogeneous algebraic equations for the coefficients $\langle a \,|\, b\rangle$. In order for the set of equations to have a non-trivial solution it is necessary that what is known as the 'secular determinant' should vanish.

$$\det \left| \langle a'|B|a\rangle - \lambda_b \delta_{a'a} \right| = 0 \tag{3.107}$$

An example illustrating Cramer's rule

The reason why this determinant is required to be zero has to do with Cramer's rule for solving a set of simultaneous algebraic equations. Suppose, for example, that we want to solve the set of algebraic equations

$$3x + 4y = 5$$
$$5x + 6y = 7 \tag{3.108}$$

Cramer's rule says that the solution will be the ratio of determinants

$$x = \frac{\begin{vmatrix} 5 & 4 \\ 7 & 6 \end{vmatrix}}{\begin{vmatrix} 3 & 4 \\ 5 & 6 \end{vmatrix}} = \frac{30 - 28}{18 - 20} = -1 \tag{3.109}$$

and

$$y = \frac{\begin{vmatrix} 3 & 5 \\ 5 & 7 \end{vmatrix}}{\begin{vmatrix} 3 & 4 \\ 5 & 6 \end{vmatrix}} = \frac{21 - 25}{18 - 20} = 2 \tag{3.110}$$

You can see that what we have to do to construct the determinant in the denominator is just to write down the array of numbers multiplying the unknowns x and y. In order to construct the determinant in the numerator, we take the denominator and replace the column corresponding to the particular unknown which we are trying to find with the constants on the right-hand side of the equals sign. This works all right, as you can see, and gives the correct answer. But suppose that we want to solve the set of equations:

$$3x + 4y = 0$$

$$5x + 6y = 0 \qquad (3.111)$$

Now the set of linear algebraic equations is 'homogeneous', (i.e., there are no constants standing on the right) and when we try to construct the numerators, following Cramer's rule, we will just get zero. This being so, the solutions will have to be zero unless the denominator also vanishes. We could think of a case where the denominator vanishes, for example,

$$3x + 4y = 0$$

$$6x + 8y = 0 \qquad (3.112)$$

Then Cramer's rule would give an indeterminant answer of the form $\frac{0}{0}$.

In fact, the solution to Eq. (3.112) is not completely determined since one of the equations is redundant.

If you are trying to solve the set of secular equations, Eq. (3.106), you start out with the $N \times N$ matrix $\langle a'|B|a \rangle$. (In general, there may be an infinite number of eigenfunctions in the set $|a\rangle$, but either as an approximation or on the basis of other considerations, such as symmetry, we usually decide to include only a finite number N of them in our series for $|b\rangle$, Eq. (3.100).) Since you know the operator B and the functions $|a\rangle$, the matrix elements $\langle a'|B|a \rangle$ can be evaluated somehow or other—if not analytically then, as a last resort, numerically. The next step is to put these into Eq. (3.107), which is, in effect, an Nth order algebraic equation for λ. Having found the N roots λ_b, you can use the secular equations, Eq. (3.106), to determine for each root λ_b the corresponding set of N coefficients $\langle a \mid b \rangle$. Although the vanishing of the secular determinant makes one of the secular equations redundant, the missing information is supplied by the unitarity condition, Eq. (3.104).

An example of matrix diagonalization

For example, suppose that $N = 2$ and suppose that

$$\langle a'|B|a \rangle = \begin{pmatrix} \delta & \varepsilon \\ \varepsilon & \delta \end{pmatrix} \qquad (3.113)$$

Then the secular equations, Eq. (3.106), are

$$(\delta - \lambda_b)\langle a_1 | b \rangle + \varepsilon \langle a_2 | b \rangle = 0$$
$$\varepsilon \langle a_1 | b \rangle + (\delta - \lambda_b)\langle a_2 | b \rangle = 0 \qquad (3.114)$$

In order for Eq. (3.114) to have a non-trivial solution, the secular determinant must be zero.

$$\det \begin{vmatrix} (\delta - \lambda_b) \cdot & \varepsilon \\ \varepsilon & (\delta - \lambda_b) \end{vmatrix} = (\delta - \lambda_b)^2 - \varepsilon^2 = 0 \qquad (3.115)$$

Equation (3.115) is a quadratic equation with two roots

$$\lambda_1 = \delta + \varepsilon$$

and

$$\lambda_2 = \delta - \varepsilon \qquad (3.116)$$

If you substitute λ_1 into Eq. (3.114) you get

$$(\delta - \delta - \varepsilon)\langle a_1 | b_1 \rangle + \varepsilon \langle a_2 | b_1 \rangle = 0 \qquad (3.117)$$

so that

$$\langle a_1 | b_1 \rangle = \langle a_2 | b_1 \rangle \qquad (3.118)$$

This does not completely determine $\langle a_1 | b_1 \rangle$ and $\langle a_2 | b_1 \rangle$, but from the unitarity condition, we have

$$\langle a_1 | b_1 \rangle^2 + \langle a_2 | b_1 \rangle^2 = 1 \qquad (3.119)$$

Equations (3.111) and (3.119) have a solution

$$\langle a_1 | b_1 \rangle = \frac{1}{\sqrt{2}}, \qquad \langle a_2 | b_1 \rangle = \frac{1}{\sqrt{2}} \qquad (3.120)$$

Similarly, by substituting λ_2 into the secular equations you find the coefficients of the other eigenfunction:

$$\langle a_1 | b_1 \rangle = \frac{-1}{\sqrt{2}}, \qquad \langle a_2 | b_2 \rangle = \frac{1}{\sqrt{2}} \qquad (3.121)$$

Now you know the entire transformation matrix

$$\langle a | b \rangle = \begin{pmatrix} \dfrac{1}{\sqrt{2}} & \dfrac{1}{\sqrt{2}} \\ \dfrac{-1}{\sqrt{2}} & \dfrac{1}{\sqrt{2}} \end{pmatrix} \equiv \frac{1}{\sqrt{2}} \begin{pmatrix} 1 & 1 \\ -1 & 1 \end{pmatrix} \qquad (3.122)$$

The quantum theory of atoms, molecules, and photons

and hence the eigenfunctions $|b\rangle$ in terms of the known functions $|a\rangle$, Eq. (3.100). You can see that $\langle a \mid b \rangle$ is unitary because when it is multiplied by its transpose, the result is the unit matrix

$$\frac{1}{2}\begin{pmatrix} 1 & 1 \\ -1 & 1 \end{pmatrix}\begin{pmatrix} 1 & -1 \\ 1 & 1 \end{pmatrix} = \begin{pmatrix} 1 & 0 \\ 0 & 1 \end{pmatrix} \tag{3.123}$$

which is to be compared with Eq. (3.104). (With a little practice you can learn to multiply matrices together quickly. Run the index finger of your left hand along a row of the left-hand matrix and the index finger of your right hand down a column of the right-hand matrix, mentally adding up the products of the elements. The total gives you the element in the corresponding row and column of the product matrix.) The unitary transformation shown in Eq. (3.102) brings $\langle a'|B|a\rangle$ into the $|b\rangle$-representation where it is diagonal. Written in algebraic notation, the transformation looks like this:

$$\sum_{a,\,a'} \langle b' \mid a'\rangle\langle a'|B|a\rangle\langle a \mid b\rangle = \langle b'|B|b\rangle = \lambda_b\delta_{b'b} \tag{3.124}$$

Written out in terms of the matrices of Eq. (3.113) and Eq. (3.123), the transformation of Eq. (3.124) becomes:

$$\frac{1}{2}\begin{pmatrix} 1 & -1 \\ 1 & 1 \end{pmatrix}\begin{pmatrix} \delta & \varepsilon \\ \varepsilon & \delta \end{pmatrix}\begin{pmatrix} 1 & 1 \\ -1 & 1 \end{pmatrix} = \frac{1}{2}\begin{pmatrix} 1 & -1 \\ 1 & 1 \end{pmatrix}\begin{pmatrix} \delta - \varepsilon & \delta + \varepsilon \\ \varepsilon - \delta & \varepsilon + \delta \end{pmatrix}$$

$$= \begin{pmatrix} \delta + \varepsilon & 0 \\ 0 & \delta - \varepsilon \end{pmatrix} \tag{3.125}$$

Problem (3.3) Try to diagonalize the matrix,

$$\langle a'|B|a\rangle = \begin{pmatrix} \delta & \varepsilon & \varepsilon \\ \varepsilon & \delta & \varepsilon \\ \varepsilon & \varepsilon & \delta \end{pmatrix}$$

following a procedure similar to that of Eqs. (3.113)–(3.125).

The analogy between functions and vectors

All of this may seem a bit familiar. In fact the whole procedure of diagonalizing a matrix to find its eigenvalues and eigenfunctions is very closely analogous to the calculation which we had to go through in Appendix I to find the small vibrations of a classical system about its equilibrium position. There is also a mathematical analogy between the set of orthonormal eigenfunctions of an Hermitian operator and a set of mutually perpendicular (orthogonal) unit vectors in a many-dimensional space. For example, think of the two-dimensional space shown in Fig. 3.2. The two unit vectors $\hat{u}_a$ and $\hat{u}_{a'}$ have the orthonormality relation

$$\hat{u}_a \cdot \hat{u}_{a'} = \delta_{aa'} \tag{3.126}$$

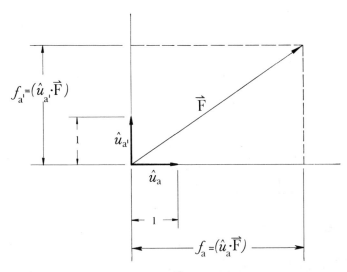

Figure 3.2 shows an arbitrary vector $\vec{F}$ in a two-dimensional space resolved into its components in the directions of the two unit vectors, $\hat{u}_a$ and $\hat{u}_{a'}$: $\vec{F} = \hat{u}_a f_a + \hat{u}_{a'} f_{a'}$. The coefficients in the expansion are found by taking the scalar product of $\vec{F}$ with $\hat{u}_a$ and $\hat{u}_{a'}$: $f_a = \hat{u}_a \cdot \vec{F}$, $f_a = \hat{u}_{a'} \cdot \vec{F}$. This is analogous to the Fourier expansion of a function in terms of a set of orthonormal basis functions. $\vec{F}$ is analogous to the original function, the unit vectors $\hat{u}_a$ and $\hat{u}_{a'}$ are analogous to the basis functions, while f_a and $f_{a'}$ are analogous to the expansion coefficients.

An arbitrary vector $\vec{F}$ can be expressed as a linear combination of the two unit vectors

$$\vec{F} = \sum_a \hat{u}_a f_a \tag{3.127}$$

The orthonormality relation can be used to solve for the expansion coefficients f_a

$$f_a = (\hat{u}_a \cdot \vec{F}) \tag{3.128}$$

We could equally well use another set of basis vectors $\hat{u}_b$ as shown in Fig. 3.3. These are related to the old basis vectors by a pure rotation through an angle θ

$$\hat{u}_b = \sum_a \hat{u}_a (\hat{u}_a \cdot \hat{u}_b) \tag{3.129}$$

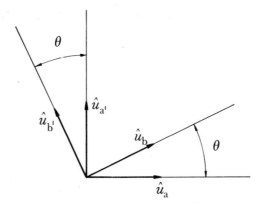

Figure 3.3 shows a second set of orthogonal unit vectors, $\hat{u}_b$ and $\hat{u}_{b'}$. They 'span' the same two-dimensional space as $\hat{u}_a$ and $\hat{u}_{a'}$, i.e., an arbitrary vector $\vec{F}$ in this space can be expanded either in terms of $\hat{u}_a$ and $\hat{u}_{a'}$ or else in terms of $\hat{u}_b$ and $\hat{u}_{b'}$. The rotation which takes us from one set of basis vectors to the other is analogous to a unitary transformation relating two different sets of orthonormal basis functions spanning the same Hilbert space.

Because the new basis vectors are also orthonormal, the transformation matrix $(\hat{u}_a \cdot \hat{u}_b)$ must be unitary

$$(\hat{u}_{b'} \cdot \hat{u}_b) = \sum_{a',a} (\hat{u}_{b'} \cdot \hat{u}_{a'})(\hat{u}_{a'} \cdot \hat{u}_a)(\hat{u}_a \cdot \hat{u}_b)$$

$$= \sum_{a',a} (\hat{u}_{b'} \cdot \hat{u}_{a'})\delta_{a'a}(\hat{u}_a \cdot \hat{u}_b)$$

$$= \sum_{a} (\hat{u}_{b'} \cdot \hat{u}_a)(\hat{u}_a \cdot \hat{u}_b) = \delta_{b'b} \tag{3.130}$$

In fact, for the example shown in Fig. 3.3 the transformation matrix is just

$$(\hat{u}_a \cdot \hat{u}_b) = \begin{pmatrix} \cos\theta & -\sin\theta \\ \sin\theta & \cos\theta \end{pmatrix} \tag{3.131}$$

which is obviously unitary since

$$\begin{pmatrix} \cos\theta & \sin\theta \\ -\sin\theta & \cos\theta \end{pmatrix}\begin{pmatrix} \cos\theta & -\sin\theta \\ \sin\theta & \cos\theta \end{pmatrix} = \begin{pmatrix} 1 & 0 \\ 0 & 1 \end{pmatrix} \tag{3.132}$$

Hilbert noticed this analogy. *An orthonormal set of eigenfunctions is analogous to a set of mutually orthonormal unit vectors. A unitary transformation to another basis set is analogous to a pure rotation of the basis vectors.* He found that the analogy helped him to think about the relationships between functions. The two unit vectors in Fig. 3.2 form a complete set in the sense that any vector $\vec{F}$ in the two-dimensional space can be expressed as a linear superposition of $\hat{u}_a$ and $\hat{u}_{a'}$. They span the space.

118

Hilbert introduced the idea of a many-dimensional function-space spanned by an orthonormal set of eigenfunctions. In general, the number of eigenfunctions in the set will be infinite and so the dimension of the space will also be infinite. In other words, a function can be thought of as a vector in an infinite dimensional space (Hilbert space). The set of eigenfunctions of an Hermitian operator is said to be complete if it spans the Hilbert space of all functions which obey the same boundary conditions. The integral

$$f_a = \int dx \phi_a^*(x) f(x) \equiv \langle a \mid f \rangle \tag{3.133}$$

corresponds to the 'projection' of the function $f(x)$ onto the eigenfunction $\phi_a(x)$, i.e., the scalar product of f and ϕ_a. (The Dirac notation is nice because it is so ambiguous. One can use it equally well both for functions and for vectors.)

Subspaces of Hilbert space; projection operators; spectral resolutions of the identity operator

A Hilbert space can be divided into subspaces. Suppose, for example, that we expand a function $f(x)$ in a Fourier sine series and that the expansion involves only the first N values of n

$$f(x) = \sum_{n=1}^{N} \sqrt{\frac{2}{L}} \sin\left(\frac{n\pi x}{L}\right) f_n \equiv \sum_{n=1}^{N} |n\rangle\langle n \mid f\rangle \tag{3.134}$$

Using a notation which is sometimes also used for vectors, we can specify the function $f(x)$ by writing out all of the expansion coefficients $f_n = \langle n \mid f \rangle$ in a long line.

$$f(x) = (f_1, f_2, f_3, f_4, \ldots, f_\infty) = (f_1, f_2, \ldots, f_N, 0, \ldots, 0) \tag{3.135}$$

Then the function f is said to fall entirely within the part of Hilbert space spanned by the N basis functions $|1\rangle, |2\rangle, \ldots, |N\rangle$. Now suppose that we have another function $g(x)$ whose Fourier sine series expansion only involves the basis functions $|N + 1\rangle, \ldots, |\infty\rangle$

$$g(x) = \sum_{n=N+1}^{\infty} |n\rangle\langle n \mid g\rangle = (g_1, g_2, g_3, g_4, \ldots, g_\infty)$$

$$= (0, \ldots, 0, g_{N+1}, \ldots, g_\infty) \tag{3.136}$$

Then the scalar product of f and g is zero:

$$\int_0^L dx f^*(x) g(x) = f_1^* g_1 + f_2^* g_2 + f_3^* g_3 + \ldots, \text{etc.}$$

$$= 0 \tag{3.137}$$

119

and this must always be so when two functions come from different parts of Hilbert space. Like the marriage of Romeo and Juliet, their union comes to nothing. The operator

$$P = \sum_{n=1}^{N} |n\rangle\langle n| \qquad (3.138)$$

acting on the function $|f\rangle$ has no effect at all

$$P|f\rangle = \left(\sum_{n'=1}^{N} |n'\rangle\langle n'| \right)\left(\sum_{n=1}^{N} |n\rangle f_n \right)$$

$$= \sum_{n',n=1}^{N} |n'\rangle \, \delta_{n'n} f_n = \sum_{n=1}^{N} |n\rangle f_n = |f\rangle \qquad (3.139)$$

If P' acts on $|g\rangle$ it annihilates it. *If P acts on a general function it preserves those parts of the function which lie inside the region of Hilbert space spanned by the basis functions $|1\rangle, \ldots, |N\rangle$. The parts which lie outside are annihilated. This kind of operator is called a 'projection operator'.* It projects out the components of a function which lie within a particular subspace of Hilbert space. When a Hilbert space is divided into a number of subspaces, the identity operator can be resolved into a series of projection operators each of which corresponds to a particular subspace. For example we could write

$$1 = \sum_{n=1}^{\infty} |n\rangle\langle n| = \sum_{n=1}^{N} |n\rangle\langle n| + \sum_{n=N+1}^{\infty} |n\rangle\langle n| = P + P' \qquad (3.140)$$

An equation like Eq. (3.140) is called a 'spectral resolution of the identity'. The effect of the projection operator corresponding to a certain subspace of Hilbert space acting on an arbitrary function, is to amputate the components of the function which lie outside the subspace. On the other hand, if the function is already entirely within the subspace then it survives without being mutilated.

So that is Hilbert space! One can either take it or else leave it alone, since it is perfectly possible to understand the properties of eigenfunctions without insisting that they are analogous to vectors.

I remember once, at a party in Chicago, hearing people singing a new version of the spiritual 'You Can't Get to Heaven'. I have forgotten most of the verses (there were very many of them), but a few that stick in my mind went something like this:

> 'Let's give a cheer for Bernard Riemann,
> He thought of those surfaces when he was dreamin'!
> Let's give a cheer for Fredrick Gauss
> He used total curvature in choosing his spouse!

Oh you can't get to Heaven in Hilbert space,
'Cause the Lord maintains there's no such place!'

Problem (3.4)   (a) Show that if P is the projection operator defined by
Eq. (3.138), then $P^2 = P$. What are the eigenvalues and eigenfunctions of P?
(b) Suppose that the complete orthonormal set of functions $|n\rangle$ obey the
equation $(\Omega - \lambda_n)|n\rangle = 0$. Show that

$$\prod_{n' \neq n} \left(\frac{\Omega - \lambda_{n'}}{\lambda_n - \lambda_{n'}} \right) = |n\rangle\langle n|$$

where the symbol $\prod$ denotes a product. (For the solution, see Appendix IV.)

4. Angular momentum

The commutation rules for orbital angular momentum operators

In discussing the properties of operators we remarked that when two operators commute with each other it is possible to find simultaneous eigenfunctions of both of them, Eqs. (3.64)–(3.69). Let us now consider the case where two operators fail to commute.

The history of non-commutative algebra goes back to the breakfast table of Sir William Rowan Hamilton whose contributions to mechanics we discussed earlier. Hamilton was trying to find an algebraic representation for the operations of rotation about the three coordinate axes x, y, and z. But these operations are non-commutative as shown in Fig. 4.1 and

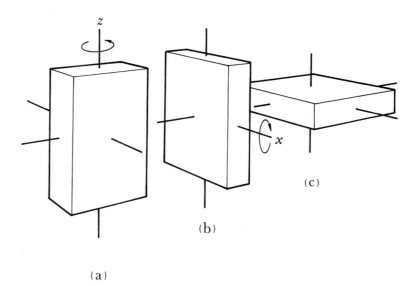

Figure 4.1 An object (a) is first rotated around the z-axis to position (b) and then about the x-axis to position (c).

122

Fig. 4.2. Hamilton struggled with the problem for some time before he realized that any algebraic representation of the rotation operations also had to be non-commutative. Every morning at breakfast his children would ask him: 'Well, Papa, can you multiply triplets?' (i.e. rotations) and he would reply sadly 'No, I can only add them'. When Hamilton finally thought of the idea of a non-commutative algebra, he was so excited that he carved his solution onto a wooden bridge which he happened to be passing!

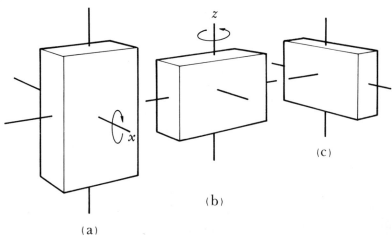

(a)   (b)   (c)

Figure 4.2 The same object (a) is first rotated about the x-axis to position (b) and then around the z-axis to position (c). The final position differs from the one shown in Fig. 4.1, showing that the x and z rotations are non-commutative: i.e., the order of the two operations makes a difference.

But how do you multiply rotations? If dx is an infinitesimal distance, then from Eq. (1.10)

$$f(x + dx) = f(x) + dx \frac{\partial f}{\partial x} \tag{4.1}$$

The operator $1 + dx(\partial/\partial x)$ acting on the function $f(x)$ has the same effect as a small displacement of the x coordinates. In the same way, the operator

$$1 + d\varphi \left(x \frac{\partial}{\partial y} - y \frac{\partial}{\partial x} \right) = 1 + d\varphi \frac{\partial}{\partial \varphi} \tag{4.2}$$

acting on a function of x, y, and z, has the same effect as a rotation of the coordinates through an infinitesimal angle $d\varphi$ about the z-axis. Comparing Eq. (4.2) with Eqs. (3.4)–(3.6) we see that

$$1 + d\varphi \frac{\partial}{\partial \varphi} = 1 + \frac{i}{\hbar} L_z \tag{4.3}$$

123

where

$$L_z = \frac{\hbar}{i}\left(x\frac{\partial}{\partial y} - y\frac{\partial}{\partial x}\right) \tag{4.4}$$

In a similar way, the operators

$$L_x = \frac{\hbar}{i}\left(y\frac{\partial}{\partial z} - z\frac{\partial}{\partial y}\right) \tag{4.5}$$

and

$$L_y = \frac{\hbar}{i}\left(z\frac{\partial}{\partial x} - x\frac{\partial}{\partial z}\right) \tag{4.6}$$

can be used to represent infinitesimal rotations about the x- and y-axes. These are just the operators whose expectation value reduces to the classical angular momentum in the limit of large quantum numbers, Eqs. (3.2)–(3.10). (Incidentally, you can also see by comparing Eq. (4.1) and Eq. (2.16) that the operator corresponding to linear momentum can be used to represent the effect of a linear translation of the coordinates.) As Hamilton discovered, the algebra of the rotation operators, Eqs. (4.3)–(4.6), is by no means commutative (see Eqs. (3.66)–(3.68)). In fact, it is easy to show by successive application of the angular momentum operators to an arbitrary function that they have the commutation rules

$$[L_x, L_y] = i\hbar L_z$$
$$[L_y, L_z] = i\hbar L_x$$
$$[L_z, L_x] = i\hbar L_y \tag{4.7}$$

It is possible to extract from the commutation relations, Eq. (4.7), quite a lot of information about the properties of the operators L_x, L_y, and L_z and their eigenfunctions. You might ask why we would want to do such a thing, since we already know all about the spherical harmonics. The answer is that when several angular momentum operators are added together, the result is a vector operator whose components commute in the same way as those of a single angular momentum. In a many-electron atom, when there is no external perturbation to destroy the spherical symmetry, this total angular momentum operator commutes with the non-relativistic many-electron Hamiltonian. The eigenvalues of the total angular momentum operators are then 'good quantum numbers' for characterizing the energy levels of the atom. If we can develop a theory of angular momentum based solely on the commutation relations, Eq. (4.7), then whatever we find out can be taken over bodily and applied to any vector operator whose components obey the same commutation rules.

The definition of a general angular momentum operator $\vec{J}$; simultaneous eigenfunctions of J^2 and J_z

In order to distinguish it from the one-electron orbital angular momentum operator $\vec{L}$ defined by Eqs. (4.4)–(4.6) we shall use the symbol $\vec{J}$ to denote any operator whatsoever which obeys the commutation rules

$$[J_x, J_y] = i\hbar J_z$$

$$[J_y, J_z] = i\hbar J_x$$

$$[J_z, J_x] = i\hbar J_y \qquad \textbf{(4.7a)}$$

One thing which is obvious immediately from Eq. (4.7a) is that since the components of $\vec{J}$ do not commute from one another, an eigenfunction of one component will not be an eigenfunction of the other two (see Eqs. (3.63)–(3.65)). For example, an eigenfunction of J_z will not be an eigenfunction of J_x and J_y. On the other hand, one can show that J_z commutes with the operator

$$J^2 = J_x^2 + J_y^2 + J_z^2 \qquad (4.8)$$

so that

$$[J_z, J^2] = 0 \qquad (4.9)$$

In order to prove Eq. (4.9) we notice that

$$[J_z, J^2] = [J_z, J_x^2] + [J_z, J_y^2] \qquad (4.10)$$

Now for any two operators A and B,

$$[A, B^2] \equiv ABB - BBA = (AB - BA)B + B(AB - BA)$$

$$\equiv [A, B]B + B[A, B] \qquad (4.11)$$

Using Eq. (4.11) and Eq. (4.7) we obtain

$$[J_z, J_x^2] = [J_z, J_x]J_x + J_x[J_z, J_x] = iJ_yJ_x + iJ_xJ_y \qquad (4.12)$$

and similarly

$$[J_z, J_y^2] = [J_z, J_y]J_y + J_y[J_z, J_y] = -iJ_xJ_y - iJ_yJ_x \qquad (4.13)$$

Adding Eq. (4.12) and Eq. (4.13) gives Eq. (4.9). (We could show in a similar way that J_x and J_y also commute with J^2.)

Since J_z and J^2 commute we can find simultaneous eigenfunctions of the two operators, i.e., there exists a set of functions $|j, m\rangle$ which satisfy the equations

$$J_z|j, m\rangle = \lambda_m|j, m\rangle \qquad (4.14)$$

$$J^2|j, m\rangle = \lambda_j|j, m\rangle \qquad (4.15)$$

125

Raising and lowering operators; the family of eigenfunctions belonging to the same eigenvalue of J^2

Using the commutation relations we can show in the following way that $J_x - iJ_y$ is a 'lowering operator' (see Eq. (2.29)).

$$J_z(J_x - iJ_y) - (J_x - iJ_y)J_z = [J_z, J_x] - i[J_z, J_y]$$

$$= i\hbar J_y - \hbar J_x = -\hbar(J_x - iJ_y)$$

(4.16)

Collecting terms we have

$$J_z(J_x - iJ_y) = (J_x - iJ_y)(J_z - \hbar) \tag{4.17}$$

From Eq. (4.17) and Eq. (4.14) we can see that

$$J_z(J_x - iJ_y)|j, m\rangle = (\lambda_m - \hbar)(J_x - iJ_y)|j, m\rangle \tag{4.18}$$

In other words $(J_x - iJ_y)|j, m\rangle$ is an eigenfunction of J_z belonging to the eigenvalue $(\lambda_m - \hbar)$. Similarly, one can show that $J_x + iJ_y$ is a 'raising operator',

$$J_z(J_x + iJ_y)|j, m\rangle = (\lambda_m + \hbar)(J_x + iJ_y)|j, m\rangle \tag{4.19}$$

The derivation of Eq. (4.19) is identical to that of Eq. (4.18) except for a change of signs. Since the raising and lowering operators commute with J^2, the raised or lowered eigenfunctions of J_z are also eigenfunctions of J^2 belonging to the eigenvalue λ_j

$$J^2(J_x \pm iJ_y)|j, m\rangle = (J_x \pm iJ_y)J^2|j, m\rangle = \lambda_j(J_x \pm iJ_y)|j, m\rangle \tag{4.20}$$

This means that a family of different eigenfunctions of J_z belonging to various values of λ_m can all be eigenfunctions of J^2 corresponding to the same eigenvalue λ_j. Like the members of a family these functions have different first names λ_m but the same last name λ_j. It is interesting to ask how many members there are in such a family. If we keep applying the raising operator to the function $|j, m\rangle$ we get eigenfunctions corresponding to higher and higher eigenvalues

$$\lambda_{m'} = \lambda_m, \lambda_m + \hbar, \lambda_m + 2\hbar, \ldots, \text{etc.} \tag{4.21}$$

Unless something happens to stop it, this process can go on for ever. The family of eigenfunctions belonging to λ_j needs some sort of birth control or else it will have an infinite number of members. Let us apply the restriction that the set of eigenvalues λ_m must have a largest member, $\lambda_m(\text{max})$. This is a reasonable restriction because in the classical limit, no component of the angular momentum vector $\vec{J}$ can be larger than the length of $\vec{J}$. If $J_x^2 + J_y^2$ is required to be a positive quantity then

$$J_x^2 + J_y^2 = J^2 - J_z^2 > 0 \qquad (4.22)$$

Therefore we impose the requirement

$$\{\lambda_m(\text{max})\}^2 = \{\lambda_m(\text{min})\}^2 < \lambda_j^2 \qquad (4.23)$$

If we define the dimensionless numbers m and j by the relations

$$\lambda_m = \hbar m \qquad (4.24)$$

and

$$\lambda_m(\text{max}) = \hbar j \qquad (4.25)$$

without any prejudice about whether m and j are integral or fractional, then we are left with the following range of possible values of λ_m.

$$\frac{\lambda_m}{\hbar} = m = j, j - 1, j - 2, \ldots, -j \qquad (4.26)$$

Equation (4.26) implies that *there are $2j + 1$ possible values of λ_m belonging to a particular value of λ_j. Therefore $2j + 1$ must be a positive integer and j must be a positive integer or half-integer.* We have still not related the number j to λ_j, the eigenvalue of J^2, but that is the next step: In order for the raising process of Eq. (4.19) and Eq. (4.21) to terminate, the raising operator, applied once too often, must annihilate the eigenfunction corresponding to $\lambda_m(\text{max}) = \hbar j$. If we call this highest eigenfunction $|j, j\rangle$ then we have

$$(J_x + iJ_y)|j, j\rangle = 0 \qquad (4.27)$$

Applying $J_x - iJ_y$ and using the commutation relations, Eq. (4.7) gives

$$(J_x - iJ_y)(J_x + iJ_y)|j, j\rangle = (J_x^2 + J_y^2 + iJ_xJ_y - iJ_yJ_x)|j, j\rangle$$
$$= (J^2 - J_z^2 - \hbar J_z)|j, j\rangle = 0 \qquad (4.28)$$

but

$$J_z|j, j\rangle = \hbar j|j, j\rangle \qquad (4.29)$$

so that finally Eq. (4.28) becomes

$$J^2|j, j\rangle = \lambda_j|j, j\rangle = \hbar^2 j(j + 1)|j, j\rangle \qquad \textbf{(4.30)}$$

Normalization of the eigenfunctions

Equations (4.28) and (4.29) show us how to manufacture all of the eigenfunctions in the set $|j, m\rangle$ $m = j, j - 1, \ldots, -j$ provided that we have got

127

one of them: introducing an unknown normalization factor, N_+, we can write

$$(J_x + iJ_y)|j, m\rangle = N_+|j, m + 1\rangle \qquad (4.31)$$

If we apply the lowering operator to $|j, m + 1\rangle$ we obtain $|j, m\rangle$ multiplied by a normalizing factor which we can call N_-:

$$(J_x - iJ_y)|j, m + 1\rangle = N_-|j, m\rangle \qquad (4.32)$$

Let us now introduce the additional condition

$$N_+ = N_- \equiv N = \text{real} \qquad (4.33)$$

As we shall see, this condition leads to matrix representations of the operators J_x, J_y, and J_z which are Hermitian. Now if we apply the lowering operator to both sides of Eq. (4.31) we obtain

$$(J_x - iJ_y)(J_x + iJ_y)|j, m\rangle = N(J_x - iJ_y)|j, m + 1\rangle = N^2|j, m\rangle \quad (4.34)$$

If we take the scalar product of Eq. (4.34) with the conjugate function $\langle j, m|$ and make use of Eqs. (4.7), (4.29), and (4.30) together with the normalization condition, then we obtain an expression for N^2.

$$
\begin{aligned}
\langle j, m|(J_x - iJ_y)(J_x + iJ_y)|j, m\rangle \\
= \langle j, m|\{J_x^2 + J_y^2 + i(J_xJ_y - J_yJ_x)\}|j, m\rangle \\
= \langle j, m|(J^2 - J_z^2 - \hbar J_z)|j, m\rangle \\
= \hbar^2\{j(j + 1) - m(m + 1)\} = N^2 \qquad (4.35)
\end{aligned}
$$

or, choosing the + sign for the square root,

$$N = \hbar\sqrt{j(j + 1) - m(m + 1)} \qquad (4.36)$$

then Eq. (4.31) becomes

$$(J_x + iJ_y)|j, m\rangle = \hbar\sqrt{j(j + 1) - m(m + 1)}|j, m + 1\rangle \qquad \textbf{(4.37)}$$

and from Eq. (4.32) we have

$$(J_x - iJ_y)|j, m + 1\rangle = \hbar\sqrt{j(j + 1) - m(m + 1)}|j, m\rangle \qquad (4.38)$$

Replacing m with $m - 1$ in Eq. (4.38) gives

$$(J_x - iJ_y)|j, m\rangle = \hbar\sqrt{j(j + 1) - m(m - 1)}|j, m - 1\rangle \qquad \textbf{(4.39)}$$

If we add Eq. (4.37) and Eq. (4.39) the parts involving J_y drop out leaving:

$$
\begin{aligned}
J_x|j, m\rangle = \frac{\hbar}{2}\sqrt{j(j + 1) - m(m + 1)}|j, m + 1\rangle \\
+ \frac{\hbar}{2}\sqrt{j(j + 1) - m(m - 1)}|j, m - 1\rangle \qquad (4.40)
\end{aligned}
$$

The matrix representation of angular momentum

Taking the scalar product of Eq. (4.40) with the conjugate function $\langle j', m'|$ gives us finally a matrix representation of J_x

$$\langle j, m'|J_x|j, m\rangle = \frac{\hbar}{2}\sqrt{j(j+1) - m(m+1)}\delta_{j',j}\delta_{m',m+1}$$

$$+ \frac{\hbar}{2}\sqrt{j(j+1) - m(m-1)}\delta_{j',j}\delta_{m',m-1}$$

$$(4.41)$$

Similarly, subtracting Eq. (4.39) from Eq. (4.37) yields a matrix representation of J_y:

$$\langle j', m'|J_y|j, m\rangle$$

$$= -\frac{i\hbar}{2}\sqrt{j(j+1) - m(m+1)}\delta_{j',j}\delta_{m',m+1}$$

$$+ \frac{i\hbar}{2}\sqrt{j(j+1) - m(m-1)}\delta_{j',j}\delta_{m',m-1} \qquad (4.42)$$

The task of finding a matrix representation of J_z is much easier. Since the functions $|j, m\rangle$ are eigenfunctions of J_z we have immediately

$$\langle j', m'|J_z|j, m\rangle = \hbar m\, \delta_{j'j}\, \delta_{m'm} \qquad (4.43)$$

The representations of the angular momentum operators are block diagonal, each block corresponding to an integral or half-integral value of j. The case $j = 0$ is trivial: J_x, J_y, and J_z are represented respectively by three numbers all of which are zero. The next higher allowed value of j, $j = \frac{1}{2}$, is more interesting. In that case, the diagonal blocks of J_x, J_y, and J_z are 2×2 matrices based on the $2j + 1 = 2$ functions (Eq. 4.26) $|\frac{1}{2}, \frac{1}{2}\rangle$ and $|\frac{1}{2}, -\frac{1}{2}\rangle$. According to Eqs. (4.41), (4.42), and (4.43) these 2×2 matrices are given by

$$\langle \tfrac{1}{2}, m'|J_x|\tfrac{1}{2}, m\rangle = \frac{\hbar}{2}\begin{pmatrix} 0 & 1 \\ 1 & 0 \end{pmatrix} \qquad (4.44)$$

$$\langle \tfrac{1}{2}, m'|J_y|\tfrac{1}{2}, m\rangle = \frac{\hbar}{2}\begin{pmatrix} 0 & -i \\ i & 0 \end{pmatrix} \qquad (4.45)$$

and

$$\langle \tfrac{1}{2}, m'|J_z|\tfrac{1}{2}, m\rangle = \frac{\hbar}{2}\begin{pmatrix} 1 & 0 \\ 0 & -1 \end{pmatrix} \qquad (4.46)$$

129

It is easy to see that these matrices obey the commutation rules, Eq. (4.7). For example,

$$\langle \tfrac{1}{2}, m' | [J_x, J_y] | \tfrac{1}{2}, m \rangle = \frac{\hbar^2}{4} \left\{ \begin{pmatrix} 0 & 1 \\ 1 & 0 \end{pmatrix} \begin{pmatrix} 0 & -i \\ i & 0 \end{pmatrix} - \begin{pmatrix} 0 & -i \\ i & 0 \end{pmatrix} \begin{pmatrix} 0 & 1 \\ 1 & 0 \end{pmatrix} \right\}$$

$$= \frac{\hbar^2}{4} \left\{ \begin{pmatrix} i & 0 \\ 0 & -i \end{pmatrix} - \begin{pmatrix} -i & 0 \\ 0 & i \end{pmatrix} \right\} = \frac{i\hbar^2}{2} \begin{pmatrix} 1 & 0 \\ 0 & -1 \end{pmatrix}$$

$$= i\hbar \langle \tfrac{1}{2}, m' | J_z | \tfrac{1}{2}, m \rangle \tag{4.47}$$

Furthermore the representation of $J^2 = J_x^2 + J_y^2 + J_z^2$ is diagonal with diagonal elements $\hbar^2 j(j+1) = \hbar^2 \tfrac{1}{2}(\tfrac{1}{2}+1)$.

$$\langle \tfrac{1}{2}, m' | J^2 | \tfrac{1}{2}, m \rangle =$$

$$\frac{\hbar^2}{4} \left\{ \begin{pmatrix} 0 & 1 \\ 1 & 0 \end{pmatrix} \begin{pmatrix} 0 & 1 \\ 1 & 0 \end{pmatrix} + \begin{pmatrix} 0 & -i \\ i & 0 \end{pmatrix} \begin{pmatrix} 0 & -i \\ i & 0 \end{pmatrix} + \begin{pmatrix} 1 & 0 \\ 0 & -1 \end{pmatrix} \begin{pmatrix} 1 & 0 \\ 0 & -1 \end{pmatrix} \right\}$$

$$= \frac{3\hbar^2}{4} \begin{pmatrix} 1 & 0 \\ 0 & 1 \end{pmatrix} \tag{4.48}$$

Finally, it is easy to see that the matrices of Eqs. (4.45)–(4.47) are Hermitian —that is, taking the conjugate transpose of one of these matrices does not change it. The diagonal blocks corresponding to $j = 1$ are 3×3 matrices based on the $2j + 1 = 2 + 1 = 3$ functions $|1, 1\rangle$, $|1, 0\rangle$, and $|1, -1\rangle$. From Eq. (4.41) we have

$$\langle 1, m' | J_x | 1, m \rangle = \frac{\hbar}{\sqrt{2}} \begin{pmatrix} 0 & 1 & 0 \\ 1 & 0 & 1 \\ 0 & 1 & 0 \end{pmatrix} \tag{4.49}$$

$$\langle 1, m' | J_y | 1, m \rangle = \frac{\hbar}{\sqrt{2}} \begin{pmatrix} 0 & -i & 0 \\ i & 0 & -i \\ 0 & i & 0 \end{pmatrix} \tag{4.50}$$

and

$$\langle 1, m' | J_z | 1, m \rangle = \hbar \begin{pmatrix} 1 & 0 & 0 \\ 0 & 0 & 0 \\ 0 & 0 & -1 \end{pmatrix} \tag{4.51}$$

When $j = \tfrac{3}{2}$ we have

$$\langle \tfrac{3}{2}, m' | J_x | \tfrac{3}{2}, m \rangle = \frac{\hbar}{2} \begin{pmatrix} 0 & \sqrt{3} & 0 & 0 \\ \sqrt{3} & 0 & 2 & 0 \\ 0 & 2 & 0 & \sqrt{3} \\ 0 & 0 & \sqrt{3} & 0 \end{pmatrix} \tag{4.52}$$

$$\langle \tfrac{3}{2}, m' | J_y | \tfrac{3}{2}, m \rangle = \frac{\hbar}{2} \begin{pmatrix} 0 & -\sqrt{3}i & 0 & 0 \\ \sqrt{3}i & 0 & -2i & 0 \\ 0 & 2i & 0 & -\sqrt{3}i \\ 0 & 0 & \sqrt{3}i & 0 \end{pmatrix} \qquad (4.53)$$

and

$$\langle \tfrac{3}{2}, m' | J_z | \tfrac{3}{2}, m \rangle = \hbar \begin{pmatrix} \tfrac{3}{2} & 0 & 0 & 0 \\ 0 & \tfrac{1}{2} & 0 & 0 \\ 0 & 0 & -\tfrac{1}{2} & 0 \\ 0 & 0 & 0 & -\tfrac{3}{2} \end{pmatrix} \qquad (4.54)$$

and so on.

Problem (4.1) Find the matrix representations of J_x, J_y, and J_z for $j = 2$. Verify that the commutation relations, Eq. (4.7a), hold for the matrices, and that $\langle j, m' | J^2 | j, m \rangle = \hbar^2 j(j + 1)\, \delta_{m'm}$

Spin angular momentum

Since the matrix representations, Eq. (4.41)–(4.43), were derived using only the commutation rules Eq. (4.7) the results can be applied to any set of three operators which commute in the same way. In our discussion of the Pauli exclusion principle, Eqs. (2.44)–(2.54), we mentioned that the electron seems to have an intrinsic angular momentum or spin of $\hbar/2$. We shall discuss the idea of spin angular momentum more thoroughly in connection with the Dirac equation (chapter 8). However, for the moment, let us take it as a matter of faith that *the spin angular momentum of an electron is represented by a vector operator whose three components obey the same commutation relations as the components of the orbital angular momentum vector.*

$$\vec{S} = (S_x, S_y, S_z) \qquad (4.55)$$

$$[S_x, S_y] = i\hbar S_z$$
$$[S_y, S_z] = i\hbar S_x$$
$$[S_z, S_x] = i\hbar S_y \qquad \textbf{(4.56)}$$

The two linearly independent spin states $|\alpha\rangle$ and $|\beta\rangle$ of Eq. (2.54) correspond to the functions which we have denoted here by $|\tfrac{1}{2}, \tfrac{1}{2}\rangle$ and $|\tfrac{1}{2}, -\tfrac{1}{2}\rangle$. In other words

$$S^2|\alpha\rangle \equiv (S_x^2 + S_y^2 + S_z^2)|\tfrac{1}{2}, \tfrac{1}{2}\rangle = \hbar^2 s(s + 1)|\tfrac{1}{2}, \tfrac{1}{2}\rangle$$
$$= \hbar^2 \tfrac{1}{2}(\tfrac{1}{2} + 1)|\tfrac{1}{2}, \tfrac{1}{2}\rangle = \hbar^2 \tfrac{3}{4}|\tfrac{1}{2}, \tfrac{1}{2}\rangle \equiv \tfrac{3}{4}\hbar^2|\alpha\rangle \qquad (4.57)$$

and similarly

$$S^2|\beta\rangle = \tfrac{3}{4}\hbar^2|\beta\rangle \qquad (4.58)$$

$|\alpha\rangle$ and $|\beta\rangle$ are also eigenfunctions of S_z belonging respectively to the eigenvalues $\hbar/2$ and $-\hbar/2$:

$$S_z|\alpha\rangle \equiv S_z\left|\tfrac{1}{2},\tfrac{1}{2}\right\rangle = \frac{\hbar}{2}\left|\tfrac{1}{2},\tfrac{1}{2}\right\rangle \equiv \frac{\hbar}{2}|\alpha\rangle \qquad (4.59)$$

and similarly

$$S_z|\beta\rangle = -\frac{\hbar}{2}|\beta\rangle \qquad (4.60)$$

The two functions $|\alpha\rangle$ and $|\beta\rangle$ form the basis for a representation of S_x, S_y, and S_z which is identical with the $l = \tfrac{1}{2}$ representation of L_x, L_y, and L_z given in Eqs. (4.44)–(4.46). We can rewrite this relationship in the form

$$\vec{S} = \frac{\hbar}{2}\,\vec{\sigma} \qquad (4.61)$$

where

$$\sigma_x \equiv \begin{pmatrix} 0 & 1 \\ 1 & 0 \end{pmatrix}, \qquad \sigma_y \equiv \begin{pmatrix} 0 & -i \\ i & 0 \end{pmatrix}, \qquad \sigma_z \equiv \begin{pmatrix} 1 & 0 \\ 0 & -1 \end{pmatrix} \qquad \textbf{(4.62)}$$

and

$$|\alpha\rangle \equiv \begin{pmatrix} 1 \\ 0 \end{pmatrix}, \qquad |\beta\rangle \equiv \begin{pmatrix} 0 \\ 1 \end{pmatrix} \qquad \textbf{(4.63)}$$

In other words, the action of one of the components of the spin angular momentum operator $\vec{S}$ of Eq. (4.61) can be found by multiplying the corresponding matrix Eq. (4.62) by the appropriate column matrix Eq. (4.63). For example

$$S_x|\alpha\rangle \equiv \frac{\hbar}{2}\begin{pmatrix} 0 & 1 \\ 1 & 0 \end{pmatrix}\begin{pmatrix} 1 \\ 0 \end{pmatrix} = \frac{\hbar}{2}\begin{pmatrix} 0 \\ 1 \end{pmatrix} \equiv \frac{\hbar}{2}|\beta\rangle \qquad (4.64)$$

In this scheme, the functions which are conjugate to $|\alpha\rangle$ and $|\beta\rangle$ are represented by 'row matrices'

$$\langle\alpha| \equiv (1, 0), \qquad \langle\beta| \equiv (0, 1) \qquad \textbf{(4.65)}$$

The scalar product of two spin functions is found by multiplying the corresponding row matrix and column matrix. The result is just a number. For example,

$$\langle\alpha\,|\,\alpha\rangle \equiv (1, 0)\begin{pmatrix} 1 \\ 0 \end{pmatrix} = 1 \qquad (4.66)$$

and

$$\langle\alpha|S_x|\alpha\rangle \equiv \frac{\hbar}{2}(1, 0)\begin{pmatrix} 0 & 1 \\ 1 & 0 \end{pmatrix}\begin{pmatrix} 1 \\ 0 \end{pmatrix} = \frac{\hbar}{2}(1, 0)\begin{pmatrix} 0 \\ 1 \end{pmatrix} = 0 \qquad (4.67)$$

Total spin of a two-electron system

It is interesting to try to represent two-electron spin functions in the same way. For example, in Eq. (2.55) we used the symbol $\alpha(1)\beta(2)$ to represent the state in which the first electron has spin 'up' ($m_s = \frac{1}{2}$) while the second electron has spin 'down' ($m_s = -\frac{1}{2}$). Let us now introduce a subscript to our spin angular momentum operator $\vec{S}$ to indicate on which electron it is supposed to act. The operator $\vec{S}_1$ is to act on electron 1 while $\vec{S}_2$ acts on electron 2. Thus, for example

$$S_{1x}\alpha(1)\beta(2) = \frac{\hbar}{2}\beta(1)\beta(2) \qquad (4.68)$$

while

$$S_{2x}\alpha(1)\beta(2) = \frac{\hbar}{2}\alpha(1)\alpha(2) \qquad (4.69)$$

It is interesting to notice that the components of the operator

$$\vec{S} \equiv \vec{S}_1 + \vec{S}_2 \qquad (4.70)$$

also obey the angular momentum commutation relations, Eq. (4.56). For example,

$$[S_x, S_y] \equiv [(S_{1x} + S_{2x}), (S_{1y} + S_{2y})] = [S_{1x}, S_{1y}] + [S_{2x}, S_{2y}]$$
$$= i\hbar(S_{1z} + S_{2z}) = i\hbar S_z \qquad (4.71)$$

We can write down a matrix representation of the two electron total spin operator based on the functions

$$\alpha(1)\alpha(2) \equiv |\alpha, \alpha\rangle = \begin{pmatrix} 1 \\ 0 \\ 0 \\ 0 \end{pmatrix} \qquad (4.72)$$

$$\beta(1)\alpha(2) \equiv |\beta, \alpha\rangle \equiv \begin{pmatrix} 0 \\ 1 \\ 0 \\ 0 \end{pmatrix} \qquad (4.73)$$

133

$$\alpha(1)\beta(2) \equiv |\alpha, \beta\rangle \equiv \begin{pmatrix} 0 \\ 0 \\ 1 \\ 0 \end{pmatrix} \tag{4.74}$$

$$\beta(1)\beta(2) \equiv |\beta, \beta\rangle \equiv \begin{pmatrix} 0 \\ 0 \\ 0 \\ 1 \end{pmatrix} \tag{4.75}$$

If we let $S_x = S_{1x} + S_{2x}$ act on $|\alpha, \alpha\rangle$ we get a sum of two terms, one from the action of S_{1x} and the other from the action of S_{2x}:

$$S_x|\alpha, \alpha\rangle = (S_{1x} + S_{2x})|\alpha, \alpha\rangle = \frac{\hbar}{2}|\beta, \alpha\rangle + \frac{\hbar}{2}|\alpha, \beta\rangle \tag{4.76}$$

This allows us to calculate the first column in the matrix representation of $S_x = S_{1x} + S_{2x}$ based on the four functions $|\alpha, \alpha\rangle$, $|\beta, \alpha\rangle$, $|\alpha, \beta\rangle$, and $|\beta, \beta\rangle$. Taking the scalar product of the conjugates of these four functions with Eq. (4.75) we have

$$\langle\alpha, \alpha|S_x|\alpha, \alpha\rangle = 0$$

$$\langle\beta, \alpha|S_x|\alpha, \alpha\rangle = \frac{\hbar}{2}$$

$$\langle\alpha, \beta|S_x|\alpha, \alpha\rangle = \frac{\hbar}{2}$$

$$\langle\beta, \beta|S_x|\alpha, \alpha\rangle = 0 \tag{4.77}$$

If we continue and calculate the other columns of the matrix in the same way, we obtain the representation

$$S_x \equiv S_{1x} + S_{2x} = \frac{\hbar}{2}\begin{pmatrix} 0 & 1 & 1 & 0 \\ 1 & 0 & 0 & 1 \\ 1 & 0 & 0 & 1 \\ 0 & 1 & 1 & 0 \end{pmatrix} \tag{4.78}$$

Similarly, we find that

$$S_y \equiv S_{1y} + S_{2y} = \frac{\hbar}{2}\begin{pmatrix} 0 & -i & -i & 0 \\ i & 0 & 0 & -i \\ i & 0 & 0 & -i \\ 0 & i & i & 0 \end{pmatrix} \tag{4.79}$$

$$S_z = S_{z1} + S_{z2} = \frac{\hbar}{2} \begin{pmatrix} 2 & 0 & 0 & 0 \\ 0 & 0 & 0 & 0 \\ 0 & 0 & 0 & 0 \\ 0 & 0 & 0 & -2 \end{pmatrix} \tag{4.80}$$

and

$$S^2 = (\vec{S}_1 + \vec{S}_2)^2 = S_1^2 + 2\vec{S}_1 \cdot \vec{S}_2 + S_2^2$$

$$= (S_{1x} + S_{2x})^2 + (S_{1y} + S_{2y})^2 + (S_{1z} + S_{2z})^2$$

$$= \hbar^2 \begin{pmatrix} 2 & 0 & 0 & 0 \\ 0 & 1 & 1 & 0 \\ 0 & 1 & 1 & 0 \\ 0 & 0 & 0 & 2 \end{pmatrix} \tag{4.81}$$

The matrix representing S_z is diagonal. This means that the basis functions $|\alpha, \alpha\rangle$, $|\beta, \alpha\rangle$, $|\alpha, \beta\rangle$, and $|\beta, \beta\rangle$ are eigenfunctions of S_z belonging respectively to the eigenvalues represented by the diagonal elements: $\hbar, 0, 0$, and $-\hbar$. On the other hand S^2 is only block diagonal. $|\alpha, \alpha\rangle$ and $|\beta, \beta\rangle$ are eigenfunctions of S^2, both belonging to the eigenvalue $2\hbar^2$. However, $|\beta, \alpha\rangle$ and $|\alpha, \beta\rangle$, by themselves, are not eigenfunctions of S^2. If we let S^2, Eq. (4.81), act on $|\beta, \alpha\rangle$, Eq. (4.71), we have

$$S^2|\beta, \alpha\rangle = \hbar^2 \begin{pmatrix} 2 & 0 & 0 & 0 \\ 0 & 1 & 1 & 0 \\ 0 & 1 & 1 & 0 \\ 0 & 0 & 0 & 2 \end{pmatrix} \begin{pmatrix} 0 \\ 1 \\ 0 \\ 0 \end{pmatrix} = \hbar^2 \begin{pmatrix} 0 \\ 1 \\ 1 \\ 0 \end{pmatrix}$$

$$= \hbar^2(|\beta, \alpha\rangle + |\alpha, \beta\rangle) \tag{4.82}$$

and similarly

$$S^2|\alpha, \beta\rangle = \hbar^2 \begin{pmatrix} 2 & 0 & 0 & 0 \\ 0 & 1 & 1 & 0 \\ 0 & 1 & 1 & 0 \\ 0 & 0 & 0 & 2 \end{pmatrix} \begin{pmatrix} 0 \\ 0 \\ 1 \\ 0 \end{pmatrix} = \hbar^2 \begin{pmatrix} 0 \\ 1 \\ 1 \\ 0 \end{pmatrix}$$

$$= \hbar^2(|\beta, \alpha\rangle + |\alpha, \beta\rangle) \tag{4.83}$$

Triplet and singlet spin states

From Eq. (4.82) and Eq. (4.83) it follows that

$$S^2 \left(\frac{|\beta, \alpha\rangle + |\alpha, \beta\rangle}{\sqrt{2}} \right) = 2\hbar^2 \left(\frac{|\beta, \alpha\rangle + |\alpha, \beta\rangle}{\sqrt{2}} \right) \tag{4.84}$$

and

$$S^2 \left(\frac{|\beta, \alpha\rangle - |\alpha, \beta\rangle}{\sqrt{2}} \right) = 0 \qquad (4.85)$$

In other words, $(1/\sqrt{2})(|\beta, \alpha\rangle + |\alpha, \beta\rangle)$ is an eigenfunction of S^2 belonging to the eigenvalue $2\hbar^2$, while $(1/\sqrt{2})(|\beta, \alpha\rangle - |\alpha, \beta\rangle)$ is an eigenfunction of S^2 belonging to the eigenvalue 0. Comparing this with Eq. (4.30) or Eq. (4.57) we can see that the eigenvalue $2\hbar^2$ must be identified with the total spin quantum number $s = 1$, since

$$2\hbar^2 = s(s + 1)\hbar^2 = 1(1 + 1)\hbar^2 \qquad (4.86)$$

According to our general arguments, Eq. (4.26), there ought to be $2s + 1 = 3$ eigenfunctions of S^2 all belonging to this eigenvalue but corresponding to different eigenvalues of S_z. From Eq. (4.80) we can see that $|\alpha, \alpha\rangle$, $(1/\sqrt{2})(|\beta, \alpha\rangle + |\alpha, \beta\rangle)$, and $|\beta, \beta\rangle$ are eigenfunctions of S_z corresponding respectively to the eigenvalues $\hbar$, 0, and $-\hbar$. *These three spin states, with $s = 1$ and $m_s = 1, 0, -1$ are all symmetric with respect to exchange of the electron spin coordinates which means that the space part of the wave function must be antisymmetric to give an overall antisymmetry. Since the energy of a two-electron wave function usually depends much more strongly on the exchange symmetry than on m_s, the three possible $s = 1$ spin states usually correspond to three nearly-degenerate energy levels called a 'triplet'.* (In a later section we shall discuss the triplet states which occur in many-electron systems such as conjugated organic molecules.) The remaining $s = 0$, $m_s = 0$, two-electron spin state, $(1/\sqrt{2})(|\beta, \alpha\rangle - |\alpha, \beta\rangle)$, is called a 'singlet' state. The representation of the three components of the total spin operator $\vec{S} = \vec{S}_1 + \vec{S}_2$ based on the three $s = 1$ two-electron spin functions is identical with the representation shown in Eqs. (4.49)–(4.51).

Addition of angular momentum; Wigner's Clebsch–Gordan coefficients

In Eqs. (4.70)–(4.86) we used a set of functions which were simultaneous eigenfunctions of the four operators S_1^2, S_2^2, S_{1z}, and S_{2z} as a set of basis functions from which to construct simultaneous eigenfunctions of the four operators S_1^2, S_2^2, S^2, and S_z, where $\vec{S}$ was the total spin, $\vec{S} = \vec{S}_1 + \vec{S}_2$. The coefficients which make up the unitary transformation matrix taking us from one set of functions to the other are called 'Wigner's Clebsch–Gordan coefficients'. In Eqs. (4.70)–(4.86) we were talking about spin angular momentum, but the procedure of finding eigenfunctions of total

angular momentum by means of such a transformation is quite general.
Suppose that

$$\vec{J} = \vec{J}_1 + \vec{J}_2 \tag{4.87}$$

where $\vec{J}_1$ and $\vec{J}_2$ are any two operators which obey the angular momentum commutation rules:

$$[J_{1x}, J_{1y}] = i\hbar J_{1z}, \text{ etc.} \tag{4.88}$$

Let us denote a simultaneous eigenfunction of J_1^2, J_2^2, J_{1z}, and J_{2z} by the symbol $|m_1, m_2\rangle$. (Since the quantum numbers j_1 and j_2 corresponding to the operators J_1^2 and J_2^2 are unaffected by the transformation, we do not need to keep writing them.) Then, if we denote a simultaneous eigenfunction of J_1^2, J_2^2, J^2, and J_z by the symbol $|j, m\rangle$, we can write the unitary transformation from one set of functions to the other set in the form:

$$|j, m\rangle = \sum_{m_1, m_2} |m_1, m_2\rangle \overset{j_1, j_2}{\langle m_1, m_2 | j, m\rangle} \tag{4.89}$$

(The quantum numbers j_1 and j_2 are not affected by the transformation. They just 'go along for the ride', and so we write them on top.) The transformation coefficients $\overset{j_1, j_2}{\langle m_1, m_2 | j, m\rangle}$ (which, as we said above, are called Wigner's Clebsch–Gordan coefficients) have been extensively studied and tabulated. Using group theory, Eugene Wigner was able to derive a general expression for the coefficients, Eq. (9.77), and tables for particular values of j_2 can be found in *The Theory of Atomic Spectra*, by E. U. Condon and G. H. Shortley, Cambridge University Press (1953), pp. 76–77. Table 4.1 shows the coefficients $\overset{\frac{1}{2}, \frac{1}{2}}{\langle m_1, m_2 | j, m\rangle}$ which took us from the four eigenfunctions of S_{1z} and S_{2z}: $|\alpha, \alpha\rangle$, $|\alpha, \beta\rangle$, $|\beta, \alpha\rangle$, and $|\beta, \beta\rangle$ to the four eigenfunctions of S^2 and S_z: $|\alpha, \alpha\rangle$, $(1/\sqrt{2})(|\alpha, \beta\rangle + |\beta, \alpha\rangle)$, $|\beta, \beta\rangle$, and $(1/\sqrt{2})(|\alpha, \beta\rangle - |\beta, \alpha\rangle)$ (i.e., the transformation which we discussed in Eqs. (4.70)–(4.86)).

In Table 4.2, the quantum number j_1 may take on any positive integral or half-integral, whereas in Table 4.1 its value is fixed at $j_1 = \frac{1}{2}$. You can easily construct Table 4.1 starting with Table 4.2. Since we are considering the case where $j_1 = \frac{1}{2}$, the two possible values of j are $j = j_1 + \frac{1}{2} = 1$ and $j = j_1 - \frac{1}{2} = 0$. For the case where $j = 1$, there are $2j + 1 = 3$ possible values of m: $m = 1$, $m = 0$, and $m = -1$. Let us consider the first case, where $m = 1$. We know that non-zero coefficients can occur only when $m = m_1 + m_2$. Therefore when $m = 1$ we can only get a non-zero coefficient in the case $m_1 = \frac{1}{2}$, $m_2 = \frac{1}{2}$, and we can immediately put zeros

Table 4.1

$$\overset{\frac{1}{2},\frac{1}{2}}{\langle m_1, m_2 \mid j, m \rangle}$$

$\frac{1}{2},\frac{1}{2}$	j	1			0
$m_1 \qquad m_2$	m	1	0	-1	0
	$\frac{1}{2}$	1	0	0	0
$\frac{1}{2}$	$-\frac{1}{2}$	0	$\dfrac{1}{\sqrt{2}}$	0	$\dfrac{1}{\sqrt{2}}$
	$\frac{1}{2}$	0	$\dfrac{1}{\sqrt{2}}$	0	$\dfrac{-1}{\sqrt{2}}$
$\frac{1}{2}$	$-\frac{1}{2}$	0	0	1	0

Table 4.2

$$\overset{j_1,\frac{1}{2}}{\langle m_1, m_2 \mid j, m \rangle}$$

$m_2 \qquad j$	$j_1 + \frac{1}{2}$	$j_1 - \frac{1}{2}$
$\frac{1}{2}$	$\sqrt{\dfrac{j_1 + m + \frac{1}{2}}{2j_1 + 1}}$	$-\sqrt{\dfrac{j_1 - m + \frac{1}{2}}{2j_1 + 1}}$
$-\frac{1}{2}$	$\sqrt{\dfrac{j_1 - m + \frac{1}{2}}{2j_1 + 1}}$	$\sqrt{\dfrac{j_1 + m + \frac{1}{2}}{2j_1 + 1}}$

into the other places in the corresponding column of Table 4.1. The non-zero coefficient can be found by looking at the upper left-hand element in Table 4.2 and inserting the values $j_1 = \frac{1}{2}$, $m = 1$. Then

$$\sqrt{\frac{j_1 + m + \frac{1}{2}}{2j_1 + 1}} = \sqrt{\frac{\frac{1}{2} + 1 + \frac{1}{2}}{2 \cdot \frac{1}{2} + 1}} = 1 \tag{4.90}$$

It is a good exercise to construct the other elements of Table 4.1 by means of Table 4.2.

It is easy to verify that the transformation matrix shown in Table 4.1 is unitary: i.e., its conjugate transpose is equal to its inverse. As we saw in chapter 3, a transformation which takes us from one set of orthogonal and normalized functions to another orthonormal set spanning the same part of Hilbert space is always unitary.

If we apply Table 4.2 to the case where $j_1 = 1$, we obtain the transformation matrix shown below:

Table 4.3

$$\overset{1,\frac{1}{2}}{\langle m_1, m_2 | j, m \rangle}$$

$1, \frac{1}{2}$		j	$\frac{3}{2}$				$\frac{1}{2}$	
m_1	m_2	m	$\frac{3}{2}$	$\frac{1}{2}$	$-\frac{1}{2}$	$-\frac{3}{2}$	$\frac{1}{2}$	$-\frac{1}{2}$
1	$\frac{1}{2}$		1	0	0	0	0	0
	$-\frac{1}{2}$		0	$\dfrac{1}{\sqrt{3}}$	0	0	$\sqrt{\dfrac{2}{3}}$	0
0	$\frac{1}{2}$		0	$\sqrt{\dfrac{2}{3}}$	0	0	$\dfrac{-1}{\sqrt{3}}$	0
	$-\frac{1}{2}$		0	0	$\sqrt{\dfrac{2}{3}}$	0	0	$\dfrac{1}{\sqrt{3}}$
-1	$\frac{1}{2}$		0	0	$\dfrac{1}{\sqrt{3}}$	0	0	$-\sqrt{\dfrac{2}{3}}$
	$-\frac{1}{2}$		0	0	0	1	0	0

Again, it is easy to verify that the transformation is unitary, as it must be, since it takes us from one set of orthonormal basis functions to another orthonormal set spanning the same part of Hilbert space. In Table 4.3, the operator $J_1^2 \equiv \vec{J}_1 . \vec{J}_1$ which has the quantum number $j_1 = 1$ might correspond to the orbital angular momentum of an electron excited to a p-state in a hydrogen atom, while the operator $J_2^2 \equiv \vec{J}_2 . \vec{J}_2$, which has the quantum number $j_2 = \frac{1}{2}$, might correspond to the spin angular momentum of the electron. In other words, if we are considering such an example, we might make the identification $\vec{J}_1 \Rightarrow \vec{L}$ and $\vec{J}_2 \Rightarrow \vec{S}$, where $\vec{L}$ is the one-electron orbital angular momentum operator defined by Eqs. (4.4)–(4.6), and $\vec{S}$ is the one-electron spin angular momentum operator defined by Eqs. (4.61)–(4.63). In the representation based on the functions $|j, m\rangle$, the total angular momentum,

$$J^2 \equiv (\vec{L} + \vec{S})^2 = L^2 + 2\vec{L}.\vec{S} + S^2 \tag{4.91}$$

is diagonal. As we shall see in chapter 8, relativistic effects produce a 'spin-orbit coupling' term in the Hamiltonian

$$H' = \xi(r)\vec{L}.\vec{S} \tag{4.92}$$

This spin-orbit coupling term produces a slight but observable splitting between the states corresponding to various values of j. Thus, in the hydrogen atom, the stationary states are not eigenfunctions of L^2, S^2, L_z, and S_z, but they are instead eigenfunctions of L^2, S^2, J^2, and J_z. As we can see from Eq. (4.89), Wigner's Clebsch–Gordan coefficients can be used to construct the eigenfunctions of total angular momentum, and thus to calculate the splitting produced by spin-orbit coupling. In chapter 9 we shall see that *in a many-electron atom, the stationary states are eigenfunctions of the total angular momentum summed over all the electrons in the atom, and also they are eigenfunctions of the total spin.* Again, Wigner's Clebsch–Gordan coefficients can be used to calculate the eigenfunctions and their corresponding energies, and this is why we have discussed the coefficients here in such detail.

Problem (4.2) Use Table 4.2 to construct a table of Wigner's Clebsch–Gordan coefficients for $j_1 = 2, j_2 = \frac{1}{2}$. (The method of construction should be similar to that used in making Table 4.3.) Show that the matrix of Clebsch–Gordan coefficients is unitary.

5. The chemical bond

The binding energy of the hydrogen molecule; molecular orbitals expressed as linear combinations of atomic orbitals

When the Schrödinger equation became available, Heitler, London, Pauling, Slater, Hund, Mullikin, Lennard-Jones, Hylleraas, Born, Oppenheimer, and many other workers immediately applied it to the study of the chemical bond. Before the advent of quantum mechanics the rules governing chemical bonding were catalogued but not understood. For example, the force which holds a hydrogen molecule together was a complete mystery. Why should two electrically neutral atoms attract one another so strongly? The Schrödinger wave equation together with the Pauli exclusion principle solved the problem. The electron in an isolated hydrogen atom is confined to a small volume around the nucleus, as though contained in a small box. The ground state of the hydrogen atom is analogous to the fundamental harmonic of an organ pipe. The effect of lengthening an organ pipe is to lower the frequency of the fundamental harmonic. Analogously, the effect of lengthening a box containing an electron is to lower the electron's energy. When two hydrogen atoms come together to form a molecule, the 'box' in which the electron is free to move becomes longer and the energy associated with the electron wave function becomes lower. Such a wave function is called a 'molecular orbital'. When we discussed the Pauli exclusion principle, Eqs. (2.44)–(2.55), we said that *two electrons with different spins can occupy the same orbital*. Therefore, according to Pauli's principle we can put both the electrons of the hydrogen molecule into the lowest energy molecular orbital and the system obtains a net energetic advantage over two isolated hydrogen atoms. The situation is a little bit like two neighbours who decide to pull down the fence between their back yards. Assuming that their children do not fight with one another, this will be an advantage, since the children will have more room to play.

The generalized Fourier analysis discussed in the preceding section gives us a mathematical method for attacking the problem of the hydrogen molecule. Since we already know the hydrogen-like atomic orbitals listed in Table 2.3 we can use these as the raw material from which to construct the molecular orbitals; that is, *we can try to represent a molecular orbital as a linear combination of atomic orbitals*. Suppose that the nucleus of the first hydrogen atom is at the position $\vec{X}_1$ and the second is at $\vec{X}_2$. Let χ_1 and χ_2 represent ground state hydrogen-like atomic orbitals localized respectively on the first and second nucleus, as shown in Fig. 5.1.

$$\chi_{1s}(\vec{x} - \vec{X}_1) = \frac{1}{\sqrt{\pi}}\left(\frac{1}{a_0}\right)^{3/2} e^{-|\vec{x} - \vec{X}_1|/a_0} \equiv \chi_1 \tag{5.1}$$

$$\chi_{1s}(\vec{x} - \vec{X}_2) = \frac{1}{\sqrt{\pi}}\left(\frac{1}{a_0}\right)^{3/2} e^{-|\vec{x} - \vec{X}_2|/a_0} \equiv \chi_2 \tag{5.2}$$

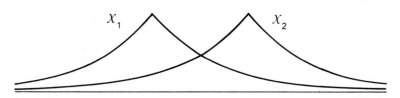

Figure 5.1 shows the two 1s atomic orbitals in the hydrogen molecule. These orbitals, localized respectively on the two nuclei, are the basis functions from which the molecular orbitals are constructed. They are plotted here as a function of position along a line passing through the two nuclei.

These two wave functions are normalized so that

$$\int d^3x |\chi_1|^2 = \int d^3x |\chi_2|^2 = 1 \tag{5.3}$$

However, they are not orthogonal to one another. It is possible to evaluate the 'overlap integral' explicitly but we shall just represent it by the constant S_{12}

$$\int d^3x \chi_1^* \chi_2 \equiv S_{12} \tag{5.4}$$

In a very crude approximation we can try to represent the wave function of the electron moving in the Coulomb field of the two hydrogen nuclei by a linear combination of the two atomic orbitals χ_2 and χ_1. If we let φ_m stand for this 'molecular orbital' we can write

$$\varphi_m = \chi_1 C_{1m} + \chi_2 C_{2m} \tag{5.5}$$

where C_{1m} and C_{2m} are unknown constants which have to be determined. We would like φ_m to be an eigenfunction of the one-electron Hamiltonian operator (neglecting inter-electron repulsions)

$$H = \frac{-\hbar^2}{2m_0}\nabla^2 - \frac{e^2}{|\vec{x} - \vec{X}_1|} - \frac{e^2}{|\vec{x} - \vec{X}_2|} \tag{5.6}$$

We require that

$$(H - E_m)\varphi_m = 0 \tag{5.7}$$

The secular equation; calculation of the molecular wave function and orbital energies

Substituting Eq. (5.5) into Eq. (5.7) gives

$$(H - E_m)(\chi_1 C_{1m} + \chi_2 C_{2m}) = 0 \tag{5.8}$$

If we take the scalar product of Eq. (5.8) first with the conjugate function χ_1^* and then with χ_2^* we obtain a set of simultaneous equations for the coefficients C_{1m} and C_{2m}.

$$(E_a - E_m)C_{1m} + (H_{12} - S_{12}E_m)C_{2m} = 0$$
$$(H_{12} - S_{12}E_m)C_{1m} + (E_a - E_m)C_{2m} = 0 \tag{5.9}$$

where we have introduced the notatión

$$\int d^3x \chi_1^* H \chi_1 = \int d^3x \chi_2^* H \chi_2 \equiv E_a$$

$$\int d^3x \chi_1^* H \chi_2 = \int d^3x \chi_2^* H \chi_1 = H_{12} \tag{5.10}$$

In order for these simultaneous algebraic equations to have a non-trivial solution, the secular determinant must vanish. (See Eqs. (3.106)–(3.115)).

$$\det \begin{vmatrix} E_a - E_m & H_{12} - S_{12}E_m \\ H_{12} - S_{12}E_m & E_a - E_m \end{vmatrix}$$
$$= (E_a - E_m)(E_a - E_m) - (H_{12} - S_{12}E_m)(H_{12} - S_{12}E_m) = 0 \tag{5.11}$$

Equation (5.11) is a quadratic equation for E_m and it has two roots:

$$E_1 = \frac{E_a + H_{12}}{1 + S_{12}} \tag{5.12}$$

and

$$E_2 = \frac{E_a - H_{12}}{1 - S_{12}} \tag{5.13}$$

With these values of E_m, one of the secular equations, Eq. (5.9), is redundant, leaving only one equation for the two unknowns C_{1m} and C_{2m}. However, the missing information is supplied by the requirement that the

143

molecular orbitals be normalized. Substituting the first root, E_1, back into Eq. (5.9) gives the normalized molecular orbital

$$\varphi_1 = \chi_1 \frac{1}{\sqrt{2(1 + S_{12})}} + \chi_2 \frac{1}{\sqrt{2(1 + S_{12})}} \qquad (5.14)$$

Similarly, the root E_2 corresponds to the molecular orbital

$$\varphi_2 = \chi_1 \frac{1}{\sqrt{2(1 - S_{12})}} - \chi_2 \frac{1}{\sqrt{2(1 - S_{12})}} \qquad (5.15)$$

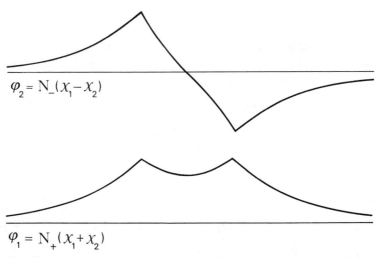

$$\varphi_2 = N_-(\chi_1 - \chi_2)$$

$$\varphi_1 = N_+(\chi_1 + \chi_2)$$

Figure 5.2 shows the bonding and antibonding molecular orbitals in the hydrogen molecule. The doubly-filled bonding orbital, $\varphi_1 = \mathcal{N}_+(\chi_1 + \chi_2)$, resembles the fundamental harmonic of a vibrating string, while the empty antibonding orbital, $\varphi_2 = \mathcal{N}_-(\chi_1 - \chi_2)$, resembles the first overtone. The normalization factors are given by $\mathcal{N}_\pm = 1/\sqrt{\{2(1 \pm S)\}}$, where S is the overlap integral.

The molecular orbitals of Eq. (5.14) and Eq. (5.15) are shown in Fig. 5.2. The overlap integral S_{12} is intrinsically positive, while E_a and

$$H_{12} = \int d^3x \chi_1^* \left(-\frac{\hbar^2}{2m_0} \nabla^2 - \frac{e^2}{|\vec{x} - \vec{X}_1|} - \frac{e^2}{|\vec{x} - \vec{X}_2|} \right) \chi_2$$

$$= E_a - \int d^3x \chi_1^* \frac{e^2}{|\vec{x} - \vec{X}_1|} \chi_2 \qquad (5.16)$$

are negative. This means that the energy $E_1 = (E_a + H_{12})(1 + S_{12})$ of the molecular orbital φ_1 is lower than E_a while the energy $E_2 = (E_a - H_{12})(1 - S_{12})$ of the molecular orbital φ_2 is higher. The low-energy

144

orbital is called a 'bonding orbital', and it is analogous to the fundamental tone of an organ pipe. The high-energy orbital φ_2 is called an 'antibonding orbital' and it is analogous to the next higher harmonic.

Motion of the nuclei; the Born–Oppenheimer approximation

The Pauli exclusion principle allows both electrons in the hydrogen molecule to occupy the bonding orbital and thus the system obtains a net energetic advantage over two isolated hydrogen atoms. As the two nuclei approach one another, the absolute values of both S_{12} and the energy of the bonding orbital is lowered more and more. However, at some internuclear separation, the energetic advantage obtained by putting both of the electrons in the bonding orbital is balanced by the Coulomb repulsion between the two nuclei and this separation corresponds to the equilibrium bond length, $R = 0.8$ angstroms. The sum of the electronic energy and nuclear repulsion can be regarded as defining an effective potential under whose influence the motion of the nuclei takes place. This method of separating electronic and nuclear motions is called the Born–Oppenheimer approximation. The nuclei are given fixed positions and the electronic energy is calculated. The nuclear positions are then changed slightly and the electronic energy is recalculated. In this way one builds up a graph of the electronic energy as a function of the nuclear positions. Adding in the nuclear repulsions gives a total-energy curve which defines an effective internuclear potential. Finally the wave functions of the nuclei moving within this effective potential are calculated. Because of the nuclear vibrations, molecular absorption and emission spectra do not consist of sharp lines like the spectra of atoms. One finds instead broad frequency-bands in which light can be absorbed or emitted. We shall discuss the nuclear vibrations in a later section. Meanwhile, let us consider the nuclei to be fixed at their equilibrium positions and let us continue our discussion of the electrons.

Equations (5.12)–(5.13) give us an explanation for the fact that helium does not form a stable molecule like hydrogen. When two helium atoms come together, there are four electrons to be disposed of. The Pauli principle allows two of them to occupy the bonding orbital, but the other two must go into the antibonding orbital, and the energy gained from the first pair of electrons is lost again. Therefore the He_2 molecule is unstable.

Heteronuclear diatomic molecules; ionic and covalent bonding

One can use a similar treatment to discuss heteronuclear diatomic molecules. In a rough approximation it is possible to represent the wave function of an electron in a many-electron atom by a hydrogen-like atomic orbital (Table 2.3). In such an atom, the electron moves not only in the attractive potential of the nucleus but also in the repulsive potential of the other electrons. The effect of the interelectron repulsion is to 'screen' the nucleus so that it does not appear to have its full positive charge. Thus, when using the hydrogen-like atomic orbitals of Table 2.3 to approximate the wave function of an electron in a heavy atom, one replaces the nuclear charge Z by an empirically determined 'effective charge' Z^*. The treatment goes through in the same way as before except that the diagonal matrix elements of the Hamiltonian, Eq. (5.10), are no longer all equal. Thus for example, in a heteronuclear diatomic molecule we might have a set of secular equations of the form

$$(H_{11} - E_m)C_{1m} + (H_{12} - S_{12}E_m)C_{2m} = 0$$

$$(H_{12} - S_{12}E_m)C_{1m} + (H_{22} - E_m)C_{2m} = 0 \qquad (5.17)$$

where $H_{11} \neq H_{22}$. (The number of simultaneous equations and unknown coefficients C_{1m}, C_{2m}, etc., may be larger if more than two atomic orbitals are needed to approximate the molecular orbital.) If $H_{11} - H_{22}$ is very large compared with H_{12} and $S_{12}E_m$, then the roots of the secular determinant are given approximately by $E_1 \approx H_{11}$ and $E_2 \approx H_{22}$. Substituting the first root, $E_1 \approx H_{11}$ into the secular equations, Eq. (5.9) yields $C_{2m} \approx 0$. Thus the root $E_1 \approx H_{11}$ corresponds to a molecular orbital which is localized almost entirely on the first atom: $\varphi_1 \approx \chi_1$. The second root $E_2 \approx H_{22}$ corresponds to a molecular orbital localized almost entirely on the second atom: $\varphi_2 \approx \chi_2$. This is in contrast to the hydrogen molecule with $H_{11} = H_{22}$ where the molecular orbitals are completely delocalized. In the intermediate case, where $|H_{11} - H_{22}|$ is comparable with $|H_{12}|$, the molecular orbitals are partly delocalized but favour one atom or the other. Now suppose that χ_1 represents a filled orbital of the first atom and suppose that χ_2 represents an empty orbital of the second atom. Suppose also that the energy H_{22} associated with the empty atomic orbital χ_2 is lower than the energy H_{11} associated with the filled orbital χ_1. Then the molecular orbital φ_2 will have a lower energy than φ_1 and will be filled while φ_1 remains empty. In effect, one or two electrons will be transferred or partially transferred from the first atom to the second. In the extreme case where the electron is almost completely transferred, the molecule is said to be 'ionically bonded'. In the intermediate case, where the transfer is incomplete the bond is said to be partially 'ionic' and partially 'covalent'. When a molecular orbital is equally distributed between one or more atoms as in the hydrogen molecule, then the bonding is said to be 'covalent' or 'homopolar'.

Löwdin-orthogonalized atomic orbitals

The method of building up a molecular orbital from a linear combination of atomic orbitals (the LCAO method) is only a rough approximation, because, in practice, the number of atomic orbitals used in the series is very limited and the set of basis functions is therefore far from complete. The entire set of hydrogen-like atomic orbitals, localized on a particular nucleus is complete provided that the set includes not only the infinite number of bound states but also all of the continuum states where the electron has sufficient energy to escape from the nucleus. We could, for example, use such a complete set to represent an electron bound to a nucleus at an entirely different point in space. In fact, we could use it to represent any arbitrary well-behaved function of the coordinates x, y, and z. However, in practice, the use of such a series is economical only if a good approximation can be obtained with a moderate number of terms. For this reason one must cleverly choose a set of basis functions which are closely related to the function which they are to represent. This is why the LCAO method uses atomic orbitals localized on different nuclei. However, as we saw in Eq. (5.4), such atomic orbitals are not mutually orthogonal. Since much of the formalism discussed in chapter 3 depends on the orthogonality of the wave functions it is convenient to begin by orthogonalizing the original set of atomic orbitals. You can see from the analogy with vectors, Fig. 3.3, that there are a great many ways in which a mutually orthogonal set of basis functions can be chosen. We shall use a particular method of orthogonalization which is due to A. Wannier and P. O. Löwdin[13], and which is described in detail in Appendix VI. *The Löwdin-orthogonalized atomic orbitals $\bar{\chi}_l$ are related to the usual atomic orbitals χ_n by the transformation*

$$\bar{\chi}_l = \sum_n \chi_n T_{nl} \qquad (5.18)$$

where the matrix T is just the reciprocal square root of the matrix of overlap integrals, S. In other words,

$$T = S^{-1/2}$$

where

$$S_{n'n} \equiv \int d^3x \chi_{n'}^* \chi_n \qquad (5.19)$$

Now you might ask how it is possible to find the reciprocal square root of a matrix. The first step is to transform S into a diagonal representation (see Eqs. (3.106)–(3.125)). Then, in the diagonal representation, it is easy to take the reciprocal square root of each element in the diagonal, and there are no off-diagonal elements. (In the Löwdin method, we always choose the positive sign for the square roots.) Finally, we transform back to the original representation, and this gives us the desired matrix, T. In this way, we obtain a set of orbitals $\bar{\chi}_l$ which obey the orthonormality relation

$$\int d^3x \bar{\chi}_{l'}^* \bar{\chi}_l = \delta_{l'l} \tag{5.20}$$

The Löwdin method of orthonormalization yields a set of orbitals $\bar{\chi}_l$ which closely resemble the original atomic orbitals χ_n. Each of them is localized predominantly on a single atom, but each contains a slight admixture of the neighbouring atomic orbitals—just enough to produce orthogonality. In the discussion of the Hückel theory, which follows now, we shall drop the bar used above to distinguish Löwdin-orthogonalized orbitals from ordinary atomic orbitals, but *we must remember throughout the discussion that the atomic orbitals (from which we hope to build molecular orbitals) are assumed to have been orthogonalized.*

The Hückel approximation[11]

Suppose that we try to represent a molecular orbital φ_m as a series of (orthogonalized) atomic orbitals

$$\varphi_m = \sum_n \chi_n C_{nm} \tag{5.21}$$

We would like φ_m to be an eigenfunction of the molecular Hamiltonian, H:

$$(H - E_m)\varphi_m = 0 \tag{5.22}$$

Substituting Eq. (5.21) into Eq. (5.22) gives

$$\sum_n (H - E_m)\chi_n C_{nm} = 0 \tag{5.23}$$

If we multiply Eq. (5.23) on the left by $\chi_{n'}^*$ and integrate, making use of the orthonormality condition, then we obtain the 'secular equations',

$$\sum_n (H_{n'n} - \delta_{n'n}E_m)C_{nm} = 0 \tag{5.24}$$

where

$$H_{n'n} \equiv \int d^3x \chi_{n'}^* H \chi_n \tag{5.25}$$

In order for the set of secular equations to have a non-trivial solution for the unknown constants C_{nm} the so-called 'secular determinant' must vanish:

$$\det |H_{n'n} - E_m \delta_{n'n}| = 0 \tag{5.26}$$

If there are N atomic orbitals involved in the series of Eq. (5.21), then Eq. (5.26) is an Nth order algebraic equation for E_m. Substituting the N roots successively into the secular equations, Eq. (5.24) and obtaining the necessary extra information from the unitarity condition

$$\sum_n C^*_{nm'} C_{nm} = \delta_{m'm} \tag{5.27}$$

we determine the expansion coefficients C_{nm}. *The lowest-energy molecular orbitals will be occupied, two electrons with opposite spins going into each molecular orbital until the available electrons are used up.* It should be noticed that this method of constructing molecular orbitals neglects interelectron repulsion and that it also neglects the antisymmetry of the many-electron wave function. When the matrix elements $H_{n'n}$ are empirical parameters, and when the method is applied to the so-called 'π-electrons' of a flat organic molecule, then it is called the 'Hückel approximation'.

Problem (5.1) Solve Eq. (5.26) and find the roots E_m for the case where

$$H_{n'n} = \begin{pmatrix} \alpha_1 & \beta \\ \beta & \alpha_2 \end{pmatrix}$$

Plot E_1 and E_2 as functions of $\beta/(\alpha_1 - \alpha_2)$.

Find the coefficients C_{nm} of Eq. (5.24) in the limits $|\beta| \ll |\alpha_1 - \alpha_2|$ and $|\beta| \gg |\alpha_1 - \alpha_2|$. How are the coefficients related to the distinction between ionic and covalent bonding?

The π-electron system of benzene treated in the Hückel approximation

The method of constructing molecular orbitals neglecting interelectron repulsion has proved to be especially useful in organic chemistry. For example, one can use it to discuss the electron wave functions in the benzene molecule. Benzene, with its six carbons and six hydrogens has a total of 42 electrons. In a molecule of this complexity, a large number of atomic orbitals have to go into the construction of the molecular wave function. However, the problem is simplified by the fact that not all of the atomic orbitals mix together significantly—that is to say, a certain subset of the molecular orbitals occurring in the complete wave function may contain only atomic orbitals drawn from some subset of the entire set of basis functions. Such a simplification may occur for two reasons. In the first place, the matrix $H_{n'n}$ may be block-diagonal. This means that the rows and columns of the matrix can be arranged so that the non-zero matrix elements occur in blocks along the diagonal. A block-diagonal matrix is shown schematically in Fig. 5.3. In that case the eigenfunctions of H can be

149

found by diagonalizing each block separately. Alternatively, two subsets of Löwdin atomic orbitals may correspond to very different energies. In that case (as we saw in the case of ionic bonding) very little mixing of the atomic orbitals will occur. In the benzene molecule, the $1s$ atomic orbitals localized on the carbon atoms do not mix (or 'hybridize') significantly with the $2s$ or $2p$ orbitals because they correspond to a very different value of energy. Because of geometrical considerations, which will be discussed later, the carbon $2p_z$ orbitals in benzene do not mix with the $2p_x$, $2p_y$, and $2s$ orbitals except through interelectron repulsion terms which in this approximation we neglect. Generally speaking, an orbital χ_n and another orbital $\chi_{n'}$ will not mix significantly (i.e., they will not occur in the same molecular orbital) if

$$|H_{n'n}| \ll |H_{n'n'} - H_{nn}| \qquad (5.28)$$

As we said above, the block of the Hamiltonian matrix corresponding to the $2p_z$ carbon atomic orbitals can be treated separately. We can number the carbon atoms consecutively around the ring, and let $\chi_1, \chi_2, \ldots, \chi_6$ denote $2p_z$ orthogonalized atomic orbitals localized on the carbon atoms $C^{(1)}, C^{(2)}, \ldots, C^{(6)}$. The interaction between next-nearest neighbours can be neglected. If we denote the interaction between nearest neighbours by α and the diagonal element by β, then

$$H_{n'n} \equiv \int d^3x \chi_{n'}^* H \chi_n$$

$$= \begin{pmatrix} \alpha & \beta & 0 & 0 & 0 & \beta \\ \beta & \alpha & \beta & 0 & 0 & 0 \\ 0 & \beta & \alpha & \beta & 0 & 0 \\ 0 & 0 & \beta & \alpha & \beta & 0 \\ 0 & 0 & 0 & \beta & \alpha & \beta \\ \beta & 0 & 0 & 0 & \beta & \alpha \end{pmatrix} \qquad (5.29)$$

The secular equations, Eq. (5.24), then become

$$\beta C_{Nm} \quad + (\alpha - E_m)C_{1m} + \beta C_{2m} = 0$$
$$\beta C_{1m} \quad + (\alpha - E_m)C_{2m} + \beta C_{3m} = 0$$
$$\vdots \qquad\qquad \vdots \qquad\qquad \vdots$$
$$\beta C_{N-1, m} + (\alpha - E_m)C_{Nm} + \beta C_{1m} = 0 \qquad (5.30)$$

(In benzene, $N = 6$, but for the sake of generality we have denoted it by a variable. The treatment which follows is valid for any cyclic polyene.) Because of the symmetry of the benzene molecule, the secular equations, Eq. (5.30), all look alike except that in each successive equation the indices

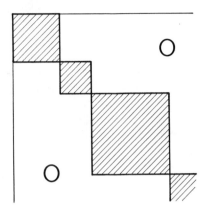

Figure 5.3 shows the form of a block-diagonal matrix. Non-zero elements occur only in the shaded blocks along the diagonal.

are shifted. Because of this symmetry we can bypass the step of setting the secular determinant equal to zero. Instead we cleverly guess the solution

$$C_{nm} = \frac{1}{\sqrt{N}} e^{in\theta} \qquad (5.31)$$

Substituting this trial solution into a typical member of the set of secular equations

$$\beta C_{n-1, m} + (\alpha - E_m)C_{nm} + \beta C_{n+1, m} = 0 \qquad (5.32)$$

we have

$$\beta e^{i(n-1)\theta} + (\alpha - E_m) e^{in\theta} + \beta e^{i(n+1)\theta} = 0 \qquad (5.33)$$

If we divide Eq. (5.33) by $e^{in\theta}$ the result is completely independent of n

$$\beta e^{-i\theta} + \alpha - E_m + \beta e^{i\theta} = 0 \qquad (5.34)$$

In other words, the trial solution, Eq. (5.31), solves all N of the secular equations by making them all redundantly require that

$$E_m = \alpha + 2\beta \cos \theta \qquad (5.35)$$

The possible values of θ are limited by the 'boundary condition' which requires that

$$C_{n, m} = C_{n+N, m} \qquad (5.36)$$

i.e., if we go all the way around the ring we must come back to the same place. Thus, we must have

$$e^{in\theta} = e^{i(n+N)\theta} \qquad (5.37)$$

151

so that

$$\theta = \frac{2\pi m}{N}, \quad m = 1, 2, 3, \ldots, N \tag{5.38}$$

Other integral values of m are possible, but they do not lead to any new linearly independent solutions. For example, the solution corresponding to $m = 0$ is the same as the one corresponding to $m = N$. Thus, finally we obtain from the N orthogonalized atomic orbitals, $\varphi_1, \ldots, \varphi_N$, the set of N molecular orbitals

$$\varphi_m = \sum_{n=1}^{N} \chi_n \frac{1}{\sqrt{N}} e^{i 2\pi mn/N}, \quad m = 1, 2, \ldots, N \tag{5.39}$$

According to Eq. (5.35) and Eq. (5.38) the molecular orbital φ_m corresponds to the energy

$$E_m = \alpha + 2\beta \cos\left(\frac{2\pi m}{N}\right) \tag{5.40}$$

Figure 5.4 shows the allowed energies E_m in the case of benzene, where $N = 6$. The interaction between neighbouring carbon atoms hybridizes the six carbon $2p_z$ atomic orbitals and splits the originally six-fold degenerate level producing three bonding molecular orbitals and three antibonding orbitals. In the benzene molecule, six electrons go into the three bonding orbitals and contribute a total of $8|\beta|$ to the bonding energy. (When we say that an electron 'goes into an orbital', we mean that the orbital appears in the antisymmetrized molecular wave functions.) The values of α and β can be determined empirically by comparing the observed properties of benzene with those predicted from the energy levels of Eq. (5.40) and Fig. 5.4. The values of α and β turn out to be approximately $\alpha = -6.9\,\text{eV}$ and $\beta = -2.4\,\text{eV}$. This approximate method of treating the π-electron system of a flat conjugated organic molecule is called the Hückel approximation. Its essential features are that the interelectron repulsion is neglected, the π-electrons are treated separately, and the matrix elements of the one-electron Hamiltonian operator (based on orthogonalized atomic orbitals) are empirical parameters.

The definition of σ- and π-orbitals; reduction of the secular equation by symmetry

The molecular orbitals which we have been describing, constructed from the carbon $2p_z$ atomic wave functions, are called 'π-orbitals'. This terminology derives from the treatment of diatomic molecules. In that case, the system is symmetric with respect to rotation around the bond axis. If φ is

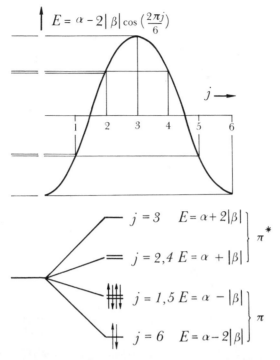

$$E = \alpha - 2|\beta|\cos\left(\frac{2\pi j}{6}\right)$$

$j \longrightarrow$

$j = 3 \quad E = \alpha + 2|\beta|$
$j = 2,4 \quad E = \alpha + |\beta|$ $\Big\} \pi^*$

$j = 1,5 \quad E = \alpha - |\beta|$
$j = 6 \quad E = \alpha - 2|\beta|$ $\Big\} \pi$

Figure 5.4 shows the energies of the 'π-orbitals' in benzene in the Hückel approximation. The interaction, β, between the six degenerate carbon $2p_z$ atomic orbitals causes them to combine into three bonding molecular orbitals (π) and three antibonding molecular orbitals (π^*). In the ground state of benzene, each of the bonding π-orbitals is doubly filled, while the anti-bonding π^*-orbitals are empty. The π-electrons thus contribute $8|\beta|$ to the binding energy of benzene.

the angle associated with this rotation, then the molecular orbitals will have a φ-dependence given by $e^{im\varphi}$ where single valuedness requires m to be an integer. Molecular orbitals with $m = 0$ are symmetric with respect to rotation through 180° around the bond axis, and these are called 'σ-orbitals'. Molecular orbitals with $m = 1$ are called 'π-orbitals'. An anti-bonding orbital is sometimes denoted by an asterisk. Thus, σ^* denotes an antibonding σ-orbital and π^* denotes an antibonding π-orbital. A non-bonding orbital is denoted by n. This notation is also used to describe the orbitals of polyatomic molecules although, as we have seen in the case of benzene, some of the orbitals do not have a definite symmetry with respect to rotation around the axis between two neighbouring atoms. In the case of flat molecules such as benzene, however, there is symmetry with respect to reflection through the plane of the molecule. The orbitals which are anti-symmetric with respect to this reflection are called π-orbitals.

153

We can now understand the reason why the matrix elements of the Hamiltonian linking the carbon $2p_z$ atomic orbitals with the $2p_x$, $2p_y$, $2s$, and $1s$ orbitals vanish. The former are antisymmetric with respect to reflection through the plane of the carbon atoms while the latter are symmetric. Thus, for example, the integral

$$H_{n'n} = \int d^3x \chi_{2p_z}^* H \chi_{2p_x} \tag{5.41}$$

vanishes because it consists of an antisymmetric factor χ_{2p_z} multiplied by a symmetric factor $H\chi_{2p_x}$. The regions on one side of the reflection plane which give a positive contribution to the integral are exactly balanced by regions on the other side which give an equal negative contribution, and the result is zero. Similarly, the overlap integral

$$\int d^3x \chi_{2p_z}^* \chi_{2p_x} \equiv S_{n'n} \tag{5.42}$$

vanishes. This means that the symmetric and antisymmetric atomic orbitals are not mixed together in the Löwdin-orthogonalized atomic orbitals. Therefore, the Löwdin orbitals are either symmetric or else antisymmetric with respect to reflection through the plane of the molecule. The matrix element of H between Löwdin orbitals vanishes if the orbitals have opposite symmetry. This is the justification for treating the π-orbitals separately as we have done.

The σ-electrons in benzene; trigonally hybridized atomic orbitals

In order to discuss the reflection-symmetric molecular orbitals of benzene, let us represent the reflection-symmetric atomic orbitals of the carbon $n = 2$ shell by

$$\chi_{2s} = \frac{1}{2\sqrt{2\pi}} \left(\frac{z^*}{a_0}\right)^{3/2} e^{-z^*r/2a_0} \left(1 - \frac{z^*r}{2a_0}\right)$$

$$\chi_{2p_x} = \frac{1}{4\sqrt{2\pi}} \left(\frac{z^*}{a_0}\right)^{5/2} e^{-z^*r/2a_0} r \sin\theta \cos\varphi$$

$$\chi_{2p_y} = \frac{1}{4\sqrt{2\pi}} \left(\frac{z^*}{a_0}\right)^{5/2} e^{-z^*r/2a_0} r \sin\theta \sin\varphi \tag{5.43}$$

We have centred the coordinate system on a particular carbon atom, and, as before, taken the z-axis perpendicular to the plane of the benzene molecule. The reflection operation with respect to which these orbitals are symmetric is $\theta \to (180° - \theta)$. It is convenient to begin by transforming to a slightly different set of basis functions

$$\chi_1 = \frac{1}{\sqrt{3}} \chi_{2s} + \sqrt{\frac{2}{3}}\chi_{2p_x}$$

$$\chi_2 = \frac{1}{\sqrt{3}} \chi_{2s} - \frac{1}{\sqrt{6}} \chi_{2p_x} + \frac{1}{\sqrt{2}} \chi_{2p_y}$$

$$\chi_3 = \frac{1}{\sqrt{3}} \chi_{2s} - \frac{1}{\sqrt{6}} \chi_{2p_x} - \frac{1}{\sqrt{2}} \chi_{2p_y} \qquad (5.44)$$

These are called 'trigonally hybridized' orbitals. You can verify that they are mutually orthogonal and normalized. The advantage of begin-

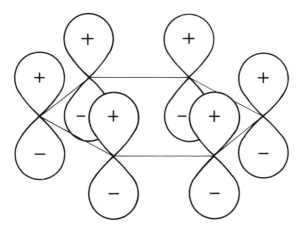

Figure 5.5 shows schematically the lowest-energy π-orbital of benzene (the one with $j = 6$ and $E = \alpha - 2|\beta|$ shown in Fig. 5.4). It is a linear combination of the carbon $2p_z$ atomic orbitals (see Fig. 2.3). The atomic orbitals all enter this molecular orbital with the same phase, so that above the plane of the carbon nuclei, the orbital is positive, while below the plane, it is negative.

ning with the trigonally hybridized atomic orbitals of Eq. (5.44) is that they allow us to separate both the matrix representation of the Hamiltonian, and the matrix into a series of 2×2 diagonal overlap integral blocks. The interactions are negligible except between overlapping hybrid orbitals of adjacent atoms. One of the three trigonal hybrids of Eq. (5.44) combines with the $1s$ atomic orbital of the neighbouring hydrogen atom to give a bonding σ-orbital and an antibonding σ^*-orbital. The bonding orbital is filled by two electrons with opposite spins, one coming from the hydrogen and the other from the carbon. Each of the other two trigonal

155

hybrids combines with an overlapping hybrid from an adjacent carbon atom. The two overlapping hybrid atomic orbitals combine to form a bonding σ molecular orbital and an antibonding σ^*-orbital, the bonding orbital being doubly filled.

Tetrahedrally hybridized atomic orbitals

Similarly, if we wish to apply the LCAO method to a molecule with tetrahedral symmetry like CH_4 or CCl_4 it is convenient to begin with the set of tetrahedrally hybridized carbon atomic orbitals

$$\chi_1 = \tfrac{1}{2}\chi_{2s} - \frac{1}{\sqrt{2}}\chi_{2p_x} - \frac{1}{\sqrt{6}}\chi_{2p_y} - \frac{1}{2\sqrt{3}}\chi_{2p_z}$$

$$\chi_2 = \tfrac{1}{2}\chi_{2s} + \frac{1}{\sqrt{2}}\chi_{2p_x} - \frac{1}{\sqrt{6}}\chi_{2p_y} - \frac{1}{2\sqrt{3}}\chi_{2p_z}$$

$$\chi_3 = \tfrac{1}{2}\chi_{2s} + \sqrt{\tfrac{2}{3}}\,\chi_{2p_y} - \frac{1}{2\sqrt{3}}\chi_{2p_z}$$

$$\chi_4 = \tfrac{1}{2}\chi_{2s} + \frac{\sqrt{3}}{2}\chi_{2p_z} \tag{5.45}$$

The geometrical meaning of the coefficients in Eq. (5.45) can be seen from the fact that the set of vectors

$$\vec{v}_1 = \left(-\frac{1}{\sqrt{2}}, -\frac{1}{\sqrt{6}}, -\frac{1}{2\sqrt{3}}\right)$$

$$\vec{v}_2 = \left(\frac{1}{\sqrt{2}}, -\frac{1}{\sqrt{6}}, -\frac{1}{2\sqrt{3}}\right)$$

$$\vec{v}_3 = \left(0, \sqrt{\tfrac{2}{3}}, \frac{-1}{2\sqrt{3}}\right)$$

$$\vec{v}_4 = \left(0, 0, \frac{\sqrt{3}}{2}\right) \tag{5.46}$$

point from the centre of a tetrahedron to its corners. You can verify that the functions χ_1, χ_2, χ_3, and χ_4 are normalized and mutually orthogonal. They span the same part of Hilbert space as the orthonormal set of functions χ_{2s}, χ_{2p_x}, χ_{2p_y}, and χ_{2p_z}. Thus, the transformation from one set to the other is a unitary transformation. The energy of each of the tetrahedral hybrids is $\tfrac{1}{4}E_{2s} + \tfrac{3}{4}E_{2p}$ so that the energy required to promote the carbon electrons from their normal configuration $(1s)^2(2s)^2(2p)^2$ to the tetrahedrally hybridized configuration $(1s)^2(2sp)^4$ is about $E_{2p} - E_{2s}$. In a

156

molecule like CH_4, this promotion energy is small compared to the energy gained from the four σ-bonds. The tetrahedral hybrids can also give us a rough understanding of the water molecule. The normal electron configuration of oxygen is $(1s)^2(2s)^2(2p)^4$. This provides six electrons in the $n = 2$ shell. In the water molecule two of the tetrahedral hybrids form σ-bonds with the hydrogen $1s$ orbitals. The two σ-bonding orbitals are filled by four electrons, two from the oxygen and two from the hydrogen. The other four electrons of the oxygen occupy the remaining two tetrahedral hybrids forming two 'lone pairs'. The angle between the two bonds in the water molecule is not exactly the same as the angle between two lines joining the centre of a tetrahedron with its corners. This is because of the electrostatic repulsion between the two positively charged nuclei. In fact for an accurate calculation of the bond-angle in the water molecule one must include the interelectron repulsion term in the Hamiltonian and take into account the antisymmetry of the electron wave function.

The effects of antisymmetry and interelectron repulsion; the variational principle

The effects of antisymmetry and interelectron repulsion are also important in the study of the π-electron system of heterocyclic organic compounds. The benzene molecule, which contains only carbon and hydrogen atoms, is an example of a homocyclic molecule. If a nitrogen were substituted into the ring it would be 'heterocyclic'—i.e., the molecule would contain more than one type of heavy atom. The energy differences between the atomic orbitals of atoms of different types militate for a non-uniform distribution of the electronic charge density. On the other hand the interelectron repulsion terms, which we have until now neglected, together with the kinetic energy terms, militate for a uniform charge distribution. In other words, there is an energetic advantage in concentrating the electronic charge density onto low-lying atomic orbitals but this concentration of the wave function is associated with the energetic disadvantage of a higher kinetic energy and a higher energy of interelectron repulsion. The actual wave function for the ground state of the system is a compromise which minimizes the total energy. We can show in the following way that the ground-state wave function minimizes the total energy. The expectation value of the energy is given, according to Eq. (3.15) by

$$\langle E \rangle = \int d\tau \Psi^* H \Psi \qquad (5.47)$$

We require the wave function to be normalized, so that

$$\int d\tau \Psi^* \Psi = 1 \qquad (5.48)$$

If a function f of some variable x is a minimum, then $df/dx = 0$. Similarly, the energy $\langle E \rangle$ depends on the form of the wave function Ψ. If the form of Ψ is such as to make $\langle E \rangle$ an extremum while retaining the normalization condition, Eq. (5.75), then an infinitesimal variation of Ψ will leave

$$\bar{E} \equiv \frac{\int d\tau \Psi^* H \Psi}{\int d\tau \Psi^* \Psi} \tag{5.49}$$

unaffected. We can take into account the fact that Ψ may be complex by varying Ψ and Ψ^* independently.

Let us consider what happens to $\bar{E}$ when Ψ^* is changed to an infinitesimally different wave function $\Psi^* + \delta\Psi^*$. The change of $\bar{E}$ will then be given by

$$\delta\bar{E} = \frac{\int d\tau (\Psi^* + \delta\Psi^*) H \Psi}{\int d\tau (\Psi^* + \delta\Psi^*) \Psi} - \frac{\int d\tau \Psi^* H \Psi}{\int d\tau \Psi^* \Psi} = 0 \tag{5.50}$$

Since $\int d\tau \Psi^* \Psi = 1$, we must have

$$\int d\tau \, \delta\Psi^* (H - \bar{E}) \Psi = 0 \tag{5.51}$$

Since the variation $\delta\Psi^*$ is arbitrary, Eq. (5.51) can be satisfied only if

$$(H - \bar{E})\Psi = 0 \tag{5.52}$$

This shows that *the time-independent Schrödinger equation is equivalent to the variational principle*

$$\delta\bar{E} \equiv \delta \left(\frac{\int d\tau \Psi^* H \Psi}{\int d\tau \Psi^* \Psi} \right) = 0 \tag{5.53}$$

In the case of excited states, the solution of the Schrödinger equation, Eq. (5.52), does not necessarily make $\bar{E}$ an absolute minimum but rather an extremum. The variational principle often provides a practical way of calculating approximate wave functions. Suppose that we put forward an approximate solution in terms of the coordinates and a number of undetermined constants. The variational principle then states that in order for the approximate solution to be as near as possible to the actual solution, the constants must take on values which make $\bar{E}$ an extremum.

The helium atom

For example, consider the case of the helium atom with nuclear charge $Z = 2$. The two electrons of helium can both fit into an atomic orbital which has the approximate form of the hydrogen $1s$ atomic orbital given in Table 2.3. We can approximately take into account the interelectron repulsion by introducing an effective nuclear charge Z^* into the anti-symmetrized two-electron wave function of the helium atom, Eq. (2.55)

$$\Psi = \frac{1}{\pi\sqrt{2}}\left(\frac{Z^*}{a_0}\right)^3 e^{-(Z^*/a_0)(|\vec{x}_1| + |\vec{x}_2|)}\{\alpha(1)\beta(2) - \beta(1)\alpha(2)\}$$

(5.54)

where $a_0 = \hbar^2/(m_0 e^2) = 0.529$ Å is the Bohr radius. We would like to determine Z^* in such a way that the energy will be a minimum.

The energy of the system is given by

$$\bar{E} = \frac{1}{\pi^2}\left(\frac{Z^*}{a_0}\right)^6 \int d\tau_1 \int d\tau_2\, e^{-(Z^*/a_0)(r_1 + r_2)}$$

$$\times \left\{\frac{\hbar^2}{2m_0}(\nabla_1^2 + \nabla_2^2) - \frac{2e^2}{r_1} - \frac{2e^2}{r_2} + \frac{e^2}{|\vec{x}_1 - x_2|}\right\}$$

$$\times e^{-(Z^*/a_0)(r_1 + r_2)}$$

(5.55)

With a certain amount of effort, the integral of Eq. (5.55) can be evaluated (see L. I. Schiff, *Quantum Mechanics*, McGraw-Hill, 2nd edition (1955), p. 174), and the result is that

$$\bar{E} = \frac{e^2}{a_0}(Z^{*2} - \tfrac{27}{8}Z^*)$$

(5.56)

The value of the effective nuclear charge Z^* which minimizes the energy $\bar{E}$ is determined by the equation

$$\frac{d\bar{E}}{dZ^*} = \frac{e^2}{a_0}(2Z^* - \tfrac{27}{8}) = 0$$

(5.57)

Thus, the optimum value of the effective charge is $Z^* = \tfrac{27}{16} = 1.69$ which is to be compared with the actual value of the nuclear charge $Z = 2$. The effect of interelectron repulsion is therefore to make the wave function spread out over a larger volume than it would do if the repulsion were not included.

The Hartree–Fock approximation for calculating many-electron wave functions

D. R. Hartree[10] and V. Fock were able to use the variational principle to attack complicated many-electron problems including the effects of inter-electron repulsion and antisymmetry. *In the Hartree–Fock scheme the*

N-electron wave function is approximated by a determinantal wave function of the form

$$\Delta = \frac{1}{\sqrt{N!}} \det \begin{vmatrix} \Phi_1(1) & \Phi_1(2) & \cdots & \Phi_1(N) \\ \Phi_2(1) & \Phi_2(2) & \cdots & \Phi_2(N) \\ \vdots & \vdots & & \vdots \\ \Phi_N(1) & \Phi_N(2) & \cdots & \Phi_N(N) \end{vmatrix} \equiv |\Phi_1 \Phi_2 \cdots \Phi_N| \tag{5.58}$$

This type of many-electron wave function was introduced by J. C. Slater and it is called a 'Slater determinant'. A Slater determinant is antisymmetric with respect to the operation which interchanges the coordinates of two electrons since when two columns of a determinant are interchanged the value is unchanged except for a minus sign. However, Eq. (5.58) obviously does not represent the most general type of antisymmetric wave function, since a sum of Slater determinants would also be antisymmetric. In the Hartree–Fock method, however, one assumes that the wave function can be represented by a single Slater determinant and that the spin-orbitals Φ_i are normalized and mutually orthogonal. Hartree and Fock used the variational principle to find a set of differential equations for the optimum one-electron spin-orbitals from which to construct this single Slater determinant.

The Slater–Condon rules for evaluating matrix elements of operators between determinantal wave functions

In order to apply the variational principle to a determinantal many-electron wave function we need to be able to evaluate integrals of the type

$$\int d\tau \Delta_v^* H \Delta_{v'} \equiv \int d\tau |\Phi_1 \Phi_2 \cdots \Phi_N|^* H |\Phi_1' \Phi_2' \cdots \Phi_N'| \tag{5.59}$$

where H is the many-electron Hamiltonian operator

$$H = \sum_i \left\{ \frac{-\hbar^2}{2m_0} \nabla_i^2 + V(i) \right\} + \sum_i \sum_{j>i} \frac{e^2}{r_{ij}} \tag{5.60}$$

If we let

$$f(i) \equiv \frac{-\hbar^2}{2m_0} \nabla_i^2 + V(i) \tag{5.61}$$

then the first term in Eq. (5.60) has the form

$$\mathscr{F} = \sum_i f(i) \tag{5.62}$$

If we let

$$g(i, j) \equiv \frac{e^2}{r_{ij}} \tag{5.63}$$

then the second term in Eq. (5.60) has the form

$$\mathscr{G} = \sum_i \sum_{j>i} g(i, j) \tag{5.64}$$

Rules for evaluating matrix elements of operators of type $\mathscr{F}$ and type $\mathscr{G}$ taken between determinantal wave functions were worked out by J. C. Slater and E. U. Condon, and a detailed discussion of these rules can be found in *The Theory of Atomic Spectra* by E. U. Condon and G. H. Shortley, Cambridge University Press (1953), on pp. 169–174. (See also Problem 5.2 of the present text.) The Slater–Condon rules can be summarized in the following way: Suppose that we let the symbol Δ_0 denote a certain Slater determinant

$$\Delta_0 \equiv |\Phi_1 \Phi_2 \ldots \Phi_i \ldots \Phi_N| \tag{5.65}$$

and suppose that we let $\Delta_{i \to j}$ represent the same determinant with the spin-orbital Φ_i replaced by Φ_j:

$$\Delta_{i \to j} \equiv |\Phi_1 \Phi_2 \ldots \Phi_j \ldots \Phi_N| \tag{5.66}$$

Similarly, we let $\Delta_{k \to l}^{i \to j}$ denote the determinant Δ_0 with Φ_i replaced by Φ_j and Φ_k replaced by Φ_l, etc. The Slater–Condon rules state that if the set of one-electron spin-orbitals Φ_1, Φ_2, ..., Φ_∞ obey the orthonormality condition

$$\int d\tau_1 \Phi_i^*(1) \Phi_j(1) = \delta_{ij} \tag{5.67}$$

then

$$\int d\tau \Delta_0^* (\mathscr{F} + \mathscr{G}) \Delta_0$$

$$= \sum_{s=1}^{N} \int d\tau_1 \Phi_s^*(1) f(1) \Phi_s(1)$$

$$+ \frac{1}{2} \sum_{s=1}^{N} \sum_{t=1}^{N} \int d\tau_1 \int d\tau_2 \Phi_s^*(1) \Phi_t^*(2) g(1, 2)$$

$$\times \{\Phi_s(1) \Phi_t(2) - \Phi_t(1) \Phi_s(2)\} \tag{5.68}$$

161

$$\int d\tau \Delta_0^*(\mathscr{F} + \mathscr{G})\Delta_{i\to j}$$

$$= \int d\tau_1 \Phi_i^*(1)f(1)\Phi_j(1)$$

$$+ \sum_{s=1}^{N} \int d\tau_1 \int d\tau_2 \Phi_i^*(1)\Phi_s^*(2)g(1,2)$$

$$\times \{\Phi_j(1)\Phi_s(2) - \Phi_s(1)\Phi_j(2)\} \tag{5.69}$$

and

$$\int d\tau \Delta_0^*(\mathscr{F} + \mathscr{G})\Delta_{k\to l}^{i\to j}$$

$$= \int d\tau_1 \int d\tau_2 \Phi_i^*(1)\Phi_k^*(2)g(1,2)$$

$$\times \{\Phi_j(1)\Phi_l(2) - \Phi_l(1)\Phi_j(2)\} \tag{5.70}$$

The matrix elements of both $\mathscr{F}$ and $\mathscr{G}$ linking Δ_0 to determinants differing from it by three or more orbitals vanish. For example,

$$\int d\tau \Delta_0^*(\mathscr{F} + \mathscr{G})\Delta_{\substack{k\to l\\m\to n}}^{i\to j} = 0 \tag{5.71}$$

Problem (5.2) Use the electron creation and annihilation operators of Eqs. (9.6)–(9.10) to prove the Slater–Condon rules, Eqs. (5.68)–(5.71).

Derivation of the Hartree–Fock equations

We are now in a position to apply the variational principle to a many-electron system. We would like to approximate the N-electron wave function by a single Slater determinant

$$\Psi = \Delta_0 \equiv |\Phi_1\Phi_2 \ldots \Phi_N| \tag{5.72}$$

Let us consider the variation

$$\delta\Psi^* = \eta\Delta_{i\to j}^* \tag{5.73}$$

where η is an infinitesimal constant and $1 \le i \le N$, $N < j$. Because of the orthonormality condition, Eq. (5.67),

$$\int d\tau \, \delta\Psi^*\Psi = \eta \int d\tau \Delta_{i\to j}^*\Delta_0 = 0 \tag{5.74}$$

so that Eq. (5.51) can be written in the form

$$\int d\tau\, \delta\Psi^* H\Psi = \eta \int d\tau \Delta_{i,\,j}^* H\Lambda_0 = 0 \qquad (5.75)$$

From Eq. (5.69) and Eqs. (5.60)–(5.64) we see that we can rewrite Eq. (5.75) in the form

$$\int d\tau_1 \Phi_j^*(1) F(1) \Phi_i(1) = 0 \qquad \textbf{(5.76)}$$

where the 'Fock operator' F is defined by

$$F(1) \equiv H^c(1) + \sum_{s=1}^{N} \int d\tau_2 \Phi_s^*(2)\, \frac{e^2}{r_{12}}\, (1 - \mathscr{P}_{12}) \Phi_s(2) \qquad \textbf{(5.77)}$$

and the 'core Hamiltonian' H^c is

$$H^c \equiv \frac{-\hbar^2}{2m}\, \nabla^2 + V \qquad \textbf{(5.78)}$$

$\mathscr{P}_{12}$ is an operator which exchanges the space and spin coordinates of electron 1 with those of electron 2, i.e.,

$$\mathscr{P}_{12}\Phi_s(2)\Phi_i(1) \equiv \Phi_s(1)\Phi_i(2) \qquad \textbf{(5.79)}$$

We know nothing at all about Φ_j except that it lies outside the part of Hilbert space spanned by the filled orbitals $\Phi_1 \ldots \Phi_N$. What Eq. (5.76) really asserts is that the function $F\Phi_i$ is orthogonal to Φ_j and therefore it must lie in the part of Hilbert space spanned by $\Phi_1 \ldots \Phi_N$. From this it follows that we can express $F\Phi_i$ as a linear combination of $\Phi_1 \ldots \Phi_N$:

$$F(1)\Phi_i(1) = \sum_{k=1}^{N} \lambda_{ik}\Phi_k(1) \qquad (5.80)$$

From the orthonormality condition we have that

$$\int d\tau_1 \Phi_l^*(1) F(1) \Phi_i(1) = \lambda_{li} \qquad (5.81)$$

Thus, the constants $\lambda_{li}(l, i = 1, 2, \ldots, N)$ constitute a matrix representation of the Fock operator F. Since the Fock operator (as defined by Eq. (5.77)) is an Hermitian operator, we can always bring it into a diagonal form by means of a unitary transformation, and we should notice that such a unitary transformation leaves Λ_0 invariant. In the diagonal representation, the equation for the one-electron spin-orbitals has the form

$$\{F(1) - \varepsilon_k\}\Phi_k(1) = 0, \quad k = 1, 2, \ldots, N \qquad \textbf{(5.82)}$$

where the constants ε_k are the eigenvalues of the matrix λ_{li}. From Eq. (5.77) and Eq. (5.79) we can see that it is possible to write the Fock operator in the form

$$F(1) = H^c(1) + \sum_{s=1}^{N} \{J_s(1) - K_s(1)\} \qquad (5.83)$$

where

$$J_s(1)\Phi_k(1) \equiv \int d\tau_2 \Phi_s^*(2) \frac{e^2}{r_{12}} \Phi_s(2)\Phi_k(1) \qquad (5.84)$$

and

$$K_s(1)\Phi_k(1) \equiv \int d\tau_2 \Phi_s^*(2) \frac{e^2}{r_{12}} \Phi_k(2)\Phi_s(1) \qquad (5.85)$$

The simultaneous equations Eq. (5.82) are called the 'Hartree–Fock equations'. We can think of a member of this set of equations as the approximate wave equation for a single electron moving in the potential produced by the nuclei and by the other electrons. The 'core Hamiltonian', $H^c = (-\hbar^2/2m)\nabla^2 + V$, includes the kinetic energy term and the attractive potential of the nuclei. The Coulomb operator, $J_s(1) \equiv \int d\tau_2 \Phi_s^*(2)(e^2/r_{12})\Phi_s(2)$ can be visualized as the potential produced by a second electron in the spin-orbital Φ_s acting on the electron which we are studying. The 'exchange operator' $K_s(1)$ of Eq. (5.85) is much less easy to visualize, but we can interpret it as arising from the interelectron repulsion and the antisymmetry of the many-electron wave function. When the spin-orbital Φ_s overlaps very little with the spin-orbital Φ_k, then the exchange term $K_s\Phi_k$ can be neglected. This is the reason why we do not have to consider all of the electrons in the universe when we are solving the Hartree–Fock equations. The exchange interaction with distant electrons can be neglected and they contribute only a repulsive Coulomb potential, which cancels the attractive Coulomb potential of the nuclei with which they are associated.

The Hartree–Fock approximation reduces the N-electron problem to a set of N simultaneous non-linear integro-differential equations. These equations can be solved by a method of successive approximations. An initial approximation for the one-electron orbitals can be used to calculate the Coulomb and exchange interactions, and hence the Fock operator F. Using this approximate Fock operator, the one-electron orbitals can be recalculated. The improved orbitals can be used to calculate an improved Fock operator and so on. When the difference between the orbitals resulting from successive iterations ceases to be appreciable, then the solution is said to be 'self-consistent'. For this reason, the Hartree–Fock method for

164

attacking a many-electron problem is sometimes called the 'self-consistent field' or 'SCF' method. Hartree applied this method with great success to the calculation of atomic orbitals. The interested reader is referred to his book: *The Calculation of Atomic Structure* by D. R. Hartree, John Wiley and Sons (1955). (Actually, most of the numerical work was done by Hartree's father who said that he enjoyed sitting by the fire and calculating in the evenings.)

Roothaan's equations

C. C. J. Roothaan[21] applied the Hartree–Fock SCF method to the case where *the electron orbitals are represented by a linear superposition of some set of M basis functions*

$$\Phi_i = \sum_{b=1}^{M} \chi_b C_{bi} \qquad (5.86)$$

For example, Φ_i might represent a molecular spin-orbital built up from a linear combination of atomic spin-orbitals. Inserting Eq. (5.86) in Eq. (5.82) and taking the scalar product with χ_a^* we obtain

$$\sum_{a=1}^{M} \int d\tau_1 \chi_a^*(1)\{F(1) - \varepsilon_i\}\chi_b(1)C_{bi} = 0 \qquad (5.87)$$

or

$$\sum_{a=1}^{M} (F_{ab} - S_{ab}\varepsilon_i)C_{bi} = 0 \qquad (5.88)$$

where

$$F_{ab} \equiv \int d\tau_1 \chi_a^*(1)F(1)\chi_b(1) \qquad (5.89)$$

and

$$S_{ab} \equiv \int d\tau_1 \chi_a^*(1)\chi_b(1) \qquad (5.90)$$

From Eqs. (5.77) and (5.86) we can see that the 'Fock matrix' F_{ab} can be expressed in the form

$$F_{ab} = H_{ab}^c + \sum_{c,d} P_{cd}\Gamma_{(ab)cd} \qquad (5.91)$$

where

$$H_{ab}^c \equiv \int d\tau_1 \chi_a^*(1)H^c(1)\chi_b(1) \qquad (5.92)$$

$$\Gamma_{(ab)cd} \equiv \int d\tau_1 \int d\tau_2 \chi_a^*(1)\chi_c^*(2) \frac{e^2}{r_{12}} (1 - \mathscr{P}_{12})\chi_d(2)\chi_b(1) \quad \textbf{(5.93)}$$

$$P_{cd} = \sum_{i=1}^{M} v_i C_{ci}^* C_{di} \quad \textbf{(5.94)}$$

and

$$v_i \equiv \begin{cases} 1 & \text{filled spin-orbitals} \\ 0 & \text{virtual spin-orbitals} \end{cases} \quad \textbf{(5.95)}$$

In Roothaan's method, a slight complication is introduced by the fact that the number of basis functions M may be much larger than the number of electrons N. The Fock matrix F_{ab} is an $M \times M$ matrix, and diagonalizing it produces M molecular orbitals, only N of which are filled. The unused spin-orbitals are called 'virtual orbitals', and one must be careful to leave them out when calculating the matrix P_{cd} of Eq. (5.94). We therefore introduce an 'occupation number' v_i which is 1 for filled orbitals and 0 for empty ones.

Problem (5.3) Show by direct substitution that Roothaan's equations, Eqs. (5.86)–(5.95), follow from the Hartree–Fock equations, Eqs. (5.77) and (5.82).

Total electronic energy; excitation energy; Koopmans' theorem

After self-consistency has been obtained, one might wish to calculate the total energy of the system. This is not merely the sum of the orbital energy parameters but must be calculated by means of Eq. (5.68).

$$\begin{aligned} \bar{E} &= \int d\tau \Delta_0^* H \Delta_0 \\ &= \sum_{s=1}^{N} \int d\tau_1 \Phi_s(1) H^c(1) \Phi_s(1) \\ &\quad + \frac{1}{2} \sum_{s=1}^{N} \sum_{t=1}^{N} \int d\tau_1 \int d\tau_2 \Phi_s^*(1)\Phi_t^*(2) \frac{e^2}{r_{12}} \\ &\quad \times (1 - \mathscr{P}_{12})\Phi_s(1)\Phi_t(2) \\ &= \frac{1}{2} \sum_{s=1}^{N} \left\{ \int d\tau_1 \Phi_s^*(1) H^c(1)\Phi_s(1) + \varepsilon_s \right\} \end{aligned} \quad \textbf{(5.96)}$$

In terms of the matrices defined in Eqs. (5.91)–(5.95) this becomes

$$\bar{E} = \tfrac{1}{2} \sum_{a,b=1}^{M} P_{ab}(H^c_{ab} + F_{ab}) \tag{5.97}$$

Equation (5.97) gives us the energy of the ground state. Now we need to ask whether there is any relationship between the 'virtual' unoccupied levels and the excited states of the system. It is tempting to assume that a Slater determinant involving one or more virtual orbitals corresponds to an excited state. However, this relationship only holds as a rough approximation. In an excited state, the occupation numbers v_i differ from the ground state occupation numbers. Therefore the Fock matrix F_{ab} is also different, and all of the molecular orbitals, both filled and virtual, will be changed when the system is excited. However, if we neglect this readjustment, we can use Eq. (5.96) and Eq. (5.97) to write down approximate expressions for the energy difference between the ground state and an excited state. Suppose that in the ground state the occupation numbers are represented by v_i and suppose that in the excited state they are represented by v'_i. Then, according to Eq. (5.96) the approximate excitation energy is given by

$$(\Delta\bar{E})_{v_i \to v_{i'}} = \sum_i (v'_i - v_i) \int d\tau_1 \Phi^*_i(1) H^c(1)\Phi_i(1)$$

$$+ \tfrac{1}{2} \sum_i \sum_j (v'_i v'_j - v_i v_j) \int d\tau_1 \int d\tau_2 \Phi^*_i(1)\Phi^*_j(2)$$

$$\times \frac{e^2}{r_{12}}(1 - \mathscr{P}_{12})\Phi_i(1)\Phi_j(2) \tag{5.98}$$

or in terms of the matrices defined in Eqs. (5.91)–(5.95),

$$(\Delta\bar{E})_{v_i \to v'_i} = \sum_{a,b} \{(P'_{ab} - P_{ab})H^c_{ab}$$

$$+ \tfrac{1}{2} \sum_{c,d} (P'_{ab}P'_{cd} - P_{ab}P_{cd})\Gamma_{(ab)cd}\} \tag{5.99}$$

where P'_{ab} is calculated using the excited state occupation numbers. An interesting special case occurs when the change of occupation numbers corresponds to the removal of an electron from the system. Then if k is the index of the removed electron,

$$v'_i = v_i - \delta_{ik} \tag{5.100}$$

The approximate change in energy, calculated from Eq. (5.98) and Eq. (5.100) is

$$\Delta\bar{E}_k = -\varepsilon_k \tag{5.101}$$

where

$$\varepsilon_k \equiv \int d\tau_1 \Phi_k^*(1) H^c(1) \Phi_k(1)$$

$$+ \sum_j v_j \int d\tau_1 \int d\tau_2 \Phi_j^*(1) \Phi_k^*(2) \frac{e^2}{r_{12}}$$

$$\times (1 - \mathscr{P}_{12}) \Phi_j(1) \Phi_k(2) \qquad (5.102)$$

is the eigenvalue of the Fock operator belonging to the molecular spin-orbital Φ_k. Equation (5.101) is known as Koopmans' theorem. It states that *if we neglect the readjustment of the orbitals resulting from ionization, the eigenvalue ε_k of the Fock operator, Eq. (5.82), is just the energy needed to remove an electron from the kth molecular orbital.*

Problem (5.4) Show that Koopmans' theorem, Eqs. (5.101)–(5.102), follows from Eq. (5.98).

Configuration interaction

Both the Fock equations and Roothaan's equations are aimed at determining optimum one-electron orbitals under the assumption that the many-electron wave function is a single Slater determinant. As we remarked above, a single Slater determinant is not the most general type of anti-symmetric wave function. For example if we express Ψ as a sum of Slater determinants it will still be antisymmetric because each determinant in the sum will change sign when the coordinates of two electrons are interchanged. It is possible to obtain an improved approximation by expressing the wave function as a series of the form

$$\Psi_\kappa = \sum_v \Delta_v B_{v\kappa} \qquad (5.103)$$

Here the B's are constants and Δ_v stands for a Slater determinant constructed from N molecular spin-orbitals. The subscript v, used here to label the various Slater determinants, stands for an electron 'configuration'; that is, it stands for a set of N occupation numbers v. Φ_m is included in the determinant provided that the occupation number v_m is equal to 1. If $v_m = 0$ then Φ_m does not appear in Δ_v. In other words, the prescription is as follows: *Solve Roothaan's equations with a particular set of occupation numbers. Take the M resulting occupied and virtual orbitals and use them to construct Slater determinants with various other sets of occupation numbers. This provides a set of basis functions Δ_v. Express the many-electron Hamiltonian operator as a matrix based on the set of functions Δ_v.*

$$H_{v'v} = \int d\tau \Delta_{v'}^* H \Delta_v = \int d\tau \Delta_{v'}^* \left\{ \sum_i \left(H_i^c + \sum_{j>i} \frac{e^2}{r_{ij}} \right) \right\} \Delta_v \qquad (5.104)$$

Then find the energies E_κ and the expansion coefficients $B_{\nu\kappa}$ by solving the secular equation

$$\sum_\nu (H_{\nu'\nu} - E_\kappa \delta_{\nu'\nu}) B_{\nu\kappa} = 0 \qquad (5.105)$$

This procedure is called 'configuration interaction'. The matrix elements $H_{\nu'\nu}$ of Eq. (5.104) can be evaluated by means of the Slater–Condon rules, Eqs. (5.68)–(5.71). Not all of the possible matrix elements need to be evaluated. We can tell in advance that some of them will be zero. For example, looking back to our variational principle, Eq. (5.75), we can see that *matrix elements of H linking Δ_0 (which is usually the ground state) with singly-excited configurations $\Delta_{i \to j}$ will vanish.* This rule is known as Brillouin's theorem. Matrix elements linking Δ_0 to doubly-excited configurations $\Delta_{i \to j \atop k \to l}$ may be non-zero, as may those linking one singly-excited configuration $\Delta_{i \to j}$ to another, $\Delta_{k \to l}$. However, from Eq. (5.71) we can see that elements linking triply- (or higher-) excited configurations to the ground state configuration will vanish. Also, since our approximate many-electron Hamiltonian does not contain spin, it follows that it commutes with the total spin operator of the system, and that, in this approximation, the eigenfunctions of H are also eigenfunctions of S^2. If a configuration belongs to a particular eigenvalue of S^2 there will be no non-zero matrix elements of linking it to a configuration belonging to a different eigenvalue of S^2. For example, there are no non-zero matrix elements linking triplet configurations to singlets.

The operator representing the perturbation caused by an incoming light wave is an operator of type $\mathscr{F}$, Eq. (5.62). Therefore, according to Eq. (5.69) and Eq. (5.70) it links the ground state to singly-excited configurations, but not to doubly-excited ones. Therefore the states of the system which are represented by linear combinations of singly-excited configurations are the excited states which are observed in molecular spectroscopy and they are called 'optical excited states'. Configuration interaction can be a very important consideration in the calculation of optical excited states, especially in cases where a degeneracy exists.

As we mentioned above, the method which is followed in configuration interaction is to begin by solving Roothaan's equations for the ground state of the system. This produces a set of N filled molecular spin-orbitals, and $M - N$ unfilled virtual spin-orbitals. (N is the number of electrons, and M is the number of atomic spin-orbitals used in the series of Eq. (5.86).) The next step is to construct all of the possible singly-excited configurations $\Delta_{i \to j}$ by replacing filled spin-orbitals Φ_i with virtual ones Φ_j. Finally, we evaluate the matrix elements of H linking the various singly-excited configurations, and diagonalize the resulting matrix. In some cases the ground state may be approximated by Δ_0, while in other cases, the mixing

The quantum theory of atoms, molecules, and photons

of Δ_0 with doubly-excited configurations must be taken into account. According to Eq. (5.70), if $i \neq k$ and $j \neq l$, $1 \leq i, k \leq N$, $N < j, l$, then

$$\int d\tau \Delta_0^* H \Delta_{\substack{i \to j \\ k \to l}}$$

$$= \int d\tau_1 \int d\tau_2 \Phi_i^*(1) \Phi_k^*(2) \frac{e^2}{r_{12}} (1 - \mathscr{P}_{12}) \Phi_j(1) \Phi_l(2) \quad (5.106)$$

Making use of Eq. (5.86) we can express this in terms of the expansion coefficients C_{ai}:

$$\int d\tau \Delta_0^* H \Delta_{\substack{i \to j \\ k \to l}} = \sum_{a,b,c,d=1}^{M} C_{ai}^* C_{bj} C_{ck}^* C_{dl} \Gamma_{(ab)cd} \quad (5.107)$$

where $\Gamma_{(ab)cd}$ is the matrix of Coulomb and exchange integrals between atomic orbitals defined by Eq. (5.93). Similarly, if $i \neq k$, $j \neq l$ ($1 \leq i, k \leq N$, and $N < j, l$), then

$$\int d\tau \Delta_{i \to j}^* H \Delta_{k \to l}$$

$$= \int d\tau_1 \int d\tau_2 \Phi_j^*(1) \Phi_k^*(2) \frac{e^2}{r_{12}} (1 - \mathscr{P}_{12}) \Phi_i(1) \Phi_l(2) \quad (5.108)$$

If $j \neq l$ ($1 \leq i \leq N$, and $N < j, l$), then from Eq. (5.69),

$$\int d\tau \Delta_{i \to j}^* H \Delta_{i \to l}$$

$$= \int d\tau_1 \Phi_j^*(1) H^c(1) \Phi_l(1)$$

$$+ \sum_{s=1}^{N} \int d\tau_1 \int d\tau_2 \Phi_j^*(1) \Phi_s^*(2) \frac{e^2}{r_{12}} (1 - \mathscr{P}_{12}) \Phi_s(2) \Phi_l(1)$$

$$- \int d\tau_1 \int d\tau_2 \Phi_j^*(1) \Phi_i^*(2) \frac{e^2}{r_{12}} (1 - \mathscr{P}_{12}) \Phi_i(2) \Phi_l(1) \quad (5.109)$$

Equation (5.109) can be simplified by noticing that

$$\int d\tau_1 \Phi_j^*(1) H^c(1) \Phi_l(1)$$

$$+ \sum_{s=1}^{N} \int d\tau_1 \int d\tau_2 \Phi_j^*(1) \Phi_s^*(2) \frac{e^2}{r_{12}} (1 - \mathscr{P}_{12}) \Phi_s(2) \Phi_l(1)$$

$$= \int d\tau_1 \Phi_j^*(1) F(1) \Phi_l(1) \quad (5.110)$$

In other words, the first two terms of Eq. (5.109) are just the matrix element of the Fock operator between Φ_j and Φ_l. However, since the configuration interaction procedure begins by calculating spin-orbitals which are eigenfunctions of F, we have for $j \neq l$,

$$\int d\tau_1 \Phi_j^*(1)F(1)\Phi_l(1) = \varepsilon_l \int d\tau_1 \Phi_j^*(1)\Phi_l(1) = \varepsilon_l \delta_{jl} = 0 \quad (5.111)$$

Therefore Eq. (5.109) reduces to

$$\int d\tau \Delta_{i\to j}^* H \Delta_{i\to l}$$

$$= \int d\tau_1 \int d\tau_2 \Phi_j^*(1)\Phi_i^*(2) \frac{e^2}{r_{12}} (1 - \mathscr{P}_{12})\Phi_i(1)\Phi_l(2), \quad \text{for } j \neq l$$
$$(5.112)$$

In a similar way, one can show that for $i \neq k$,

$$\int d\tau \Delta_{i\to j}^* H \Delta_{k\to j}$$

$$= \int d\tau_1 \int d\tau_2 \Phi_j^*(1)\Phi_k^*(2) \frac{e^2}{r_{12}} (1 - \mathscr{P}_{12})\Phi_i(1)\Phi_j(2) \quad (5.113)$$

We still have to consider the diagonal elements of $H_{v'v}$ linking singly-excited configurations. From Eq. (5.98) and Eq. (5.102) we have that

$$\int d\tau \Delta_{i\to j}^* H \Delta_{i\to j} - \int d\tau \Delta_0^* H \Delta_0$$

$$= \int d\tau_1 \int d\tau_2 \Phi_j^*(1)\Phi_i^*(2) \frac{e^2}{r_{12}} (1 - \mathscr{P}_{12})\Phi_i(1)\Phi_j(2) + \varepsilon_j - \varepsilon_i \quad (5.114)$$

Comparing Eq. (5.108) and Eqs. (5.112)–(5.114), we see that they can be summarized in a single formula, which holds for all values of i, j, k, and l provided that i and k are the indices of filled spin-orbitals while j and l are the indices of empty ones:

$$\int d\tau \Delta_{i\to j}^* H \Delta_{k\to l}$$

$$= \int d\tau_1 \int d\tau_2 \Phi_j^*(1)\Phi_k^*(2) \frac{e^2}{r_{12}} (1 - \mathscr{P}_{12})\Phi_i(1)\Phi_l(2)$$

$$+ \delta_{ik}\delta_{jl}\left(\varepsilon_j - \varepsilon_i + \int d\tau \Delta_0^* H \Delta_0 \right), \quad 1 \leq i, k \leq N; \ N < j, l$$
$$\mathbf{(5.115)}$$

In terms of the matrices defined by Eqs. (5.88)–(5.95), this becomes,

$$\int d\tau \Delta_{i \to j}^* H \Delta_{k \to l}$$

$$= \sum_{a, b, c, d = 1}^{M} C_{aj}^* C_{bi} C_{ck}^* C_{dl} \Gamma_{(ab)cd}$$

$$+ \delta_{ik} \delta_{jl} \left(\varepsilon_j - \varepsilon_i + \int d\tau \Delta_0^* H \Delta_0 \right), \quad 1 \le i, k \le N; \quad N < j, l$$

$$(5.116)$$

Problem (5.5)   Use the creation and annihilation operators of Eqs. (9.6)–(9.10) to establish Eq. (5.116).

Closed shell calculations of π-electron systems; the semi-empirical method of Pople, Pariser, and Parr[18]

In order to actually carry out self-consistent-field, linear-combination-of-atomic-orbitals (SCF, LCAO) calculations of molecular wave functions, it is necessary to have some way of evaluating the matrices S_{ab}, H_{ab}^c, and $\Gamma_{(ab)cd}$ of Eqs. (5.90)–(5.93). In the *ab initio* approach (as exemplified by the work of E. Clementi and F. Harris), all of the necessary integrals are evaluated numerically. The work is, of course, carried out by high-speed digital computers, but even so, the very large number of integrals involved makes *ab initio* calculations rather cumbersome and limits the applicability of the method to small molecules. Therefore other authors have tried to develop semi-empirical approximations. For example, Pople, Pariser, and Parr (PPP) have developed a semi-empirical method for carrying out SCF, LCAO calculations on the π-electron systems of flat organic molecules. In the PPP method, the basis functions, $\chi_1, \ldots, \chi_M$, are a set of Löwdin-orthogonalized atomic spin-orbitals constructed from the $2p_z$ atomic orbitals of the carbon, nitrogen, and oxygen atoms in the planar organic molecule. Because of the orthonormalization of the orbitals, the matrix of overlap integrals reduces to the unit matrix: $S_{ab} = \delta_{ab}$. The atomic spin-orbitals in the basis set are eigenfunctions of the z-component of spin. If we use a bar to denote a spin-down spin-orbital, then we can write:

$$\chi_a(1) \equiv \chi_a(\bar{x}_1) \alpha(1)$$

$$\bar{\chi}_a(1) \equiv \chi_a(\bar{x}_1) \beta(1) \tag{5.117}$$

The ground state configuration of the system is assumed to be a Slater determinant of the form

$$\Delta_0 = \left| \Phi_1 \bar{\Phi}_1 \Phi_2 \bar{\Phi}_2 \ldots \Phi_{N/2} \bar{\Phi}_{N/2} \right| \tag{5.118}$$

where

$$\Phi_i(1) \equiv \varphi_i(\bar{x}_1)\alpha(1) = \sum_{a=1}^{M/2} \chi_a(1)C_{ai}$$

$$\overline{\Phi}_i(1) \equiv \varphi_i(\bar{x}_1)\beta(1) = \sum_{a=1}^{M/2} \overline{\chi}_a(1)C_{ai} \qquad (5.119)$$

A configuration of the form shown in Eq. (5.118) is called a 'closed-shell' configuration. In a closed-shell configuration, all of the electrons are paired, so that the space part of each spin-orbital appears twice in the Slater determinant: once with spin 'up', and once with spin 'down'. One says that each molecular orbital is 'doubly filled'. Obviously closed-shell configurations can only enter the wave functions of systems with an even number of electrons. If Δ_0 is restricted to the form given by Eq. (5.118) and Eq. (5.119), then the number of undetermined expansion coefficients is cut in half: i.e., there are only $M/2$ unknown coefficients, rather than M. These are found, as before, by an iterative diagonalization and recalculation of the Fock matrix, i.e., by solving the reduced set of Roothaan's equations,

$$\sum_{a,b=1}^{M/2} (F_{ab} - \delta_{ab}\varepsilon_i)C_{bi} = 0 \qquad (5.120)$$

where

$$F_{ab} = H_{ab}^c + \sum_{c,d=1}^{M/2} \sum_{i=1}^{N/2} C_{ci}C_{di}$$

$$\times \int d^3x_1 \int d^3x_2 \chi_a(\bar{x}_1)\chi_c(\bar{x}_2) \frac{e^2}{r_{12}} (2 - \mathscr{P}_{12})\chi_d(\bar{x}_2)\chi_b(\bar{x}_1) \qquad (5.121)$$

Notice that since the $2p_z$ orbitals are real, we do not need complex numbers in Eq. (5.121). Notice also, that because of the orthonormality of the spin functions, the Coulomb integrals enter the Fock matrix with twice the weight of the exchange integrals. The PPP method introduces a further simplification called the 'zero differential overlap' approximation (ZDO), in which one assumes that

$$\chi_a(\bar{x}_1)\chi_b(\bar{x}_1) \cong \delta_{ab}|\chi_a(\bar{x}_1)|^2 \qquad (5.122)$$

so that

$$\int d^3x_1 \int d^3x_2 \chi_a(\bar{x}_1)\chi_c(\bar{x}_2) \frac{e^2}{r_{12}} (2 - \mathscr{P}_{12})\chi_d(\bar{x}_2)\chi_b(\bar{x}_1)$$

$$\cong (2\delta_{ab}\delta_{cd} - \delta_{ad}\delta_{cb})\gamma_{bd} \qquad (5.123)$$

where

$$\gamma_{bd} \equiv \int d^3x_1 \int d^3x_2 |\chi_b(\bar{x}_1)|^2 \frac{e^2}{r_{12}} |\chi_d(\bar{x}_2)|^2 \qquad (5.124)$$

The quantum theory of atoms, molecules, and photons

In the early papers of Pople, Pariser, and Parr, the integrals γ_{bd} were evaluated by assuming figure-8 shaped charge distributions for $|\chi_b|^2$ and $|\chi_d|^2$. Mataga and Nishimoto[15] have introduced the approximation

$$\gamma_{bd} \cong \frac{e^2}{R_{bd} + a_{bd}} \tag{5.125}$$

where R_{bd} is the distance between atom b and atom d, while

$$a_{bd} \equiv \frac{2e^2}{I_b - A_b + I_d - A_d} \tag{5.126}$$

Here I_b, I_d, A_b, and A_d are respectively the ionization energies and electron affinities of atoms b and d. Alternatively, Ohno[16] has introduced the approximation

$$\gamma_{bd} \cong \frac{e^2}{\sqrt{R_{bd}^2 + a_{bd}^2}} \tag{5.127}$$

where R_{bd} and a_{bd} are defined in the same way as in the approximation of Mataga and Nishimoto.[15] The PPP method also makes use of an approximation due to Goeppert–Mayer and Sklar[29] in which the diagonal elements of the core Hamiltonian are represented by the formula

$$H_{aa}^c = -I_a - \sum_{b \neq a} Z_b \gamma_{ba} \tag{5.128}$$

Here I_a is the ionization energy of the ath atom, Z_b is the number of electrons which the bth atom contributes to the π-pool, and γ_{ba} is given by Eq. (5.125) or Eq. (5.127). The off-diagonal elements of the core Hamiltonian are empirical parameters. One begins by considering a series of 'calibration molecules' and choosing the off-diagonal elements of H_{ab}^c in such a way as to match the spectroscopic properties as well as possible. Then one hopes that the same values of H_{ab}^c will lead to a reasonable agreement with experiment when the properties of a different series of molecules are calculated. In the PPP method, the interaction of the ground state configuration with doubly-excited configurations is neglected. The optical excited states of the system are represented by a linear combination of singly-excited configurations. They can be divided into singlet states, corresponding to the total-spin quantum number $S = 0$, and triplet states, with total spin $S = 1$. As we mentioned above, in this approximation there is no mixing between singlets and triplets. Let us introduce the notation $\Delta_{i \rightarrow \bar{j}}$ to represent a Slater determinant in which the spin-up molecular spin-orbital Φ_i in the closed-shell configuration Δ_0 of Eq. (5.118) has been replaced by the spin-down virtual spin-orbital $\bar{\Phi}_j$. One can show (by means of Eq. (9.6) and Eq. (9.19)) that $\Delta_{i \rightarrow \bar{j}}$ is a triplet state with $M_s = -1$. The other two members of the triplet are $\Delta_{\bar{i} \rightarrow j}$ with $M_s = 1$ and

174

$(1/\sqrt{2})(\Delta_{i \to j} - \Delta_{\bar{i} \to \bar{j}})$ with $M_s = 0$. In the same notation, a singlet state with $S = 0$ and $M_s = 0$ is represented by $(1/\sqrt{2})(\Delta_{i \to j} + \Delta_{\bar{i} \to \bar{j}})$. From Eq. (5.116)

$$\tfrac{1}{2} \int d\tau (\Delta_{i \to j} + \Delta_{\bar{i} \to \bar{j}}) H (\Delta_{k \to l} + \Delta_{\bar{k} \to \bar{l}})$$

$$= \sum_{a,b=1}^{M/2} (2 C_{ai} C_{aj} C_{bk} C_{bl} - C_{ai} C_{ak} C_{bj} C_{bl}) \gamma_{ab}$$

$$+ \delta_{ik} \delta_{jl} \left(\varepsilon_i - \varepsilon_j + \int d\tau \Delta_0 H \Delta_0 \right) \tag{5.129}$$

while the triplet-triplet configuration interaction becomes:

$$\int d\tau \Delta_{i \to \bar{j}} H \Delta_{k \to \bar{l}} = \int d\tau \Delta_{\bar{i} \to j} H \Delta_{\bar{k} \to l}$$

$$= \tfrac{1}{2} \int d\tau (\Delta_{i \to j} - \Delta_{\bar{k} \to \bar{l}}) H (\Delta_{i \to j} - \Delta_{\bar{k} \to \bar{l}})$$

$$= - \sum_{a,b=1}^{M/2} C_{ai} C_{ak} C_{bj} C_{bl} \gamma_{ab}$$

$$+ \delta_{ik} \delta_{jl} \left(\varepsilon_j - \varepsilon_i + \int d\tau \Delta_0 H \Delta_0 \right) \tag{5.130}$$

Figure 5.6 shows schematically the six linearly independent Slater determinants which it is possible to construct from two molecular orbitals. Of these, the ground state, Δ_0, and the doubly-excited state, $\Delta_{\bar{1} \to \bar{2}}^{1 \to 2}$, are eigenfunctions of total spin with the quantum number $s = 0$, i.e., they are singlet states. Two of the singly-excited states, $\Delta_{1 \to \bar{2}}$ and $\Delta_{\bar{1} \to 2}$, are eigenfunctions of total spin belonging to the quantum number $s = 1$, i.e., they are members of a triplet. The third member of the triplet, and another singlet state, can be constructed from the two remaining singly-excited Slater determinants, $\Delta_{1 \to 2}$ and $\Delta_{\bar{1} \to \bar{2}}$.

Problem (5.6) (a) Verify that the closed-shell form of Roothaan's equations, Eqs. (5.120)–(5.121), follow from substituting Eq. (5.119) into Eq. (5.77) and Eq. (5.82).

(b) Verify that Eq. (5.129) and Eq. (5.130) follow from substituting Eq. (5.122) and Eq. (5.124) into Eq. (5.116).

The CNDO approximation

In the PPP method, only one atomic orbital per atom enters the basis set, (a $2p_z$ orbital on each of the carbon, nitrogen, or oxygen atoms of the flat organic compound). The σ-electrons do not enter the calculation at all. Actually, this is not a completely valid procedure, because the σ and π electrons influence each other through $\Gamma_{(ab)cd}$. For non-planar molecules, the σ–π separation disappears altogether, since there is no longer a plane of symmetry. In a non-planar molecule, the σ and π electrons are linked, not only through $\Gamma_{(ab)cd}$, but also through S_{ab} and H_{ab}^c. A calculation of the molecular orbitals of such a system must necessarily involve more than one atomic orbital per atom. Semi-empirical methods for dealing with this type of system have been developed by Pople, Segal, and others.[19] One such method is called the complete-neglect-of-differential-overlap (CNDO) approximation. In the CNDO method, as in the PPP method, the basis functions are Löwdin-orthogonalized atomic orbitals, and the coefficients are found by the iterative diagonalization and recalculation of the reduced Fock matrix, Eq. (5.120). The approximations of Eqs. (5.122)–(5.124) are also used. However, in the evaluation of the integrals γ_{bd}, Eq. (5.124), the approximations of Mataga, Nishimoto, and Ohno are often not used. Instead, one uses the spherical-average (SA) approximation, in which $\chi_b(\bar{x}_1)$ and $\chi_d(\bar{x}_2)$ of Eq. (5.124) are represented by spherically symmetric Slater-type orbitals (STO's). (An STO is a function of the form $N r^{n-1} e^{-\zeta r}$ where N and ζ are constants.) There may be more than one orbital per atom, but in the SA approximation, one does not distinguish between them. Thus, γ_{bd} depends only on the nature of the two atoms and the distance between them, rather than on the specific indices of the atomic orbitals. If we use capital letters to denote the indices of the atoms, and small letters near the beginning of the alphabet to denote the indices of atomic orbitals, then in the CNDO method the diagonal elements of the Fock matrix are approximated by the formula

$$F_{aa} \cong -\tfrac{1}{2}(I_a + A_a) + [(P_{AA} - Z_A) - \tfrac{1}{2}(P_{aa} - 1)]\gamma_{AA}$$
$$+ \sum_{B \neq A} (P_{BB} - Z_B)\gamma_{AB} \quad (5.131)$$

while the off-diagonal elements are given by

$$F_{ab} \cong \beta_{AB}^0 S_{ab} - \tfrac{1}{2}P_{ab}\gamma_{AB}, \quad a \neq b \quad (5.132)$$

Here γ_{AA} and γ_{AB} are the integrals of Eq. (5.124), evaluated using the SA approximation, Z_A is the number of electrons which the Ath atom contributes to the calculation, (i.e., the number of valence electrons), I_a and A_a are, as before, the ionization energy and electron affinity of the ath orbital, and P_{ab} is the matrix defined by Eq. (5.94). However, because we are confining the discussion to cases where the ground state is assumed to be a closed shell, we can write,

$$P_{ab} = \sum_{i=1}^{N/2} 2C_{ai}C_{bi} \tag{5.133}$$

Notice that in Eq. (5.132), the off-diagonal elements of the core Hamiltonian are represented by

$$H_{ab}^c \cong \beta_{AB}^0 S_{ab} \tag{5.134}$$

In other words, H_{ab}^c is assumed to be proportional to the overlap integral S_{ab}. The constants of proportionality, β_{AB}^0, are empirical parameters which are fitted to the properties of a series of calibration molecules. There are many other ways of doing CNDO calculations. For example, the method can be extended to open shells, and a variety of approximations can be used to evaluate H_{ab}^c and γ_{ab}.

Restricted and unrestricted Hartree–Fock calculations; the symmetry dilemma

Closed-shell calculations of the type described here are examples of restricted Hartree–Fock calculations. The Slater determinant Δ_0 representing the ground-state configuration of the system is restricted to the closed-shell form given in Eq. (5.118). A simple example can illustrate the difference between a restricted Hartree–Fock calculation and an unrestricted one: Suppose that we wish to calculate the ground state of the H$^-$ ion. If we restrict Δ_0 to the closed-shell form, Eq. (5.118), then we obtain a certain optimum wave function subject to the restriction, and it will have the form,

$$\Delta_0 = |\Phi_{1s}\bar{\Phi}_{1s}| \tag{5.135}$$

On the other hand, a Hartree–Fock calculation without this restriction would lead to a ground-state configuration with different orbitals for different spins (DODS), i.e., it would have the form:

$$\Delta_0' = |\Phi_{1s}\bar{\Phi}_{1s'}| \tag{5.136}$$

where

$$\Phi_{1s}(1) \equiv \varphi_{1s}(\bar{x}_1)\alpha(1)$$

$$\Phi_{1s'}(1) \equiv \varphi_{1s'}(\bar{x}_1)\beta(1) \tag{5.137}$$

177

with φ_{1s} and $\varphi_{1s'}$ different functions of $\bar{x}_1$. The DODS configuration, Δ'_0 of Eq. (5.136), is not an eigenfunction of total spin, however. If we wish it to be an eigenfunction of S^2 (and we do), we must operate on Δ'_0 with the appropriate projection operator, $(S^2 - 1)$, Eq. (9.19). In this way we can obtain an approximate singlet ground state of the form

$$\Psi_0 = \frac{1}{\sqrt{2}} (|\Phi_{1s}\overline{\Phi}_{1s'}| + |\overline{\Phi}_{1s}\Phi_{1s'}|) \tag{5.138}$$

While both Δ_0 of Eq. (5.135) and Ψ_0 of Eq. (5.138) fulfil the symmetry requirement which requires the eigenfunctions of H to be simultaneous eigenfunctions of S^2, Ψ_0 corresponds to a lower energy than Δ_0. Thus the unrestricted calculation leads to a more accurate representation of the ground state, and this representation is a sum of several Slater determinants. We have seen here an example of the so-called 'symmetry dilemma' for Hartree–Fock calculations. On the one hand, we know in advance that the wave functions of a system ought to have certain symmetry properties. However, if we impose this restriction before performing our variational calculation, then the resulting Slater determinant does not correspond very closely to the real ground state. If we wished to improve such a restricted ground state, we would have to perform a configuration interaction calculation involving a very large number of doubly-excited configurations. P. O. Löwdin[14] has emphasized in numerous papers and lectures that the way around the symmetry dilemma is to *forget about the symmetry until after the Hartree–Fock variational calculation is finished. Then we should remember the symmetry, and apply the appropriate projection operators. The resulting ground-state wave function is a sum of Slater determinants.*

The discussion given here by no means exhausts the methods for performing Hartree–Fock calculations of molecular orbitals. The current literature is very rich in such methods, and equally rich in abbreviations for them. But now, at least, if someone tells you that he has performed an SCF, LCAO, CS, PPP, ZDO, MO calculation with CI, you will know exactly what he means.

6. Translational symmetry

Crystals and polymers; reduction of the secular equation by means of symmetry; review of benzene, treated in the Hückel approximation; cyclic boundary conditions

A long polymer is sometimes so big that it is called a macromolecule. A crystal actually is macroscopic. Neither a long polymer nor a crystal differs very much from an ordinary molecule except in its size. The number of electrons in a crystal is so enormous that if there were no symmetry to help us there would be no hope of solving the secular equations. However, the translational symmetry of a crystal or a polymer can be used to reduce the secular equations to a manageable size.

In a previous section we discussed the π-electrons of benzene in the Hückel approximation. The molecular orbital of a π-electron was represented as a linear combination of $2p_z$ atomic orbitals localized on the nth carbon atom and represented by the symbol $|n\rangle$

$$|k\rangle = \sum_n |n\rangle\langle n|k\rangle \tag{6.1}$$

The molecular orbital $|k\rangle$ was to be an eigenfunction of the Hamiltonian operator H so that

$$H|k\rangle = E_k|k\rangle \tag{6.2}$$

Substituting Eq. (6.1) into Eq. (6.2) and multiplying on the left by the conjugate atomic orbital $\langle n'|$ we obtained the secular equations

$$\sum_n \{\langle n'|H|n\rangle - E_k \langle n'|n\rangle\} \langle n|k\rangle = 0 \tag{6.3}$$

We considered the case where the set of atomic orbitals were orthogonalized so that

$$\langle n'|n\rangle = \delta_{n'n} \tag{6.4}$$

179

and where only interactions between nearest neighbours are taken into account so that

$$\langle n'|H|n\rangle = \begin{cases} \alpha & n = n' \\ \beta & n = n' \pm 1 \\ 0 & \text{otherwise} \end{cases} \tag{6.5}$$

Then the set of secular equations (6.3) had the form

$$\beta\langle N\,|\,k\rangle + (\alpha - E_k)\langle 1\,|\,k\rangle + \beta\langle 2\,|\,k\rangle \quad\;\; = 0$$
$$\beta\langle 1\,|\,k\rangle + (\alpha - E_k)\langle 2\,|\,k\rangle + \beta\langle 3\,|\,k\rangle \quad\;\; = 0$$
$$\vdots \qquad\qquad \vdots \qquad\qquad \vdots$$
$$\beta\langle N-1\,|\,k\rangle + (\alpha - E_k)\langle N\,|\,k\rangle + \beta\langle N+1\,|\,k\rangle = 0 \tag{6.6}$$

We saw that these equations could all be made redundant by the trial solution.

$$\langle n|k\rangle = \frac{1}{\sqrt{N}}\,e^{inkd}, \quad n = 1, 2, \ldots, N; \; N = 6 \tag{6.7}$$

where the boundary condition of single-valuedness required that

$$kd = \frac{2\pi}{N}, \frac{4\pi}{N}, \ldots, \frac{2N\pi}{N}, \quad N = 6 \tag{6.8}$$

Then the secular equations (6.6) all redundantly required that

$$E_k = \alpha + 2\beta \cos{(kd)} \tag{6.9}$$

giving six allowed values of the energy corresponding to the six allowed values of kd, Eq. (6.8).

Linear polymers with one atom per unit cell; homogeneous boundary conditions

We might ask what would happen if we broke the benzene ring, added an extra hydrogen at each end and thus made it into a linear polymer. The set of secular equations corresponding to Eq. (6.6) would then have the form

$$0 \qquad\;\; + (\alpha - E_k)\langle 1\,|\,k\rangle + \beta\langle 2\,|\,k\rangle = 0$$
$$\beta\langle 1\,|\,k\rangle + (\alpha - E_k)\langle 2\,|\,k\rangle + \beta\langle 3\,|\,k\rangle = 0$$
$$\vdots \qquad\qquad \vdots \qquad\qquad \vdots$$
$$\beta\langle N-1\,|\,k\rangle + (\alpha - E_k)\langle N\,|\,k\rangle + \quad 0 \quad\;\; = 0 \tag{6.10}$$

In other words, the matrix element of the Hamiltonian corresponding to the coupling between the two ends of the chain would disappear. The symmetry of the secular equations is now spoiled by the zeros in the first and last equations. We can restore the symmetry by introducing at the two ends fictitious coefficients which are required to be zero,

$$\langle 0 \,|\, k \rangle \equiv 0 \tag{6.11}$$

$$\langle N + 1 \,|\, k \rangle \equiv 0 \tag{6.12}$$

Then we can rewrite Eq. (6.10) as

$$
\begin{aligned}
\beta\langle 0 \,|\, k \rangle + (\alpha - E_k)\langle 1 \,|\, k \rangle + \beta\langle 2 \,|\, k \rangle &= 0 \\
\beta\langle 1 \,|\, k \rangle + (\alpha - E_k)\langle 2 \,|\, k \rangle + \beta\langle 3 \,|\, k \rangle &= 0 \\
\vdots \qquad\qquad \vdots \qquad\qquad \vdots &
\end{aligned}
$$

$$\beta\langle N - 1 \,|\, k \rangle + (\alpha - E_k)\langle N \,|\, k \rangle + \beta\langle N + 1 \,|\, k \rangle = 0 \tag{6.13}$$

A solution of the form

$$\langle n \,|\, k \rangle \sim \mathrm{e}^{\pm inkd} \tag{6.14}$$

will now make all of the equations in the set (6.13) redundantly require that

$$E_k = \alpha + 2\beta \cos (kd) \tag{6.15}$$

But now instead of single-valuedness as a boundary condition determining the allowed values of kd we have the requirements of Eq. (6.11) and Eq. (6.12). Equation (6.11) together with the requirement of normalization will be satisfied if we let

$$\langle n \,|\, k \rangle = \sqrt{\frac{2}{N + 1}} \sin (nkd) \tag{6.16}$$

Equation (6.12) requires that

$$\sin \{(N + 1)kd\} = 0 \tag{6.17}$$

which will be satisfied if

$$kd = \frac{\pi}{N + 1}, \frac{2\pi}{N + 1}, \ldots, \frac{N\pi}{N + 1} \tag{6.18}$$

We have left N as a variable for the sake of generality. Just as Eqs. (6.7)–(6.9) describe the π-electron system not only for benzene with $N = 6$ but also for a general cyclic conjugated polyolefin with arbitrary N, equations (6.15)–(6.18) describe the π-electron system of any polyene, $C_N H_{N+2}$ with arbitrary N. For example, in the case of butadiene with $N = 4$ the allowed values of kd are

$$kd = \frac{\pi}{5}, \frac{2\pi}{5}, \frac{3\pi}{5}, \frac{4\pi}{5} \tag{6.19}$$

and the corresponding energy eigenvalues are

$$\frac{E_k - \alpha}{\beta} = 2 \cos (kd) = -1{\cdot}62, \; -0{\cdot}62, \; +0{\cdot}62, \; +1{\cdot}62 \qquad (6.20)$$

The unitary matrix of coefficients $\langle n \mid k \rangle$ used in constructing the molecular orbitals from the atomic orbitals (Eq. (6.1)), is given by

$$\langle n \mid k \rangle = \sqrt{\frac{2}{N + 1}} \sin (nkd)$$

$$= \begin{pmatrix} 0{\cdot}37 & 0{\cdot}60 & 0{\cdot}60 & 0{\cdot}37 \\ 0{\cdot}60 & 0{\cdot}37 & -0{\cdot}37 & -0{\cdot}60 \\ 0{\cdot}60 & -0{\cdot}37 & -0{\cdot}37 & 0{\cdot}60 \\ 0{\cdot}37 & -0{\cdot}60 & 0{\cdot}60 & -0{\cdot}37 \end{pmatrix} \qquad (6.21)$$

Figures (6.1) and (6.2) illustrate schematically the π-electron molecular orbitals and energies of butadiene. It is an interesting exercise to apply Eqs. (6.15)–(6.18) to the case of ethylene ($N = 2$) and to allyl ($N = 3$) calculating also the charge and bond-order matrix and the free-valence index.

When N is very large, end effects become relatively unimportant and it becomes approximately valid to treat the polymer just as though the two ends were joined together. In other words it becomes approximately valid to use the periodic (Born–von Kàrmàn) boundary conditions Eq. (6.8) and the solution of Eq. (6.7) in place of Eqs. (6.16) and (6.18).

Linear polymers with more than one atom per unit cell; crystal orbitals; Brillouin zones

If we are dealing with more complicated polymers where it is necessary to use more than one atomic orbital per monomer, it is still possible to use symmetry to simplify the problem. Let us continue to use the index n for labelling the N monomers which form the polymer, but let us now introduce another index, j, which labels the m different atomic orbitals of a particular monomer. Thus we can use the symbol $|n, j\rangle$ to represent the jth atomic orbital of the nth monomer. Similarly the molecular orbitals of the whole polymer will now need two indices and we can represent them by the symbol $|k, b\rangle$. As before we can think of k as the wave number associated with the wave-like molecular orbital $|k, b\rangle$ (see Fig. 6.1). The index b is called the 'band index' for reasons which will soon become clear. Let us try a solution of the form

$$|k, b\rangle = \frac{1}{\sqrt{N}} \sum_{n, j} |n, j\rangle \; C_{jb}(k) \, e^{inkd} \qquad (6.22)$$

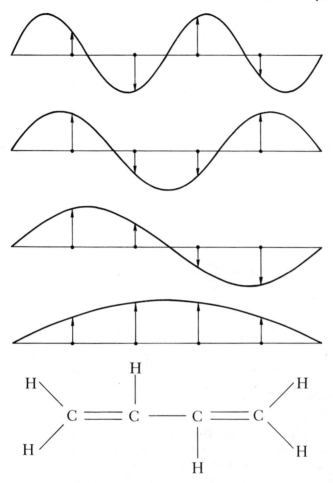

Figure 6.1 shows the structural formula of butadiene, and also illustrates schematically the π-orbitals of the molecule, Eq. (6.21). The amplitude with which each of the carbon $2p_z$ atomic orbitals enters a molecular orbital is indicated by an arrow.

to see whether it will allow us to reduce the order of the secular equations. (For the moment let us assume that N is very large so that it is approximately valid to use the periodic boundary conditions of Eq. (6.8).) The polymer orbital $|k, b\rangle$, which is sometimes called a 'crystal orbital' or a 'Bloch function', must be an eigenfunction of the Hamiltonian operator in the Hückel approximation so that

$$H \,|k, b\rangle = E_b(k) \,|k, b\rangle \qquad (6.23)$$

183

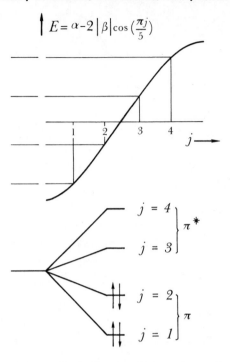

$$E = \alpha - 2|\beta|\cos\left(\frac{\pi j}{5}\right)$$

Figure 6.2 shows the π-orbital energies of butadiene, Eq. (6.20), which should be compared with the corresponding energies in benzene, Fig. 5.4, and with the energies of the conduction electrons in a metal, Fig. 6.6.

Substituting Eq. (6.22) into Eq. (6.23) taking the scalar product with the conjugate function $\langle n', j'|$ and assuming that the basic set of atomic orbitals $|n, j\rangle$ have been orthogonalized so that

$$\langle n'j' \mid nj \rangle = \delta_{n'n}\,\delta_{j'j} \tag{6.24}$$

we have

$$\sum_{n,j} \langle n'j'|H|n, j\rangle\, C_{jb}(k)\, e^{inkd}$$

$$E_b(k) \sum_{n,j} \langle n'j' \mid n, j\rangle\, C_{jb}(k)\, e^{inkd} = E_b(k)C_{j'b}(k)\, e^{in'kd} \tag{6.25}$$

If we let

$$\sum_n \langle n', j'|H|n, j\rangle\, e^{i(n-n')kd} \equiv H_{j'j}(k) \tag{6.26}$$

then Eq. (6.25) can be written in the form

$$\sum_j \{H_{j'j}(k) - E_b(k)\,\delta_{j'j}\}C_{jb}(k) = 0 \tag{6.27}$$

You might ask what has happened to the index n' in Eq. (6.26) and Eq. (6.27). The answer is that provided N is sufficiently large so that it is valid to treat the polymer as though its two ends were joined together, the left-hand side of Eq. (6.26) is independent of n'. This is because $\langle n', j' | H | n, j \rangle \times e^{i(n'-n)kd}$ depends only on the relative position of the two monomers n' and n, not on their absolute position. If we start at the monomer n' and perform the sum $\sum_n$ over nearest neighbours, next nearest neighbours, etc., we shall get the same result regardless of the position of n'. In fact, this is precisely the meaning of translational symmetry: if end effects can be neglected, the environment of a unit cell gives no indication of its absolute position. The trial function of Eq. (6.22) has thus allowed us to reduce the order of the set of secular equations from Nm to m where N is the number of monomers in the polymer and m is the number of atomic orbitals per monomer. In simple cases the m secular equations (6.27) can sometimes be solved analytically to give C_{jb} and E_b as functions of k. Alternatively, they can be solved numerically for various values of k. Then the coefficients $C_{jb}(k)$ and energies $E_b(k)$ can be found for other values of k by means of interpolation.

As an example consider a long polymer composed of two kinds of atoms so that it has the form A–B–A–B–A–B–A–B, etc. Suppose that the Hückel Hamiltonian matrix corresponding to this polymer has the form shown in Table 6.1.

$\langle n', j' | H | n, j \rangle =$

Table 6.1

n' / j' \ n / j	1 / 1	1 / 2	2 / 1	2 / 2	3 / 1	3 / 2	4 / 1	4 / 2	
1 / 1	α_A	β							
1 / 2	β	α_B	β						
2 / 1		β	α_A	β					
2 / 2			β	α_B	β				etc.
3 / 1				β	α_A	β			
3 / 2					β	α_B	β		
4 / 1						β	α_A	β	
4 / 2							β	α_B	

etc.

185

Then the matrix $H_{j'j}(k)$ of Eq. (6.26) is given by

$$H_{j'j}(k) = \begin{pmatrix} \alpha_A & \beta(1 + e^{-ikd}) \\ \beta(1 + e^{ikd}) & \alpha_B \end{pmatrix} \qquad (6.28)$$

In order for the secular equations, Eq. (6.27), to have a non-trivial solution we must have

$$\det \begin{vmatrix} \alpha_A - E_b(k) & \beta(1 + e^{-ikd}) \\ \beta(1 + e^{ikd}) & \alpha_B - E_b(k) \end{vmatrix} = 0 \qquad (6.29)$$

Solving the resulting quadratic equation for $E_b(k)$ we have the two roots

$$E_{\pm}(k) = \frac{\alpha_A + \alpha_B}{2} \pm \sqrt{\left(\frac{\alpha_A - \alpha_B}{2}\right)^2 + \left(2\beta \cos \frac{kd}{2}\right)^2} \qquad (6.30)$$

The allowed values of kd are determined by the boundary conditions, Eq. (6.8), so that $E_+(k)$ and $E_-(k)$ each correspond to a closely spaced 'band' of energy eigenvalues, as shown in Fig. 6.3. The parameter d is the

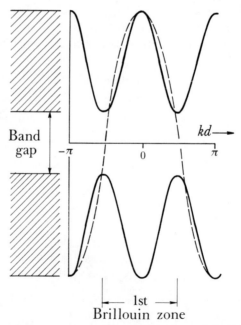

Figure 6.3 shows the two bands of closely spaced (almost continuous) energy levels for electrons in a long polymer containing two kinds of atoms, A and B, Eq. (6.30). When $\alpha_A = \alpha_B$, there is only one band, whose energy as a function of the wave number k is given by the dotted line. When $\alpha_A \neq \alpha_B$, a gap forms in the middle of the band, the size of the unit cell is doubled, and the first Brillouin zone becomes half as large.

lattice spacing; in other words it represents the length of a complete repeat unit A–B. The energy in the two bands as a function of the wave number k repeats itself with a period such that $E_\pm(k + \pi/d) = E_\pm(k)$. The region where $-\pi/2 < kd < \pi/2$ is called the 'first Brillouin zone'. We do not need to consider the behaviour of $E_b(k)$ outside the first Brillouin zone, since it just repeats the behaviour inside the zone. We can ask what will happen if $\alpha_A = \alpha_B$. Then Eq. (6.30) will have to reduce to Eq. (6.15) and it does, if we take the plus sign for the square root. $E(k)$ for the case $\alpha_A = \alpha_B$ is indicated by a dotted line in Fig. 6.3 which has the periodicity $E(k + 2\pi/d) = E(k)$. By letting $\alpha_A = \alpha_B$ we have made the repeat unit of the polymer half as big, and the effect is to double the size of the repeat unit of $E(k)$.

Two- and three-dimensional structures with translational symmetry treated in the crystal orbital approximation

In an exactly similar way we can use translational symmetry to reduce the order of the secular equation in a two- or three-dimensional periodic structure. Suppose that $\vec{X}_n$ is a vector from the origin of the coordinates to a chosen point in the nth unit cell. If (as before) we let $|n, j\rangle$ represent the jth atomic orbital or the nth repeat unit we can try writing down crystal orbitals of the form

$$|\vec{k}, b\rangle = \frac{1}{\sqrt{N}} \sum_{n, j} |n, j\rangle C_{jb}(\vec{k})\, e^{i\vec{k}\cdot X_n} \tag{6.31}$$

to see whether trial functions of this form will allow us to reduce the order of the set of secular equations. We want the crystal orbital of Eq. (6.31) to satisfy

$$H|\vec{k}, b\rangle = E_b(\vec{k})\,|\,\vec{k}, b\rangle \tag{6.32}$$

From Eqs. (6.31) and (6.32) we have (assuming orthonormality of the atomic orbitals $|n, j\rangle$)

$$\sum_{n, j} \langle n', j'|H|n, j\rangle C_{jb}(\vec{k})\, e^{i\vec{k}\cdot X_n}$$

$$= \sum_{n, j} \langle n', j' \,|\, n, j\rangle C_{jb}(\vec{k})\, e^{i\vec{k}\cdot X_n}$$

$$= C_{j'b}(\vec{k})\, e^{i\vec{k}\cdot X_{n'}} \tag{6.33}$$

If we let

$$\sum_{n} \langle n', j'|H|n, j\rangle\, e^{i\vec{k}\cdot(X_n - X_{n'})} \equiv H_{j'j}(\vec{k}) \tag{6.34}$$

then Eq. (6.33) can be written in the form

$$\sum_{j'} H_{j'j}(\vec{k})C_{jb}(\vec{k}) = E_b(\vec{k})C_{j'b}(\vec{k}) \tag{6.35}$$

The sum on the left-hand side of Eq. (6.34) is independent of n' because

$$\langle n', j'|H|n, j\rangle \, e^{i\vec{k}\cdot(X_n - X_{n'})}$$

depends only on the relative coordinates $\vec{X}_n - \vec{X}_{n'}$. Equation (6.35) can be solved numerically for certain values of k and the energies and eigenfunctions corresponding to other values of k can be found by interpolation.

Basis vectors of the direct lattice and the reciprocal lattice; periodicity of energy in the reciprocal lattice

In order to discuss the translational symmetry of a two- or three-dimensional periodic structure it is convenient to introduce a set of basis vectors $\vec{a}_1, \vec{a}_2$, and $\vec{a}_3$ which lead from a chosen point in one unit cell to the corresponding point in a neighbouring unit cell. The position vector of the nth unit cell in the lattice can be expressed in terms of integral multiples of these three basis vectors:

$$\vec{X}_n = n_1\vec{a}_1 + n_2\vec{a}_2 + n_3\vec{a}_3, \quad n_i = 0, \pm 1, \pm 2, \pm 3, \text{ etc.} \tag{6.36}$$

$\vec{X}_n$ is called a direct lattice vector. We can also define a set of reciprocal basis vectors defined by the relation

$$\vec{a}_i.\vec{b}_j = \delta_{ij} \tag{6.37}$$

A set of 'reciprocal lattice vectors', $\vec{G}_l$, can then be formed from integral multiples of the reciprocal basis vectors $\vec{b}_1, \vec{b}_2$, and $\vec{b}_3$.

$$\vec{G}_l \equiv 2\pi(l_1\vec{b}_1 + l_2\vec{b}_2 + l_3\vec{b}_3)$$
$$l_i = 0, \pm 1, \pm 2, \pm 3, \ldots \tag{6.38}$$

We would now like to show that the matrix elements $H_{j'j}(\vec{k})$ defined by Eq. (6.34) have a periodicity in 'k-space' such that displacement by any reciprocal lattice vector will bring us back to the same value. In other words we would like to show that

$$H_{j'j}(\vec{k} + \vec{G}_l) = H_{j'j}(\vec{k}) \tag{6.39}$$

Going back to Eq. (6.34) we can write

$$H_{j'j}(\vec{k} + \vec{G}_l) = \sum_n \langle n'j'|H|n, j\rangle \, e^{i(\vec{k} + \vec{G}_l)\cdot(X_n - X_{n'})} \tag{6.40}$$

But

$$\vec{G}_l.(\vec{X}_n - \vec{X}_{n'}) = 2\pi(l_1\vec{b}_1 + l_2\vec{b}_2 + l_3\vec{b}_3)$$
$$\times \{(n_1 - n'_1)\vec{a}_1 + (n_2 - n'_2)\vec{a}_2 + (n_3 - n'_3)\vec{a}_3\}$$
$$= 2\pi\{l_1(n_1 - n'_1) + l_2(n_2 - n'_2) + l_3(n_3 - n'_3)\}$$
$$= 2\pi p \tag{6.41}$$

where p is an integer. Then

$$e^{i\vec{G}_l.(\vec{X}_n - \vec{X}_{n'})} = e^{i2\pi p} = 1 \tag{6.42}$$

Substituting Eq. (6.42) into Eq. (6.40) we obtain Eq. (6.39). From this and from Eq. (6.35) it follows that $E_b(\vec{k})$ has a periodicity such that for any reciprocal lattice vector $\vec{G}_l$,

$$E_b(\vec{k} + \vec{G}_l) = E_b(\vec{k}) \tag{6.43}$$

We can imagine, in k-space, a lattice of points which are connected to the origin by reciprocal lattice vectors. The first Brillouin zone is defined as the volume of k-space around the origin bounded by planes which are the perpendicular bisectors of reciprocal lattice vectors. As in the one-dimensional case, we need only consider the behaviour of $E_b(\vec{k})$ inside the first Brillouin zone since, according to Eq. (6.43), this behaviour is repeated periodically in the remainder of k-space.

The Hückel approximation applied to a plane of graphite

For example, we might consider the two-dimensional structure formed by the carbon atoms in a plane of graphite[3] (see Fig. 6.4). If we neglect the weak interactions between two planes then we can treat the π-electron system of the graphite plane as though it were the π-electron system of an enormous flat conjugated molecule. If d represents the distance between two neighbouring carbon atoms, then the basis vectors for the direct lattice are

$$\vec{a}_1 = \left\{\frac{3}{2}d, -\frac{\sqrt{3}}{2}d\right\}$$
$$\vec{a}_2 = \{0, \sqrt{3}\,d\} \tag{6.44}$$

Equation (6.37) gives us two simultaneous equations for the two components of the reciprocal lattice vector $\vec{b}_1 = \{b_{11}, b_{12}\}$

$$\vec{a}_1.\vec{b}_1 = 1$$
$$\vec{a}_2.\vec{b}_1 = 0 \tag{6.45}$$

or

$$\tfrac{3}{2}\, d\, b_{11} - \frac{\sqrt{3}}{2}\, d\, b_{12} = 1$$

$$0 + \sqrt{3}\, d\, b_{12} = 0 \qquad (6.46)$$

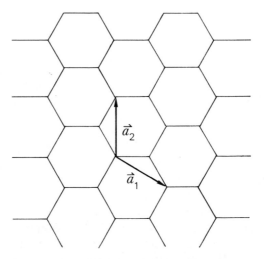

Figure 6.4 shows the structure of a plane of graphite. The plane resembles an enormous conjugated hydrocarbon. The π-electrons in a graphite plane can be treated in the Hückel approximation, neglecting the weak interaction between the planes.

Solving Eq. (6.46) and the corresponding equations for $\vec{b}_2$ we find that

$$\vec{b}_1 = \left\{ \frac{2}{3d},\; 0 \right\}$$

$$\vec{b}_2 = \left\{ \frac{1}{3d},\; \frac{1}{\sqrt{3}\, d} \right\} \qquad (6.47)$$

The direct lattice vectors have the form

$$\vec{X}_n = n_1 \vec{a}_1 + n_2 \vec{a}_2 \qquad (6.48)$$

where n_1 and n_2 are integers. Thus the basis set of $2p_z$ carbon orbitals has three indices $|n, j\rangle \rightarrow |n_1, n_2, j\rangle$. You can see from Fig. 6.4 that there are two carbon atoms per unit cell so that the index j takes on two values. Let us use a Hückel Hamiltonian for the graphite plane in exactly the same way that we did for benzene and butadiene; i.e., the diagonal matrix elements are represented by the symbol α. The matrix elements between

190

the orbitals of neighbouring carbon atoms are represented by β, and all other elements are zero.

$$\langle n'_1, n'_2, j' | H | n_1, n_2, j \rangle = \begin{cases} \alpha & \text{diagonal elements} \\ \beta & \text{nearest neighbours} \\ 0 & \text{otherwise} \end{cases} \quad (6.49)$$

Then

$$H_{j'j}(\vec{k}) = \sum_{n_1, n_2} \langle n'_1, n'_2, j' | H | n_1, n_2, j \rangle \, e^{i\vec{k}\{(n_1 - n'_1)\vec{a}_1 + (n_2 - n'_2)\vec{a}_2\}}$$

$$= \sum_{n_1, n_2} \langle 0, 0, j' | H | n_1, n_2, j \rangle \, e^{i\vec{k}\{n_1\vec{a}_1 + n_2\vec{a}_2\}}$$

$$= \begin{pmatrix} \alpha & \beta\{1 + e^{-i\vec{k}\cdot\vec{a}_1} + e^{-i\vec{k}(\vec{a}_1 + \vec{a}_2)}\} \\ \beta\{1 + e^{i\vec{k}\cdot\vec{a}_1} + e^{i\vec{k}(\vec{a}_1 + \vec{a}_2)}\} & \alpha \end{pmatrix}$$

$$(6.50)$$

Solving the quadratic equation,

$$\det |H_{j'j}(\vec{k}) - E_b(\vec{k})\,\delta_{j'j}| = 0 \quad (6.51)$$

we find two bands of allowed energy levels

$$E_{\pm}(\vec{k}) = \alpha \pm |\beta|\{3 + 2\cos(\vec{k}\cdot\vec{a}_1) + 2\cos(\vec{k}\cdot\vec{a}_2)$$
$$+ 2\cos(\vec{k}\cdot\vec{a}_1 + \vec{k}\cdot\vec{a}_2)\}^{\frac{1}{2}} \quad (6.52)$$

The bands $E_{\pm}(\vec{k})$ are illustrated in Fig. 6.5. The allowed values of $\vec{k}$ can be determined using periodic boundary conditions. Suppose that we impose periodic boundary conditions at the edges of a parallelogram in the graphite plane and that two of the edges are defined by the vectors $n\vec{a}_1$ and $n\vec{a}_2$. Then the parallelogram will contain $N = n^2$ unit cells. The periodic boundary conditions then require that

$$e^{in\vec{k}\cdot\vec{a}_1} = e^{in\vec{k}\cdot\vec{a}_2} = 1 \quad (6.53)$$

The values of k which fulfil this requirement and which fall within the first Brillouin zone are given by

$$\vec{k} = \frac{2\pi}{n}\left\{\left(l_1 - \frac{n}{2}\right)\vec{b}_1 + \left(l_2 - \frac{n}{2}\right)\vec{b}_2\right\}$$

$$l_1 = 1, 2, 3, \ldots, n$$
$$l_2 = 1, 2, 3, \ldots, n \quad (6.54)$$

Other integral values of l_1 and l_2 satisfy the boundary conditions, Eq. (6.53), but they do not lead to any new linearly independent solutions. From Eq. (6.54) we can see that the number of allowed values of $\vec{k}$ which fall within the first Brillouin zone is $N = n^2$; that is, it is just the same as

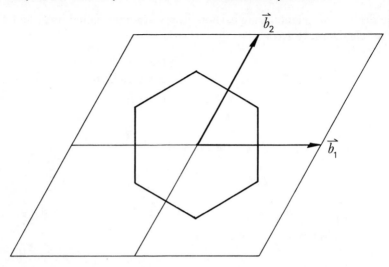

Figure 6.5a shows two basis vectors of the graphite reciprocal lattice, $\vec{b}_1$ and $\vec{b}_2$. All other reciprocal lattice vectors can be expressed as integral multiples of $\vec{b}_1$ and $\vec{b}_2$. The Brillouin zone boundaries are formed by perpendicular bisectors of the reciprocal lattice vectors.

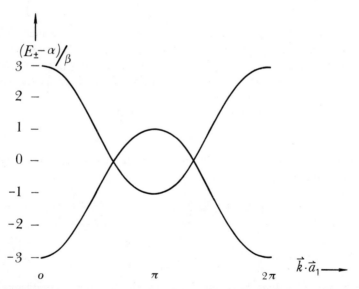

Figure 6.5b shows the two π-electron bands of graphite:
$$E_\pm = \alpha \pm |\beta|\{3 + 2 \cos (\vec{k}\cdot\vec{a}_1) + 2 \cos (\vec{k}\cdot\vec{a}_2) + 2 \cos (\vec{k}\cdot\vec{a}_1 + \vec{k}\cdot\vec{a}_2)\}^{1/2}$$
plotted along the line $\vec{k}\cdot\vec{a}_1 = \vec{k}\cdot\vec{a}_2$.

the number of unit cells inside the region at the edges of which the boundary conditions were applied. This result is independent of the shape of the boundary and it holds also if we instead require the wave function to vanish at the edges as in Eq. (6.18). In the case of our graphite plane lattice, each unit cell contains two carbon atoms each of which contributes two π-electrons to the pool giving a total of $2N$. If each of the crystal orbitals is doubly-filled, then the N lowest-energy orbitals will be occupied. This means that if the two bands of Eq. (6.52) were separated by an energy gap, the lower band would be completely filled and the upper band would be completely empty. However, as it happens, the two bands touch at the point where $\vec{k}.\vec{a}_1 = \vec{k}.\vec{a}_2 = 2\pi/3$, and for this reason graphite conducts electricity.

Problem (6.1) Try to carry out a similar calculation on the electron bands of diamond.

The Fermi surface; the electrical conductivity and binding energy of metals

In the absence of an electric field, the filled levels of a polymer or crystal are bounded by a surface of constant energy called the 'Fermi surface' which is symmetrically placed with respect to the origin of the coordinates in k-space. Thus in the absence of an electric field each filled orbital with wave number $\vec{k}$ is balanced by another filled orbital with wave number $-\vec{k}$. The effect of the field is to shift the Fermi surface so that the origin of the k coordinates no longer lies at its centre. The result is that some of the filled orbitals are now not balanced by filled orbitals with the opposite value of momentum. This situation corresponds to a net electron momentum which shows itself as a current. *The conductivity of metals results from the incomplete filling of a band.* For example, in a monovalent metal the highest filled orbital of an isolated atom is only singly occupied. When the constituent atoms are brought together to form the metallic crystal, the interaction between them broadens this singly occupied energy level into a half-filled band. The high cohesive energy results from the fact that the filled crystal orbitals in the lower half of the valence band all have a lower energy than the highest filled orbital of the isolated metal atom. For example, consider a metal with a simple cubic lattice structure and only one atom per unit cell. Then only one atomic orbital per unit cell will enter the crystal orbital. This means that in this simple example both the orbital index j and the band index b of our previous formalism can be dropped. Equation (6.35) becomes unnecessary and we can evaluate the energy as a function of $\vec{k}$ directly from the lattice sum, Eq. (6.34)

$$E(\vec{k}) = \sum_n \langle n'|H|n\rangle\, e^{i\vec{k}(X_n - X_{n'})} \qquad (6.55)$$

If we neglect all interactions except between nearest neighbours as in the Hückel approximation, then $\langle n'|H|n \rangle$ has the form

$$\langle n'|H|n \rangle = \begin{cases} \alpha & \text{diagonal elements} \\ \beta & \text{nearest neighbours} \\ 0 & \text{otherwise} \end{cases} \qquad (6.56)$$

and

$$E(\vec{k}) = \alpha - 2|\beta|\{\cos(k_1 d) + \cos(k_2 d) + \cos(k_3 d)\} \qquad (6.57)$$

where d is the lattice spacing. Figure 6.6 shows the surfaces of constant energy in k-space defined by Eq. (6.57). The Fermi surface is the surface which divides the filled orbitals from the empty ones. In this example the lattice has a simple cubic structure so that the direct lattice vectors are given by

$$\vec{a}_1 = (d, 0, 0)$$
$$\vec{a}_2 = (0, d, 0)$$
$$\vec{a}_3 = (0, 0, d) \qquad (6.58)$$

where d is the lattice spacing. Let us apply periodic boundary conditions at the faces of a cube three of whose edges are defined by the vectors $n\vec{a}_1$, $n\vec{a}_2$, and $n\vec{a}_3$. The periodic boundary conditions then require that

$$e^{in\vec{k}\cdot\vec{a}_1} = e^{in\vec{k}\cdot\vec{a}_2} = e^{in\vec{k}\cdot\vec{a}_3} = 1 \qquad (6.59)$$

The allowed values of k which fall into the first Brillouin zone are then given by

$$\vec{k} = \frac{2\pi}{n}\left\{\left(l_1 - \frac{n}{2}\right)\vec{b}_1 + \left(l_2 - \frac{n}{2}\right)\vec{b}_2 + \left(l_3 - \frac{n}{2}\right)\vec{b}_3\right\}$$

$$l_1 = 1, 2, 3, \ldots, n$$
$$l_2 = 1, 2, 3, \ldots, n$$
$$l_3 = 1, 2, 3, \ldots, n \qquad (6.60)$$

where $\vec{b}_1$, $\vec{b}_2$, and $\vec{b}_3$ are the reciprocal lattice vectors

$$\vec{b}_1 = \left\{\frac{1}{d}, 0, 0\right\}$$

$$\vec{b}_2 = \left\{0, \frac{1}{d}, 0\right\}$$

$$\vec{b}_3 = \left\{0, 0, \frac{1}{d}\right\} \qquad (6.61)$$

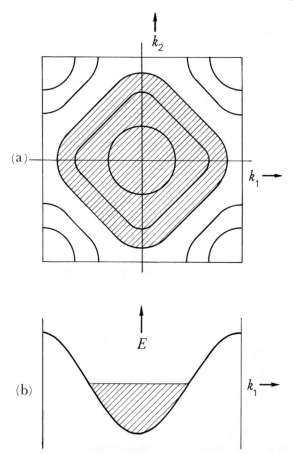

Figures 6.6a and **6.6b** show the energy as a function of wave number for electrons in a simple monovalent metal with cubic crystal structure. In Fig. 6.6a contours of constant energy are plotted as functions of k_1 and k_2 in the plane $k_3 = 0$. Near the origin of k-space, the constant-energy surfaces are spheres, but near the boundary of the first Brillouin zone, the surfaces are distorted, so that they intersect the zone boundary perpendicularly. The filled levels are indicated by shading, i.e., in a simple monovalent metal, the valence band is half filled. The surface in k-space separating the filled levels from the empty ones is known as the 'Fermi surface'.

The cubical volume of the crystal at the faces of which we applied the boundary conditions contains $n^3 \equiv N$ unit cells and each unit cell contains one atom of the monovalent metal and hence contributes one electron. From Eq. (6.60) we can see that there are $n^3 \equiv N$ allowed values of $\vec{k}$ within the first Brillouin zone. Thus the number of different linearly independent crystal orbitals which result from the solution of the secular equation just equals the number of atomic orbitals in the original basis set, as it must. The N electrons will doubly fill the lowest of the crystal orbitals and thus the $\frac{1}{2}N$ orbitals in the lower half of the band will be filled. A metallic crystal is analogous to the hydrogen molecule which obtains an energetic advantage over the isolated atoms because the bonding orbital is doubly-filled while the antibonding orbital is empty. The $\frac{1}{2}N$ doubly-filled crystal orbitals in the bottom of the band correspond to bonding molecular orbitals while the remaining $\frac{1}{2}N$ unfilled orbitals in the top of the band correspond to antibonding molecular orbitals.

Molecular crystals in the Frenkel exciton approximation

The approximation which we have been using is essentially the same as the Hückel LCAO approximation in that it does not explicitly consider the effects of electron-electron repulsion or the effects of the antisymmetry of the many-electron wave function. We could, if we wished, carry through a Hartree–Fock SCF treatment of a polymer or crystal. In that case the entire many-electron wave function of the crystal would be treated as antisymmetric with respect to electron exchange. There is an intermediate model which can be used in the case of a 'molecular crystal' such as crystalline benzene or naphthalene. A molecular crystal is a weakly bound periodic aggregate of tightly bonded constituent molecules. The low melting point of a benzene crystal reflects the small amount of energy required to separate the benzene molecules from one another. A much larger amount of energy would be needed to break the strong covalent bonds of all the benzene rings. The electron wave function of a molecular crystal can be built up from products of molecular wave functions. Suppose that we have found the ground state and excited state wave functions of an isolated constituent molecule. We might do this by the Hartree–Fock SCF method in which case the molecular wave functions would be antisymmetrized. We can separate the Hamiltonian of the crystal into two parts, H_0 and H', where H_0 represents the Hamiltonian of the isolated monomeric subunits and H' represents the interaction between them. The eigenfunctions of H_0 will then just be products of molecular wave functions. The lowest-energy member of this set of zeroth order crystal wave functions will represent all of the constituent molecules in their ground state. If $\Delta_0(n)$ represents the nth molecule in its ground state, then the lowest energy wave function of a crystal containing N subunits is represented by the product

$$|0\rangle \equiv \Delta_0(1)\Delta_0(2)\ldots\Delta_0(N) \tag{6.62}$$

Above this state in energy are N degenerate eigenfunctions of H_0 which represent all of monomeric subunits in their ground state except the nth one which is in the excited state $\Delta_\xi(n)$:

$$|n\rangle = \Delta_0(1)\Delta_0(2)\ldots\Delta_\xi(n)\ldots\Delta_0(N) \qquad (6.63)$$

In the simplest approximation, we can say that the effect of the small intermonomer interaction H' is to hybridize the N degenerate wave functions of Eq. (6.63). We can try to build up eigenfunctions of the complete crystal Hamiltonian $H_0 + H'$ from a linear combination of these N functions

$$|\vec{k}\rangle = \sum_n |n\rangle\langle n \mid \vec{k}\rangle \qquad (6.64)$$

The state $|\vec{k}\rangle$ is to be an eigenfunction of $H = H_0 + H'$ so that we require

$$(H - E_{\vec{k}})|\vec{k}\rangle = \sum_n (H - E_{\vec{k}})|n\rangle\langle n \mid \vec{k}\rangle = 0 \qquad (6.65)$$

Taking the scalar product of Eq. (6.65) with the conjugate function $\langle n'|$ and making use of the orthonormality relation $\langle n' \mid n\rangle = \delta_{n'n}$ we obtain the set of secular equations

$$\sum_n \langle n'|H|n\rangle\langle n \mid \vec{k}\rangle = E_{\vec{k}}\langle n' \mid \vec{k}\rangle \qquad (6.66)$$

Inserting the trial solution

$$\langle n \mid \vec{k}\rangle = \frac{1}{\sqrt{N}} e^{i\vec{k}\cdot\vec{X}_n} \qquad (6.67)$$

into Eq. (6.66) we obtain

$$E_{\vec{k}} = \sum_n \langle n'|H|n\rangle\, e^{i\vec{k}(\vec{X}_n - \vec{X}_{n'})} \qquad (6.68)$$

Because of the translational periodicity of the Hamiltonian the right-hand side of Eq. (6.68) depends only on the relative position of the two unit cells $\vec{X}_n - \vec{X}_{n'}$. It is thus independent of n'. All of the N secular equations redundantly require that $E_{\vec{k}}$ be given by the lattice sum, Eq. (6.68). The argument may by now seem a bit familiar. Equations (6.64)–(6.68) strongly resemble Eqs. (6.1)–(6.9) or Eqs. (6.22)–(6.27) or Eqs. (6.31)–(6.35). This is because the method of solving the set of secular equations always depends on the translational symmetry of the crystal or polymer. However, the wave functions which we are now describing are quite different from the delocalized one-electron crystal orbitals of our previous discussion. Written out in full, the many-electron crystal wave function $|\vec{k}\rangle$ of Eqs. (6.64)–(6.68) becomes

$$|\vec{k}\rangle = \frac{1}{\sqrt{N}} \sum_n \Delta_0(1)\Delta_0(2)\ldots\Delta_\xi(n)\ldots\Delta_0(N)\, e^{i\vec{k}\cdot\vec{X}_n} \qquad \textbf{(6.69)}$$

The quantum theory of atoms, molecules, and photons

States of this kind were introduced by J. Frenkel[8] and R. Peierls[17] in 1931 to explain the optical properties of molecular crystals and have come to be known as 'Frenkel excitons'. *A Frenkel exciton represents an excited state of the entire crystal or polymer* and it involves all of the electrons. *Each of the electrons is localized on its own monomeric subunit although the excitation energy is completely delocalized.* For every excited state of the monomer Δ_ξ there is a band of Frenkel exciton states $|\bar{k}\rangle$ of the form shown in Eq. (6.69). We can try to find the energy distribution of the states in the band by evaluating the lattice sum, Eq. (6.68). To do this we need to know the matrix elements $\langle n'|H|n\rangle$ of the Hamiltonian operator based on the degenerate zeroth-order functions of Eq. (6.63). H_0 is just the sum of the Hamiltonians of the separated monomers

$$H_0 = \sum_n H(n) \tag{6.70}$$

The ground state and excited state monomer wave functions $\Delta_0(n)$ and $\Delta_\xi(n)$ are eigenfunctions of the monomer Hamiltonian H

$$H(n)\Delta_0(n) = E_0\Delta_0(n)$$
$$H(n)\Delta_\xi(n) = E_\xi\Delta_\xi(n)$$
$$n = 1, 2, \ldots, N \tag{6.71}$$

and $|n\rangle$ is an eigenfunction of the sum of monomer Hamiltonians

$$H_0|n\rangle = \{(N-1)E_0 + E_\xi\}|n\rangle \tag{6.72}$$

The interaction part of the Hamiltonian has the form

$$H' = \sum_n \sum_{n'>n} H'(n', n)$$

where $H'(n', n)$ represents the interaction between the monomer n' and the monomer n and involves only the coordinates of electrons in these two monomers.

$$H'(n', n) = \sum_i \sum_j \frac{e^2}{|\bar{x}_i - \bar{x}_j|} \tag{6.73}$$

Here $\bar{x}_i$ represents the position of the ith electron in the nth monomer while $\bar{x}_j$ represents the position of the jth electron in the n'th monomer. Then

$$\langle n'|H'|n\rangle = \int d\tau_1 \int d\tau_2 \ldots \int d\tau_N \Delta_0^*(1) \ldots \Delta_\xi^*(n') \ldots \Delta_0^*(N)$$

$$\times \sum_{n''} \sum_{n'''>n''} H'(n'', n''')\Delta_0(1) \ldots \Delta_\xi(n) \ldots \Delta_0(N)$$

$$= \int d\tau_n \int d\tau_{n'} \Delta_0^*(n)\Delta_\xi^*(n')H'(n, n')\Delta_\xi(n)\Delta_0(n') \tag{6.74}$$

In Eq. (6.74) we have used the orthonormality relation.

$$\int d\tau_n \Delta_\xi^*(n)\Delta_\xi(n) = \int d\tau_n \Delta_0^*(n)\Delta_0(n) = 1$$

$$\int d\tau_n \Delta_\xi^*(n)\Delta_0(n) = 0 \qquad (6.75)$$

The next step is to make a multipole expansion of $H'(n, n')$. This will allow us to relate the width of the exciton band to the monomer transition dipole moment, and hence to relate the optical properties of the crystal or polymer to the optical properties of a monomer. We can expand the function $1/|\bar{x}_i - \bar{x}_j|$ in a Taylor series about the position of the nth monomer $\vec{X}_n$ and the position of the n'th monomer $\vec{X}_{n'}$.

$$\frac{1}{|\bar{x}_i - \bar{x}_j|} = \left[1 + (\bar{x}_i - \vec{X}_n) \cdot \frac{\partial}{\partial \vec{X}_n} + (\bar{x}_j - \vec{X}_{n'}) \cdot \frac{\partial}{\partial \vec{X}_{n'}} \right. $$
$$\left. + \tfrac{1}{2} \left\{ (\bar{x}_i - \vec{X}_n) \cdot \frac{\partial}{\partial \vec{X}_n} \right\} \left\{ (\bar{x}_j - \vec{X}_{n'}) \cdot \frac{\partial}{\partial \vec{X}_{n'}} \right\} + \cdots \right] \frac{1}{|\vec{X}_n - \vec{X}_{n'}|} \quad (6.76)$$

If we substitute this series into Eq. (6.73) and Eq. (6.74) we find that the first three terms vanish because of the orthogonality relationships, Eq. (6.75). The first non-zero term is the fourth term in the series, which corresponds to an interaction between the transition dipole moments of the two monomers. Approximating the series by the first non-zero term we have the off-diagonal matrix element of the Hamiltonian

$$\langle n'|H|n \rangle = \left\{ e \int d\tau_n \Delta_0^*(n) \sum_i (\bar{x}_i - \vec{X}_n) \Delta_\xi(n) \right\} \cdot \frac{\partial}{\partial \vec{X}_n}$$
$$\times \left\{ e \int d\tau_{n'} \Delta_\xi^*(n') \sum_j (\bar{x}_j - \vec{X}_{n'}) \Delta_0(n') \right\} \cdot \frac{\partial}{\partial \vec{X}_{n'}} \frac{1}{|\vec{X}_n - \vec{X}_{n'}|}, \quad n \neq n' \qquad (6.77)$$

The quantity

$$\vec{D}_n \equiv e \int d\tau_n \Delta_0^*(n) \sum_i (\bar{x}_i - \vec{X}_n) \Delta_\xi(n) \qquad \textbf{(6.78)}$$

is called the transition dipole moment of the nth monomer. Using the fact that

$$\frac{\partial^2}{\partial X_n^\alpha \partial X_{n'}^\beta} \frac{1}{|\vec{X}_n - \vec{X}_{n'}|} = \frac{\delta_{\alpha\beta}}{R^3} - \frac{3 R_\alpha R_\beta}{R^5} \qquad (6.79)$$

where $\vec{R}$ is the intermonomer separation

$$\vec{R} \equiv \vec{X}_n - \vec{X}_{n'} \qquad (6.80)$$

we can rewrite the off-diagonal matrix element of Eq. (6.77) in the form

$$\langle n'|H|n\rangle = \frac{\vec{D}_n \cdot \vec{D}_{n'}^*}{R^3} - \frac{3(\vec{D}_n \cdot \vec{R})(\vec{D}_{n'}^* \cdot \vec{R})}{R^5} \tag{6.81}$$

From Eq. (6.72), the diagonal matrix element is

$$\langle n|H|n\rangle = (N-1)E_0 + E_\xi \equiv E_{0\to\xi} \tag{6.82}$$

Then the energy of the Frenkel exciton state $|\vec{k}\rangle$ is given by the lattice sum of Eq. (6.68)

$$E_{\vec{k}} = E_{0\to\xi} + \sum_{n \ne n'} \left\{ \frac{\vec{D}_n \cdot \vec{D}_{n'}^*}{R_{nn'}^3} - \frac{3(\vec{D}_n \cdot \vec{R}_{nn'})(\vec{D}_{n'}^* \cdot \vec{R}_{nn'})}{R_{nn'}^5} \right\} \times e^{i\vec{k} \cdot \vec{R}_{nn'}} \tag{6.83}$$

The dipole-dipole lattice sum, Eq. (6.83) has been evaluated explicitly for simple cubic crystals by Cohen and Keffer[25] using mathematical methods introduced by Ewald, Born, and Bradburn.[26] The result is that

$$E_{\vec{k}} = E_{0\to\xi} + \frac{4\pi e^2}{3d^3} D^2 (1 - 3\cos^2 \theta) \tag{6.84}$$

where d is the lattice spacing, D is the magnitude of the transition dipole moment vector $\vec{D} \equiv \vec{D}_n = \vec{D}_{n'}$ and θ is the angle between $\vec{D}$ and $\vec{k}$. An exciton whose wave number $\vec{k}$ is perpendicular to $\vec{D}$ so that $\cos^2 \theta = 0$ is called a transverse exciton. An exciton where $\vec{k}$ is parallel to $\vec{D}$ so that $\cos^2 \theta = 1$ is called a longitudinal exciton. From Eq. (6.84) we can see that the energy difference between a transverse exciton and a longitudinal exciton in a simple cubic crystal is given by

$$E = \frac{4\pi e^2 D^2}{d^3} \tag{6.85}$$

Measured values of this splitting do not agree well with the calculated values. Craig has proposed that the discrepancies may be due to long-range retardation terms which are neglected in the simple Coulomb interaction of Eq. (6.73).

We said above that a polymer can be treated as a molecular crystal provided that the monomeric subunits do not interact too strongly with one another. The excited states of such a polymer are Frenkel exciton states. Moffit has used this model to develop a theory of the optical properties of polymers.

Problem (6.2) Include one higher term in the expansion of Eq. (6.76) and Eq. (6.81) (i.e., calculate the dipole–quadrupole interaction). How does it decrease as a function of internuclear separation?

High melting-point crystals treated in the crystal orbital approximation; effective mass

In a tightly bound, high melting-point crystal, the constituent subunits interact strongly with one another and it is not by any means valid to discuss the excited states by means of the Frenkel exciton approximation. For example, the valence electrons of a metallic crystal, far from being localized on a particular unit cell, behave almost like free electrons confined to a box the size of the crystal. For a free electron the time-independent Schrödinger equation is

$$-\frac{\hbar^2}{2m_0} \nabla^2 |\vec{k}\rangle = E |\vec{k}\rangle \tag{6.86}$$

which has solutions of the form

$$|\vec{k}\rangle = \frac{1}{\sqrt{Nd^3}} e^{i\vec{k}\cdot\vec{x}} \tag{6.87}$$

where Nd^3 is the volume of the box within which the electron is confined. If the electron is in a cubical box three of whose edges are given by $n\vec{a}_1$, $n\vec{a}_2$, and $n\vec{a}_3$ (Eq. (6.58)), then the allowed values of $\vec{k}$ are given by Eq. (6.60) except that l_1, l_2, and l_3 can now take on any integral value at all and still lead to new linearly independent solutions whereas before, all of the different linearly independent solutions lay in the range $l_1, l_2, l_3 = 1$, ..., n. The energy $E(\vec{k})$ of the free electron in the box can be found by substituting the wave function $|\vec{k}\rangle$ of Eq. (6.87) into the Schrödinger equation, Eq. (6.86),

$$E(\vec{k}) = \frac{\hbar^2}{2m_0} (k_1^2 + k_2^2 + k_3^2) \equiv \frac{\hbar^2}{2m_0} k^2 \tag{6.88}$$

Thus, for a free electron, the surfaces of constant energy in k-space will be spheres. We can compare $E(\vec{k})$ for the free electron, Eq. (6.88), with $E(\vec{k})$ for the electron in the cubic metal lattice, Eq. (6.57), by expanding the cosines in a Taylor series. Then for small values of k Eq. (6.57) becomes approximately

$$E(\vec{k}) = \alpha - 6|\beta| + |\beta| d^2(k_1^2 + k_2^2 + k_3^2)$$
$$\equiv E_0 + |\beta| d^2 k^2 \equiv E_0 + \frac{\hbar^2 k^2}{2m_0^*} \tag{6.89}$$

This means that at the bottom of the band (i.e., for small values of k) the surfaces of constant energy for an electron moving in a cubic metal lattice will be spheres just as they are in the case of a free electron. The

201

quantity which appears in Eq. (6.89) in place of the free electron mass m_0 is

$$m_0^* = \frac{\hbar^2}{2|\beta|d^2} \tag{6.90}$$

The behaviour of an electron moving in a cubic metal lattice, under the influence of electric and magnetic fields, is therefore similar to the behaviour of a free electron except that it seems to have an 'effective mass' given by Eq. (6.90). If we express the ratio of the effective mass m_0^* to the free electron mass m_0 in terms of the Bohr radius $a_0 = \hbar^2/m_0 e^2$ then we have

$$\frac{m_0^*}{m_0} = \left(\frac{a_0}{d}\right)^2 \left(\frac{e^2/a_0}{2|\beta|}\right) \tag{6.91}$$

The larger the interatomic interaction energy β the smaller the effective mass. Wide bands correspond to small effective mass m_0^* and narrow bands to large m_0^*. The example of a cubic crystal which we have discussed here is a rather special case. In other types of lattices, the lattice sum, Eq. (6.55), can lead to an $E(\vec{k})$ whose Taylor series contains an anisotropic quadratic term. In general, an expansion of $E(\vec{k})$ around the point $\vec{k} = 0$ has the form

$$E(\vec{k}) \approx E(0) + \tfrac{1}{2} \sum_{i,j} \left[\frac{\partial^2 E}{\partial k_i \, \partial k_j}\right]_{\vec{k}=0} k_i k_j + \cdots$$

$$\equiv E(0) + \frac{\hbar^2}{2} \sum_{i,j} \left(\frac{1}{m^*}\right)^{ij} k_i k_j + \cdots \tag{6.92}$$

where the 'reciprocal effective mass tensor' is defined as

$$\left(\frac{1}{m^*}\right)^{ij} \equiv \frac{2}{\hbar^2} \left[\frac{\partial^2 E}{\partial k_i \, \partial k_j}\right]_{\vec{k}=0} \tag{6.93}$$

In the general case, Eq. (6.92), where the quadratic term in $E(\vec{k})$ is not isotropic, the surfaces of constant energy at the bottom of the band are ellipsoids rather than spheres.

Wannier excitons and mixed excitons

Now suppose that we consider an ionic crystal. In the ground state of such a crystal the highest filled band will be completely filled. If an electron is removed from this band the state of highest energy will be empty. If an electric field is applied, the highest energy crystal orbital in the band will have a non-zero momentum vector $\hbar\vec{k}$. Since that state is empty while all of the other states in the band are filled, the situation corresponds to a net transport of negative charge in the direction opposite to $\vec{k}$. This is equivalent to a transport of positive charge in the direction of $\vec{k}$. In other words, the hole in the filled band behaves like a particle with a unit positive charge. In fact, if an electron is lifted up from the filled band to an empty band, the hole which is left in the filled band can attract the electron and the two can form a bound state analogous to the hydrogen atom. (It is even more closely analogous to positronium—the bound system formed by an electron and an antielectron or positron.) If the effective mass of the hole is m_h^* and if m_e^* is the effective mass of the electron then the 'reduced mass' which enters the equation of motion of the relative coordinates (see Eqs. (1.102)–(1.105)), is

$$\mu \equiv \frac{m_e^* m_h^*}{m_e^* + m_h^*} \tag{6.94}$$

The bound states of the electron-hole system are just like the bound states of the hydrogen atom except that reduced mass μ of Eq. (6.94) enters the expression for the energy, Eq. (2.8), in place of the electron mass m_0.

$$E = -\frac{1}{2}\left(\frac{1}{137n}\right)^2 \mu c^2 \tag{6.95}$$

This discrete hydrogen-like (or positronium-like) spectrum of bound states appears just below a continuum of excited states where the electron-hole pair are not bound. The concept of a bound state of an electron-hole pair was first introduced by G. Wannier,[27] and such a state is called a 'Wannier exciton'. Wannier exciton states can be observed in the spectra of many high melting-point insulating crystals such as ZnS. Rice and co-workers have suggested that something resembling an electron-hole bound state can occur even in a low melting-point molecular crystal such as benzene or naphthalene. In discussing the excited states of molecular crystals (Frenkel excitons) we approximated the eigenfunctions $|\vec{k}\rangle$ of the crystal Hamiltonian $H = H_0 + H'$ by a linear combination of N degenerate eigenfunctions of H_0, Eq. (6.63). Rice[20] improves the approximation by enlarging the set of basis functions so that it includes 'charge transfer states'. For example, one might include states of the form

$$|n, n'\rangle \equiv \Delta_0(1)\Delta_0(2)\ldots\Delta_e(n)\ldots\Delta_h(n')\ldots\Delta_0(N) \tag{6.96}$$

This represents all of the monomeric subunits in their ground state except the nth monomer to which an extra electron has been added and the n'th monomer from which an electron has been taken away. Rice has shown that when charge transfer states of this kind are added to the basis set, the resulting Frenkel excitons include electron-hole bound states reminiscent of Wannier excitons. Rice calls these states 'mixed excitons'. It should be noticed that the wave function of a mixed exciton is more closely related to that of a Frenkel exciton than it is to that of a Wannier exciton. In a Wannier exciton, the starting point is a set of electron orbitals which are delocalized over the entire crystal. In a Frenkel exciton or in a mixed exciton the starting point is a set of many-electron wave functions each of which is a product of Slater determinants as in Eq. (6.63) or Eq. (6.69). Such a product represents each electron as localized on its own monomeric subunit. The Frenkel exciton model and the mixed exciton model are appropriate for describing the excited states of low melting-point molecular crystals. The Wannier exciton model is appropriate for describing the excited states of tightly bound, high melting-point non-conducting crystals.

In discussing Wannier exciton states we introduced the concept of effective mass, Eq. (6.93). It is possible to observe the effective mass of an electron in a metallic lattice by applying a magnetic field and observing the 'cyclotron frequency'. For simplicity let us consider the case of a cubic lattice where the effective mass is isotropic. According to classical electrodynamics, an electron of mass m_0^*, under the influence of a magnetic field in the z direction $\vec{H} = (0, 0, \mathscr{H})$, follows a helical path such that the x, y, and z coordinates as functions of time are given by Eq. (1.179):

$$x = r_0 \sin \omega_0 t$$
$$y = r_0 \cos \omega_0 t$$
$$z = v_{\parallel} t \tag{6.97}$$

The frequency ω_0 is called the cyclotron frequency and according to Eq. (1.180) it is proportional to the magnetic field strength $\mathscr{H}$ and inversely proportional to the electron mass m_0^*:

$$\omega_0 = \frac{e\mathscr{H}}{m_0^* c} \tag{6.98}$$

This frequency is independent of r_0, the radius of the orbit. Radiation of the cyclotron frequency can be absorbed by an electron in such an orbit, the energy of the radiation being used to increase the radius r_0 and hence to increase the kinetic energy of the electron. For a particular magnetic field strength $\mathscr{H}$, the frequency at which this absorption occurs is a measure of the effective mass m_0^*. A quantum mechanical treatment of the 'cyclotron resonance' leads to the same result.

Nearly-free electrons perturbed by a periodic potential; three-dimensional Brillouin zones

The free-electron picture gives us another way of approaching the problem of an electron moving in a crystal lattice. *Instead of starting with atomic orbitals and using them to build up the crystal orbitals we can alternatively begin by regarding the electrons, in the first approximation, as moving freely in a box the size of the crystal. From this point of view, the periodic potential of the lattice of atomic cores is a perturbation which modifies the free-electron wave functions and energies.* The effective potential $V(\vec{x})$ experienced by an electron in a crystal lattice has translational symmetry such that displacement by any lattice vector $\vec{X}_n$, Eq. (6.36), leaves $V(\vec{x})$ unaltered

$$V(\vec{x} + \vec{X}_n) = V(\vec{x}) \tag{6.99}$$

In the same way that a periodic function of a single coordinate can be expanded in a Fourier sine series, (see Eq. (1.66)), a function of the three space coordinates which displays the lattice periodicity can be expanded in a series of sinusoidal functions involving the reciprocal lattice vectors $\vec{G}_l$

$$V(\vec{x}) = \sum_{\vec{G}_l} V_{\vec{G}_l} e^{-i\vec{G}_l \cdot \vec{x}} \tag{6.100}$$

where $\vec{G}_l$ is defined by Eq. (6.38). It is easy to see that a function of this form will have the periodicity of the lattice. If we displace $\vec{x}$ by a direct lattice vector $\vec{X}_n$ we have

$$V(\vec{x} + \vec{X}_n) = \sum_{\vec{G}_l} V_{\vec{G}_l} e^{-i\vec{G}_l \cdot (\vec{x} + \vec{X}_n)}$$

$$= \sum_{\vec{G}_l} V_{\vec{G}_l} e^{-i\vec{G}_l \cdot \vec{x}} = V(\vec{x}) \tag{6.101}$$

Here, as in Eq. (6.43), we have used the fact that the scalar product of a direct and a reciprocal lattice vector is always an integral multiple of 2π, Eq. (6.41) and Eq. (6.42). The basis functions $e^{-i\vec{G}_l \cdot \vec{x}}$ used in the Fourier series, Eq. (6.100), are orthogonal but not normalized. If $\vec{a}_1$, $\vec{a}_2$, and $\vec{a}_3$ are the vectors defining a unit cell then the volume of the cell is

$$|a_{ij}| = \det \begin{vmatrix} a_{11} & a_{12} & a_{13} \\ a_{21} & a_{22} & a_{23} \\ a_{31} & a_{32} & a_{33} \end{vmatrix}$$

$$= (\vec{a}_1 \wedge \vec{a}_2) \cdot \vec{a}_3 \tag{6.102}$$

(Think of the parallelogram two of whose edges are the direct-lattice basis vectors $\vec{a}_1$ and $\vec{a}_2$. The area of the parallelogram is given by their cross product $\vec{a}_1 \wedge \vec{a}_2$. Taking the scalar product with the third lattice vector gives the volume of the parallelepiped three of whose edges are $\vec{a}_1$, $\vec{a}_2$, and $\vec{a}_3$, that is, the volume of the unit cell.)

The quantum theory of atoms, molecules, and photons

The orthonormality relationship can thus be written in the form

$$\frac{1}{|a_{ij}|} \int\limits_{\substack{\text{unit}\\\text{cell}}} d^3x \; e^{-i(\vec{G}_l - \vec{G}_{l'})\cdot\vec{x}} = \delta_{l_1 l_1'} \delta_{l_2, l_2'} \delta_{l_3 l_3'}$$

$$\equiv \delta_{l,l'} \tag{6.103}$$

Then the Fourier coefficients $V_{\vec{G}_l}$ in the series of Eq. (6.100) can be found by multiplying on the left by the conjugate function ϕ_l^*, and integrating over the unit cell

$$V_{\vec{G}_l} = \frac{1}{|a_{ij}|} \int\limits_{\substack{\text{unit}\\\text{cell}}} d^3x \; e^{i\vec{G}_l \cdot \vec{x}} V(\vec{x}) \tag{6.104}$$

Our programme is to treat the periodic potential $V(\vec{x}) \equiv H'$ as a small perturbation which slightly distorts the free-electron wave functions and energies. If the free-electron wave-functions are normalized over a volume containing N unit cells then these wave functions are given by Eq. (6.87)

$$|\psi_{\vec{k}}^{(0)}\rangle \equiv |\vec{k}\rangle = \frac{1}{\sqrt{N|a_{ij}|}} e^{i\vec{k}\cdot\vec{x}} \tag{6.105}$$

The corresponding 'zeroth-order' energies are

$$E_{\vec{k}}^{(0)} = \frac{\hbar^2}{2m_0} \vec{k}.\vec{k} \equiv \frac{\hbar}{2m_0} k^2 \tag{6.106}$$

Then, according to time-independent perturbation theory, Eqs. (V.18) and (V.19), the perturbed wave functions and energies are given by

$$|\psi_{\vec{k}}\rangle = |\psi_{\vec{k}}^{(0)}\rangle + |\psi_k^{(')}\rangle + \cdots$$

$$= |\vec{k}\rangle + \frac{2m_0}{\hbar^2} \sum_{\vec{k}' \neq \vec{k}} \frac{|\vec{k}'\rangle\langle\vec{k}'|V|\vec{k}\rangle}{(k'^2 - k^2)} + \cdots \tag{6.107}$$

and

$$E_{\vec{k}} = E_{\vec{k}}^{(0)} + E_{\vec{k}}^{(1)} + E_{\vec{k}}^{(2)} + \cdots$$

$$= \frac{\hbar^2}{2m_0} k^2 + \langle\vec{k}|V|\vec{k}\rangle$$

$$+ \frac{2m_0}{\hbar^2} \sum_{k' \neq k} \frac{\langle\vec{k}|V|\vec{k}'\rangle\langle\vec{k}'|V|\vec{k}\rangle}{(k'^2 - k^2)} + \cdots \tag{6.108}$$

It is easy to evaluate the matrix elements $\langle\vec{k}'|V|\vec{k}\rangle$; we just use the Fourier expansion of $V(\vec{x})$, Eq. (6.100), and the requirement that $\vec{k}$ and $\vec{k}'$ must obey periodic boundary conditions at the edges of the volume of normalization. Then

$$\langle \vec{k}'|V|\vec{k}\rangle = \frac{1}{\sqrt{N|a_{ij}|}} \sum_{\vec{G}_l} V_{\vec{G}_l} \int d^3x\, e^{i(\vec{k}-\vec{k}'-\vec{G}_l)\cdot\vec{x}}$$

$$= \sum_{\vec{G}_l} V_{\vec{G}_l}\, \delta_{\vec{k}',\vec{k}-\vec{G}_l} \qquad (6.109)$$

In other words, we get a non-zero value for the matrix element $\langle \vec{k}'|V|\vec{k}\rangle$ only when $\vec{k}' - \vec{k}$ is a reciprocal lattice vector. Using Eq. (6.109) we can rewrite Eq. (6.108) in the form

$$E_{\vec{k}} = \frac{\hbar^2}{2m_0} k^2 + V_0$$

$$+ \frac{2m_0}{\hbar^2} \sum_{\vec{k}'\neq\vec{k}} \sum_{\vec{G}_l} \frac{|V_{\vec{G}_l}|^2\, \delta_{\vec{k}',\vec{k}-\vec{G}_l}}{\vec{k}'.\vec{k}' - \vec{k}.\vec{k}}$$

$$= \frac{\hbar^2 k^2}{2m_0} + V_0 + \frac{2m_0}{\hbar^2} \sum_{\vec{G}_l\neq 0} \frac{|V_{\vec{G}_l}|^2}{(\vec{k}-\vec{G}_l).(\vec{k}-\vec{G}_l) - \vec{k}.\vec{k}} + \cdots \qquad (6.110)$$

The denominator of the second-order term vanishes when

$$(\vec{k} - \vec{G}_l).(\vec{k} - \vec{G}_l) - \vec{k}.\vec{k} = (\vec{G}_l - 2\vec{k}).\vec{G}_l = 0 \qquad (6.111)$$

This condition will be fulfilled whenever the vector $\vec{k}$ touches a plane perpendicularly bisecting a reciprocal lattice vector. Such a plane is, by definition, the boundary of a Brillouin zone.

Problem (6.3) Construct the boundaries of the first few Brillouin zones in the case of the plane of graphite, Fig. 6.4.

The band-gap at the edge of a Brillouin zone

As we approach the boundary of a Brillouin zone (i.e., as we approach a plane which is the perpendicular bisector of a reciprocal lattice vector) the effect of the periodic potential becomes more and more pronounced. Finally very near to the boundary the perturbation series fails to converge. The reason for this divergence is basically a degeneracy in the zeroth-order energies. At the boundary of a Brillouin zone the unperturbed free-electron energy $E^{(0)}(\vec{k}) = (\hbar^2/2m_0)k^2$ is exactly matched by the energy $E^{(0)}(\vec{k} - \vec{G}_l) = (\hbar^2/2m_0)(\vec{k} - \vec{G}_l).(\vec{k} - \vec{G}_l)$ corresponding to the wave number $\vec{k}$ displaced by a reciprocal lattice vector $\vec{G}_l$. Near to the zone boundary we can approximate the wave function as a linear combination of the two degenerate zeroth-order functions $|\vec{k}\rangle$ and $|\vec{k} - \vec{G}_l\rangle$

$$|\psi_{\vec{k}}\rangle \approx |\vec{k}\rangle C_1 + |\vec{k} - \vec{G}_l\rangle C_2 \qquad (6.112)$$

Then

$$(H - E_k)|\psi_{\bar{k}}\rangle = 0$$

$$= \left(-\frac{\hbar^2}{2m_0}\nabla^2 + V - E_{\bar{k}}\right)(|\bar{k}\rangle C_1 + |\bar{k} - \bar{G}_l\rangle C_2) \quad (6.113)$$

Taking the scalar product of Eq. (6.113) first with $\langle\bar{k}|$ and then with $\langle\bar{k} - \bar{G}_l|$ we obtain the two secular equations

$$\left(\frac{\hbar^2}{2m_0}k^2 + \langle\bar{k}|V|\bar{k}\rangle - E_{\bar{k}}\right)C_1 + \langle\bar{k}|V|\bar{k} - \bar{G}_l\rangle C_2 = 0 \quad (6.114)$$

$$\langle\bar{k} - \bar{G}_l|V|\bar{k}\rangle C_1 + \left(\frac{\hbar^2}{2m_0}k^2 + \langle\bar{k} - \bar{G}_l|V|\bar{k} - \bar{G}_l\rangle - E_{\bar{k}}\right)C_2 = 0$$

$$(6.115)$$

Equation (6.109) relates the matrix elements of V to the Fourier coefficients,

$$\langle\bar{k}|V|\bar{k}\rangle = \langle\bar{k} - \bar{G}|V|\bar{k} - \bar{G}\rangle = \frac{1}{|a_{ij}|}\int_{\substack{\text{unit}\\\text{cell}}} d^3x V(\bar{x}) \equiv V_0 \quad (6.116)$$

and

$$\langle\bar{k}|V|\bar{k} - \bar{G}_l\rangle = \langle\bar{k} - \bar{G}_l|V|\bar{k}\rangle$$

$$= V_{\bar{G}_l} \quad (6.117)$$

The secular equations, Eqs. (6.114) and (6.115), will thus have a non-trivial solution only if

$$\det\begin{vmatrix} \dfrac{\hbar^2}{2m_0}k^2 + V_0 - E_{\bar{k}} & V_{\bar{G}_l} \\[2ex] V_{\bar{G}_l} & \dfrac{\hbar^2}{2m_0}k^2 + V_0 - E_{\bar{k}} \end{vmatrix} = 0 \quad (6.118)$$

This is a quadratic equation for $E_{\bar{k}}$ with two roots

$$E_{\bar{k}} = \frac{\hbar^2 k^2}{2m_0} + V_0 \pm V_{\bar{G}_l} \quad \textbf{(6.119)}$$

In other words *according to the approach which starts with free-electron wave functions as a basis set and which treats the periodic potential of the lattice as a perturbation, energy gaps will occur at the boundaries of the Brillouin zones. The energy discontinuity which occurs at the zone boundary perpendicularly bisecting the reciprocal lattice vector $\bar{G}_l$ will be $2V_{\bar{G}_l}$ where $V_{\bar{G}_l}$ is a coefficient in the Fourier series for V, Eq. (6.100). We have ap-*

proached the problem of a periodic structure from two opposite directions. In the LCAO approach, we started with atomic orbitals or unit cell orbitals. When the separate atoms or unit cells were assembled to form a periodic polymer or crystal, the interaction broadened each monomer level into a band of allowed energy levels. In the second approach we started with free-electron wave functions. The allowed energies of these free electrons formed a continuum. However, the effect of a periodic perturbing potential was to produce energy gaps at the Brillouin zone boundaries. It is interesting (and encouraging) that these two opposite approximations both predict more or less the same thing, i.e., the existence of allowed and forbidden energy bands.

Problem (6.4) Consider the one-dimensional Schrödinger equation for an electron moving in the periodic square-well potential,

$$V(x) = \begin{cases} E & 0 < x \le L/2 \\ 0 & L/2 < x \le L \end{cases}$$
$$V(x + L) = V(x)$$

Make a Fourier series expansion of $V(x)$ using Eq. (6.101) and Eq. (6.104). Use Eq. (6.110) and Eq. (6.119) to find $E_{\bar{k}}$ near the boundary of the first Brillouin zone and far from the boundary, and make a sketch of $E_{\bar{k}}$. Is there a relationship between the band gap and the effective mass of the electron at the zone boundary?

Diffraction of electrons, neutrons, and X-rays; the phase problem

In chapter 1, Eq. (1.124), we discussed Young's experiment to demonstrate interference effects in optics. Just before the First World War, a father and son scientific team, W. H. Bragg and W. L. Bragg, were working with J. J. Thomson at the Cavendish Laboratory in Cambridge when word arrived from Germany that Max von Laue had succeeded in performing a variation of Young's experiment using a beam of Roentgen's X-rays instead of a beam of light. The beam of X-rays was scattered from a crystal lattice. Each atom of the lattice was the source of a spherical wavelet (in accordance with Huygens' principle). At certain angles the wavelets added together constructively and at other angles they cancelled one another. Von Laue's observation of interference effects using a beam of X-rays showed conclusively that X-rays have a wavelike nature and that the wave length is comparable with the lattice spacing of a crystal. Thomson and the Braggs were very much excited by von Laue's experiments and they set out to repeat them. The Braggs discovered that the diffraction pattern from a molecular crystal was very much complicated by the fact that there is more than one atom per unit cell. They showed that an analysis of the diffraction pattern can be used to determine the relative positions of the atoms within the unit-cell. This was the beginning of chemical crystallography. Both the Braggs were later knighted and they both received the Nobel prize for their work. Some of the credit should go to J. J. Thomson, whose scientific style influenced not only the Braggs but also Rutherford. Through Rutherford, Thomson's outlook and style came down to Bohr, and through Bohr the tradition was passed to the many outstanding scientists who were produced by Bohr's institute in Copenhagen. J. J. Thomson's own son, G. P. Thomson, inherited a knack for doing things with electrons from his father, who had discovered them. Together with Davisson and Germer he directed a monoenergetic beam of electrons at the surface of a crystal, and he observed that at certain angles the electrons were strongly scattered. At other angles there was almost no scattering at all. This experiment is exactly analogous to Young's experiment. Each atom of the crystal is a source of spherical wavelets which can be constructed by means of Huygens principle. At certain angles the wavelets interfere constructively and at other angles, destructively. Equation (6.107) allows us to make the discussion of such an electron diffraction experiment a little more quantitative. Suppose that the incoming electron beam is represented by the plane wave $|\vec{k}\rangle$ of Eq. (6.105). Then, according to perturbation theory, the probability that such an electron will be scattered into a state $|\vec{k}'\rangle \neq |\vec{k}\rangle$ by the periodic lattice potential V is given by

$$
\left| \langle \vec{k}' \mid \psi_{\vec{k}} \rangle \right|^2 = \frac{2m_0}{\hbar^2} \left| \frac{\langle \vec{k}' | V | \vec{k} \rangle}{(k'^2 - k^2)} \right|^2
$$

$$
= \left| \frac{2m_0}{\hbar^2} \frac{\sum_{\vec{G}_l} V_{\vec{G}_l} \, \delta_{\vec{k}', \vec{k} - \vec{G}_l}}{k'^2 - k^2} \right|^2 \tag{6.120}
$$

There are three things to notice about Eq. (6.120). First of all, in this approximation, there is no scattering at all unless the difference between the initial and final electron momenta is equal to a reciprocal lattice vector

$$
\vec{k} - \vec{k}' = \vec{G}_l \tag{6.121}
$$

Secondly, the scattering is largest when the energies of the incoming and outgoing states are nearly equal,

$$
k'^2 \approx k^2 \tag{6.122}
$$

Finally, when the scattered electron wave number fulfils Eqs. (6.121) and (6.122) the scattering probability is proportional to the square of the Fourier coefficient $V_{\vec{G}_l}$.

$$I_e(\vec{G}_l) = \left| \langle \vec{k}' \mid \psi_{\vec{k}} \rangle \right|^2 \sim \left| V_{\vec{G}_l} \right|^2 = \left| V_{\vec{k}-\vec{k}'} \right|^2$$

$$= \left| \frac{1}{\left| a_{ij} \right|} \int_{\substack{\text{unit} \\ \text{cell}}} d^3x \; e^{i(\vec{k}-\vec{k}')\cdot\vec{x}} V(\vec{x}) \right|^2 \tag{6.123}$$

Suppose that we do an electron diffraction experiment by allowing a beam of monoenergetic electrons of momentum $\hbar\vec{k}$ to fall on a crystal lattice and suppose that we allow the scattered electrons to fall onto a counting device such as a photographic plate. The plate will exhibit a spot at each point where the angle between $\vec{k}$ and $\vec{k}'$ satisfies Eqs. (6.121) and (6.122). Each spot will correspond to a particular reciprocal lattice vector $\vec{G}_l$. The number of electrons arriving at each allowed spot will be proportional to the square of the corresponding Fourier coefficient. By measuring this number and taking the square root we could find the values of all the Fourier coefficients in the series of Eq. (6.104). This would allow us to find the potential $V(\vec{x})$ by inserting the coefficients in the series. The only trouble is that we do not know what sign to give to the square roots. In fact the Fourier coefficients $V_{\vec{G}_l}$ are determined only up to a complex multiplicative factor of modulus 1. This is the famous 'phase problem' of chemical crystallography. The same problem turns up also if we use high energy photons (X-rays) instead of electrons in the diffraction experiment. It can be shown that if the electron charge density $\rho(\vec{x})$ in a large crystal is represented by the Fourier series

$$\rho(\vec{x}) = \sum_{\vec{G}_l} F_{\vec{G}_l} \, e^{-i\vec{G}_l \cdot \vec{x}} \tag{6.124}$$

then the probability that an X-ray of wave number $\vec{k}$ will be elastically scattered into the direction of the wave number $\vec{k}'$ is zero unless $\vec{k} - \vec{k}'$ fulfils Eqs. (6.121) and (6.122). If these two conditions are fulfilled the scattering probability is approximately proportional to the square of the Fourier coefficient $F_{\vec{G}_l}$ provided we are not in an energy range where the X-rays are strongly absorbed.

$$I_x(\vec{G}_l) \sim \left| F_{\vec{G}_l} \right|^2 = \left| F_{\vec{k}-\vec{k}'} \right|^2$$

$$\sim \left| \int_{\substack{\text{unit} \\ \text{cell}}} d^3x \; \rho(\vec{x}) \, e^{i(\vec{k}-\vec{k}')\cdot\vec{x}} \right|^2 \tag{6.125}$$

Again if we knew how to assign the phases we could calculate the Fourier coefficients from the relative intensities of the various reflections, and thus build up a Fourier synthesis of the charge densities within the unit cell, Eq. (6.124). In a neutron diffraction experiment the intensity of a reflection associated with a reciprocal lattice vector $\vec{G}_l = \vec{k} - \vec{k}'$ is proportional to

$$I_N(\vec{G}_l) = \left| \sum_j f_j \, e^{i\vec{G}_l \cdot \vec{x}_j} \right|^2$$

$$= \left| \sum_j f_j \, e^{i(\vec{k} - \vec{k}') \cdot \vec{x}_j} \right|^2 \tag{6.126}$$

In Eq. (6.126) f_j is a measure of the effectiveness of the jth nucleus in scattering neutrons. $\vec{x}_j$ is the position of the jth nucleus measured with respect to the corner of the unit cell. The sum is taken over all the nuclei within a unit cell. The neutron scattering parameters f_j are known from other experiments. If it were possible to assign the correct phase to the square root of the intensity for each reflection it would be possible to determine the positions $\vec{x}_j$ of all the nuclei within the unit cell.

When they are dealing with small molecules, chemical crystallographers usually solve the phase problem by a trial and error method. They have some notion of the position of the atoms in the unit cell, and so they begin by guessing a set of nuclear coordinates $\vec{x}_j$. These guessed coordinates provide a rough approximation of the electron charge density

$$\rho(\vec{x}) \approx \sum_j e_j \, \delta(\vec{x} - \vec{x}_j) \tag{6.127}$$

Putting this rough estimate of $\rho(\vec{x})$ back into the expression for the intensity of an X-ray reflection, Eq. (6.125), one obtains

$$I_x(\vec{G}_l) \sim \left| \int_{\substack{\text{unit} \\ \text{cell}}} d^3x \, e^{i\vec{G}_l \cdot \vec{x}} \sum_j e_j \, \delta(\vec{x} - \vec{x}_j) \right|^2$$

$$= \left| \sum_j e_j \, e^{i\vec{G}_l \cdot \vec{x}_j} \right|^2 \tag{6.128}$$

A computer program calculates the intensities of the various reflections using the guessed values of the nuclear coordinates $\vec{x}_j$ and compares the result with the measured diffraction pattern. The computer then 'refines' the coordinates by trying closely neighbouring values of $\vec{x}_j$ until it obtains the best possible fit with the X-ray diffraction pattern. Then the computer takes the square roots of the actual reflection intensities assigning the phases in accordance with the rough estimate, Eq. (6.128). The properly phased square roots of the reflection intensities are the coefficients $F_{\vec{G}_l}$ needed for a Fourier synthesis of the charge density, Eq. (6.124). In crystals formed of more complicated molecules, the phase problem is sometimes attacked by the method of 'isomorphous substitution'. Suppose that we are studying a crystal formed from some chemical compound. In some cases it is possible to make a chemical substitution which replaces an atom of the compound by a heavy element while leaving the structure of the compound almost unchanged (isomorphous). One can then study the X-ray diffraction pattern of a crystal formed from the substituted compound. The phases are assigned as though all of the scattering came from the heavy atom and since the heavy atom does in fact dominate the diffraction pattern, this corresponds to a correct assignment of the phases.

7. Vibration and rotation

Motion of the nuclei in an effective potential due to the electrons; the classical Hamiltonian of the nuclei

Up to this point, we have been concentrating on the electrons and neglecting the motion of the nuclei. Using the Born–Oppenheimer approximation we solved the electronic problem at the fixed equilibrium positions of the nuclear coordinates. This gave us the total energy of a molecule or a crystal, the sum of an attractive term due to the electrons, and a term due to the mutual repulsion of the positively charged nuclei. We could move the nuclei to slightly different positions and find a new value of electronic energy. If we patiently did this for very many points we could map out the electronic energy as a function of the nuclear coordinates. This function is, in effect, a potential in which the nuclei are moving. For example, in a diatomic molecule, the energy of the ground state and the first excited state are both functions of the internuclear separation R as shown in Fig. 7.1. If the molecule is in the ground state, the lower curve $E_0(R)$ can be thought of as representing potential energy in the equation of motion of the nuclear coordinates. Near the minimum, this function will be approximately quadratic, so that the allowed nuclear wave functions in terms of R will be solutions of the harmonic oscillator problem, and the vibrational energy levels will be evenly spaced. The vibrational levels are split still further into sublevels corresponding to various values of the rotational quantum numbers, but the magnitude of this splitting is very small compared with the separation of the vibrational levels.

Let us now try to make our discussion more quantitative. Suppose that there are N_A nuclei and hence $N = 3N_A$ nuclear coordinates which we can call $x^1, x^2, \ldots, x^N$. Let us also suppose that the centre of mass and orientation of the molecule or crystal are fixed so that each nucleus has a definite equilibrium position, which we will take as the origin of each of the co-

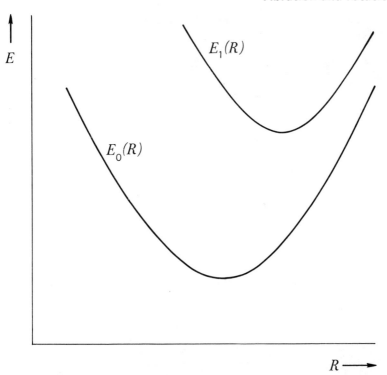

Figure 7.1 shows schematically the ground-state electronic energy, $E_0(R)$, and the first electronic excited state energy, $E_1(R)$, of a diatomic molecule as functions of the interatomic separation R.

ordinates $x^1, \ldots, x^N$. Then we can expand the potential energy function $V(x^1, \ldots, x^N)$ as a Taylor series about the equilibrium positions

$$V = [V]_{x^i = 0} + \sum_i x^i \left[\frac{\partial V}{\partial x^i} \right]_{x^i = 0}$$

$$+ \tfrac{1}{2} \sum_{i, j} x^i x^j \left[\frac{\partial^2 V}{\partial x^i \partial x^j} \right]_{x^i, x^j = 0} + \cdots \tag{7.1}$$

The first term $[V]_{x^i = 0}$ can be set equal to zero if we choose to measure the energy with respect to the equilibrium energy. The second term,

$$\sum_i x^i \left[\frac{\partial V}{\partial x^i} \right]_{x^i = 0},$$

is automatically zero because that is the definition of the equilibrium position. Therefore, provided the displacements from equilibrium are small so

215

that higher terms can be neglected, we can represent the whole series by the third term,

$$V = \tfrac{1}{2} \sum_{i,j} V_{ij} x^i x^j \tag{7.2}$$

where

$$V_{ij} = \left[\frac{\partial^2 V}{\partial x^i \partial x^j} \right]_{x^i, x^j = 0} \tag{7.3}$$

Then the classical Hamiltonian of the system can be written in the form

$$H = \tfrac{1}{2} \sum_{i,j} \left\{ m(i) \delta_{ij} \frac{dx^i}{dt} \frac{dx^j}{dt} + V_{ij} x^i x^j \right\} \tag{7.4}$$

In Appendix 1 we see that it is possible to go over to a set of 'normal coordinates' in terms of which the cross-terms in H disappear. We must first write down the mass-weighted potential energy matrix

$$V'_{ij} \equiv \frac{V_{ij}}{\sqrt{m(i)m(j)}} \tag{7.5}$$

and then diagonalize V'_{ij} either algebraically or else by means of a computer program. First, however, we must somehow evaluate the potential energy coefficients V_{ij}.

Normal modes of a system of point masses joined by springs

In the simplest possible approximation, we can regard a molecule as a collection of point masses held together by springlike bonds. Let us use the symbols $\vec{R}_s$ to represent the equilibrium position of atom s and $\vec{X}_s$ to represent the displacement of the atom from its equilibrium position. Then in our simple model, the potential energy of the molecule can be written in the form

$$V = \tfrac{1}{2} \sum_{t > s}^{NA} \sum_{s=1}^{NA} k_{st} (|\vec{X}_s + \vec{R}_s - \vec{X}_t - \vec{R}_t| - |\vec{R}_s - \vec{R}_t|)^2 \tag{7.6}$$

Here k_{st} represents the force constant of the 'spring' which connects atom s with atom t. Let us also introduce the notation

$$\vec{R}_{st} \equiv \vec{R}_s - \vec{R}_t \tag{7.7}$$

Then, if we assume $|\vec{X}_s - \vec{X}_t| \ll |\vec{R}_{st}|$ and expand Eq. (7.6) in a Taylor series, we obtain as the leading term:

$$V = \tfrac{1}{2} \sum_{s,\,t>s}^{N_A} \frac{k_{st}\{\vec{R}_{st}\cdot(\vec{X}_s - \vec{X}_t)\}^2}{|\vec{R}_{st}|^2}$$

$$\equiv \tfrac{1}{2} \sum_{s,\,t=1}^{N_A} \sum_{\mu,\,\nu=1}^{3} V_{s,\,\mu;\,t,\,\nu} X_s^\mu X_t^\nu \tag{7.8}$$

where

$$\vec{X}_s \equiv (X_s^1, X_s^2, X_s^3)$$

and

$$V_{s,\,\mu;\,s,\,\nu} = \sum_{t\ne s}^{N_A} k_{st} \frac{R_{st}^\mu R_{st}^\nu}{|\vec{R}_{st}|^2}$$

$$\underset{s\ne t}{V_{s,\,\mu;\,t,\,\nu}} = -k_{st} \frac{R_{st}^\mu R_{st}^\nu}{|\vec{R}_{st}|^2} \tag{7.9}$$

with the notation

$$\vec{R}_{st} \equiv (R_{st}^1, R_{st}^2, R_{st}^3) \tag{7.10}$$

If we let i stand for the pair of indices s, μ and if we let j stand for the pair of indices t, ν, then *Eq. (7.9) gives us the potential energy matrix V_{ij}. The next step is to diagonalize the mass-weighted potential energy matrix, $V'_{ij} = V_{ij}/\sqrt{\{m(i)m(j)\}}$, Eq. (7.5). The matrix V'_{ij} can be diagonalized by means of a standard computer program which finds a unitary matrix U_{jk} such that*

$$\sum_{j=1}^{N} (V'_{ij} - \delta_{ij}\omega_k^2)U_{jk} = 0 \tag{7.11}$$

In Eq. (7.11), ω_k is the vibrational frequency of the kth normal mode of the system. The normal coordinates are related to the original coordinates by the transformation

$$q^k = \sum_j x^j \sqrt{m(j)}\, U_{jk} \tag{7.12}$$

Problem (7.1) Try to calculate the normal vibrational modes of water.

As we see in Appendix I, classical mechanics predicts that if we start the system in motion by displacing one of the normal coordinates while leaving the others at rest, the system will continue indefinitely to oscillate in that mode with simple harmonic motion. This means, for example, that if we have three equal masses connected by equal springs sitting on a frictionless

217

surface and if we carefully pull them all away from the centre of mass in a symmetrical way and then release them, then the system will continue indefinitely to oscillate in the 'breathing mode' shown in Fig. 7.3. The same

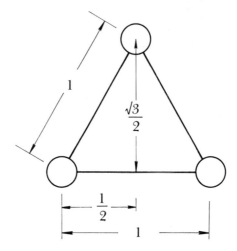

Figure 7.2 shows an idealized triatomic molecule. Unit atomic masses are placed at the vertices of an equilateral triangle.

would be true of the other modes. According to classical mechanics, if we can manage to establish pure motion in any of these modes, then in the absence of friction the system will continue to oscillate in that mode with simple harmonic motion. This is because the classical Lagrangian, expressed in terms of the normal coordinates, separates into a sum of simple harmonic oscillator Lagrangians

$$L = \sum_{k=1}^{N} L_k \equiv \tfrac{1}{2} \sum_{k=1}^{N} \left\{ \left(\frac{dq^k}{dt} \right)^2 - \omega_k^2 (q^k)^2 \right\} \qquad (7.13)$$

Each of the N Euler–Lagrange equations, Eq. (1.88), then involves only one of the normal coordinates, (the cross terms having been eliminated)

$$\frac{d}{dt} \frac{\partial L}{\partial (dq^k/dt)} = \frac{d^2 q^k}{dt^2} = \frac{\partial L}{\partial q^k} = \omega_k^2 q^k, \quad k = 1, \dots, N \qquad (7.14)$$

with the solutions

$$q^k \sim e^{\pm i\omega_k t} \qquad (7.15)$$

218

The six zero-frequency normal modes corresponding to translation of the centre of mass and rotation of the molecule as a whole; the moment of inertia tensor

It is interesting to notice that there are six zero-frequency modes corresponding to pure translation of the molecule in the directions of the three coordinate axes, Fig. 7.3(d, e, f), and pure rotation about three axes passing through the centre of mass, Fig. 7.3(g, h, i). This will be true for any

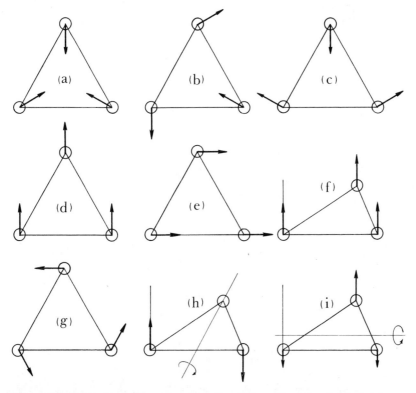

Figure 7.3 shows the nine normal modes of the triatomic molecule, shown in Fig. 7.2. There are six zero-frequency normal modes: three pure translations, *d, e,* and *f,* and three pure rotations, *g, h,* and *i.* These six zero-frequency modes will, of course exist for any molecule, regardless of the number of atoms.

molecule whatever. *There will be three modes corresponding to translation of the centre of mass and three modes corresponding to rotation about axes passing through that centre, and the classical vibrational frequency of these six modes will be zero because they do not stretch any bonds.* The zero-frequency modes can also be found without diagonalizing V'_{ij}. The normal

219

coordinates corresponding to the three translational modes are just the coordinates of the centre of mass

$$\vec{q}_{cm} = \frac{\sum_s m_s(\vec{X}_s + \vec{R}_s)}{\sum_s m_s} \tag{7.16}$$

We should remember that $\vec{X}_s$ was defined as the displacement of atom s from the equilibrium position $\vec{R}_s$. In discussing rotations it is convenient to introduce a new symbol, $\vec{r}_s \equiv \vec{X}_s + \vec{R}_s - \vec{q}_{cm}$, *which stands for the position of atom s referred to an origin fixed at the centre of mass.* It is also convenient to introduce three angles θ_x, θ_y, and θ_z, which measure rotation about the three coordinate axes passing through the centre of mass. If the molecule is spinning around some arbitrary axis which passes through the centre of mass, then the vector

$$\frac{d\vec{\theta}}{dt} \equiv \left(\frac{d\theta_x}{dt}, \frac{d\theta_y}{dt}, \frac{d\theta_z}{dt} \right) \tag{7.17}$$

points in the direction of that axis. If the centre of mass is at rest, then the velocity of one of the atoms is given by

$$\frac{d\vec{r}_s}{dt} = \frac{d\vec{\theta}}{dt} \wedge \vec{r}_s \tag{7.18}$$

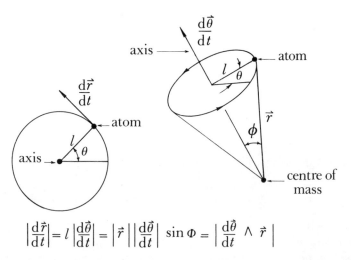

$$\left| \frac{d\vec{r}}{dt} \right| = l \left| \frac{d\vec{\theta}}{dt} \right| = |\vec{r}| \left| \frac{d\vec{\theta}}{dt} \right| \sin \Phi = \left| \frac{d\vec{\theta}}{dt} \wedge \vec{r} \right|$$

Figure 7.4 shows the relationship between the velocity of an atom, $d\vec{r}/dt$, in a rotating molecule, its position vector $\vec{r}$, and the angular velocity with which the whole molecule rotates about its axis, $d\vec{\theta}/dt$, Eq. (7.18).

as shown in Fig. 7.4 and the angular momentum pseudo-vector, (Eqs. (3.2)–(3.3)) of the molecule becomes

$$\vec{L} = \sum_{s=1}^{NA} \vec{r}_s \wedge \vec{p}_s$$

$$= \sum_{s=1}^{NA} m_s \vec{r}_s \wedge \left(\frac{d\vec{\theta}}{dt} \wedge \vec{r}_s\right) \qquad (7.19)$$

Introducing the moment of inertia tensor defined by

$$I_{\mu\nu} = \sum_{s=1}^{NA} m_s(\delta_{\mu\nu}|\vec{r}_s|^2 - r_s^\mu r_s^\nu) \qquad \textbf{(7.20)}$$

we can rewrite Eq. (7.19) in the form

$$L_\mu = \sum_{\nu=1}^{3} I_{\mu\nu} \frac{d\theta^\nu}{dt} \qquad (7.21)$$

Written in terms of the moment of inertia tensor, the kinetic energy of a rigid rotor with a stationary centre of mass becomes

$$T_{\text{rot}} = \tfrac{1}{2} \sum_{\mu,\nu=1}^{3} I_{\mu\nu} \frac{d\theta^\mu}{dt} \frac{d\theta^\nu}{dt} \qquad (7.22)$$

(If a molecule is vibrating, the kinetic energy will contain vibration-rotation interaction terms. The interested reader can find a discussion of these terms in *Molecular Vib-Rotors* by H. C. Allan, Jr. and P. C. Cross, Wiley, (1963).) *In general, the tensor $I_{\mu\nu}$ may have off-diagonal terms. However, we can eliminate them by going over to a different set of coordinates by means of a so-called 'principal axis' transformation*

$$r_s^{\nu'} = \sum_{\mu=1}^{3} r_s^\mu U_{\mu\nu} \qquad (7.23)$$

Here $U_{\mu\nu}$ is a 3×3 unitary transformation matrix which diagonalizes the moment of intertia tensor. In other words, $U_{\mu\nu}$ satisfies

$$\sum_{\nu=1}^{3} (I_{\mu\nu} - I'_{\lambda\lambda}\delta_{\mu\nu})U_{\nu\lambda} = 0 \qquad (7.24)$$

In terms of the new angular velocity pseudo-vector

$$\frac{d\theta^{\nu'}}{dt} = \sum_{\mu=1}^{3} \frac{d\theta^\mu}{dt} U_{\mu\nu} \qquad (7.25)$$

221

and the new diagonalized moment of inertia tensor $I'_{\lambda\lambda}$, the rotational kinetic energy becomes

$$T_{rot} = \tfrac{1}{2} \sum_{\lambda=1}^{3} I'_{\lambda\lambda} \left(\frac{d\theta^{\lambda'}}{dt}\right)^2 \tag{7.26}$$

Letting $I'_{\lambda\lambda} \equiv I_x$, $d\theta^{\lambda'}/dt \equiv d\theta_x/dt$, etc., and $\dot{L}_x \equiv I_x(d\theta_x/dt)$, we have

$$T_{rot}\ddot{} = H_{rot} = \tfrac{1}{2}\left(\frac{L_x^2}{I_x} + \frac{L_y^2}{I_y} + \frac{L_z^2}{I_z}\right) \tag{7.27}$$

Problem (7.2) Calculate the moment of inertia tensor of ammonia, and bring it into its diagonal form.

Quantum mechanical treatment of rotation

Now we are finally ready to begin our quantum mechanical treatment of rotation and vibration. As we saw in chapter 3 the angular momenta L_x, L_y, and L_z have the commutation relations

$$[L_x, L_y] = i\hbar L_z$$

$$[L_y, L_z] = i\hbar L_x$$

$$[L_z, L_x] = i\hbar L_y \tag{7.28}$$

We showed from the commutation relations that the matrix representations of L_x, L_y, and L_z, based on eigenfunctions of L^2 and L_z have the form

$$\langle m'|L_x|m\rangle = \frac{\hbar}{2}\sqrt{l(l+1) - m(m+1)}\ \delta_{m', m+1}$$

$$+ \frac{\hbar}{2}\sqrt{l(l+1) - m(m-1)}\ \delta_{m', m-1} \tag{7.29}$$

$$\langle m'|L_y|m\rangle = -\frac{i\hbar}{2}\sqrt{l(l+1) - m(m+1)}\ \delta_{m', m+1}$$

$$+ \frac{i\hbar}{2}\sqrt{l(l+1) - m(m-1)}\ \delta_{m', m-1} \tag{7.30}$$

and

$$\langle m'|L_z|m\rangle = m\delta_{m'm} \tag{7.31}$$

We can easily square these matrices and find the representations of L_x^2, L_y^2, and L_z^2:

$$\langle m'|L_x^2|m\rangle = \sum_{m''} \langle m'|L_x|m''\rangle\langle m''|L_x|m\rangle$$

$$= \frac{\hbar^2}{4} \sum_{m''} \{\sqrt{l(l+1) - m''(m''+1)}\, \delta_{m',\,m''+1}$$

$$+ \sqrt{l(l+1) - m''(m''-1)}\, \delta_{m',\,m''-1}\}$$

$$\times \{\sqrt{l(l+1) - m(m+1)}\, \delta_{m'',m+1}$$

$$+ \sqrt{l(l+1) - m(m-1)}\, \delta_{m'',m-1}\} \qquad (7.32)$$

Because of the Kronecker δ-functions in Eq. (7.32) the only non-vanishing terms in the sum over m'' are those for which $m'' = m + 1$ or $m'' = m - 1$. Carrying out the sum, we have:

$$\langle m'|L_x^2|m\rangle =$$

$$\frac{\hbar^2}{4}\left[\sqrt{\{l(l+1) - (m+1)(m+2)\}\{l(l+2) - m(m+1)\}} \right.$$

$$\times \delta_{m',m+2} + 2\{l(l+1) - m^2\}\delta_{m',m}$$

$$+ \sqrt{\{l(l+1) - (m-1)(m-2)\}\{l(l+1) - m(m-1)\}}$$

$$\left. \times \delta_{m',m-2} \right] \qquad (7.33)$$

and similarly,

$$\langle m'|L_y^2|m\rangle =$$

$$\frac{\hbar^2}{4}\left[-\sqrt{\{l(l+1) - (m+1)(m+2)\}\{l(l+1) - m(m+1)\}} \right.$$

$$\times \delta_{m',m+2} + 2\{l(l+1) - m^2\}\delta_{m',m}$$

$$- \sqrt{\{l(l+1) - (m-1)(m-2)\}\{l(l+1) - m(m-1)\}}$$

$$\left. \times \delta_{m',m-2} \right] \qquad (7.34)$$

while

$$\langle m'|L_z^2|m\rangle = \hbar^2 m^2 \delta_{m',m} \qquad (7.35)$$

It is encouraging to see that by adding Eqs. (7.33)–(7.35) we get back the right representation of total angular momentum

$$\langle m'|(L_x^2 + L_y^2 + L_z^2)|m\rangle = \hbar^2 l(l+1)\delta_{m',m} \qquad (7.36)$$

From Eqs. (7.33)–(7.35) it follows that the non-zero matrix elements of the rotational Hamiltonian, based on eigenfunctions of L^2 and L_z have the form

$$\langle m \pm 2|H_{rot}|m\rangle = \frac{\hbar^2}{8}\left(\frac{1}{I_x} - \frac{1}{I_y}\right)$$

$$\times \sqrt{\{l(l + 1) - (m \pm 1)(m \pm 2)\}\{l(l + 1) - m(m \pm 1)\}} \quad (7.37)$$

and

$$\langle m|H_{rot}|m\rangle = \frac{\hbar^2}{4}\left[\left(\frac{1}{I_x} + \frac{1}{I_y}\right)\{l(l + 1) - m^2\} + \frac{2m^2}{I_z}\right]$$

$$l = 0, 1, 2, \ldots, \text{etc.}, m = -l, \ldots, l \quad (7.38)$$

This finally gives us a recipe for finding the rotational energy levels of a molecule (neglecting the interaction between the rotational and vibrational modes). *The first step is to find the moment of inertia tensor $I_{\mu\nu}$ using Eq. (7.20). One then diagonalizes $I_{\mu\nu}$, and the diagonal elements are I_x, I_y, and I_z. These can be substituted into Eqs. (7.37)–(7.38) and a matrix representation of H_{rot} can be calculated. This matrix is block-diagonal, each block corresponding to one of the allowed integral or half-integral values of l. The final step is to diagonalize the blocks (one at a time).* The diagonal elements will then be eigenvalues of H_{rot}; in other words, they will correspond to rotational energy levels of the molecule.

In the matrix treatment of the rigid rotor given above we have not said what sort of functions are the basis of the representation except that they are eigenfunctions of L^2 and L_z (and we must be careful not to assume that we are dealing with spherical harmonics). It is possible to express the rigid-rotor Hamiltonian in terms of the so-called 'Eulerian angles' and to carry through a differential treatment of the problem. In such a treatment one finds the eigenfunctions explicitly, and it turns out to be possible to express these somewhat exotic functions of the Eulerian angles in terms of the hypergeometric function (see Eq. 2.37). The interested reader is referred to *Introduction to Quantum Mechanics* by L. Pauling and E. B. Wilson, McGraw-Hill (1935).

Problem (7.3) Calculate the energy of the first few rotational excited states of ammonia.

A simple harmonic oscillator treated by means of commutation relations

Let us now turn to the quantum mechanical treatment of the $N - 6$ vibrational normal modes. As in the case of the rotational modes two treatments are possible—a differential approach and a matrix approach. Let us begin with the matrix method. *The vibrational Hamiltonian, expressed in terms of the normal modes, becomes a sum of simple harmonic oscillator Hamiltonians*

$$H_{\text{vib}} = \sum_{k=1}^{N-6} H_k \tag{7.39}$$

where

$$H_k = \tfrac{1}{2}\left\{ \left(\frac{\mathrm{d}q^k}{\mathrm{d}t}\right)^2 + \omega_k^2 (q^k)^2 \right\}$$
$$= \tfrac{1}{2}\{p_k^2 + \omega_k^2 (q^k)^2\} \tag{7.40}$$

and

$$p_k = \frac{\partial L}{\partial(\mathrm{d}q^k/\mathrm{d}t)} = \frac{\mathrm{d}q^k}{\mathrm{d}t} \tag{7.41}$$

When the momentum p_k is defined by Eq. (7.41) it is said to be canonically conjugate to the coordinate q^k and the usual quantum mechanical commutation relations hold between them (see Appendix III)

$$[p_{k'}, q_k] = -i\hbar\delta_{k',k}$$
$$[p_{k'}, p_k] = 0, \quad [q^{k'}, q^k] = 0 \tag{7.42}$$

Let us try to use commutation to discuss the eigenfunctions and eigenvalues of a single simple harmonic oscillator Hamiltonian

$$H_k \rightarrow H = \tfrac{1}{2}(p^2 + \omega^2 q^2) \tag{7.43}$$

(Because we are now discussing a single oscillator we can drop the index k.) Using the commutation relation $[p, q] = -i\hbar$ we have

$$[H, p] = \tfrac{1}{2}\omega^2 [q^2, p]$$
$$= \tfrac{1}{2}\omega^2 (q[q, p] + [q, p]q)$$
$$= +i\hbar\omega^2 q \tag{7.44}$$

and

$$[H, q] = \tfrac{1}{2}[p^2, q]$$
$$= \tfrac{1}{2}(p[p, q] + [p, q]p)$$
$$= -i\hbar p \tag{7.45}$$

where H is defined by Eq. (7.43). Now suppose that we have found an eigenfunction of H so that

$$H|n\rangle = E_n|n\rangle \tag{7.46}$$

225

The quantum theory of atoms, molecules, and photons

We can show by means of the commutation relations, Eqs. (7.42)–(7.45), that when the operator $p \pm i\omega q$ acts on $|n\rangle$ the resulting function is also an eigenfunction of H. Letting H act on this function and commuting it through the operator we have

$$H(p \pm i\omega q)|n\rangle = \{[H, p] \pm i\omega[H, q] + (p \pm i\omega q)H\}|n\rangle$$
$$= \{+i\hbar w^2 q \pm i\omega(-i\hbar p) + (p \pm i\omega q)E_n\}|n\rangle$$
$$= (E_n \pm \hbar\omega)(p \pm i\omega q)|n\rangle \qquad (7.47)$$

Equation (7.47) shows that the function $(p \pm i\omega q)|n\rangle$ *is an eigenfunction of H corresponding to the energy* $E_n \pm \hbar\omega$. *In other words, $p - i\omega q$ is a 'lowering operator'.* Now we know that any physical system must have a ground state. If the possible energy states of our harmonic oscillator could become infinitely negative, then what would happen when it established thermal equilibrium with its surroundings? It would become a heat-sink and all the energy in the universe would eventually drain away into it. Clearly this does not happen, so we must require the energy eigenvalues to have a lower bound E_0. If we use the symbol $|o\rangle$ to represent the ground state then

$$H|o\rangle = E_0|o\rangle \qquad (7.48)$$

The lowering operator $(p - i\omega q)$ acting on $|o\rangle$ must give zero since it cannot give an eigenfunction corresponding to a lower energy. Thus we must have

$$(p - i\omega q)|o\rangle = 0 \qquad (7.49)$$

and also

$$(p + iwq)(p - iwq)|o\rangle = (p^2 + \omega^2 q^2 + i\omega[p, q])|o\rangle$$
$$= (2H - \hbar\omega)|o\rangle$$
$$= (2E_0 - \hbar\omega)|o\rangle = 0 \qquad (7.50)$$

so that

$$E_0 = \frac{\hbar\omega}{2} \qquad (7.51)$$

Combining this with Eq. (7.47) we have

$$E_n = (n + \tfrac{1}{2})\hbar\omega$$
$$n = 0, 1, 2, 3, \ldots, \infty \qquad (7.52)$$

Phonon creation and annihilation operators

It is convenient to define the normalized raising operator or 'creation operator''

$$a^\dagger \equiv \mathcal{N}(-ip + \omega q) \tag{7.53}$$

and the normalized lowering operator or 'annihilation operator'

$$a \equiv \mathcal{N}(ip + \omega q) \tag{7.54}$$

The normalization constant $\mathcal{N}$ is to be chosen in such a way that

$$a^\dagger |n\rangle = \sqrt{n + 1}\, |n + 1\rangle \tag{7.55}$$

and

$$a|n + 1\rangle = \sqrt{n + 1}\, |n\rangle \tag{7.56}$$

Then

$$
\begin{aligned}
aa^\dagger |n\rangle &= \sqrt{n + 1}\, a|n + 1\rangle \\
&= (n + 1)|n\rangle \\
&= \mathcal{N}^2(p - i\omega q)(p + i\omega q)|n\rangle \\
&= \mathcal{N}^2\{p^2 + \omega^2 q^2 + i\omega[p, q]\}\,|n\rangle \\
&= \mathcal{N}^2\{2H + i\omega(-i\hbar)\}|n\rangle \\
&= \mathcal{N}^2\{2(n + \tfrac{1}{2})\hbar\omega + \hbar\}|n\rangle \\
&= \mathcal{N}^2(n + 1)2\hbar\omega|n\rangle
\end{aligned}
\tag{7.57}
$$

Cancelling the factor $(n + 1)$ from both sides of Eq. (7.57) we are left with the requirement

$$\mathcal{N} = \frac{1}{\sqrt{2\hbar\omega}} \tag{7.58}$$

so that the definitions

$$a^\dagger = \frac{1}{\sqrt{2\hbar\omega}}\,(-ip + \omega q) \tag{7.59}$$

and

$$a = \frac{1}{\sqrt{2\hbar\omega}}\,(ip + \omega q) \tag{7.60}$$

227

The quantum theory of atoms, molecules, and photons

are consistent with Eq. (7.55) and Eq. (7.56). Solving for p and q we have

$$p = i\sqrt{\frac{\hbar\omega}{2}}\,(a^\dagger - a) \tag{7.61}$$

and

$$q = \sqrt{\frac{\hbar}{2\omega}}\,(a^\dagger + a) \tag{7.62}$$

From the commutation relations for p and q, Eq. (7.42) we can obtain the commutation relations for a and $a^\dagger$.

$$[a, a^\dagger] = 1$$
$$[a, a] = 0, \quad [a^\dagger, a^\dagger] = 0 \tag{7.63}$$

Then substituting Eq. (7.61) and Eq. (7.62) into Eq. (7.43) we have

$$H = \tfrac{1}{2}(p^2 + \omega^2 q^2)$$

$$= \frac{\hbar\omega}{4}\{(a^\dagger + a)^2 - (a^\dagger - a)^2\}$$

$$= \frac{\hbar\omega}{2}(a^\dagger a + aa^\dagger)$$

$$= \hbar\omega(a^\dagger a + \tfrac{1}{2}) \tag{7.64}$$

The operator $a^\dagger a$ is called the 'number operator' because the states $|n\rangle$ are eigenfunctions of $a^\dagger a$ belonging to the eigenvalue n:

$$a^\dagger a|n\rangle = ([a^\dagger, a] + aa^\dagger)|n\rangle$$
$$= \{-1 + (n + 1)\}|n\rangle$$
$$= n|n\rangle \tag{7.65}$$

This of course also implies that the states $|n\rangle$ are eigenfunctions of H belonging to the eigenvalue $E_n = \hbar\omega(n + \tfrac{1}{2})$ in agreement with Eq. (7.52).

We are now in a position to write down matrix representations of the various operators. Taking the scalar product of Eq. (7.55) with the conjugate function $\langle n'|$ we have

$$\langle n'|a^\dagger|n\rangle = \sqrt{n + 1}\,\langle n'|n + 1\rangle = \sqrt{n + 1}\,\delta_{n', n+1}$$

$$= \begin{pmatrix} 0 & 0 & 0 & 0 & \cdots \\ 1 & 0 & 0 & 0 & \cdots \\ 0 & \sqrt{2} & 0 & 0 & \cdots \\ 0 & 0 & \sqrt{3} & 0 & \cdots \\ \vdots & \vdots & \vdots & \vdots & \\ & & \text{etc.} & & \end{pmatrix} \tag{7.66}$$

while

$$\langle n'|a|n\rangle = \sqrt{n}\langle n'|n-1\rangle = \sqrt{n}\delta_{n',n-1}$$

$$= \begin{pmatrix} 0 & 1 & 0 & 0 & \cdots \\ 0 & 0 & \sqrt{2} & 0 & \cdots \\ 0 & 0 & 0 & \sqrt{3} & \cdots \\ 0 & 0 & 0 & 0 & \\ \vdots & \vdots & \vdots & \vdots & \\ & & \text{etc.} & \end{pmatrix} \qquad (7.67)$$

The operators a and $a^\dagger$ are obviously not self-adjoint (Hermitian) but they are adjoints of one another. On the other hand, since the operators p and q represent physically measurable dynamical variables, the matrices which represent them must be Hermitian, and we can see that they are:

$$\langle n'|p|n\rangle = i\sqrt{\frac{\hbar\omega}{2}}\left(\langle n'|a^\dagger|n\rangle - \langle n'|a|n\rangle\right)$$

$$= \sqrt{\frac{\hbar\omega}{2}} \begin{pmatrix} 0 & -i & 0 & \cdots \\ i & 0 & -i\sqrt{2} & \cdots \\ 0 & i\sqrt{2} & 0 & \cdots \\ \vdots & \vdots & \vdots & \\ & & \text{etc.} & \end{pmatrix} \qquad (7.68)$$

while

$$\langle n'|q|n\rangle = \sqrt{\frac{\hbar}{2\omega}}\left(\langle n'|a^\dagger|n\rangle + \langle n'|a|n\rangle\right)$$

$$= \sqrt{\frac{\hbar}{2\omega}} \begin{pmatrix} 0 & 1 & 0 & \cdots \\ 1 & 0 & \sqrt{2} & \cdots \\ 0 & \sqrt{2} & 0 & \cdots \\ \vdots & \vdots & \vdots & \\ & & \text{etc.} & \end{pmatrix} \qquad (7.69)$$

Problem (7.4) An anharmonic oscillator has a Hamiltonian of the form $H = \frac{1}{2}(p^2 + \omega^2 q^2) + \varepsilon q^3$. Use perturbation theory to calculate the effect of the small anharmonic term on the first few energy levels.

The Schrödinger equation of an harmonic oscillator; Hermite polynomials; the Franck–Condon principle

It is interesting to compare this matrix treatment of the simple harmonic oscillator with a differential treatment. If p and q are related to each other

The quantum theory of atoms, molecules, and photons

and to the Lagrangian by Eq. (7.41), then in quantum theory p is represented by the differential operator $(\hbar/i)(\partial/\partial q)$. Then the harmonic oscillator Hamiltonian, Eq. (7.43), becomes

$$H = \tfrac{1}{2}\left(-\hbar^2 \frac{\partial^2}{\partial q^2} + \omega^2 q^2 \right) \tag{7.70}$$

It is convenient to introduce the dimensionless parameter defined by

$$\xi \equiv \sqrt{\frac{\omega}{\hbar}}\, q \tag{7.71}$$

Written in terms of ξ, the Hamiltonian of Eq. (7.70) becomes

$$H = \hbar\omega\left(-\frac{\partial^2}{\partial \xi^2} + \xi^2 \right) \tag{7.72}$$

The eigenfunctions $|n\rangle \equiv \psi_n(\xi)$ should then obey the differential equation

$$\hbar\omega\left(-\frac{\partial^2}{\partial \xi^2} + \xi^2 \right)\psi_n(\xi) = E_n\psi_n(\xi) \tag{7.73}$$

If we replace E_n by $(n + \tfrac{1}{2})\hbar\omega$, then Eq. (7.73) has the solutions

$$|n\rangle = \psi_n(\xi) = N_n\, e^{-\frac{1}{2}\xi^2} H_n(\xi) \tag{7.74}$$

where N_n is a normalizing factor and $H_n(\xi)$ is a type of polynomial first studied by the French mathematician Hermite, whose name is also associated with self-adjointness. The first few Hermite polynomials are

$$
\begin{aligned}
H_0 &= 1 & H_1 &= 2\xi \\
H_2 &= 4\xi^2 - 2 & H_3 &= 8\xi^3 - 12\xi
\end{aligned}
\tag{7.75}
$$

The Hermite polynomials obey the differential equation

$$\frac{\partial^2 H_n}{\partial \xi^2} + 2\xi \frac{\partial H_n}{\partial \xi} + 2nH_n = 0 \tag{7.76}$$

and the recursion relations

$$\frac{\partial H_n}{\partial \xi} = 2nH_{n-1}$$

$$H_{n+1} = 2\xi H_n - 2nH_{n-1} \tag{7.77}$$

The solutions to Eq. (7.76) are finite polynomials only if $n = 0, 1, 2, 3, \ldots, \infty$, and therefore n is restricted to these values by the boundary condition which requires $\psi_n(\xi)$ to be finite at $\xi \to \infty$. The recursion relations, Eq. (7.77), give us a practical method for generating higher Hermite polynomials if we want them. For example, we can see from Eqs. (7.77) and (7.75) that

$$H_4 = 2\xi H_3 - 6H_2$$
$$= 16\xi^4 - 48\xi^2 + 12 \tag{7.78}$$

If the wave functions ψ_n are normalized in such a way that

$$\int_{-\infty}^{\infty} dq \psi_{n'} \left(\sqrt{\frac{\omega}{\hbar}} q\right) \psi_n \left(\sqrt{\frac{\omega}{\hbar}} q\right) = \delta_{n'n} \tag{7.79}$$

then the normalization factor N_n of Eq. (7.74) turns out to be

$$N_n = \left(\frac{\sqrt{\dfrac{\omega}{\hbar}}}{\sqrt{\pi}\, 2^n n!}\right)^{1/2} \tag{7.80}$$

The harmonic oscillator wave function corresponding to $n = 5$ is shown in Fig. 7.5. In classical mechanics, a particle moving in an harmonic oscillator potential has its highest velocity at the deepest part of the potential well. As it reaches one of the classical turning points (the points at which the energy becomes negative) the particle slows down, stops, and reverses its motion. We can see these features also in the quantum mechanical wave function, Fig. 7.5. The wave length is shortest where the well is deepest. Near the turning points, the amplitude of the wave function becomes large, which corresponds to the fact that the probability of finding the particle at a given position is larger the smaller the velocity. You might object that at the turning points themselves, where the particle momentarily stops, the amplitude of the wave function ought to approach infinity. In fact, in the limit $n \to \infty$ (which is the classical limit) the amplitude of the wave function at the turning point does approach infinity. Even for moderate values of n the amplitude of the harmonic oscillator wave function is appreciably larger at the turning points, and this is the quantum mechanical reason for the Franck–Condon principle (chapter 8).

A collection of harmonic oscillators; the vibrational Hamiltonian of a molecule or crystal

Having discussed a simple harmonic oscillator from the quantum mechanical standpoint, we should now remember that the vibrational Hamiltonian, Eq. (7.43), is a sum of simple harmonic oscillator Hamiltonians:

$$H = \sum_k H_k$$
$$= \sum_k \tfrac{1}{2}(p_k^2 + \omega_k^2 q_k^2)$$
$$= \sum_k \hbar\omega_k \{a_k^\dagger a_k + \tfrac{1}{2}\} \tag{7.81}$$

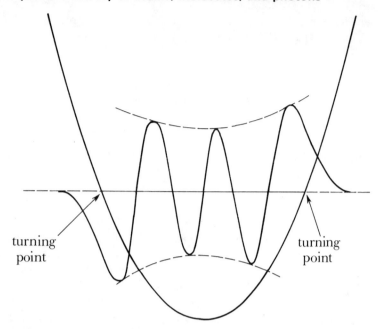

Figure 7.5 shows an harmonic oscillator potential with the energy level corresponding to $n = 5$ and the associated wave function, Eq. (7.74), superimposed. The wave function has its largest amplitude near the turning points where a classical particle would be moving slowly. This feature becomes more pronounced as n increases, and is responsible for the Franck–Condon principle.

The commutation relations corresponding to Eq. (7.63) are

$$[a_{k'}, a_k^\dagger] = \delta_{k', k}$$
$$[a_{k'}, a_k] = 0$$
$$[a_{k'}^\dagger, a_k^\dagger] = 0 \qquad \textbf{(7.82)}$$

The eigenfunctions of the Hamiltonian are just products of simple harmonic oscillator eigenfunctions:

$$H|n_1, n_2, \ldots\rangle = E|n_1, n_2, \ldots\rangle$$
$$= \sum_k \hbar\omega_k(n_k + \tfrac{1}{2})|n_1, n_2, \ldots\rangle \qquad \textbf{(7.83)}$$

These eigenfunctions are labelled by the set of quantum numbers $n_1, n_2, \ldots, n_k, \ldots$, a quantum number for each vibrational normal mode of the system. If the creation operator $a_k^\dagger$ acts on such an eigenfunction it affects only the quantum number corresponding to the kth normal mode

$$a_k^\dagger |\ldots, n_k, \ldots\rangle = \sqrt{(n_k + 1)} |\ldots, n_k + 1, \ldots\rangle \qquad (7.84)$$

and similarly,

$$a_k |\ldots, n_k + 1, \ldots\rangle = \sqrt{(n_k + 1)} |\ldots, n_k, \ldots\rangle \qquad (7.85)$$

Vibrational modes of a system with translational symmetry; dispersion; the cut-off frequency

It is interesting to try to apply these methods to a system with translational symmetry. For example, we might consider a system of N equal point masses constrained to move in the x direction and connected to each other by weightless springs as shown in Fig. 7.6. If κ represents the force constant

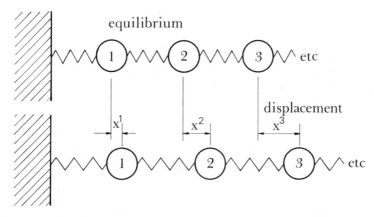

Figure 7.6 shows the idealized system whose Lagrangian is given in Eqs. (7.86)–(7.87). It consists of a set of equal point masses connected by weightless springs. In this simple example we neglect gravitation and assume that the masses are constrained to move parallel to the line of springs. The coordinates x^j represent the displacement of the jth mass from its equilibrium position.

of the springs and x^i represents the displacement of the ith mass from its equilibrium position, then the classical Lagrangian of the system has the form

$$L = \tfrac{1}{2} \sum_{i=1}^{N} \sum_{j=1}^{N} \left(m\, \delta_{ij} \frac{dx^i}{dt} \frac{dx^j}{dt} - V_{ij} x^i x^j \right) \qquad (7.86)$$

where

$$V_{ij} = \begin{cases} 2\kappa & i = j \\ -\kappa & i = j \pm 1 \end{cases} \qquad (7.87)$$

233

Then the secular equations, Eq. (7.11), become

$$-\kappa U_{j-1,k} + \{2\kappa - \mathcal{V}(k)\}U_{jk} - \kappa U_{j+1,k} = 0$$
$$j = 1, 2, \ldots, N \qquad (7.88)$$

As in the case of the electronic wave functions of a linear polymer, Eq. (6.13), the trial solution

$$U_{jk} = \sqrt{\frac{2}{N+1}} \sin(jkd) \qquad (7.89)$$

makes all of the secular equations redundant. All of the equations, Eq. (7.88), redundantly require that

$$\mathcal{V}(k) = 2\kappa\{1 - \cos(kd)\} \qquad (7.90)$$

Imposing homogeneous boundary conditions (i.e., clamping the two ends of the line) restricts the allowed values of k and we must have

$$k = \frac{\pi}{L}, \frac{2\pi}{L}, \ldots, \frac{N\pi}{L} \qquad (7.91)$$

where $L = (N+1)d$ is the length of the chain and d is the spacing between the equilibrium positions of the masses. (In other words d is the 'lattice parameter'.) The frequency spectrum

$$\omega_k \equiv \frac{\mathcal{V}(k)}{m} = \sqrt{\frac{2\kappa\{1 - \cos(kd)\}}{m}} \qquad (7.92)$$

is shown in Fig. 7.7 as a function of k. According to Eqs. (7.89) and (7.12), the normal mode which corresponds to the frequency ω_k is

$$q^k = \sum_{j=1}^{N} x^j \sqrt{\frac{2m}{N+1}} \sin(jkd) \qquad (7.93)$$

Because of the unitarity of the transformation we can easily write down the inverse of Eq. (7.93):

$$x^j = \sum_{k=\pi/L}^{N\pi/L} q^k \sqrt{\frac{2}{m(N+1)}} \sin(jkd) \qquad (7.94)$$

According to classical mechanics (Appendix I), the time-dependence of q^k is given by

$$\frac{d^2 q^k}{dt^2} + \omega_k^2 q^k = 0 \qquad (7.95)$$

so that

$$q^k = [q^k]_{t=0} \cos \omega_k t + \left(\frac{1}{\omega_k}\right)\left[\frac{dq^k}{dt}\right]_{t=0} \sin \omega_k t \qquad (7.96)$$

234

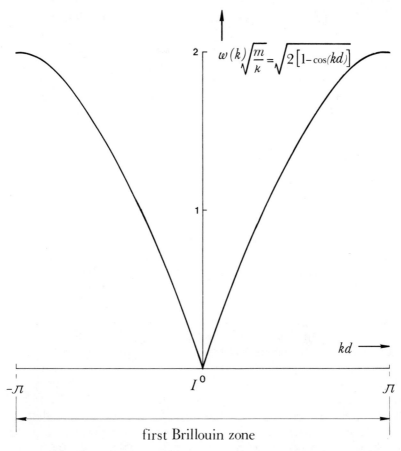

$$\omega(k)\sqrt{\frac{m}{\kappa}} = \sqrt{2\left[1-\cos(kd)\right]}$$

first Brillouin zone

Figure 7.7 shows the frequency as a function of wave number, Eq. (7.92), for the vibrational modes of the system illustrated in Fig. 7.6.

We might try to calculate the motion of the system following the initial conditions

$$[q^k]_{t=0} = D\,\delta_{kk'}$$

$$\left[\frac{dq^k}{dt}\right]_{t=0} = 0 \qquad (7.97)$$

In that case we would have

$$x^j = D\sqrt{\frac{2}{N+1}}\,\cos\omega_k t\,\sin kx \qquad (7.98)$$

where $x \equiv jd$. In other words, when only one of the normal modes is excited, the displacement of the jth point mass is a sinusoidal function of

235

its index j and hence also a sinusoidal function of its equilibrium position $x = jd$ (d being the lattice spacing). We can see that the normal modes in this example are 'standing waves' and that they are very similar to the harmonics of a vibrating string, Eqs. (1.33)–(1.72). One difference is that in this case we are considering longitudinal waves (the masses here are constrained to move in the x direction) whereas in our earlier discussion of the vibrating string we considered transverse waves. Another difference is that in our earlier discussion we began by considering a set of point masses elastically joined together, but then, following Daniel Bernoulli's treatment, we passed over to the continuum. In the case of a continuum, the number of harmonics is infinite because although the possible values of ω are restricted by the boundary conditions, ω can become infinitely large. However, these infinitely large frequencies are not physically meaningful. A vibrating string is not really continuous but consists of very small particles held together by chemical forces. If we try to make a sound wave of higher and higher frequency propagate through a piece of matter, we will eventually come to a frequency which corresponds to a wave length shorter than the interatomic spacing. At this point there is a 'cut-off'. We can see from Eq. (7.92) that in the case of our elastically connected point masses, the cut-off occurs at $\omega = 2\sqrt{\kappa/m}$. We can also see that higher frequencies might be achieved, if we allowed imaginary values of k. Such imaginary wave numbers would correspond physically to a wave of exponentially decaying amplitude. In other words, if we were to drive one of the ends of our linear chain at a frequency higher than the cut-off, the disturbance would not propagate but would be exponentially damped. The linear chain of Fig. 7.6 is thus a 'low pass' mechanical filter. The mathematical treatment of electrical filters is very similar to Eqs. (7.88)–(7.98) and an excellent discussion of both problems can be found in Prof. L. Brillouin's book *Wave Propagation in Periodic Structures*, Dover (1953); McGraw-Hill (1946).

8. The interaction between matter and radiation

The need for a first-order Lorentz-invariant wave equation

In 1926, when Erwin Schrödinger wrote down his wave equation, the special theory of relativity was already a very well-established and important part of physics. In fact the first equation which Schrödinger tried was the relativistically invariant one, Eq. (2.12)

$$(\Box^2 - k_0^2)\psi = 0 \tag{8.1}$$

This equation fulfils the relativistic requirement that the space and time coordinates should enter on an equal footing. However, it presents a difficulty because of the second-order partial derivative with respect to time. You may remember that according to the Copenhagen interpretation of the wave function ψ the state of the system at a particular time was specified by a knowledge of the wave function at that time. The future evolution of the system could then be calculated by solving the wave equation and finding the wave function $\psi(t)$ at a future time. On the other hand the solution of the Schrödinger's relativistic equation is not determined at a future time unless we possess not only the initial value of ψ at all points in space but also the initial values of $\partial\psi/\partial t$. Because of these and other difficulties, Schrödinger abandoned the search for a relativistically invariant wave equation for matter. Meanwhile P. A. M. Dirac (6) took up the project. Because of the difficulties connected with the second-order relativistic equation, Eq. (8.1), Dirac looked for an equation which would contain only a first-order partial derivative with respect to time. Since special relativity requires the space and time coordinates to enter on an equal footing, only first-order partial derivatives with respect to the space coordinates could be allowed. This reasoning led Dirac to write down an equation of the form

$$\left(\gamma^1 \frac{\partial}{\partial x^1} + \gamma^2 \frac{\partial}{\partial x^2} + \gamma^3 \frac{\partial}{\partial x^3} + \gamma^4 \frac{\partial}{\partial x^4}\right)\psi = -k_0\psi \tag{8.2}$$

237

where

$$k_0 = \frac{m_0 c}{\hbar} \tag{8.3}$$

$$(x^1, x^2, x^3, x^4) = (x, y, z, ict) \tag{8.4}$$

and $\gamma^1, \gamma^2, \gamma^3, \gamma^4$ represent constant multiplicative factors which still have to be determined. According to Dirac's reasoning, a first-order equation of this form must govern the motion of the electron. But the second-order equation cannot be wrong because if we make the substitutions

$$\frac{\hbar}{i} \frac{\partial}{\partial \vec{x}} = \vec{p}, \qquad -\frac{\hbar}{i} \frac{\partial}{\partial t} = E \tag{8.5}$$

it gives back the right relativistic equation relating momentum, energy, and rest mass, Eq. (2.18), in accordance with Bohr's correspondence principle.

The gamma matrices

Dirac concluded that the second-order equation Eq. (8.1) was not wrong but too weak. The first-order equation Eq. (8.2) was stronger but it had to be consistent with Eq. (8.1). Now suppose that we apply the operator

$$\left(\sum_{\mu=1}^{4} \gamma^\mu \frac{\partial}{\partial x^\mu} \right)^2 \equiv \left(\gamma^\mu \frac{\partial}{\partial x^\mu} \right)^2 \tag{8.6}$$

to a wave function ψ which is a solution of Eq. (8.2). Then we should get k_0^2. In other words we require

$$\gamma^1 \gamma^1 \frac{\partial^2}{\partial x^1 \partial x^1} + \gamma^1 \gamma^2 \frac{\partial^2}{\partial x^1 \partial x^2} + \cdots$$

$$+ \gamma^2 \gamma^1 \frac{\partial^2}{\partial x^2 \partial x^1} + \gamma^2 \gamma^2 \frac{\partial^2}{\partial x^2 \partial x^2} + \cdots + \cdots = k_0^2 \tag{8.7}$$

This can be consistent with Eq. (8.1.) only if

$$\gamma^1 \gamma^1 = \gamma^2 \gamma^2 = \gamma^3 \gamma^3 = \gamma^4 \gamma^4 = 1 \tag{8.8}$$

and

$$\gamma^1 \gamma^2 + \gamma^2 \gamma^1 = \gamma^1 \gamma^3 + \gamma^3 \gamma^1 = \gamma^1 \gamma^4 + \gamma^4 \gamma^1 = \gamma^2 \gamma^3 + \gamma^3 \gamma^2$$

$$= \gamma^2 \gamma^4 + \gamma^4 \gamma^2 = \gamma^3 \gamma^4 + \gamma^4 \gamma^3 = 0 \tag{8.9}$$

In shorthand notation Eq. (8.8) and Eq. (8.9) can be rewritten as

$$\gamma^\mu \gamma^\nu + \gamma^\nu \gamma^\mu = 2 \delta^{\mu\nu} \tag{8.10}$$

238

The mystery deepened. What could these γ's be? They could not be simple constants because if they were, the order of multiplication would not make any difference. Dirac decided that to have a non-commutative law of multiplication like Eq. (8.10) his γ's had to be matrices. The smallest matrices which would multiply in this way were 4×4 matrices. For example suppose that we represent γ^1, γ^2, γ^3, and γ^4 by the matrices

$$\gamma^1 = \begin{pmatrix} 0 & 0 & 0 & -i \\ 0 & 0 & -i & 0 \\ 0 & i & 0 & 0 \\ i & 0 & 0 & 0 \end{pmatrix} \tag{8.11}$$

$$\gamma^2 = \begin{pmatrix} 0 & 0 & 0 & -1 \\ 0 & 0 & 1 & 0 \\ 0 & 1 & 0 & 0 \\ -1 & 0 & 0 & 0 \end{pmatrix} \tag{8.12}$$

$$\gamma^3 = \begin{pmatrix} 0 & 0 & -i & 0 \\ 0 & 0 & 0 & i \\ i & 0 & 0 & 0 \\ 0 & -i & 0 & 0 \end{pmatrix} \tag{8.13}$$

and

$$\gamma^4 = \begin{pmatrix} 1 & 0 & 0 & 0 \\ 0 & 1 & 0 & 0 \\ 0 & 0 & -1 & 0 \\ 0 & 0 & 0 & -1 \end{pmatrix} \tag{8.14}$$

You can verify that these matrices square up to the unit matrix and 'anti-commute' as required by Eq. (8.10). If we introduce a set of 2×2 matrices (see Eqs. (4.44)–(4.67))

$$\sigma_1 = \begin{pmatrix} 0 & 1 \\ 1 & 0 \end{pmatrix} \quad \sigma_2 = \begin{pmatrix} 0 & -i \\ i & 0 \end{pmatrix}$$

$$\sigma_3 = \begin{pmatrix} 1 & 0 \\ 0 & -1 \end{pmatrix} \quad I = \begin{pmatrix} 1 & 0 \\ 0 & 1 \end{pmatrix} \tag{8.15}$$

then we can rewrite Eqs. (8.11)–(8.14) in a streamlined notation

$$\vec{\gamma} = \left(\begin{array}{c|c} 0 & -i\vec{\sigma} \\ \hline i\vec{\sigma} & 0 \end{array} \right) \quad \gamma^4 = \left(\begin{array}{c|c} I & 0 \\ \hline 0 & -I \end{array} \right) \tag{8.16}$$

239

Problem (8.1)   The solution of Dirac's free-electron equation, Eq. (8.2), can be written in the form

$$\psi = U(k)\, e^{ik_\mu x^\mu}$$

where $U(k)$ is a four-component column matrix which depends on k_μ but is independent of x^μ. Find the four linearly independent solutions $U(k)$ for the case of an electron propagating in the z direction, with $k_\mu = \{0, 0, k_3, k_4\}$.

Dirac's relativistic wave equation for an electron in an external electromagnetic field

Dirac's first-order relativistically invariant wave equation (8.2) represents a free electron in the absence of any electromagnetic field. Having got this equation he then proceeded to put in the electromagnetic vector potential A_μ, (see Eq. (1.163)) in the only possible way that would satisfy both the requirements of relativistic invariance and the correspondence principle. In this way P. A. M. Dirac obtained his famous relativistic wave equation for an electron in an external electromagnetic field

$$\gamma^\mu \left(\frac{\partial}{\partial x^\mu} - \frac{ie}{\hbar c} A_\mu \right) \psi = -k_0 \psi \qquad (8.17)$$

Here, as in chapter 1, we have used the convention of summing over a repeated index, so that $\gamma^\mu (\partial/\partial x^\mu)$ means

$$\gamma^1 \frac{\partial}{\partial x^2} + \gamma^2 \frac{\partial}{\partial x^2} + \gamma^3 \frac{\partial}{\partial x^3} + \gamma^4 \frac{\partial}{\partial x^4}$$

In his original work Dirac used a slightly different notation with three α matrices and a β matrix. We have used a more modern 'γ notation' which helps to show clearly the symmetry between the space and time coordinates.

It is interesting to apply the squared operator

$$\left\{ \gamma^\mu \left(\frac{\partial}{\partial x^\mu} - \frac{ie}{\hbar c} A_\mu \right) \right\}^2$$

to the wave function ψ. This will give us a second-order equation similar to Schrödinger's relativistic equation, Eq. (8.1), but containing the effects of

240

the electromagnetic field. From Eqs. (8.15)–(8.17), and Eqs. (1.170)–(1.171) it follows that

$$\left\{ \gamma^\mu \left(\frac{\partial}{\partial x^\mu} - \frac{ie}{\hbar c} A_\mu \right) \right\}^2 \psi$$

$$= \left\{ \left(\frac{\partial}{\partial \vec{x}} - \frac{ie}{\hbar c} \vec{A} \right)^2 + \frac{e}{\hbar c}\, \vec{\sigma}.\vec{H} - \frac{ie}{\hbar c}\, \vec{\alpha}.\vec{E} + \left(\frac{\partial}{\partial x^4} - \frac{ie}{\hbar c} A_4 \right)^2 \right\} \psi$$

$$= k_0^2 \psi$$

where $\vec{\alpha} \equiv i\gamma^4 \vec{\gamma}$ $\qquad\qquad$ **(8.18)**

The non-relativistic limit; spin magnetic moment

We can ask what this second-order equation reduces to in the non-relativistic limit. In the limit where $pc \ll m_0 c^2$ the energy of an electron is approximately represented by Eq. (2.20)

$$\pm E = \sqrt{(pc)^2 + (m_0 c^2)^2} \cong m_0 c^2 + \frac{p^2}{2m_0} \qquad (8.19)$$

It is interesting to notice that the sign of the E in Eq. (8.19) can be negative as well as positive. This seems to imply the existence of negative-energy solutions. We shall come back to this point, but for the moment, let us confine our attention to the positive energies. In the non-relativistic limit it is convenient to redefine the energy by subtracting off the rest energy

$$E_{\text{N.R.}} = E - m_0 c^2 \qquad (8.20)$$

It is also convenient to define a non-relativistic wave function by factoring out

$$e^{k_0 x^4} = e^{i(m_0 c^2/\hbar)t}$$

so that

$$\psi = e^{k_0 x^4} \psi_{\text{N.R.}} \qquad (8.21)$$

Then

$$\frac{\partial \psi}{\partial x^4} = \frac{\partial}{\partial x^4} (e^{k_0 x^4} \psi_{\text{N.R.}}) = e^{k_0 x^4} \left(k_0 + \frac{\partial}{\partial x^4} \right) \psi_{\text{N.R.}} \qquad (8.22)$$

If we neglect the terms which become very small in the non-relativistic limit, this gives us

$$\left\{ \left(\frac{\partial}{\partial x^4} - \frac{ie}{\hbar c} A_4 \right)^2 - k_0^2 \right\} e^{k_0 x^4} \psi_{\text{N.R.}} \cong 2k_0\, e^{k_0 x^4} \left(\frac{\partial}{\partial x^4} - \frac{ie}{\hbar c} A_4 \right) \psi_{\text{N.R.}}$$

$$= \frac{2m_0}{\hbar^2}\, e^{k_0 x^4} \left(\frac{\hbar}{i} \frac{\partial}{\partial t} + e\phi \right) \psi_{\text{N.R.}} \quad (8.23)$$

241

Putting Eq. (8.23) back into Eq. (8.18) we finally arrive at something similar to the non-relativistic Schrödinger equation but containing several extra terms.

$$-i\hbar \frac{\partial \psi_{\text{N.R.}}}{\partial t} = \left\{ \frac{-\hbar^2}{2m_0}\left(\frac{\partial}{\partial \bar{x}} - \frac{ie}{\hbar c}\vec{A}\right)^2 - \frac{e\hbar}{2m_0 c}\vec{H}.\vec{\sigma} \right.$$

$$\left. + \frac{ie\hbar}{2m_0 c}\vec{E}.\alpha + e\phi \right\}\psi_{\text{N.R.}} \equiv H_{\text{N.R.}}\psi_{\text{N.R.}} \quad (8.24)$$

This is a really splendid result because the extra terms are just exactly the ones needed to explain the observed effects of electric and magnetic fields on the behaviour of an electron. For example, in 1927 when Dirac wrote down his equation, Pauli, Uhlenbeck, and Goudschmidt had been forced by experimental evidence to postulate the existence of a mysterious spin quantum number. It had been observed that in the presence of a magnetic field spectral lines are split by an amount $e\hbar H/2m_0 c$. The term $(e\hbar/2m_0 c)\vec{\sigma}.\vec{H}$ is precisely what was needed to explain this splitting. The two possible linearly-independent spin states, (which we have represented by α and β in our discussion of chemical bonding), correspond to the two possible linearly independent positive-energy solutions of the Dirac equation. The term $(ie\hbar/2m_0)\vec{E}.\vec{\alpha}$, with $\vec{\alpha}$ defined by Eq. (8.29) is responsible for spin-orbit coupling in atoms and will be discussed in detail later.

Problem (8.2) Show that the vector potential

$$\vec{A} = \frac{\mathscr{H}_0}{2}(y, -x, 0)$$

represents a uniform magnetic field in the z direction. By substituting this into Eq. (8.24), find the magnetic moment, Eq. (2.53), of an electron whose wave function ψ satisfies $L_z\psi = \hbar\psi$ and $\sigma_z\psi = (\hbar/2)\psi$.

Dirac's prediction of the positron

But, you may ask, what about the negative-energy solutions? What do the negative energy solutions mean? Can such states actually exist? At the time, the idea seemed like nonsense, and the fact that the Dirac equation predicted the existence of negative energy states was raised as a criticism against it. Why, the critics asked, don't all electrons fall down into negative energy states giving up twice their rest-energy as radiation? Dirac answered that the negative energy states are all filled. The situation of an ordinary positive-energy electron is something like that of an extra electron added to the lowest empty band of a non-conducting crystal. There is no room for the electron in the filled band below and so it must stay in the higher band. On the other hand, the absorption of a photon can lift an electron up from the filled band to the empty band producing an electron-hole pair. Dirac predicted that a photon of energy greater than $2m_0c^2$ could produce an analogous electron-positron pair (positron being the name given to an unoccupied negative energy state). He showed that the positron, (which can be thought of as a hole or bubble in the sea of filled negative-energy states), ought to behave very much as though it were a particle with the same mass as the electron but with the opposite charge. Five years later, in 1932, C. D. Anderson in the United States actually observed the creation of an electron-positron pair.

The four-dimensional current vector

Using arguments based on the correspondence principle, Dirac showed that the four-dimensional current vector associated with a particle obeying his wave equation is represented by

$$j_\mu = eci\psi^+\gamma^4\gamma^\mu\psi \equiv ec\bar{\psi}\gamma^\mu\psi \tag{8.25}$$

where

$$\bar{\psi} \equiv i\psi^+\gamma^4 \tag{8.26}$$

and ψ^+ is the conjugate transpose of the wave function ψ. The space part of the current 4-vector is

$$\vec{j} = ec\psi^+\vec{\alpha}\psi \tag{8.27}$$

This is to be compared with the non-relativistic theory. *The velocity of the electron is represented by the operator $c\vec{\alpha}$* where

$$\vec{\alpha} \equiv i\gamma''\vec{\gamma} = \left(\begin{array}{c|c} 0 & \vec{\sigma} \\ \hline \vec{\sigma} & 0 \end{array}\right) \tag{8.28}$$

while in the non-relativistic theory, velocity is represented by $(\hbar/m_0 i)(\partial/\partial\vec{x})$. *The quantum mechanical entity which corresponds in the classical limit to an oscillating current is*

$$j_\mu(\vec{x}, t)_{n'n} \equiv ec\bar{\psi}_{n'}\gamma^\mu\psi_n \tag{8.29}$$

where $\psi_{n'}$ and ψ_n are eigenfunctions of the energy operator. Factoring out the time-dependence we can write

$$j_\mu(\vec{x}, t)_{n'n} = \text{Re}\{j_\mu(\vec{x})_{n'n}\, e^{i\{(E_{n'} - E_n)/(h)\}t}\} \quad \mu = 1, 2, 3 \tag{8.30}$$

In our discussion of classical electrodynamics, Eqs. (1.183)–(1.187), we treated the particular case of a current which oscillates harmonically with

243

The quantum theory of atoms, molecules, and photons

time. We showed that an oscillating current produces, at very large distances, an outgoing electromagnetic wave. If the current is given by

$$A_\mu(\vec{x}, t) = \mathrm{Re} \left\{ e^{-ikct} \int d^3x' j_\mu(\vec{x}') \frac{e^{ik|\vec{x}-\vec{x}'|}}{c|\vec{x}-\vec{x}'|} \right\} \qquad (8.31)$$

In the electric-dipole approximation only the space part of the current contributes to the radiation. Also in this approximation we can set $\vec{x}' = 0$ in the factor $e^{ik|\vec{x}-\vec{x}'|}/|\vec{x}-\vec{x}'|$ and take it outside the integral. Then we have

$$A_\mu(\vec{x}, t) \cong \mathrm{Re} \left\{ \frac{e^{ik(ct-|\vec{x}|)}}{|\vec{x}|} \int d^3x' j_\mu(\vec{x}') \right\} \quad \mu = 1, 2, 3 \qquad (8.32)$$

In classical electrodynamics the flow of energy across a unit area per unit time is given by $\hat{n}, \vec{S}$ where $\hat{n}$ is a unit vector normal to the surface and $\vec{S}$ is the 'Poynting vector' defined by

$$\vec{S} = \frac{c}{4\pi} \vec{E} \wedge \vec{H} \qquad (8.33)$$

Using Eqs. (8.32)–(8.33) and Eqs. (1.170)–(1.171) one can calculate the rate at which energy flows out across a large surface surrounding the region in which the oscillating current is confined. This turns out to be

$$r^2 \int d\Omega \hat{n} \cdot \vec{S} = \frac{2k^2}{3c} \left\{ \int d^3x' \vec{j}(\vec{x}') \right\}^2 \qquad (8.34)$$

In order to calculate the rate of spontaneous photon emission by this semi-classical method, we just replace the harmonically oscillating current, Eq. (8.31), by the transition current, Eq. (8.30), and divide by the energy per quantum $\hbar\omega = \hbar kc$.

$$\frac{1}{\tau} = \frac{4}{3} \frac{e^2}{\hbar c} kc \left(\int d^3x \psi_{n'}^\dagger \vec{\alpha} \psi_n \right)^2 \cong \frac{4}{3} \frac{ke^2\hbar}{m_0^2 c} \left(\int d^3x \psi_{n'}^* \frac{\partial}{\partial x} \psi_n \right)^2 \quad (8.35)$$

Problem (8.3) (a) Calculate the probability per unit time for spontaneous photon emission from a hydrogen atom in a $2p_z$ excited state.

(b) Repeat the calculation for a spherically symmetric harmonic oscillator in its first excited state. If the force constant of the oscillator is adjusted so that the photon energy is the same as in part (a), what is the ratio of the two transition rates?

Semiclassical treatment of induced absorption and induced emission of photons; the Dirac Hamiltonian; the vector potential representing a plane wave; transition probability and cross-section calculated by means of perturbation theory

The semiclassical treatment can also be used to discuss 'induced absorption' and 'induced emission' of radiation. When a wave of electromagnetic radiation is incident on a charged particle obeying the Dirac equation, the extra terms in the Hamiltonian can be regarded as a time-dependent perturbation (see Appendix V) which induces the particle to make a transition. In the non-relativistic limit, the terms on the right-hand side of Eq. (8.24) constitute the Hamiltonian of an electron in an external electromagnetic field. We can find the relativistic Hamiltonian by multiplying the Dirac equation on the left by $\hbar c \gamma^4$. This gives

$$\hbar c \gamma^4 \gamma^\mu \left(\frac{\partial}{\partial x^\mu} - i \frac{e}{\hbar c} A_\mu \right) \psi = \left\{ i \hbar c \vec{\alpha} . \left(\frac{\partial}{\partial \vec{x}} - \frac{ie}{\hbar c} \vec{A} \right) - i \hbar \frac{\partial}{\partial t} + e\phi \right\} \psi$$

$$= -\hbar c \gamma^4 k_0 \psi = -m_0 c^2 \gamma^4 \psi \qquad (8.36)$$

which can be rewritten in the form

$$i\hbar \frac{\partial \psi}{\partial t} = H\psi \qquad (8.37)$$

where

$$H = i\hbar c \vec{\alpha} . \left(\frac{\partial}{\partial \vec{x}} - \frac{ie}{\hbar c} \vec{A} \right) + e\phi + m_0 c^2 \gamma^4 \qquad (8.38)$$

The operator H defined by Eq. (8.38) is the relativistic Hamiltonian for an electron in an external electromagnetic field. This field may be due in part to the other charged particles of the atom or molecule in which the electron is moving, and in part to waves of electromagnetic radiation which are incident on the electron. The extra terms in the Hamiltonian produced by the incident wave constitute a perturbation H' which can induce transitions from one eigenstate of the unperturbed Hamiltonian to another. For example suppose that the perturbation is due to a beam of radiation whose vector potential has the form

$$\vec{A}(\vec{x}, t) = \vec{A}_0 \, \text{Re}\{e^{i(\vec{k}.\vec{x} - kct)}\} \qquad (8.39)$$

and whose scalar potential is zero

$$A_4 = i\phi = 0 \qquad (8.40)$$

The quantum theory of atoms, molecules, and photons

Such a wave must, of course, satisfy Maxwell's equations, Eqs. (1.163) and (1.164). Since the electromagnetic wave is propagating through a vacuum, the current term on the right-hand side of Eq. (1.163) disappears leaving

$$\Box^2 A_\mu \equiv \left(\nabla^2 - \frac{1}{c^2} \frac{\partial^2}{\partial t^2} \right) A_\mu = 0 \tag{8.41}$$

The vector potential of Eq. (8.39) certainly satisfies Eq. (8.41) because

$$\left(\nabla^2 - \frac{1}{c^2} \frac{\partial^2}{\partial t^2} \right) e^{i(\vec{k}\cdot\vec{x} - kct)} = -(\vec{k}\cdot\vec{k} - k^2) e^{i(\vec{k}\cdot\vec{x} - kct)} = 0 \tag{8.42}$$

Maxwell's other equation, Eq. (1.164), requires that

$$\frac{\partial}{\partial \vec{x}} \cdot \vec{A}_0 \, e^{i(\vec{k}\cdot\vec{x} - kct)} = i\vec{k}\cdot\vec{A}_0 \, e^{i(\vec{k}\cdot\vec{x} - kct)} = 0 \tag{8.43}$$

so that the 'photon momentum vector' $\hbar\vec{k}$ and the 'polarization and amplitude vector' $\vec{A}_0$ must be perpendicular to one another. *Such a wave corresponds to a beam radiation of frequency kc propagating in the direction of $\vec{k}$ and linearly polarized in the direction of $\vec{A}_0$.* It can be shown from Maxwell's equations that an electromagnetic wave carries energy and that the amount of energy crossing a unit area per unit time is given by the Poynting vector, Eq. (8.33). The electric and magnetic fields $\vec{E}$ and $\vec{H}$ are related to the vector potential $\vec{A}$ by Eq. (1.171). If $\vec{A}$ is the vector potential of a linearly polarized plane wave, Eq. (8.39), then

$$\vec{E} = -\frac{1}{c} \frac{\partial \vec{A}}{\partial t} - \frac{\partial \phi}{\partial \vec{x}} = -\frac{\vec{A}_0}{c} \frac{\partial}{\partial t} \cos(\vec{k}\cdot\vec{x} - kct)$$
$$= -k\vec{A}_0 \sin(\vec{k}\cdot\vec{x} - kct) \tag{8.44}$$

and

$$\vec{H} = \frac{\partial}{\partial \vec{x}} \wedge \vec{A} = -\vec{k} \wedge \vec{A} = -\vec{k} \wedge \vec{A}_0 \sin(\vec{k}\cdot\vec{x} - kct) \tag{8.45}$$

so that

$$\vec{S} = \frac{c}{4\pi} k\vec{A}_0 \wedge (\vec{k} \wedge \vec{A}_0) \sin^2(\vec{k}\cdot\vec{x} - kct)$$

$$= \frac{c}{4\pi} |\vec{A}_0|^2 \vec{k} \sin\{2(\vec{k}\cdot\vec{x} - kct)\} \tag{8.46}$$

The Poynting vector indicates that the energy of the electromagnetic wave moves in the direction of the photon momentum vector $\hbar\vec{k}$. The average amount of energy crossing a unit area per unit time is

$$\lim_{t \to \infty} \frac{1}{t} \int_0^t S(t') \, dt' = \frac{c}{8\pi} (kA_0)^2 \tag{8.47}$$

Knowing the frequency $\omega = kc$ and the intensity

$$I = \frac{c}{8\pi}(kA_0)^2 = \frac{1}{8\pi c}(\omega A_0)^2 \qquad (8.48)$$

of a beam of monochromatic, linearly polarized, radiation we can calculate the vector potential of the wave, Eq. (8.39). Then from Eq. (8.38) or from Eq. (8.24) we can write down the perturbation which it produces in the Hamiltonian of an electron.

$$H' = e\vec{\alpha}.\vec{A} \qquad (8.49)$$

According to time-dependent perturbation theory (Appendix V), the probability per unit time that such a perturbation will induce a transition between two states, $\psi_{n'}$, ψ_n, is proportional to $|H'_{n,n'}|^2$ where $H'_{n,n'}$ is the matrix element of the perturbation H' taken between those two states.

$$H'_{n,n'} = e \int d^3x \psi_{n'}^\dagger . \vec{\alpha} . \vec{A} \psi_n$$

$$\equiv \frac{eA_0}{2}\left\{ e^{-ikct} \int d^3x \psi_{n'}^\dagger . e^{i\vec{k}.\vec{x}} \hat{u}.\vec{\alpha}\psi_n + e^{ikct} \int d^3x \psi_{n'}^\dagger . e^{-i\vec{k}.\vec{x}} \hat{u}.\vec{\alpha}\psi_n \right\}$$

$$(8.50)$$

where $\hat{u} \equiv \vec{A}_0/A$ is a unit vector in the direction of polarization of the incoming wave. According to perturbation theory, the transition rate is given by

$$\frac{1}{\tau} = \frac{2\pi}{\hbar}|H'_{n',n}|^2\rho = \frac{2\pi}{\hbar}\frac{(eA_0)^2}{4}\left|\int d^3x \psi_{n'}^\dagger . e^{i\vec{k}.\vec{x}} \hat{u}.\vec{\alpha}\psi_n\right|^2 \rho \qquad (8.51)$$

where ρ is the density of final states. For example if we are considering a spectral line with a Lorentzian shape and halfwidth Γ, then the density of final states is given by

$$\rho = \frac{\Gamma/\pi}{\hbar\{(kc - \omega_{n'n})^2 + \Gamma^2\}} \qquad (8.52)$$

Eq. (8.48) allows us to express the amplitude A_0 in terms of the intensity. In a beam of intensity I, the number of photons crossing a unit area in a unit time is $I/\hbar kc$. We can express the probability that one of these photons will induce the transition $\psi_{n'} \to \psi_n$ in terms of a 'cross-section'

$$\sigma = \frac{\hbar kc}{It} = \frac{e^2}{\hbar c}\left(\frac{2\pi}{k}\right)^2\left|\int d^3x \psi_{n'}^\dagger . e^{i\vec{k}.\vec{x}} \hat{u}.\vec{\alpha}\psi_n\right|^2 \hbar kc\rho \qquad (8.53)$$

One imagines this cross-section as a tiny target in the path of the beam. If a photon hits the target, it will induce a transition—otherwise not. In making

The quantum theory of atoms, molecules, and photons

comparisons between calculated cross-sections and experiment it is convenient to introduce a parameter called the molar extinction coefficient. As a beam of light passes through a solution containing absorbing molecules, its intensity diminishes exponentially. The molar extinction coefficient ε is defined as the rate of change of the intensity of a beam of radiation passing through a molar solution of absorbing molecules

$$I(x) = I_0\, e^{-2\cdot 3026\varepsilon Cx} \tag{8.54}$$

where C is the concentration in moles/litre.

The molar extinction coefficient is proportional to the absorption cross-section σ of Eq. (8.53).

$$I(x) = I_0 e^{-N\sigma Cx} \qquad \sigma = \frac{2\cdot 3026\varepsilon}{N}$$

$$N = 6\cdot 0254 \times 10^{23} \text{ molecules/mole}$$

$$2\cdot 3026 = \log_e (10) \tag{8.55}$$

Problem (8.4) Evaluate the commutator $[H, \bar{x}]$, where H is the Dirac Hamiltonian, Eq. (8.38). Use the result to show that if $H\psi_n = E_n\psi_n$ and $H\psi_{n'} = E_{n'}\psi_{n'}$ then

$$\int d^3x\psi_{n'}^*\hat{u}\cdot\bar{\alpha}\psi_n = \frac{i(E_{n'} - E_n)}{\hbar c} \int d^3x\psi_{n'}^*\hat{u}\cdot\bar{x}\psi_n$$

Calculate the transition dipole moment matrix element

$$\int d^3x\chi_{2p_z}\bar{x}\,\chi_{1s}$$

where χ_{2p_z} and χ_{1s} are the hydrogen atom eigenfunctions listed in Table 2.3.

Circular dichroism and linear dichroism

The absorption of circularly polarized light can be treated in a very similar way. A circularly polarized light-wave can be treated as a superposition of a plane polarized wave (like the one given in Eq. (8.39)) and another wave polarized perpendicular to the first but 90° out of phase. For example, think of an electromagnetic wave whose scalar potential ϕ is zero and whose vector potential is given by

$$\bar{A} = A_0 \, \mathrm{Re}\left\{ \left(\frac{\hat{u}_1 \pm i\hat{u}_2}{\sqrt{2}} \right) e^{i(\bar{k}\cdot\bar{x} - kct)} \right\} \tag{8.56}$$

where $\hat{u}_1$ and $\hat{u}_2$ are unit vectors perpendicular to each other and perpendicular to the direction of $\vec{k}$. Now imagine an observer located at the point $\vec{x} = 0$. He will see the vector potential

$$\vec{A}(\vec{x} = 0, t) = \frac{A_0}{\sqrt{2}} \{\hat{u}_1 \cos{(kct)} \pm \hat{u}_2 \sin{(kct)}\} \tag{8.57}$$

At time $t = 0$ the polarization vector of the combined wave will be observed to be pointing in the direction of $\hat{u}_1$. At the slightly later time $t = \pi/2kc$, the polarization vector will have rotated so that it points either in the direction of $\hat{u}_2$ or in the opposite direction depending on whether we take the plus or the minus sign. Thus the vector potential of Eq. (8.56) corresponds to a right or left circularly polarized wave depending on the sign. We can calculate the absorption cross-sections for the right and left circularly polarized waves just as we did for the linearly polarized wave. The difference between σ_+ and σ_- is called the 'circular dichroism' and in a way exactly analogous to Eqs. (8.50)–(8.53) we obtain

$$\sigma_+ - \sigma_- = \frac{e^2}{\hbar c}\left(\frac{2\pi}{k}\right)^2 \frac{kcp}{2} \left\{\left|\int d^3x \psi_{n'}^\dagger\, e^{i\vec{k}\cdot\vec{x}}(\alpha_1 + i\alpha_2)\psi_n\right|^2 \right.$$
$$\left. - \left|\int d^3x \psi_{n'}^\dagger\, e^{i\vec{k}\cdot\vec{x}}(\alpha_1 - i\alpha_2)\psi_n\right|^2\right\} \tag{8.58}$$

In a similar way, we can define 'linear dichroism' as the difference between the absorption cross-sections corresponding to two directions of linear polarization:

$$\sigma_1 - \sigma_2 = \frac{e^2}{\hbar c}\left(\frac{2\pi}{k}\right)^2 kcp \left\{\left|\int d^3x \psi_{n'}^\dagger\, e^{i\vec{k}\cdot\vec{x}}\alpha_1\psi_n\right|^2 \right.$$
$$\left. - \left|\int d^3x \psi_{n'}^\dagger\, e^{i\vec{k}\cdot\vec{x}}\alpha_2\psi_n\right|^2\right\} \tag{8.59}$$

In the non-relativistic limit the velocity operator $c\vec{\alpha}$ goes over into $\vec{p}/m_0$ so that $\vec{\alpha}$ can be approximated by $(\hbar/im_0c)(\partial/\partial\vec{x})$ in Eqs. (8.53), (8.58), and (8.59).

Separation of electronic and nuclear coordinates, the Franck–Condon factor

We have thus far been considering a transition $\psi_n \to \psi_{n'}$ from one single-electron eigenfunction to another. Now we would like to generalize our results so that they will apply to a many-particle system such as a molecule. *In the Born–Oppenheimer approximation (chapter 7) we solve the wave equation for the electrons at a fixed value of the nuclear coordinates. Then we move the nuclei to slightly different positions and solve again for the electronic wave functions and energy. The electronic energy as a function of the nuclear coordinates forms a potential in which the nuclei move.* One can then find the vibrational normal modes of the nuclei and treat each mode as an harmonic oscillator. If we denote the nuclear coordinates by q and the electron coordinates by x, then the wave equation of the electrons will have the form

$$H(q, x)\Psi_\kappa(q, x) = E_\kappa(q)\Psi_\kappa(q, x) \tag{8.60}$$

Since it is the solution of an eigenvalue equation, the electron wave function $\Psi_n(q, x)$ will obey the orthonormality relation

$$\int dx \Psi_{\kappa'}^\dagger(q, x)\Psi_\kappa(q, x) = \delta_{\kappa'\kappa} \tag{8.61}$$

which holds for all values of q. Now let $H'(x) + H'(q)$ be the perturbation produced by the incoming light-wave, and let $\xi_{\kappa, n}(q)$ be the nuclear wave function. Then the matrix element corresponding to absorption of a photon will have the form:

$$\langle \kappa', n'|H'|\kappa, n\rangle$$

$$= \int dx \int dq \Psi_{\kappa'}^\dagger(qx)\xi_{\kappa', n'}^\dagger(q)\{H'(x) + H'(q)\}\Psi_\kappa(q, x)\xi_{\kappa, n}^\dagger(q)$$

$$= \int dq \xi_{\kappa', n'}^\dagger(q)\xi_{\kappa, n}(q) \int dx \Psi_{\kappa'}(q, x)H'(x)\Psi_\kappa(q, x)$$

$$+ \delta_{\kappa'\kappa} \int dq \xi_{\kappa, n'}^\dagger(q)H'(q)\xi_{\kappa, n}(q)$$

$$\cong S_{\kappa'n'; \kappa n} \int dx \Psi_{\kappa'}^\dagger(q_0, x)H'(x)\Psi_\kappa(q_0, x)$$

$$+ \delta_{\kappa'\kappa} \int dq \xi_{\kappa, n'}^\dagger(q)H'(q)\xi_{\kappa, n}(q) \tag{8.62}$$

where q_0 is the equilibrium value of the nuclear coordinates and $S_{\kappa'n'; \kappa n}$ is the nuclear overlap integral (sometimes called the Franck–Condon factor)

$$S_{\kappa'n'; \kappa n} \equiv \int dq \xi_{\kappa'n'}^\dagger(q)\xi_{\kappa, n}(q) \tag{8.63}$$

Notice that in Eq. (8.62) the term involving $H'(q)$ vanishes when $\kappa \neq \kappa'$ because of the orthogonality relation, Eq. (8.61). Also notice that the electronic wave function has been approximated by its value at q_0. In the case of an allowed transition, this is a sufficiently good approximation. However, if the transition is forbidden, all of the intensity comes from higher terms in the expansion of $\Psi_\kappa(q, x)$ about q_0.

From Eq. (8.62) we can see that the matrix element between the ground state of a molecule and an excited state will be zero unless there is some overlap between the nuclear wave functions of the two states, and the matrix element will of course be small if the overlap is small. For example, consider the nuclear wave functions in a diatomic molecule. The radial

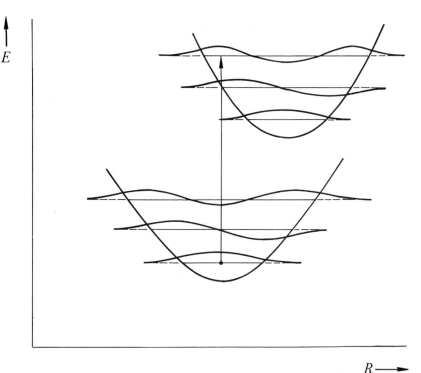

Figure 8.1 is the same as Fig. 7.1 but with the vibrational energy levels added, and the corresponding harmonic oscillator wave functions superimposed. The absorption of a photon, (indicated by the arrow) usually leaves the molecule both vibrationally and electronically excited because the overlap of nuclear wave functions is greatest for this type of transition. (Franck–Condon principle).

parts of the nuclear wave functions are shown schematically in Fig. 8.1. These functions have their maximum amplitude in the neighbourhood of the classical turning points (i.e., at the values of the internuclear coordinate q where the classical kinetic energy is equal to zero.) Therefore, when a molecule is in the lowest vibrational level of the

The quantum theory of atoms, molecules, and photons

electronic ground state, the largest photon absorption cross-section corresponds to a transition to a higher vibrational level of the electronic excited state. When a molecule in a condensed medium undergoes a transition of this kind and becomes both vibrationally and electronically excited, the vibrational energy is very rapidly converted into the kinetic energy of adjacent molecules. The molecule is then in the lowest vibrational level of the electronic excited state. From this state, the most likely photon emission process is the transition to an excited vibrational level of the electronic ground state, following which there is again a vibrational energy loss. The whole cycle is indicated by the arrows in Fig. 8.2. Thus we have a principle

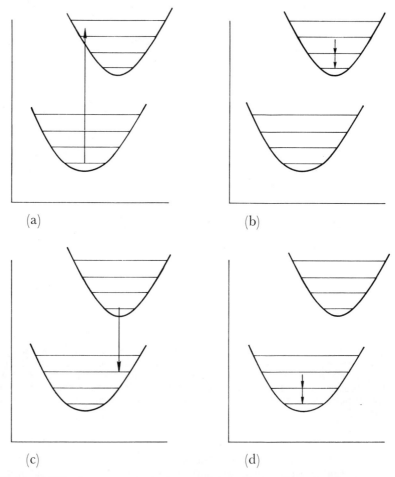

(a)   (b)

(c)   (d)

Figure 8.2 illustrates a typical sequence of events following the absorption of a photon. The difference in energy between the absorbed and emitted photon, (a) and (c), is due to the loss of vibrational energy, (b) and (d).

(first put forward by James Franck[7] and E. U. Condon), which states that electronic transitions are most likely when the initial and final nuclear wave functions have maximum overlap. We can see from Fig. 8.2 that because of the Franck–Condon principle, there will be a shift of energy between the absorption maximum and the fluorescence maximum of a band. The bands shown in Fig. 8.3 are composed of a large number of broadened lines which

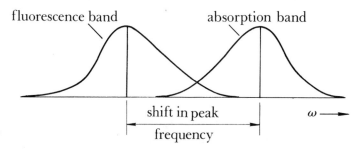

fluorescence band   absorption band

shift in peak frequency $\omega \longrightarrow$

Figure 8.3 shows the absorption and fluorescence bands which result from the sequence of events shown in Fig. 8.2. The peak frequency in the absorption band corresponds to the upward-pointing arrow of Fig. 8.2c, while less probable transitions account for the rest of the band. The peak frequency of the emission band corresponds to the downward-pointing arrow in Fig. 8.2c.

overlap one another so that the individual vibrational levels cannot be distinguished. The individual vibrational levels can however be observed by spectroscopy at infrared frequencies. Infrared spectroscopy provides us with a way to observe the vibrational potential energy curves, and it is thus an extremely valuable means for studying chemical bonding.

Vibrational transitions

In the case of infrared transitions $\kappa = \kappa'$ but $n \neq n'$, i.e., the electron quantum numbers are unchanged by the transition, but the vibrational and rotational quantum numbers are changed. When $\kappa = \kappa'$ but $n \neq n'$ the nuclear overlap integral $S_{\kappa'n';\kappa n}$ of Eq. (8.63) vanishes because in that case $\xi_{\kappa n'}(q)$ and $\xi_{\kappa n}(q)$ are different eigenfunctions of the same Hamiltonian. Therefore, in the case of infrared spectroscopy, the transition matrix element of Eq. (8.62) contains only the nuclear factor

$$\langle \kappa, n' | H' | \kappa, n \rangle = \int dq \xi^\dagger_{\kappa, n'}(q) H'(q) \xi_{\kappa, n}(q) \qquad (8.64)$$

253

The matrix element of Eq. (8.64) can be evaluated by means of Eq. (8.49) and Eqs. (7.39)–(7.69). Substituting into Eq. (8.51) and letting $e^{i\vec{k}\cdot\vec{x}} \approx 1$ we obtain the cross-section for absorption of an infrared photon by the lth vibrational normal mode of a molecule

$$\sigma = \frac{e^2}{\hbar c}(2\pi)^2 \hbar k c \rho |\vec{D}_l \cdot \hat{u}|^2$$

$$\vec{D}_l \equiv \sum_j \sqrt{\frac{\hbar}{2\omega M_j}} Z_j \hat{u}_j U_{jl}^*$$

$$\rho \cong \frac{\Gamma/\pi}{\hbar\{(kc - \omega_l)^2 + \Gamma^2\}} \tag{8.65}$$

Here U_{lj} is the unitary transformation matrix which diagonalizes the mass-weighted vibrational potential energy matrix Eq. (7.11); M_j and Z_j are the mass and atomic number associated with the jth nuclear coordinate; $\hat{u}_j$ is a unit vector in the direction of the jth coordinate; and $\omega_l \cong kc$ is the frequency of the lth normal mode. In using Eq. (8.52) for the density of final states we have neglected the complexity of the rotational spectrum and assumed that the line-shape of the vibrational levels is Lorentzian.

Electronic transitions; sum over configurations; the electric dipole approximation; the zero differential overlap LCAO approximation

When the electron quantum numbers change, as they do in visible and ultraviolet transitions, then we have the opposite situation: $\kappa \neq \kappa'$ and Eq. (8.62) reduces to

$$\langle \kappa'n'|H'|\kappa n \rangle$$

$$\cong S_{\kappa'n';\kappa n} \int dx \psi_{\kappa'}^\dagger(q_0, x) H'(x) \psi_\kappa(q_0, x)$$

$$= S_{\kappa'n';\kappa n} eA_0 e^{-ikct} \int dx \psi_{\kappa'}^\dagger \sum_j e^{i\vec{k}\cdot\vec{x}_j} \hat{u} \cdot \vec{\alpha}_j \psi_k \tag{8.66}$$

the sum being taken over the coordinates of all the electrons in the molecule. Suppose that the ground-state electronic wave function of the molecule is represented by a Slater determinant of the form

$$\Psi_0 = \Delta_0 = A\{\Phi_1 \Phi_{\bar{1}} \cdots \Phi_m \Phi_{\bar{m}} \cdots \Phi_{n_f} \Phi_{\bar{n}_f}\} \tag{8.67}$$

while a singlet or triplet excited state is represented by a linear combination of singly excited configurations

$$\Psi_\kappa = \frac{1}{\sqrt{2}} \sum_{m \to m'} (\Delta_{m \to m'} \pm \Delta_{\bar{m} \to \bar{m}'}) B_{m \to m', \kappa}$$

$$\Delta_{m \to m'} \equiv |\Phi_1 \Phi_{\bar{1}} \cdots \Phi_m \Phi_{\bar{m}} \cdots \Phi_{n_f} \Phi_{\bar{n}_f}|$$

$$\Delta_{\bar{m} \to \bar{m}'} \equiv |\Phi_1 \Phi_{\bar{1}} \cdots \Phi_m \Phi_{\bar{m}'} \cdots \Phi_{n_f} \Phi_{\bar{n}_f}| \tag{8.68}$$

with a plus sign for the singlet state, and a minus for the triplet. Then, according to the Slater–Condon rules for evaluating an operator of 'type F',

$$\int dx \Psi_\kappa^\dagger \sum_j e^{i\vec{k} \cdot \vec{x}_j} \hat{u} \cdot \vec{\alpha}_j \Psi_0$$

$$= \frac{1}{\sqrt{2}} \sum_{m \to m'} \left\{ \int d^3 x \Phi_m^\dagger e^{i\vec{k} \cdot \vec{x}} \hat{u} \cdot \vec{\alpha} \Phi_{m'} \pm \int d^3 x \Phi_{\bar{m}}^\dagger e^{i\vec{k} \cdot \vec{x}} \hat{u} \cdot \vec{\alpha} \Phi_{\bar{m}'} \right\} B_{m \to m', \kappa}^* \tag{8.69}$$

where Φ_m and $\Phi_{\bar{m}}$ are respectively spin-up and spin-down molecular orbitals. If we are dealing with a small molecule then it is a good approximation to expand the factor $e^{i\vec{k} \cdot \vec{x}_j}$ of Eq. (8.66) in a Taylor series about the centre of the molecule so that

$$\int dx \Psi_{\kappa'}^\dagger \sum_j e^{i\vec{k} \cdot \vec{x}_j} \hat{u} \cdot \vec{\alpha}_j \Psi_\kappa \cong \int dx \Psi_{\kappa'}^\dagger \sum_j (1 + i\vec{k} \cdot \vec{x}_j + \cdots) \hat{u} \cdot \vec{\alpha}_j \Psi_\kappa \tag{8.70}$$

The approximation which retains only the first term in the Taylor series is called the 'electric dipole' approximation. The matrix element of the electric dipole term $\sum_j \hat{u} \cdot \vec{\alpha}_j$ can be converted into a more familar form by means of the commutation relation

$$[H, \sum_j \hat{u} \cdot \vec{x}_j] = \frac{\hbar c}{i} \hat{u} \cdot \vec{\alpha}_j \tag{8.71}$$

where H is the many-electron Hamiltonian

$$H = \sum_j \left\{ \frac{\hbar c}{i} \vec{\alpha}_j \cdot \frac{\partial}{\partial \vec{x}_j} + V(\vec{x}_j) + \gamma_j^4 m_0 c^2 \right\} + \sum_{j' > j} \frac{e^2}{|\vec{x}_{j'} - \vec{x}_j|} \tag{8.72}$$

Thus, in the electric dipole approximation, Eq. (8.69) becomes

$$\int dx \Psi_\kappa^\dagger \sum_j e^{i\vec{k} \cdot \vec{x}_j} \hat{u} \cdot \vec{\alpha}_j \Psi_0 \cong \frac{i(E_\kappa - E_0)}{\hbar c} \hat{u} \cdot \vec{D}_{\kappa, 0} \cong ik \hat{u} \cdot \vec{D}_{\kappa, 0} \tag{8.73}$$

255

where $\vec{D}_{\kappa,0}$ is the transition dipole moment

$$\vec{D}_{\kappa,0} \equiv \sum_{m \to m'} \int d^3x \Phi_m^\dagger \vec{x} \Phi_{m'} B_{m \to m',\kappa}^* \tag{8.74}$$

Notice that in the electric dipole approximation, there is vanishing probability for the absorbed photon to induce a transition from the ground state to a triplet excited state. If the molecular orbitals Φ_m and $\Phi_{m'}$ are expressed as a linear combination of atomic orbitals

$$\Phi_m^* = \sum_l \chi_l^* C_{lm}^*$$

$$\Phi_{m'} = \sum_l \chi_{l'} C_{l'm'} \tag{8.75}$$

then in the zero differential overlap approximation

$$\int d^3x \chi_l^* \vec{x} \chi_{l'} \cong \delta_{l'l} \vec{X}_l \tag{8.76}$$

the transition dipole moment vector becomes

$$\vec{D}_{\kappa,0} \cong \sum_l \sum_{m \to m'} C_{lm}^* C_{lm'} B_{m \to m',\kappa}^* \vec{X}_l \tag{8.77}$$

where $\vec{X}_l$ is the position of the lth atom. Thus finally we have the approximate cross-section for absorption of a photon linearly polarized in the direction $\hat{u}$ accompanied by a transition of the molecule from the ground state, Eq. (8.67), to a singlet excited state Eq. (8.68).

$$\sigma = \frac{e^2}{\hbar c} (2\pi)^2 \hbar k c \rho |S_{Kn;\,0n'} \hat{u} \cdot \vec{D}_{K,0}|^2 \tag{8.78}$$

where ρ is the density of final states, given by Eq. (8.52), $S_{\kappa n;\,0n'}$ is the Franck–Condon factor given by Eq. (8.63) and $\vec{D}_{\kappa,0}$ is the transition dipole vector, given by Eq. (8.77).

Dispersion; a classical model of frequency-dependent polarizibility; the connection between absorption and scattering

Besides absorbing light, a material system can also diffract or scatter it. At frequencies where the photon absorption cross-section and the coefficient of extinction are large, the photon scattering cross-section and the index of refraction associated with the material system are also large. We can see that the two phenomena are related by considering the induced electric dipole moment of a damped harmonic oscillator. For simplicity let us begin by considering the classical equation of motion of a particle of charge e and mass m_0 elastically bound to the origin. If we subject the particle to an oscillating electric field $\vec{E} \, e^{i\omega t}$ then the classical equation of motion can be written in the form

$$\frac{d^2\vec{x}}{dt^2} + \Gamma \frac{d\vec{x}}{dt} + \omega_0^2 \vec{x} = \frac{e}{m_0} \vec{E} \, e^{i\omega t} \tag{8.79}$$

If we assume that the induced dipole moment has the form

$$e\vec{x} = \alpha \vec{E} \, e^{i\omega t} \tag{8.80}$$

then

$$\frac{d^2\vec{x}}{dt^2} + \Gamma \frac{d\vec{x}}{dt} + \omega_0^2 \vec{x} = \frac{\alpha \vec{E}}{e} e^{i\omega t}(-\omega^2 + i\omega\Gamma + \omega_0^2) \tag{8.81}$$

Comparing Eq. (8.81) and Eq. (8.79) we can see that

$$\alpha = \frac{e^2}{m_0(\omega_0^2 - \omega^2 + i\omega\Gamma)} \tag{8.82}$$

The complex constant of proportionality, α, which relates the induced dipole moment to the electric field which produces it is called the 'polarizability' associated with the oscillator. The rate at which energy is dissipated by the oscillator is proportional both to the damping constant Γ and to the amplitude of the oscillation. When the driving frequency ω approaches the resonant frequency ω_0 the amplitude $\vec{x}$ becomes large and the rate of energy absorption likewise increases. At the same time, the induced dipole moment is the source of a scattered electromagnetic wave whose amplitude is also proportional to $\vec{x}$. *Thus the rates of both absorption and scattering are large near the resonant frequency.*

The effect of an harmonic perturbation on the expectation value of an operator; susceptibility and double-refraction phenomena

One can show that if the harmonic perturbation $H' \sin \omega t$ is applied to a quantum mechanical system in the state $|n\rangle$, and if F is some dynamical variable (such as polarization), then the first-order change induced in the expectation value $\langle n|F|n\rangle$ is given by

$$\Delta(\langle n|F|n\rangle) = \sin(\omega t)\frac{2}{\hbar} \sum_{n' \neq n} \frac{\omega_{n'n}\langle n|F|n'\rangle\langle n'|H'|n\rangle}{\omega_{n'n}^2 - \omega^2 + i\omega\Gamma_{n'n}} \tag{8.83}$$

where $\hbar\omega_{n'n} = E_{n'} - E_n$ and $\Gamma_{n'n}$ is the half-width associated with the transition $|n\rangle \rightarrow |n'\rangle$. If we used Eq. (8.83) to calculate the polarizability of an electron moving in the potential $V = (m_0/2)\omega_0^2 r^2$, we would obtain a result in agreement with Eq. (8.82).

Equation (8.83) is quite a general result and it has been used by Kramers, Heisenberg, Rosenfeld, Condon, Van Vleck, Born, Jordan, and others[2] to discuss a variety of phenomena. These include magnetic susceptibility, the Faraday and Cotton–Mouton effects (double-refraction induced in transparent media by a magnetic field), the Kerr effect (double refraction induced by an electric field), circular dichroism (the difference in absorption between right and left circularly polarized light), and optical rotatory dispersion (a rotation of the angle of linear polarization as light passes through matter). The reader who is interested in this approach can find it reviewed in an article by E. U. Condon. Alternatively, M. J. Stephen[23] has shown how double refraction phenomena can be treated by means of the more general and powerful techniques of quantum field theory.

Since quantum field theory is a vast and somewhat esoteric discipline we shall only quote in a superficial way some of the results which are important for quantum chemistry. A more detailed treatment can be found in chapters 14 and 15 of *Quantum Mechanics* by L. I. Schiff.

Problem (8.5) Use Eq. (8.83) to calculate the electric polarizability of a simple harmonic oscillator. How does the result compare with Eq. (8.82)? (Hint: Let $H' = e\vec{E}.\vec{x}$ and $F = e\vec{x}$.)

A simplified treatment of quantum field theory; photon creation and annihilation operators

The one-electron Dirac equation and the semi-classical treatment of radiation which we have been using are limiting cases of the more general modern theory of quantum electrodynamics. This theory was developed in its original form by Dirac, and later in a more modern form by Dirac, Heisenberg, Kramers, Dyson, Tomonaga, Schwinger, Feynman, and many other workers. It regards the electromagnetic field as having degrees of freedom of its own. *The normal modes of the electromagnetic field are treated in a way which is analogous to our treatment of the normal modes of a crystal lattice (chapter 7). Each normal mode obeys an harmonic oscillator wave equation* and the state of the radiation field is specified by giving the harmonic oscillator quantum number corresponding to every normal mode. If n_k represents the quantum number associated with the kth normal mode, then the state of the electromagnetic field can be represented by a symbol of the form $|\ldots, n_k, \ldots\rangle$. We can define raising and lowering operators $a_k^\dagger$ and a_k which act on the state-symbol to raise or lower the quantum number n_k.

$$a_k^\dagger |\ldots, n_k\rangle = \sqrt{n_k + 1}\,|\ldots, n_k + 1, \ldots\rangle \qquad (8.84)$$

$$a_k |\ldots, n_k, \ldots\rangle = \sqrt{n_k}\,|\ldots, n_k - 1, \ldots\rangle \qquad (8.85)$$

From these definitions it follows that

$$a_k^\dagger a_k |\ldots, n_k, \ldots\rangle = n_k |\ldots, n_k, \ldots\rangle \qquad (8.86)$$

The normal modes of the electromagnetic field are specified by a wave number $\vec{k}$ and a polarization vector $\hat{u}_k$. The energy associated with a particular mode is $(n_k + \frac{1}{2})\hbar\omega_k = (n_k + \frac{1}{2})\hbar ck$ so that the Hamiltonian of the radiation field by itself (not interacting with matter) can be written in the form

$$H_{\text{radiation}} = \sum_k (a_k^\dagger a_k + \tfrac{1}{2})\hbar ck \qquad (8.87)$$

The state of the system where there are neither photons nor electrons is called the 'vacuum state' and is represented by the symbol $|0\rangle$. From Eq. (8.84) it follows that the state where there is only one 'photon' in the system can be represented by the symbol $a_k^\dagger |0\rangle$, (k being an index representing the wave number and polarization of the photon). Other states of the radiation field can be generated by acting on the vacuum state with other raising operators.

Electron creation and annihilation operators; commutation and anticommutation relations

In quantum field theory one also represents the state of the electrons in the system by a series of creation operators acting on the vacuum state. For example, the state where there is a single electron in the spin-orbital Φ_n is represented by the symbol $b_n^\dagger |0\rangle$. $b_n^\dagger$ is called the electron electron 'creation operator' associated with the spin-orbital Φ_n. Similarly, one defines an electron 'annihilation operator' b_n which gives back the vacuum state when it acts on the state $b_n^\dagger |0\rangle$

$$b_n b_n^\dagger |0\rangle \equiv |0\rangle \qquad (8.88)$$

There is a difference however between the photons and the electrons. The electrons obey the Pauli exclusion principle while the photons do not. In order to make sure that we can never get states where there are two electrons in the same spin-orbital, it is convenient to include in the definition of $b_n^\dagger$ the stipulation that acting twice on the vacuum state with the same creation operator must give zero

$$b_n^\dagger b_n^\dagger |0\rangle \equiv 0 \qquad (8.89)$$

The quantum theory of atoms, molecules, and photons

Also since we cannot have states with a negative number of electrons we require that

$$b_n|0\rangle = 0 \qquad (8.90)$$

The operator $b_n^\dagger b_n$ is a 'number operator' analogous to $a_k^\dagger a_k$. When $b_n^\dagger b_n$ acts on a state with no electrons in the spin orbital Φ_n, the result is zero. For example when $b_n^\dagger b_n$ acts on the vacuum state we have from Eq. (8.90)

$$b_n^\dagger b_n|0\rangle = 0 \qquad (8.91)$$

On the other hand, if $b_n^\dagger b_n$ acts on a state where the spin-orbital Φ_n is filled it gives back the state unchanged, (i.e., multiplied by 1). From Eq. (8.88) we have

$$(b_n^\dagger b_n)b_n^\dagger|0\rangle = b_n^\dagger(b_n b_n^\dagger)|0\rangle$$
$$= b_n^\dagger|0\rangle \qquad (8.92)$$

In general, the number operator $b_n^\dagger b_n$ acting on any state $|A\rangle$ gives $v_n|A\rangle$ where v_n is 0 or 1 depending on whether the spin-orbital Φ_n is occupied or unoccupied. The operator $b_n^\dagger$ is the Hermitian conjugate of b_n and the state $\langle 0|b_n$ is the conjugate of $b_n^\dagger|0\rangle$. We can see that these states are properly normalized because, from Eq. (8.88),

$$\langle 0|b_n b_n^\dagger|0\rangle = \langle 0 | 0 \rangle = 1 \qquad (8.93)$$

However, a state containing more than one photon in a particular mode needs a normalization factor. For example consider the state with two photons in the mode k. We would need to write it as $\dfrac{1}{\sqrt{2}} a_k^\dagger a_k^\dagger|0\rangle$, in order to assure that the scalar product with the conjugate state $\dfrac{1}{\sqrt{2}} \langle 0|a_k a_k$ will be equal to 1. Looking back at Eq. (8.84) and Eq. (8.85) we can see that

$$\tfrac{1}{2}\langle 0|a_k a_k a_k^\dagger a_k^\dagger|0\rangle = \langle 0|a_k a_k^\dagger|0\rangle = \langle 0 | 0 \rangle = 1 \qquad (8.94)$$

From Eqs. (8.84)–(8.86) it is easy to see that

$$(a_k a_k^\dagger - a_k^\dagger a_k)|\ldots, n_k, \ldots\rangle = \{(n_k + 1) - n_k\}|\ldots, n_k, \ldots\rangle \qquad (8.95)$$

which gives us the commutation relation

$$a_{k'}a_k^\dagger - a_k^\dagger a_{k'} = \delta_{k'k}$$
$$a_{k'}^\dagger a_k^\dagger - a_k^\dagger a_{k'}^\dagger = 0$$
$$a_{k'}a_k - a_{k'}a_k = 0 \qquad (8.96)$$

By contrast we include in the definition of the electron creation and annihilation operators the 'anticommutation' relations

$$b_{n'}^\dagger b_n^\dagger + b_n^\dagger b_{n'}^\dagger = 0$$

$$b_{n'} b_n + b_n b_{n'} = 0$$

$$b_{n'}^\dagger b_n + b_n b_{n'}^\dagger = \delta_{nn'} \qquad \text{(8.97)}$$

This definition ensures that a many-electron state shall be antisymmetric with respect to the exchange of two electrons. For example, the symbol $b_{n'}^\dagger b_n^\dagger |0\rangle$ represents the state $1/\sqrt{2}\,\det|\Phi_n(1)\Phi_{n'}(2)|$ while $b_n^\dagger b_{n'}^\dagger |0\rangle$ represents the exchanged state $1/\sqrt{2}\,\det|\Phi_n(2)\Phi_{n'}(1)|$. From Eq. (8.97) we can see that

$$b_{n'}^\dagger b_n^\dagger |0\rangle = (b_{n'}^\dagger b_n^\dagger + b_n^\dagger b_{n'}^\dagger - b_n^\dagger b_{n'}^\dagger)|0\rangle = - b_n^\dagger b_{n'}^\dagger |0\rangle \qquad \text{(8.98)}$$

Problem (8.6)   Suppose that

$$|B\rangle = \frac{1}{\sqrt{n_k + 1}}\, b_{n'}^\dagger b_n a_k^\dagger |A\rangle$$

and $\langle A\,|\,A\rangle = 1$. Use Eq. (8.96) and Eq. (8.97) to show that if

$$\langle B| = \frac{1}{\sqrt{n_k + 1}}\, \langle A|a_k b_n^\dagger b_{n'}$$

then $\langle B\,|\,B\rangle = 1$. Show that if

$$H' = \sum_{r,s,\kappa} b_r^\dagger b_s \{a_\kappa M_{rs}(\kappa) + a_\kappa^\dagger M_{rs}^\dagger(\kappa)\}$$

then

$$\langle B|H'|A\rangle = M_{nn'}(k)$$

The postulated Hamiltonian of the electron–photon system; alternative derivation of the total energy of a system of electrons

What we have said so far is only a mathematical definition of the operators $a_k^\dagger, a_k, b_n^\dagger$ and b_n with no physical content at all. The next step is to postulate that the Hamiltonian of a system of electrons and photons can be represented to a close approximation by an operator of the form

$$H = H_{\text{electrons}} + H_{\text{radiation}} + H_{\text{interaction}}$$

$$= \sum_n b_n^\dagger b_n E_n + \tfrac{1}{2} \sum_{n,n',n'',n'''} b_n^\dagger b_{n'}^\dagger b_{n''} b_{n'''} \langle n, n'|\frac{e^2}{r}|n''', n''\rangle$$

$$+ \sum_k \hbar c k(a_k^\dagger a_k + \tfrac{1}{2}) + \sum_{n,n',k} b_n^\dagger b_{n'}\{a_k M_{nn'}(k) + a_k^\dagger M_{nn'}^\dagger(k)\} \qquad \text{(8.99)}$$

where

$$\left\{ i\hbar c\vec{\alpha} \cdot \left(\frac{\partial}{\partial \vec{x}} - \frac{ie}{\hbar c} \vec{A} \right) + e\phi + m_0 c^2 \gamma^4 \right\} \Phi_n = E_n \Phi_n \qquad (8.100)$$

$$\langle n, n' | \frac{e^2}{r} | n''', n'' \rangle \equiv \int d\tau_1 \int d\tau_2 \Phi_n^\dagger(1) \Phi_{n'}^\dagger(2) \frac{e^2}{r_{12}} \Phi_{n''}(2) \Phi_{n'''}(1) \quad (8.101)$$

$$M_{n,n'}(k) \equiv e \sqrt{\frac{2\pi\hbar c}{kL^3}} \int d\tau \Phi_n^\dagger \, e^{i\vec{k}\cdot\vec{x}} \hat{u}_k \cdot \vec{\alpha} \Phi_{n'} \qquad (8.102)$$

and

$$M_{nn'}^\dagger(k) \equiv e \sqrt{\frac{2\pi\hbar c}{kL^3}} \int d\tau \Phi_n^\dagger \, e^{-i\vec{k}\cdot\vec{x}} \hat{u}_k \cdot \vec{\alpha} \Phi_{n'} \qquad (8.103)$$

Here $\hat{u}_k$ is a unit vector in the direction of polarization of the normal mode k. L^3 is the volume of a large box at the edges of which periodic boundary conditions are applied in order to count the normal modes. The set of spin-orbitals Φ_n associated with the creation and annihilation operators $b_n^\dagger$ and b_n are eigenfunctions of the one-electron Dirac Hamiltonian, Eq. (8.38), and E_n is the corresponding eigenvalue. Alternatively, in the non-relativistic limit, we could let Φ_n be an eigenfunction of $H_{N.R.}$, Eq. (8.24)

$$\left\{ \frac{-\hbar^2}{2m_0} \left(\frac{\partial}{\partial \vec{x}} - \frac{ie}{\hbar c} \vec{A} \right)^2 - \frac{e\hbar}{2m_0 c} \vec{H} \cdot \vec{\sigma} + \frac{e\hbar^2}{2m_0^2 c^2} \vec{E} \cdot \frac{\partial}{\partial \vec{x}} + e\phi \right\} \Phi_n = E_n \Phi_n$$
$$(8.104)$$

The electromagnetic potentials and fields which are included in Eqs. (8.100) and (8.104) are due to nuclei, external electric and magnetic fields, etc. In other words, they are due to charges and currents which are external to the system of electrons under consideration. The one-electron Hamiltonian of Eq. (8.100) or Eq. (8.104) is the same as the 'core Hamiltonian' of the Hartree–Fock SCF theory except for the added magnetic terms. The Coulomb interaction between the electrons is contained in the second term,

$$\frac{1}{2} \sum_{n, n', n'', n'''} b_n^\dagger b_{n'}^\dagger b_{n''} b_{n'''} \langle n, n' | \frac{e^2}{r} | n''', n'' \rangle$$

It is interesting to verify that in this approximation the Hamiltonian of Eq. (8.99) gives the same expectation value for the energy of a system of interacting electrons as that which we found by using the Slater–Condon rules. Let $|A\rangle$ be an N-electron state characterized by the orbital occupation numbers v_n and the photon quantum numbers n_k. Then

$$\langle A|H|A\rangle = \langle A|H_{\mathrm{el.}}|A\rangle + \langle A|H_{\mathrm{rad.}}|A\rangle + \langle A|H_{\mathrm{int.}}|A\rangle$$

$$= \sum_n v_n E_n + \tfrac{1}{2} \sum_{n, n', n'', n'''} \langle A|b_n^\dagger b_{n'}^\dagger b_{n''} b_{n'''}|A\rangle \langle n, n' \left| \frac{e^2}{r} \right| n''', n'' \rangle$$

$$+ \sum_k \hbar c k(n_k + \tfrac{1}{2}) \tag{8.105}$$

(The term $\langle A|H_{\mathrm{int.}}|A\rangle$ vanishes because $\langle A|a_k^\dagger|A\rangle = \langle A|a_k|A\rangle = 0$.) In order to evaluate $\langle A|b_n^\dagger b_{n'}^\dagger b_{n''} b_{n'''}|A\rangle$ we should notice that a non-zero term can result only if $n = n''$ and $n' = n'''$ or if $n = n'''$ and $n' = n''$. Otherwise the matrix element vanishes because of orthogonality. Then, using the anticommutation relations, Eq. (8.98), we have

$$\tfrac{1}{2} \sum_{n, n', n'', n'''} \langle A|b_n^\dagger b_{n'}^\dagger b_{n''} b_{n'''}|A\rangle \langle n, n' \left| \frac{e^2}{r} \right| n''', n'' \rangle$$

$$= \tfrac{1}{2} \sum_{n, n'} \left(\langle A|b_n^\dagger b_{n'}^\dagger b_n b_{n'}|A\rangle \langle n, n' \left| \frac{e^2}{r} \right| n', n \rangle \right.$$

$$\left. + \langle A|b_n^\dagger b_{n'}^\dagger b_{n'} b_n|A\rangle \langle n, n' \left| \frac{e^2}{r} \right| n, n' \rangle \right)$$

$$= \tfrac{1}{2} \sum_{n, n'} \langle A|b_n^\dagger b_{n'}^\dagger b_n b_{n'}|A\rangle \left(\langle n, n' \left| \frac{e^2}{r} \right| n', n \rangle - \langle n, n' \left| \frac{e^2}{r} \right| n, n' \rangle \right)$$

$$= \tfrac{1}{2} \sum_{n, n'} \langle A|b_n^\dagger(-b_n b_{n'}^\dagger + \delta_{nn'})b_{n'}|A\rangle \langle n, n' \left| \frac{e^2}{r} (1 - \mathscr{P}_{12}) \right| n', n \rangle$$

$$= \tfrac{1}{2} \sum_{n, n'} v_n v_{n'} \int \mathrm{d}\tau_1 \int \mathrm{d}\tau_2 \Phi_n^\dagger(1)\Phi_{n'}^\dagger(2) \frac{e^2}{r_{12}} (1 - \mathscr{P}_{12})\Phi_{n'}(2)\Phi_n(1) \tag{8.106}$$

Since E_n is the expectation value of the 'core Hamiltonian',

$$E_n = \int \mathrm{d}\tau_1 \Phi_n^\dagger(1) H^c(1) \Phi_{n'}(1) \tag{8.107}$$

equations (8.105) and (8.106) give us the same value for the expectation value of energy as we found in chapter 5.

Perturbation treatment of the electron-photon interaction; spontaneous photon emission

We can divide the Hamiltonian of the photon–electron system into two parts: $H = H_0 + H'$, where

$$H_0 = H_{\mathrm{electrons}} + H_{\mathrm{radiation}} \tag{8.108}$$

263

The quantum theory of atoms, molecules, and photons

and

$$H' = H_{\text{interaction}} = \sum_{n,\,n',\,k} b_n^\dagger b_{n'} \{a_k M_{nn'}(k) + a_k^\dagger M_{nn'}^\dagger(k)\} \quad \textbf{(8.109)}$$

Then we can use time-dependent perturbation theory to calculate the probability per unit time that H' will cause a transition from one eigenstate of H_0 to another. For example, we might consider the case of spontaneous photon emission which we treated earlier by means of the semiclassical theory. Suppose that the final state $|B\rangle$ differs from the initial state $|A\rangle$ by containing an extra photon in the mode k and by the electron transition $\Phi_n \to \Phi_{n'}$

$$|B\rangle = \frac{1}{\sqrt{n_k + 1}} b_{n'}^\dagger b_n a_k^\dagger |A\rangle \quad (8.110)$$

(If the initial state $|A\rangle$ contains no photons at all in the mode k then $n_k = 0$ and $\sqrt{n_k + 1} = 1$.) Then the matrix element of H' linking the initial and final states is given by

$$\langle A|H'|B\rangle$$
$$= \sum_{n'',\,n''',\,k'} \langle A|b_{n''}^\dagger b_{n'''} \{a_{k'} M_{n'',\,n'''}(k) + a_{k'}^\dagger M_{n'',\,n'''}^\dagger(k')\} b_{n'}^\dagger b_n a_k^\dagger |A\rangle$$
$$= \sum_{n'',\,n'''} \langle A|b_{n''}^\dagger b_{n'''} b_{n'}^\dagger b_n a_k a_k^\dagger |A\rangle M_{n'',\,n'''}(k)$$
$$= \langle A|b_n^\dagger b_{n'} b_{n'}^\dagger b_n |A\rangle M_{n,\,n'}(k) = (1 - v_{n'})v_n M_{n,\,n'}(k) = M_{n,\,n'}(k)$$
$$(8.111)$$

Remembering 'Golden Rule Number 2' from perturbation theory, we have for the rate of spontaneous photon emission:

$$\frac{1}{\tau} = \frac{2\pi}{\hbar} |\langle A|H'|B\rangle|^2 \rho(B) = \frac{2\pi e^2}{\hbar} \left(\frac{2\pi\hbar c}{kL^3}\right) \left| \int d\tau \, \Phi_n^\dagger \, e^{i\vec{k}\cdot\vec{x}} \hat{u}_k \cdot \vec{\alpha} \Phi_{n'} \right|^2 \rho(B)$$
$$(8.112)$$

where $\rho(B)$ is the density of final states. The allowed values of the photon momentum vector $\vec{k}$ are restricted by periodic boundary conditions applied at the faces of the cubical volume L^3. This restricts the components of $\vec{k}$ to the values

$$k_i = 0, \pm \frac{2\pi}{L}, \pm \frac{4\pi}{L}, \cdots$$
$$i = 1, 2, 3 \quad (8.113)$$

If we let L become very large, then the allowed values of k merge into a quasi-continuum and we can see from Eq. (8.113) that the number of allowed values per volume of k-space will be $(L/2\pi)^3$. We can imagine an element of volume in k-space expressed in terms of spherical polar coordinates

$$d^3k = k^2 \, dk \, \sin \theta \, d\theta \, d\phi \qquad (8.114)$$

The number of states lying within this volume element is

$$dN = \left(\frac{L}{2\pi}\right)^3 k^2 \, dk \, \sin \theta \, d\theta \, d\phi \qquad (8.115)$$

If the electron levels are sharp, then $dE = \hbar c \, dk$ and the density of final states

$$\rho(B) = \frac{dN}{dE} = \left(\frac{L}{2\pi}\right)^3 \frac{k^2}{\hbar c} \sin \theta \, d\theta \, d\phi \qquad (8.116)$$

Substituting this result into Eq. (8.112) gives us the probability for the spontaneous emission of a photon linearly polarized in the direction $\hat{u}_k$ into the element of solid angle $d\Omega = \sin \theta \, d\theta \, d\phi$

$$\frac{d}{d\Omega}\left(\frac{1}{\tau}\right) = \frac{e^2}{\hbar c} \frac{kc}{2\pi} \left| \int d\tau \Phi_n^\dagger \, e^{i\vec{k}\cdot\vec{x}} \hat{u}_k \cdot \vec{\alpha} \Phi_n \right|^2 \qquad (8.117)$$

If we use the electric dipole approximation and Eq. (8.84) and if we integrate over all angles and sum over the two possible directions of polarization, we obtain the total rate of spontaneous photon emission.

$$\frac{1}{\tau} = \frac{e^2}{\hbar c} \frac{k^3 c}{\pi} \int_0^{2\pi} d\varphi \int_0^\pi \sin \theta \, d\theta |\hat{u}_k \cdot \vec{D}_{n'n}|^2 = \frac{4}{3} \frac{e^2}{\hbar c} k^3 c |\vec{D}_{n'n}|^2 \quad (8.118)$$

which agrees with our earlier result, Eq. (8.35).

Induced absorption and emission of photons

The treatment of induced photon absorption and emission is very similar. In that case, the initial state $|A\rangle$ already contains n_k photons in the mode k so that

$$a_k^\dagger a_k |A\rangle = n_k |A\rangle \qquad (8.119)$$

The final state $|B\rangle$ differs from $|A\rangle$ by the electron transition $\Phi_n \to \Phi_{n'}$, and by having one more or one less photon in the mode k. In induced absorption a photon is lost so that

$$|B\rangle = \frac{1}{\sqrt{n_k}} b_{n'}^\dagger b_n a_k |A\rangle \qquad (8.120)$$

The matrix element of H' then becomes

$$\langle A|H'|B\rangle$$

$$= \frac{1}{\sqrt{n_k}} \sum_{n'', n''', k'} \langle A|b_{n'''}^\dagger b_{n''}\{a_{k'}M_{n'', n'''}(k') + a_k^\dagger \cdot M_{n'', n'''}^\dagger(k')\}b_{n'}^\dagger b_n a_k|A\rangle$$

$$= \frac{1}{\sqrt{n_k}} \sum_{n'', n'''} \langle A|b_{n'''}^\dagger b_{n''} b_{n'}^\dagger b_n a_k^\dagger a_k|A\rangle M_{n'', n'''}(k) = \sqrt{n_k}\, M_{n, n'}(k) \quad (8.121)$$

The rate of photon absorption is therefore

$$\frac{1}{\tau} = \frac{2\pi}{\hbar}|\langle A|H'|B\rangle|^2 \rho(B) = \frac{2\pi}{\hbar}\frac{n_k}{L^3}\frac{e^2 2\pi\hbar c}{k}\left|\int d\tau \Phi_n^\dagger\, e^{-i\vec{k}\cdot\vec{x}}\hat{u}_k\cdot\vec{\alpha}\Phi_{n'}\right|^2 \rho(B)$$

$$(8.122)$$

We would like to relate n_k to the intensity of the illuminating beam. The energy density for photons in the mode k is $n_k \hbar c k/L^3$. Since the photons move with velocity c, the energy flux or intensity is given by

$$I(k) = n_k \frac{\hbar c^2 k}{L^3} \qquad (8.123)$$

If the illuminating beam is strictly monochromatic while the final electron level $\Phi_{n'}$ has a finite width Γ as in Eq. (8.62) then

$$\rho(B) = \frac{\Gamma}{\pi\hbar\{(kc - E_{n'} - E_n)^2 + \Gamma^2\}} \qquad (8.124)$$

Finally, we can use the electric dipole approximation and Problem 8.4 to convert the matrix element of $e^{-i\vec{k}\cdot\vec{x}}\hat{u}_k\cdot\vec{\alpha}$ into a matrix element of

$$\int d\tau \Phi_n^\dagger\, e^{-i\vec{k}\cdot\vec{x}}\hat{u}_k\cdot\vec{\alpha}\Phi_{n'} \cong \int d\tau \Phi_n^\dagger \hat{u}_k\cdot\vec{\alpha}\Phi_{n'}$$

$$= \frac{E_n - E_{n'}}{i\hbar c}\int d\tau \Phi_n^\dagger \hat{u}_k\cdot\vec{x}\Phi_{n'}$$

$$\equiv i\frac{\omega_{n'n}}{c}\hat{u}_k\cdot\vec{D}_{nn'} \qquad (8.125)$$

Combining Eqs. (8.122)–(8.125) and summing over the possible final states n' we have for the photon absorption cross-section

$$\sigma = \frac{\hbar c k}{I\tau} = \frac{4\pi e^2}{\hbar c k}\sum_{n'}\frac{\Gamma_{n'}\omega_{n'n}^2|\hat{u}_k\cdot\vec{D}_{nn'}|^2}{(kc - \omega_{n'n})^2 + \Gamma_{n'}^2} \qquad (8.126)$$

in agreement with Eq. (8.53).

266

Second-order effects; scattering of photons; the generalized polarizability tensor

We can also consider cases where a photon is absorbed in one mode and emitted coherently in another mode. Such effects have to be treated by means of second-order perturbation theory since the first-order matrix elements of H' linking the initial and final states vanish. According to time-dependent perturbation theory, we can still use 'Golden Rule Number 2' for second-order processes provided we replace $\langle B|H'|A \rangle$ by a sum over intermediate states $|C\rangle$. Thus when $\langle B|H'|A \rangle = 0$, the transition rate is given by

$$\frac{1}{\tau} = \frac{2\pi}{\hbar} \left| \sum_C \frac{\langle B|H'|C \rangle \langle C|H'|A \rangle}{E_C - E_A} \right|^2 \rho(B) \qquad (8.127)$$

Let us begin by considering processes where the photon is scattered elastically. Suppose that the initial state $|A\rangle$ contains n_k photons in the mode k, and no photons in the mode k' so that

$$a_k^\dagger a_k |A\rangle = n_k |A\rangle$$

$$a_{k'}^\dagger a_{k'} |A\rangle = 0 \qquad (8.128)$$

Let us also suppose that the final state $|B\rangle$ differs from $|A\rangle$ by the annihilation of a photon in the mode k and the creation of a photon in the mode k'

$$|B\rangle = \frac{1}{\sqrt{n_k}} a_k a_{k'}^\dagger |A\rangle \qquad (8.129)$$

There are two types of intermediate states which can link $|A\rangle$ and $|B\rangle$. The first type differs from $|A\rangle$ by the electron transition $\Phi_n \rightarrow \Phi_{n'}$ and by the annihilation of a photon in the mode k.

$$|C\rangle = \frac{1}{\sqrt{n_k}} b_{n'}^\dagger b_n a_k |A\rangle \qquad (8.130)$$

The second type of intermediate state differs from $|A\rangle$ by the electron transition $\Phi_n \rightarrow \Phi_{n'}$ and by the creation of a photon in the mode k'

$$|C'\rangle = b_{n'}^\dagger b_n a_{k'}^\dagger |A\rangle \qquad (8.131)$$

Then

$$\langle B|H'|C \rangle = \frac{1}{n_k} \sum_{n'',n''',k''} \langle A|a_k^\dagger a_{k'}$$

$$\times b_{n''}^\dagger b_{n'''} \{ a_{k''} M_{n'',n'''}(k'') + a_{k''}^\dagger M_{n'',n'''}^\dagger(k'') \} b_{n'}^\dagger b_n a_k |A\rangle$$

$$= \sum_{n'',n'''} \langle A|b_{n''}^\dagger b_{n'''} b_{n'}^\dagger b_n |A\rangle M_{n'',n'''}^\dagger(k')$$

$$= \langle A|b_{n'}^\dagger b_{n'} b_{n'}^\dagger b_n |A\rangle M_{n,n'}^\dagger(k') = M_{n,n'}^\dagger(k') \qquad (8.132)$$

and similarly, one finds that

$$\langle C|H'|A\rangle = \sqrt{n_k}\, M_{n',n}(k)$$
$$\langle B|H'|C'\rangle = \sqrt{n_k}\, M_{n,n'}(k)$$
$$\langle C'|H'|A\rangle = M_{n',n}^{\dagger}(k') \tag{8.133}$$

From Eqs. (8.121) and (8.122) we can see that $E_C - E_A = E_{n'} - E_n - \hbar ck$ while $E_{C'} - E_A = E_{n'} - E_n + \hbar ck'$. Putting all of these results back into Eq. (8.127) we have

$$
\begin{aligned}
\frac{1}{\tau} &= \frac{2\pi}{\hbar}\, \rho(B)n_k \left| \sum_{n'} \left\{ \frac{M_{n,n'}^{\dagger}(k')M_{n',n}(k)}{E_{n'} - E_n - \hbar ck} + \frac{M_{n,n'}(k)M_{n',n}^{\dagger}(k')}{E_{n'} - E_n + \hbar ck} \right\} \right|^2 \\
&= \frac{2\pi}{\hbar}\, \rho(B)n_k e^4 \left(\frac{2\pi\hbar c}{kL^3} \right)^2 \left| \sum_{n'} \left\{ \frac{\langle n|\mathrm{e}^{-i\vec{k}'\cdot\vec{x}}\hat{u}_{k'}\cdot\vec{\alpha}|n'\rangle\langle n'|\mathrm{e}^{i\vec{k}\cdot\vec{x}}\hat{u}_k\cdot\vec{\alpha}|n\rangle}{E_{n'} - E_n - \hbar ck} \right. \right. \\
&\quad \left. \left. + \frac{\langle n|\mathrm{e}^{i\vec{k}\cdot\vec{x}}\hat{u}_k\cdot\vec{\alpha}|n'\rangle\langle n'|\mathrm{e}^{-i\vec{k}'\cdot\vec{x}}\hat{u}_{k'}\cdot\vec{\alpha}|n\rangle}{E_{n'} - E_n + \hbar ck} \right\} \right|^2
\end{aligned}
\tag{8.134}
$$

(Since the scattering is elastic $k = k'$ although $\vec{k}$ is not necessarily in the same direction as $\vec{k}'$ and $\hat{u}_k$ is not necessarily the same as $\hat{u}_{k'}$.) Using Eqs. (8.116) and (8.123) we can now write down the differential cross-section for scattering a photon of momentum $\hbar\vec{k}$ into the infinitesimal solid angle $\mathrm{d}\Omega = \sin\theta\, \mathrm{d}\theta\, \mathrm{d}\phi$ around the direction $\vec{k}'$ and at the same time changing the polarization direction from $\hat{u}_k$ to $\hat{u}_{k'}$:

$$
\begin{aligned}
\frac{\mathrm{d}\sigma}{\mathrm{d}\Omega} &= e^4 \left| \sum_{n'} \left\{ \frac{\langle n|\mathrm{e}^{-i\vec{k}'\cdot\vec{x}}\hat{u}_{k'}\cdot\vec{\alpha}|n'\rangle\langle n'|\mathrm{e}^{i\vec{k}\cdot\vec{x}}\hat{u}_k\cdot\vec{\alpha}|n\rangle}{E_{n'} - E_n - \hbar ck} \right. \right. \\
&\quad \left. \left. + \frac{\langle n|\mathrm{e}^{i\vec{k}\cdot\vec{x}}\hat{u}_k\cdot\vec{\alpha}|n'\rangle\langle n'|\mathrm{e}^{-i\vec{k}'\cdot\vec{x}}\hat{u}_{k'}\cdot\vec{\alpha}|n\rangle}{E_{n'} - E_n + \hbar ck} \right\} \right|^2 \\
&= \frac{k^4}{4} \left| \sum_{i,j=1}^{3} (\hat{u}_{k'})_i R_n^{ij}(\vec{k}, \vec{k}')(\hat{u}_k)_j \right|^2
\end{aligned}
\tag{8.135}
$$

where $R_n^{ij}(\vec{k}, \vec{k}')$ is a 'linear response function' or generalized polarizability tensor

$$
\begin{aligned}
R_n^{ij}(\vec{k}, \vec{k}') &\equiv \frac{2e^2}{k^2} \sum_{n'} \left\{ \frac{\langle n|\mathrm{e}^{-i\vec{k}'\cdot\vec{x}}\alpha^i|n'\rangle\langle n'|\mathrm{e}^{i\vec{k}\cdot\vec{x}}\alpha^j|n\rangle}{E_{n'} - E_n - \hbar ck} \right. \\
&\quad \left. + \frac{\langle n|\mathrm{e}^{i\vec{k}\cdot\vec{x}}\alpha^j|n'\rangle\langle n'|\mathrm{e}^{-i\vec{k}'\cdot\vec{x}}\alpha^i|n\rangle}{E_{n'} - E_n + \hbar ck} \right\}
\end{aligned}
\tag{8.136}
$$

In the electric dipole approximation, $R_n^{ij}(\vec{k}, \vec{k}')$ reduces to the ordinary electric polarizability tensor α_n^{ij}:

$$
\begin{aligned}
R_n^{ij}(\vec{k}, \vec{k}') &\cong \frac{2e^2}{k^2} \sum_{n'} \left\{ \frac{\langle n|\alpha^i|n'\rangle\langle n'|\alpha^j|n\rangle}{E_{n'} - E_n - \hbar c k} + \frac{\langle n|\alpha^j|n'\rangle\langle n'|\alpha^i|n\rangle}{E_{n'} - E_n + \hbar c k} \right\} \\
&= \frac{2e^2}{k^2} \sum_{n'} \left(\frac{E_{n'} - E_n}{\hbar c} \right)^2 \left\{ \frac{\langle n|x^i|n'\rangle\langle n'|x^j|n\rangle}{E_{n'} - E_n - \hbar c k} + \frac{\langle n|x^j|n'\rangle\langle n'|x^i|n\rangle}{E_{n'} - E_n + \hbar c k} \right\} \\
&\cong \frac{2e^2}{\hbar} \sum_{n'} \frac{\omega_{n'n}\langle n|x^i|n'\rangle\langle n'|x^j|n\rangle}{(\omega_{n'n})^2 - (kc)^2} \equiv \alpha_n^{ij}
\end{aligned}
\tag{8.137}
$$

(It is unfortunate that the symbol α has to be used here in two contexts: α^j stands for the jth component of the Dirac operator representing velocity, Eq. (8.28), while α_n^{ij} stands for the electric polarizability tensor.)

From Eqs. (8.136) and (8.137) we can see that in the electric dipole approximation, the differential cross-section for elastically scattering a photon from the mode with wave number $\vec{k}$ and polarization $\hat{u}_k$ into a mode whose wave number lies in an infinitesimal solid angle $d\Omega$ around $\vec{k}'$ with polarization $\hat{u}_{k'}$ becomes

$$
\frac{d\sigma}{d\Omega} \cong \frac{k^4}{4} \left| \sum_{i,j=1}^{3} (\hat{u}_{k'})_i \alpha_n^{ij} (\hat{u}_k)_j \right|^2
\tag{8.138}
$$

We can check that this has the right dimensions for a cross-section, since the electric polarizability α_n^{ij} has the dimensions of length cubed while k is a reciprocal length.

Problem (8.7) Use Eqs. (8.138) and (8.137) to evaluate $d\sigma/d\Omega$ for a spherically symmetric harmonic oscillator.

Optical rotatory dispersion

As M. J. Stephen[23] has shown, the Faraday, Cotton–Mouton, and Kerr effects, as well as optical rotatory dispersion can be calculated as special cases of Eq. (8.135). Optical rotatory dispersion is a very beautiful and easily observed effect which is important in determining the absolute configurations of chemical isomers and in the study of biopolymers. If you happen to have two sheets of polaroid material you can easily see this phenomenon for yourself. Hold a few bits of cellophane between the polaroid sheets and look through them at a window or lamp. As you slowly rotate one of the polarizers, the cellophane will appear to take on a series of beautiful colours. The reason for this effect is that the amount by which the plane of polarization is rotated depends on the frequency of the light. Some colours are rotated by the right amount and pass through the second sheet of polaroid material to your eye. Other colours are rotated by the wrong amount and are blocked.

Equation (8.135) can be used to calculate the optical rotatory dispersion of a polymer, but when one is dealing with a large molecule, such as a polymer, the dipole approximation has to be avoided. This is because the dimensions of a very large molecule are comparable with $1/k$ and no matter what point we take as the origin of our coordinate system, there will be some regions of the molecule where it is not legitimate to use the approximation $e^{i\vec{k}\cdot\vec{x}} \cong 1$. Generally speaking, the electric dipole approximation is always less valid in molecular spectroscopy than it is in atomic spectroscopy, since molecules are always larger than atoms. If we are dealing with a molecule of moderate size, then we ought to retain at least the second term in the series

$$e^{i\vec{k}\cdot\vec{x}} = 1 + i\vec{k}\cdot\vec{x} + \frac{1}{2!}(i\vec{k}\cdot\vec{x})^2 + \cdots \qquad (8.139)$$

However, if we keep the term $i\vec{k}\cdot\vec{x}$ we are faced with matrix elements of the form $\langle n|(i\vec{k}\cdot\vec{x})(\hat{u}_k\cdot\vec{\alpha})|n\rangle$. In order to evaluate matrix elements of this type it is helpful to notice that if H is the Dirac Hamiltonian defined by Eq. (8.37) then

$$[H,\ x^i x^j] = \left[i\hbar c\vec{\alpha}\cdot\frac{\partial}{\partial\vec{x}},\ x^i x^j \right]$$

$$= i\hbar c(x^i\alpha^i + x^j\alpha^i) \qquad \textbf{(8.140)}$$

$$\langle n|x^3\alpha^1|n'\rangle = \tfrac{1}{2}\langle n|(x^3\alpha^1 - x^1\alpha^3)|n'\rangle + \tfrac{1}{2}\langle n|(x^3\alpha^1 + x^1\alpha^2)|n'\rangle$$

$$\cong \frac{1}{2m_0 c}\langle n|\frac{\hbar}{i}\left(x^3\frac{\partial}{\partial x^1} - x^1\frac{\partial}{\partial x^3}\right)|n'\rangle + \frac{1}{2i\hbar c}(E_n - E_{n'})\langle n|x^3 x^1|n'\rangle$$

$$(8.141)$$

More generally, we have

$$(i\vec{k}\cdot\vec{x})(\hat{u}_k\cdot\vec{\alpha}) = \frac{i}{2}(\vec{k}\wedge\hat{u}_k)\cdot(\vec{x}\wedge\vec{\alpha}) + \frac{1}{2\hbar c}[H,\ (\vec{k}\cdot\vec{x})(\hat{u}_k\cdot\vec{x})] \qquad (8.142)$$

so that

$$\langle n|\ e^{i\vec{k}\cdot\vec{x}}\hat{u}_k\cdot\vec{\alpha}|n'\rangle$$

$$\cong \langle n|\{\hat{u}_k\cdot\vec{\alpha} + (i\vec{k}\cdot\vec{x})(\hat{u}_k\cdot\vec{\alpha})\}|n'\rangle$$

$$= \left(\frac{E_n - E_{n'}}{i\hbar c}\right)\hat{u}_k\cdot\langle n|\vec{x}|n'\rangle + \frac{i}{2}(\vec{k}\wedge\hat{u}_k)\cdot\langle n|\vec{x}\wedge\vec{\alpha}|n'\rangle$$

$$+ \left(\frac{E_n - E_{n'}}{2\hbar c}\right)\langle n|(\vec{k}\cdot\vec{x})(\hat{u}_k\cdot\vec{x})|h'\rangle \qquad (8.143)$$

The first term is the familiar electric dipole term. In the limit of small velocities we have

$$\langle n|\vec{x} \wedge \vec{\alpha}|n'\rangle \cong \frac{1}{m_0 c} \langle n\left|\frac{\hbar}{i}\vec{x} \wedge \frac{\partial}{\partial\vec{x}}\right|n'\rangle$$

$$\equiv \frac{1}{m_0 c} \vec{L}_{nn'} \tag{8.144}$$

so that the second term (called the 'magnetic dipole' term) involves the transition matrix element of the angular momentum operator. Finally we have a term involving $\langle n|x^i x^j|n'\rangle$ which is called the electric quadrupole term. The magnetic dipole and electric quadrupole terms both result from the inclusion of $i\vec{k}.\vec{x}$ in the series $e^{i\vec{k}.\vec{x}} \cong 1 + i\vec{k}.\vec{x} + \cdots$. Optical rotatory dispersion is produced by the cross-terms linking the transition electric dipole moments with the magnetic dipole moments in Eq. (8.135).

Problem (8.8) Letting $\hat{u}_{k'} = (1, 0, 0)$, $\hat{u}_k = (0, 1, 0)$ and $\vec{k} = \vec{k'} = (0, 0, k)$ in Eq. (8.135), and making use of Eqs. (8.143) and (8.144), find an expression for $d\sigma/d\Omega$. (Use the approximation $e^{i\vec{k}.\vec{x}} = 1 + i\vec{k}.\vec{x}$ and neglect the electric quadrupole moment.)

9. Ions and ligands

Hund's rule; high spin states in transition metal ions

When we discussed the π-electron systems of planar organic molecules we encountered singly-excited states with total spin $s = 0$ and $s = 1$, but not states of higher spin. On the other hand, higher spin states frequently occur in heavy atoms or in molecules containing heavy atoms. The reason for this difference is that the spin-orbitals Φ_{n, l, m_l, m_s} in an atomic subshell have a $2(2l + 1)$-fold degeneracy. Consider the antisymmetrized n-electron wave function built up from orbitals in a subshell

$$\Delta = \left| \Phi_{n, l, m_l, m_s} \; \Phi_{n, l, m_l', m_s'} \; \Phi_{n, l, m_l'', m_s''} \cdots \right|$$

$$\equiv \left| \Phi_{m_l m_s} \; \Phi_{m_l' m_s'} \; \Phi_{m_l'' m_s''} \cdots \right| \tag{9.1}$$

(We do not need to write the quantum numbers n and l since they are the same for all the orbitals.) According to the Slater–Condon rules, Eqs. (4.92)–(4.103), the expectation value for the energy of such a state is

$$\int d\tau \, \Delta^* \left\{ \sum_i H^c(i) + \sum_{i, j > i} \frac{e^2}{r_{ij}} \right\} \Delta = \sum_{m_l, m_s} \int d\tau_1 \, \Phi_{m_l m_s}^*(1) H^c(1) \, \Phi_{m_l m_s}(1)$$

$$+ \tfrac{1}{2} \sum_{m_l m_s} \sum_{m_l' m_s'} \int d\tau_1 \int d\tau_2 \, \Phi_{m_l m_s}^*(1) \, \Phi_{m_l' m_s'}^*(2)$$

$$\times \frac{e^2}{r_{12}} (1 - \mathscr{P}_{12}) \, \Phi_{m_l m_s}(1) \, \Phi_{m_l' m_s'}(2) \tag{9.2}$$

where the sum runs over all of the values of m_l and m_s which appear in the determinantal wave function Δ. The negative exchange term vanishes unless $m_s = m_s'$ and the energy will therefore be lowest if all of the orbitals in Δ have the same value of m_s. This is the reason for Hund's rule, which says that in the ground state of an atom the electrons in the valence shell have the highest possible spin consistent with the Pauli exclusion principle. When the valence subshell of an isolated atom is completely filled, the ground state spin is zero because the Pauli principle requires the spins to be paired for every orbital in the subshell. For such elements, the states

272

of higher spin appear only as excited states because the energy needed to incorporate an orbital from a higher subshell into the wave function is greater than the energy which would be gained from the exchange term. As one moves along the periodic table towards elements with half-filled subshells, the spin of the ground state increases to a maximum because in a half-filled shell the values of m_s can be the same for all the orbitals without violating the Pauli principle (the values of m_l being different). For example, the ground states of Be, B, C, N, O, F, and Ne have total spin quantum numbers respectively of $0, \frac{1}{2}, 1, \frac{3}{2}, 1, \frac{1}{2}$, and 0, as shown in Fig. 9.1.

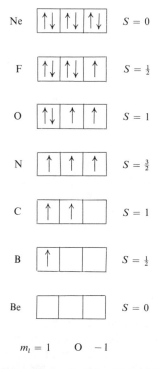

Figure 9.1 shows the filling of the $2 . (2l + 1) = 6$-fold degenerate atomic orbitals in the $2p$ subshell in accordance with Hund's rule. The total spin is always as large as possible, consistent with the Pauli exclusion principle.

The Russel–Saunders coupling scheme; total orbital and spin angular momentum as good quantum numbers

The energy of a free atom obviously does not depend on its orientation. This is another way of saying that the Hamiltonian of the atom commutes with the total angular momentum operator $\vec{J} = \vec{L} + \vec{S}$. If we use the approximate many-electron Hamiltonian

$$
\begin{aligned}
H_0 &= \sum_i H^c(i) + \sum_{i,\,j>i} \frac{e^2}{r_{ij}} \\
&= \sum_i \left(-\frac{\hbar^2}{2m_0} \nabla_i^2 + \frac{Ze^2}{r_i} \right) + \sum_{i,\,j>i} \frac{e^2}{r_{ij}}
\end{aligned}
\tag{9.3}
$$

(which neglects spin-orbit coupling) then the total orbital angular momentum operator

$$
\vec{L} = \vec{L}_1 + \vec{L}_2 + \vec{L}_3 + \cdots + \vec{L}_N
\tag{9.4}
$$

and the total spin angular momentum operator

$$
\vec{S} = \vec{S}_1 + \vec{S}_2 + \vec{S}_3 + \cdots + \vec{S}_N
\tag{9.5}
$$

also commute with H. This means that we can find simultaneous eigenfunctions of L^2, L_z, S^2, S_z, and H. To put it differently, *the eigenfunctions of H_0 are characterized (although not completely) by the quantum numbers L, M_L, S, and M_s.* If we start with the one-electron spin-orbitals of a subshell as a basis set and use them to build up antisymmetrized N-electron wave functions which are eigenfunctions of L^2, L_z, S^2, and S_z, then we will have gone a long way towards finding eigenfunctions of the free-atom Hamiltonian H. This method of constructing eigenfunctions of H (neglecting spin-orbit coupling or treating it afterwards as a small perturbation) is called the Russel–Saunders coupling scheme.

Electron creation and annihilation operators; commutation relations for orbital and spin angular momentum

In order to take antisymmetry into account it is convenient to use the electron creation and annihilation operators which were introduced in chapter 8. Let $b_m^\dagger$ and $b_{m'}$ represent the creation and annihilation operators corresponding to the orbital $\Phi_{n,\,l,\,m_l,\,m_s}$. Then, remembering the anticommutation rules, we have

$$
\begin{aligned}
b_m^\dagger b_{m'} + b_{m'} b_m^\dagger &= \delta_{m,\,m'} \\
b_m^\dagger b_{m'}^\dagger + b_{m'}^\dagger b_m^\dagger &= 0 \\
b_m b_{m'} + b_{m'} b_m &= 0
\end{aligned}
\tag{9.6}
$$

The antisymmetrized wave function Δ of Eq. (9.1) can be written in the form

$$
\Delta = b_m^\dagger b_{m'}^\dagger b_{m''}^\dagger \cdots |0\rangle
\tag{9.7}
$$

while the conjugate wave function becomes

$$\Delta^* = \langle 0| \ldots b_{m''} b_{m'} b_m \tag{9.8}$$

It is easy to show that if one-electron operators are written in the form

$$F = \sum_{p,q} \langle p|f|q \rangle b_p^\dagger b_q \tag{9.9}$$

and if two-electron operators are written in the form

$$G = \tfrac{1}{2} \sum_{p,q,r,s} \langle p, q|g|r, s \rangle b_p^\dagger b_q^\dagger b_s b_r \tag{9.10}$$

then the Slater–Condon rules follow from the anticommutation relations Eq. (9.6). The total orbital angular momentum $\vec{L}$, Eq. (9.4), is an operator of type F so we can write

$$L_x \equiv L_x + iL_y = \sum_{m,m'} \langle m|(L_x + iL_y)|m' \rangle b_m^\dagger b_{m'}$$

$$= \sum_m \sqrt{l(l+1) - m(m+1)}\, b_{m+1}^\dagger b_m \tag{9.11}$$

and similarly

$$L_- \equiv L_x - iL_y = \sum_m \sqrt{l(l+1) - m(m-1)}\, b_{m-1}^\dagger b_m$$

$$L_z = \sum_m m b_m^\dagger b_m \tag{9.12}$$

where we have let m stand for m_l and used units in which $\hbar = 1$. Then from Eq. (9.6) we have the commutation relations

$$[L_+, b_m^\dagger] = \sqrt{l(l+1) - m(m+1)}\, b_{m+1}^\dagger$$

$$[L_-, b_m^\dagger] = \sqrt{l(l+1) - m(m-1)}\, b_{m-1}^\dagger$$

$$[L_z, b_m^\dagger] = m b_m^\dagger \tag{9.13}$$

Using the relations

$$[AB, C] = A[B, C] + [A, B]C \tag{9.14}$$

and

$$L^2 = L_- L_+ + L_z^2 + L_z \tag{9.15}$$

we have

$$[L^2, b_m^\dagger] = [L_- L_+, b_m^\dagger] + [L_z L_z, b_m^\dagger] + [L_z, b_m^\dagger]$$

$$= L_-[L_+, b_m^\dagger] + [L_-, b_m^\dagger]L_+ + L_z[L_z, b_m^\dagger]$$

$$+ [L_z, b_m^\dagger]L_z + [L_z, b_m^\dagger] \tag{9.16}$$

Substituting Eq. (9.13) into Eq. (9.15) we finally obtain the commutation relation between the creation operator $b_m^\dagger$ and the total angular momentum operator L^2.

$$[L^2, b_m^\dagger] = b_m^\dagger\{l(l + 1) + 2mL_z\}$$
$$+ \sqrt{l(l + 1) - m(m + 1)}\, b_{m+1}^\dagger L_-$$
$$+ \sqrt{l(l + 1) - m(m - 1)}\, b_{m-1}^\dagger L_+ \qquad (9.17)$$

Let us now distinguish between the spin-up and spin-down states, by defining $b_m^\dagger$ as the creation operator corresponding to the spin-orbital $\Phi_{n,l,m,1/2}$ while $b_{\bar{m}}^\dagger$ corresponds to $\Phi_{n,l,m,-1/2}$. Then, by an argument similar to Eqs. (9.11)–(9.15) we have for the total spin operator $\vec{S}$,

$$S_+ = S_x + iS_y = \sum_m b_m^\dagger b_{\bar{m}}$$

$$S_- = S_x - iS_y = \sum_m b_{\bar{m}}^\dagger b_m$$

$$S_z = \tfrac{1}{2} \sum_m (b_m^\dagger b_m - b_{\bar{m}}^\dagger b_{\bar{m}}) \qquad (9.18)$$

and

$$[S^2, b_m^\dagger] = b_m^\dagger(\tfrac{3}{4} + S_z) + b_{\bar{m}}^\dagger S_+$$
$$[S^2, b_{\bar{m}}^\dagger] = b_{\bar{m}}^\dagger(\tfrac{3}{4} + S_z) + b_m^\dagger S_- \qquad (9.19)$$

Problem (9.1)   Use Eqs. (9.6), (9.18), and (9.19) to show that if $S^2|0\rangle = 0$, and $S_z|0\rangle = 0$, then $b_j^\dagger|0\rangle$, $b_{\bar{j}}^\dagger|0\rangle$, $1/\sqrt{2}\,(b_j^\dagger b_{\bar{k}}^\dagger + b_{\bar{j}}^\dagger b_k^\dagger)|0\rangle$, $b_j^\dagger b_k^\dagger|0\rangle$, $b_{\bar{j}}^\dagger b_{\bar{k}}^\dagger|0\rangle$ and $1/\sqrt{2}\,(b_j^\dagger b_{\bar{k}}^\dagger - b_{\bar{j}}^\dagger b_k^\dagger)|0\rangle$ are all eigenfunctions of S^2 and S_z. Try to find the 3-electron and 4-electron eigenfunctions of S^2 and S_z.

The Kramers pair creation operator; the seniority quantum number

One can show by means of the commutation relationships that *the 'pair creation operator'*

$$B^\dagger \equiv \frac{1}{\sqrt{2l + 1}} \sum_{m=-l}^{l} (-1)^m b_m^\dagger b_{-\bar{m}}^\dagger \qquad (9.20)$$

commutes with both $\vec{L}$ and $\vec{S}$

$$[\vec{L}, B^\dagger] = 0$$
$$[\vec{S}, B^\dagger] = 0 \qquad (9.21)$$

We can now use Eqs. (9.13)–(9.21) to build up simultaneous eigenfunctions of L^2, L_z, S^2, and S_z. Suppose that the state $|A\rangle$ is a closed-shell eigenfunction. For example $|A\rangle$ might represent the electron configuration $(1s)^2(2s)^2$, a configuration in which the $1s$ shell and the $2s$ subshell are both completely filled. Then

$$L^2|A\rangle = 0$$
$$L_z|A\rangle = 0$$
$$S^2|A\rangle = 0$$
$$S_z|A\rangle = 0 \qquad (9.22)$$

If we act on $|A\rangle$ with the pair creation operator $B^\dagger$ we will obtain a state with two added electrons but still (because $B^\dagger$ commutes with L^2 and S^2) having no spin and no orbital angular momentum. For example, suppose that we are considering the filling of the $2p$ subshell, Fig. 9.1, so that $l = 1$. Then

$$B^\dagger = \frac{1}{\sqrt{3}}(-b_1^\dagger b_{-\bar 1}^\dagger + b_0^\dagger b_0^\dagger - b_{-1}^\dagger b_{\bar 1}^\dagger) \qquad \textbf{(9.23)}$$

Acting on $|A\rangle$ with $B^\dagger$, we obtain

$$|p^N,\ ^{2s+1}_v L,\ M_L,\ M_S\rangle = |p^2,\ ^1_0 S,\ 0,\ 0\rangle$$

$$= \frac{1}{\sqrt{3}}(-b_1^\dagger b_{-\bar 1}^\dagger + b_0^\dagger b_0^\dagger - b_{-1}^\dagger b_{\bar 1}^\dagger)|A\rangle \qquad (9.24)$$

The notation here requires a little explanation. For historical reasons, *states with total angular momentum quantum numbers L = 0, 1, 2, 3, 4, 5, etc., are denoted respectively by the capital letters S, P, D, F, G, H, etc. The 'spin multiplicity' 2S + 1 is denoted by a superscript to the left. Thus for example a ^1S state has L = 0 and S = 0 while a ^3P state has L = 1 and S = 1. The subscript v which appears below the spin multiplicity in Eq. (9.24) is called the 'seniority' of the state. This is defined as the numbers of electrons in the subshell for the parent state.* In this case, the parent state $|A\rangle$ has no electrons in the subshell, so that the seniority is $v = 0$. If we act twice on the closed-shell state $|A\rangle$ then we obtain a state with $N = 4$ electrons in the p shell.

$$|p^N,\ ^{2S+1}_v L,\ M_L,\ M_S\rangle = |p^4,\ ^1_0 S,\ 0,\ 0\rangle$$

$$= \mathcal{N}\, B^\dagger B^\dagger|A\rangle$$

$$= \frac{\mathcal{N}}{3}(-b_1^\dagger b_{-\bar 1}^\dagger + b_0^\dagger b_0^\dagger - b_{-1}^\dagger b_{\bar 1}^\dagger)(-b_1^\dagger b_{-\bar 1}^\dagger + b_0^\dagger b_0^\dagger - b_{-1}^\dagger b_{\bar 1}^\dagger)|A\rangle$$

$$= \frac{2\mathcal{N}}{3}(-b_1^\dagger b_{-\bar 1}^\dagger b_0^\dagger b_0^\dagger + b_1^\dagger b_{-\bar 1}^\dagger b_{-1}^\dagger b_{\bar 1}^\dagger - b_0^\dagger b_0^\dagger b_{-1}^\dagger b_{\bar 1}^\dagger)|0\rangle \qquad (9.25)$$

(Because of Eq. (9.6), $b_m^\dagger b_m^\dagger = 0$, and factors containing repeated creation operators vanish.) In order for the state to be properly normalized we must let $\mathcal{N} = \sqrt{3}/2$. The seniority of the $N = 4$ state $|p^4, {}_0^1 S, 0, 0\rangle$ is still $v = 0$, since the $N = 0$ state $|A\rangle$ is still considered to be the parent state. In other words, the parent of a state is a state from which it can be derived by repeated application of the pair creation operator. A third application of $B^\dagger$ gives us the closed shell state

$$
\begin{aligned}
|p^N, {}^{2S+1}_v L, M_L, M_S\rangle &= |p^6, {}_0^1 S, 0, 0\rangle \\
&= \mathcal{N} \, B^\dagger B^\dagger B^\dagger |A\rangle \\
&= \mathcal{N} \, B^{\dagger 2}_{\frac{1}{3}}(- b_1^\dagger b_{-\bar{1}}^\dagger b_0^\dagger b_0^\dagger + b_1^\dagger b_{-\bar{1}}^\dagger b_{-1}^\dagger b_{\bar{1}}^\dagger - b_0^\dagger b_0^\dagger b_{-1}^\dagger b_{\bar{1}}^\dagger)|A\rangle \\
&= \mathcal{N} \, 2(b_1^\dagger b_{-\bar{1}}^\dagger b_0^\dagger b_0^\dagger b_{-1}^\dagger b_{\bar{1}}^\dagger)|A\rangle
\end{aligned}
\tag{9.26}
$$

which will be properly normalized if we let $\mathcal{N} = \frac{1}{2}$.

Problem (9.2) The state $b_1^\dagger |A\rangle$ is a normalized d^1 eigenfunction of L^2, L_z, S^2, and S_z. Use Eqs. (9.6)–(9.19) and Eq. (9.23) to evaluate $\mathcal{N} \, B^\dagger b_1^\dagger |A\rangle$ and show that it is also an eigenfunction of these operators. To what set of eigenvalues does it belong? What value should be given to $\mathcal{N}$ in order that $\mathcal{N} \, B^\dagger b_1 |A\rangle$ should be normalized?

The ${}_1^2 P$ multiplet for p^1, p^3, and p^5 configurations

Now suppose that we act on $|A\rangle$ with the single-electron creation operator $b_m^\dagger$. Let us try to show that the resulting state is an eigenfunction of L^2, L_z, S^2, and S_z. Using Eq. (9.17) and Eq. (9.19) we have

$$
\begin{aligned}
L^2 b_m^\dagger |A\rangle &= b_m^\dagger L^2 |A\rangle + [L^2, b_m^\dagger]|A\rangle \\
&= [b_m^\dagger \{L^2 + l(l + 1) + 2mL_z\} \\
&\quad + \sqrt{l(l + 1) - m(m + 1)} \, b_{m+1}^\dagger L_- \\
&\quad + \sqrt{l(l + 1) - m(m - 1)} \, b_{m-1}^\dagger L_+]|A\rangle \\
&= l(l + 1)b_m^\dagger |A\rangle
\end{aligned}
\tag{9.27}
$$

(since L^2, L_z, L_-, and L_+ acting on the closed-shell state $|A\rangle$ all give zero). Similarly,

$$
\begin{aligned}
S^2 b_m^\dagger |A\rangle &= \{b_m^\dagger (S^2 + \tfrac{3}{4} + S_z) + b_{\bar{m}}^\dagger S_+\}|A\rangle \\
&= \tfrac{3}{4} b_m^\dagger |A\rangle \\
L_z b_m^\dagger |A\rangle &= b_m^\dagger (L_z + m)|A\rangle = m b_m^\dagger |A\rangle
\end{aligned}
\tag{9.28}
$$

and

$$S_z b_m^\dagger |A\rangle = b_m^\dagger (S_z + \tfrac{1}{2})|A\rangle = \tfrac{1}{2} b_m^\dagger |A\rangle \qquad (9.29)$$

Thus, we can write down the $N = 1$, $L = 1$, $S = \tfrac{1}{2}$ multiplet

$$|p^1, {}_1^2 P, 1, \tfrac{1}{2}\rangle = b_1^\dagger |A\rangle$$

$$|p^1, {}_1^2 P, 0, \tfrac{1}{2}\rangle = b_0^\dagger |A\rangle$$

$$|p^1, {}_1^2 P, -1, \tfrac{1}{2}\rangle = b_{-1}^\dagger |A\rangle$$

$$|p^1, {}_1^2 P, 1, -\tfrac{1}{2}\rangle = b_{\bar{1}}^\dagger |A\rangle$$

$$|p^1, {}_1^2 P, 0, -\tfrac{1}{2}\rangle = b_{\bar{0}}^\dagger |A\rangle \; \cdot$$

$$|p^1, {}_1^2 P, -1, -\tfrac{1}{2}\rangle = b_{-\bar{1}}^\dagger |A\rangle \qquad (9.30)$$

The seniority of these $N = 1$ states is $v = 1$, since they cannot be derived from states of lower N by an application of $B^\dagger$. The states of Eq. (9.30) are themselves the parents of $N = 3$ and $N = 5$ states. Thus we can write

$$|p^3, {}_1^2 P, 1, \tfrac{1}{2}\rangle = \mathcal{N} B^\dagger b_1^\dagger |A\rangle$$

$$= \frac{\mathcal{N}}{\sqrt{3}}(-b_1^\dagger b_{-\bar{1}}^\dagger + b_0^\dagger b_{\bar{0}}^\dagger - b_{-1}^\dagger b_{\bar{1}}^\dagger)b_1^\dagger |A\rangle$$

$$= \frac{1}{\sqrt{2}}(b_0^\dagger b_{\bar{0}}^\dagger b_1^\dagger - b_{-1}^\dagger b_{\bar{1}}^\dagger b_1^\dagger)|A\rangle \qquad (9.30a)$$

$$|p^5, {}_1^2 P, 1, \tfrac{1}{2}\rangle = \mathcal{N} B^\dagger B^\dagger b_1^\dagger |A\rangle$$

$$= \frac{\mathcal{N}}{\sqrt{3}} B^\dagger (b_0^\dagger b_{\bar{0}}^\dagger b_1^\dagger - b_{-1}^\dagger b_{\bar{1}}^\dagger b_1^\dagger)|A\rangle$$

$$= b_{-1}^\dagger b_{\bar{1}}^\dagger b_0^\dagger b_{\bar{0}}^\dagger b_1^\dagger |A\rangle \qquad (9.30b)$$

and so on for the other members of the multiplet in Eq. (9.30).

The $\tfrac{1}{2}D$ multiplet for p^2 and p^4 configurations

Now let us try to show that

$$|p^2, \tfrac{1}{2}D, 2, 0\rangle = b_1^\dagger b_{\bar{1}}^\dagger |A\rangle \qquad (9.31)$$

Remembering that

$$|p^1, {}_1^2 P, 1, -\tfrac{1}{2}\rangle = b_{\bar{1}}^\dagger |A\rangle \qquad (9.32)$$

we have from Eq. (9.17)

$$
\begin{aligned}
L^2 b_1^\dagger b_{\bar{1}}^\dagger |A\rangle &= \{b_1^\dagger (L^2 + 2 + 2L_z) + \sqrt{2}\, b_0^\dagger L_+\} b_{\bar{1}}^\dagger |A\rangle \\
&= \{1(1 + 1) + 2 + 2\} b_1^\dagger b_{\bar{1}}^\dagger |A\rangle \\
&= 2(2 + 1) b_1^\dagger b_{\bar{1}}^\dagger |A\rangle
\end{aligned}
\tag{9.33}
$$

Thus $b_1^\dagger b_{\bar{1}}^\dagger |A\rangle$ is an eigenfunction of L^2 with the total angular momentum quantum number $L = 2$, i.e., it is a D-state. It is also an eigenfunction of S^2, with the quantum number $S = 0$ since

$$
\begin{aligned}
S^2 b_1^\dagger b_{\bar{1}}^\dagger |A\rangle &= \{b_1^\dagger (S^2 + \tfrac{3}{4} + S_z) + b_{\bar{1}}^\dagger S_+\} b_{\bar{1}}^\dagger |A\rangle \\
&= \{b_1^\dagger (\tfrac{3}{4} + \tfrac{3}{4} + \tfrac{1}{2}) b_{\bar{1}}^\dagger \\
&\quad + b_{\bar{1}}^\dagger \sqrt{\tfrac{3}{4} - (-\tfrac{1}{2})(-\tfrac{1}{2} + 1)}\, b_1^\dagger \} |A\rangle \\
&= (b_1^\dagger b_{\bar{1}}^\dagger + b_{\bar{1}}^\dagger b_1^\dagger) |A\rangle = 0
\end{aligned}
\tag{9.34}
$$

This is, of course not surprising, since the spins are obviously paired. M_S must then be zero, and from Eq. (9.13) we have

$$
\begin{aligned}
L_z b_1^\dagger b_{\bar{1}}^\dagger |A\rangle &= b_1^\dagger (L_z + 1) b_{\bar{1}}^\dagger |A\rangle \\
&= 2 b_1^\dagger b_{\bar{1}}^\dagger |A\rangle
\end{aligned}
\tag{9.35}
$$

Equations (9.33)–(9.35) establish the assertion of Eq. (9.31). The other members of the multiplet can then be written down by successive application of the lowering operator, Eq. (9.13). Thus, for example, we have

$$
\begin{aligned}
L_- b_1^\dagger b_{\bar{1}}^\dagger |A\rangle &= (b_1^\dagger L_- b_{\bar{1}}^\dagger + \sqrt{2}\, b_0^\dagger b_{\bar{1}}^\dagger) |A\rangle \\
&= \sqrt{2} (b_1^\dagger b_{\bar{0}}^\dagger + b_0^\dagger b_{\bar{1}}^\dagger) |A\rangle \\
&= 2 |p^2, \tfrac{1}{2}D, 1, 0\rangle
\end{aligned}
\tag{9.36}
$$

Continuing this process we obtain all $(2S + 1) \cdot (2L + 1) = 5$ members of the $\tfrac{1}{2}D$ multiplet as shown in Table 9.1. From these states we can obtain the $N = 4$ multiplet

$$
|p^4, \tfrac{1}{2}D, M_L, M_S\rangle = \mathcal{N}\, B^\dagger |p^2, \tfrac{1}{2}D, M_L, M_S\rangle
\tag{9.37}
$$

For example

$$
\begin{aligned}
\mathcal{N}\, B^\dagger b_1^\dagger b_{\bar{1}}^\dagger |A\rangle &= b_0^\dagger b_{\bar{0}}^\dagger b_1^\dagger b_{\bar{1}}^\dagger |A\rangle \\
&= |p^4, \tfrac{1}{2}D, 2, 0\rangle
\end{aligned}
\tag{9.38}
$$

A second application of $B^\dagger$ gives zero identically since there is a repeated creation operator in every factor, and $b_m^\dagger b_m^\dagger = 0$. Thus the state $|p^6, \tfrac{1}{2}D, 2, 0\rangle$ does not exist. In fact the only p-shell $N = 6$ state which the Pauli exclusion principle allows is the closed shell state $|p^6, \tfrac{1}{0}S, 0, 0\rangle$. It is

Table 9.1

L	S	M_L	M_S	Russel–Saunders $(p)^2$ eigenfunction	Name
2	0	2	0	$b_1^\dagger b_{\bar 1}^\dagger \,|A\rangle$	
		1	0	$1/\sqrt{2}\,(b_0^\dagger b_{\bar 1}^\dagger - b_{\bar 0}^\dagger b_1^\dagger)\,|A\rangle$	
		0	0	$1/\sqrt{6}\,(2b_0^\dagger b_{\bar 0}^\dagger + b_{-1}^\dagger b_{\bar 1}^\dagger - b_{\overline{-1}}^\dagger b_1^\dagger)\,|A\rangle$	$_2^1 D$
		-1	0	$1/\sqrt{2}\,(b_0^\dagger b_{\overline{-1}}^\dagger - b_{\bar 0}^\dagger b_{-1}^\dagger)\,|A\rangle$	
		-2	0	$b_{-1}^\dagger b_{\overline{-1}}^\dagger \,|A\rangle$	
1	1	1	1	$b_0^\dagger b_1^\dagger \,|A\rangle$	
			0	$1/\sqrt{2}\,(b_0^\dagger b_{\bar 1}^\dagger + b_{\bar 0}^\dagger b_1^\dagger)\,|A\rangle$	
			-1	$b_{\bar 0}^\dagger b_{\bar 1}^\dagger \,|A\rangle$	
		0	1	$b_{-1}^\dagger b_1^\dagger \,|A\rangle$	
			0	$1/\sqrt{2}\,(b_{-1}^\dagger b_{\bar 1}^\dagger + b_{\overline{-1}}^\dagger b_1^\dagger)\,|A\rangle$	$_2^3 P$
			-1	$b_{\overline{-1}}^\dagger b_{\bar 1}^\dagger \,|A\rangle$	
		-1	1	$b_0^\dagger b_{-1}^\dagger \,|A\rangle$	
			0	$1/\sqrt{2}\,(b_0^\dagger b_{\overline{-1}}^\dagger + b_{\bar 0}^\dagger b_{-1}^\dagger)\,|A\rangle$	
			-1	$b_{\bar 0}^\dagger b_{\overline{-1}}^\dagger \,|A\rangle$	
0	0	0	0	$1/\sqrt{3}\,(b_1^\dagger b_{\overline{-1}}^\dagger - b_{\bar 1}^\dagger b_{-1}^\dagger - b_0^\dagger b_{\bar 0}^\dagger)\,|A\rangle$	$_0^1 S$

interesting to notice that the state $|p^4, {}_2^1 D, 2, 0\rangle$ can be expressed in terms of the annihilation operators acting on the closed shell $N = 6$ state:

$$|p^4, {}_2^1 D, 2, 0\rangle = b_{-1} b_{\bar 1} |p^6, {}_0^1 S, 0, 0\rangle \qquad (9.39)$$

One can either think of such a state as containing four electrons in the p-shell or else two holes, i.e., the electron annihilation operators can be thought of as hole creation operators.

The $_2^3 P$ multiplet for p^2 and p^4 configurations; the $_3^4 S$ and $_3^2 D$ multiplets for p^3 configurations

It is easy to show by the method which we used in Eqs. (9.31)–(9.35) that

$$|p^N, {}_v^{2S+1}L, M_L, M_S\rangle = |p^2, {}_2^3 P, 1, 1\rangle = b_0^\dagger b_1^\dagger |A\rangle \qquad (9.40)$$

281

The $\frac{3}{2}P$ multiplet which contains $(2S + 1).(2L + 1) = 9$ states is shown in Table 9.1. The other members can be found from Eq. (9.40) by successive application of the lowering operators L_- and S_-. This completes the list of $N = 2$ states, no others being allowed by the Pauli exclusion principle. For each $N = 2$ state of the p-shell there is a related $N = 4$ state which can be found by application of the pair creation operator

$$|p^4, {}^{2S+1}_v L, M_L, M_S\rangle = \mathcal{N} \, B^\dagger |p^2, {}^{2S+1}_v L, M_L, M_S\rangle \qquad (9.41)$$

and this exhausts the $N = 4$ states of the p-shell. Similarly, the $N = 5$ states of the p-shell are exhausted by applying $B^\dagger$ twice to the $N = 1$ states listed in Eq. (9.30).

$$|p^5, {}^2_1 P, M_L, M_S\rangle = \mathcal{N} \, B^\dagger B^\dagger |p^1, {}^2_1 P, M_L, M_S\rangle \qquad (9.42)$$

However, applying $B^\dagger$ once to the $N = 1$ states, as in Eq. (9.30a), does not exhaust the possible $N = 3$ states. We can show, using the same method as in Eqs. (9.31)–(9.35), that the state $b_1^\dagger b_0^\dagger b_{-1}^\dagger |A\rangle$ is an eigenfunction of L^2, L_z, S^2, and S_z with a total spin of $\frac{3}{2}$ and zero orbital angular momentum and that $b_0^\dagger b_1^\dagger b_{\bar{1}}^\dagger |A\rangle$ is an eigenfunction with $L = 2$ and $S = \frac{1}{2}$.

$$|p^3, {}^2_3 D, 2, \tfrac{1}{2}\rangle = b_0^\dagger b_1^\dagger b_{\bar{1}}^\dagger |A\rangle \qquad (9.43)$$

The other members of the $\frac{4}{3}S$ and $\frac{2}{3}D$ multiplets can be found by applying the lowering operators L_- and S_-. This finally exhausts the p-shell Russel–Saunders eigenfunctions allowed by the Pauli exclusion principle. Table 9.2 shows the complete list of p-shell multiplets with one member in each multiplet specifically written out. You may ask how we can be sure that we have found all of the possible multiplets. We can check this point by counting up the total degeneracy of the Russel–Saunders eigenfunctions for a given value of N and seeing whether this is the same as the number of exclusion-principle-allowed basis functions for that value of N. We can also check that the number of times that particular values of M_L and M_S occur together in the original basis set is the same as the number of times that they occur in the Russel–Saunders eigenfunctions. For example, when $N = 2$, there are 15 possible linearly independent basis functions: $b_1^\dagger b_0^\dagger |A\rangle$, $b_1^\dagger b_{-1}^\dagger |A\rangle$, $b_1^\dagger b_{\bar{1}}^\dagger |A\rangle$, $b_1^\dagger b_0^\dagger |A\rangle$, $b_1^\dagger b_{-\bar{1}}^\dagger |A\rangle$, $b_0^\dagger b_{-1}^\dagger |A\rangle$, $b_0^\dagger b_{\bar{1}}^\dagger |A\rangle$, $b_0^\dagger b_{\bar{0}}^\dagger |A\rangle$, $b_0^\dagger b_{-\bar{1}}^\dagger |A\rangle$, $b_{-1}^\dagger b_{\bar{1}}^\dagger |A\rangle$, $b_{-1}^\dagger b_{\bar{0}}^\dagger |A\rangle$, $b_{-1}^\dagger b_{-\bar{1}}^\dagger |A\rangle$, $b_{\bar{1}}^\dagger b_{\bar{0}}^\dagger |A\rangle$, $b_{\bar{1}}^\dagger b_{-\bar{1}}^\dagger |A\rangle$, and $b_{\bar{0}}^\dagger b_{-\bar{1}}^\dagger |A\rangle$, which checks the 15 Russel–Saunders eigenfunctions listed in Table 9.1. The quantum numbers $M_L = 2$, $M_S = 0$ occur once in the basis set (for the function $b_1^\dagger b_{\bar{1}}^\dagger |A\rangle$) and once in the Russel–Saunders eigenfunctions (for the highest member of the $\frac{1}{2}D$ multiplet), etc. It is possible in this way to infer the allowed multiplets for a shell without specifically constructing them (see, for example C. J. Ballhausen, *Introduction to Ligand Field Theory*, McGraw-Hill (1962), p. 9).

Table 9.2

N	v	L	S	M_L	M_S	Name	Russel–Saunders $(p)^N$ eigenfunction	$(2S+1)$ $\times (2L+1)$
1	1	1	$\frac{1}{2}$	1	$\frac{1}{2}$	^2P	$b_1^\dagger \lvert A\rangle$	6
2	0	0	0	0	0	^1_0S	$1/\sqrt{3}\,(-b_1^\dagger b_{-1}^\dagger + b_0^\dagger b_0^\dagger \\ - b_{-1}^\dagger b_1^\dagger)\lvert A\rangle = B^\dagger \lvert A\rangle$	1
	2	2	0	2	0	^1_2D	$b_1^\dagger b_1^\dagger \lvert A\rangle$	5
		1	1	1	1	^3_2P	$b_0^\dagger b_1^\dagger \lvert A\rangle$	9
3	1	1	$\frac{1}{2}$	1	$\frac{1}{2}$	^2_1P	$B^\dagger b_1^\dagger \lvert A\rangle$	6
	3	0	$\frac{3}{2}$	0	$\frac{3}{2}$	^4_3S	$b_1^\dagger b_0^\dagger b_{-1}^\dagger \lvert A\rangle$	4
		2	$\frac{1}{2}$	2	$\frac{1}{2}$	^2_3D	$b_0^\dagger b_1^\dagger b_1^\dagger \lvert A\rangle$	10
4	0	0	0	0	0	^1_0S	$B^\dagger B^\dagger \lvert A\rangle$	1
	2	2	0	2	0	^1_2D	$B^\dagger b_1^\dagger b_1^\dagger \lvert A\rangle$	5
		1	1	1	1	^3_2P	$B^\dagger b_0^\dagger b_1^\dagger \lvert A\rangle$	9
5	1	1	$\frac{1}{2}$	1	$\frac{1}{2}$	^2_1P	$B^\dagger B^\dagger b_1^\dagger \lvert A\rangle$	6
6	0	0	0	0	0	^1_0S	$B^\dagger B^\dagger B^\dagger \lvert A\rangle$	1

Russel–Saunders eigenfunctions in the d-shell; the d-shell Kramers pair creation operator; generation of Clebsch–Gordan coefficients by means of creation operator commutation rules

We have been illustrating the Russel–Saunders scheme with the p-shell eigenfunctions because, in the p-shell, the number of multiplets is small and it is easy to construct all of them. However, from the point of view of applications, the d-shell is more interesting. A complete list of d-shell Russel–Saunders eigenfunctions is given in Appendix (3.1) of H. Watanabe *Operator Methods in Ligand Field Theory*, Prentice Hall (1966). We shall not construct all of the d-shell multiplets here since they are very numerous. However, it is interesting to construct the $(d)^2$ multiplets since they illustrate a point which is not encountered in the p-shell.

In a d-shell the pair creation operator, Eq. (9.20), is given by

$$B^\dagger = \frac{1}{\sqrt{5}}(b_2^\dagger b_{-\bar{2}}^\dagger - b_1^\dagger b_{-\bar{1}}^\dagger + b_0^\dagger b_{\bar{0}}^\dagger - b_{-1}^\dagger b_{\bar{1}}^\dagger + b_{-2}^\dagger b_{\bar{2}}^\dagger) \quad \textbf{(9.44)}$$

We can immediately get a zero-seniority $N = 2$ eigenfunction by acting on the closed-shell state $|A\rangle$ with the $B^\dagger$ of Eq. (9.44)

$$|d^2, {}_0^1S, 0, 0\rangle = B^\dagger|A\rangle \quad (9.45)$$

It is easy to guess that the Russel–Saunders eigenfunction with $L = l + l = 4$ and $M_L = L = 4$ is

$$|d^2, {}_2^1G, 4, 0\rangle = b_2^\dagger b_{\bar{2}}^\dagger|A\rangle \quad (9.46)$$

and we can show by means of Eq. (9.17) and Eq. (9.19) that this is really an eigenfunction of L^2, L_z, S^2, and S_z. Similarly one can show that $b_2^\dagger b_{\bar{1}}^\dagger|A\rangle$ is a Russel–Saunders eigenfunction with $L = 3$ and $S = 1$:

$$|d^2, {}_2^3F, 3, 1\rangle = b_2^\dagger b_1^\dagger|A\rangle \quad (9.47)$$

Now suppose that we act with L^2 on the trial function $b_1^\dagger b_{\bar{1}}^\dagger|A\rangle$. Then remembering that $l = 2$, we get

$$\begin{aligned}
L^2 b_1^\dagger b_{\bar{1}}^\dagger|A\rangle &= b_1^\dagger\{L^2 + l(l + 1) + 2mL_z\}b_{\bar{1}}^\dagger|A\rangle \\
&\quad + \sqrt{l(l + 1) - m(m + 1)}\, b_2^\dagger L_- b_{\bar{1}}^\dagger|A\rangle \\
&\quad + \sqrt{l(l + 1) - m(m - 1)}\, b_0^\dagger L_+ b_{\bar{1}}^\dagger|A\rangle \\
&= 14 b_1^\dagger b_{\bar{1}}^\dagger|A\rangle + 4\sqrt{3}\left\{\frac{1}{\sqrt{2}}(b_2^\dagger b_{\bar{0}}^\dagger + b_0^\dagger b_{\bar{2}}^\dagger)\right\}|A\rangle \quad (9.48)
\end{aligned}$$

and similarly

$$\begin{aligned}
L^2\left\{\frac{1}{\sqrt{2}}(b_2^\dagger b_{\bar{0}}^\dagger + b_0^\dagger b_{\bar{2}}^\dagger)|A\rangle\right\} \\
= 12\left\{\frac{1}{\sqrt{2}}(b_2^\dagger b_{\bar{0}}^\dagger + b_0^\dagger b_{\bar{2}}^\dagger)|A\rangle\right\} + 4\sqrt{3}\, b_1^\dagger b_{\bar{1}}^\dagger|A\rangle \quad (9.49)
\end{aligned}$$

Let us introduce the simplified notation

$$b_1^\dagger b_{\bar{1}}^\dagger|A\rangle \equiv |P\rangle \qquad \frac{1}{\sqrt{2}}(b_2^\dagger b_{\bar{0}}^\dagger + b_0^\dagger b_{\bar{2}}^\dagger)|A\rangle \equiv |Q\rangle \quad (9.50)$$

From Eqs. (9.48)–(9.49) we can see that neither $|P\rangle$ nor $|Q\rangle$ is an eigenfunction of L^2. However, since L^2 'mixes' only the functions $|P\rangle$ and

$|Q\rangle$, we can construct a linear superposition of them which will be an eigenfunction of L^2.

$$|R\rangle = |P\rangle\langle P|R\rangle + |Q\rangle\langle Q|R\rangle$$
$$(L^2 - \lambda)|R\rangle = 0 \tag{9.51}$$

Using Eqs. (9.48)–(9.51) and the orthonormality of $|P\rangle$ and $|Q\rangle$ we obtain the secular equations:

$$(14 - \lambda)\langle P|R\rangle + 4\sqrt{3}\,\langle Q|R\rangle = 0$$
$$4\sqrt{3}\,\langle P|R\rangle + (12 - \lambda)\langle Q|R\rangle = 0 \tag{9.52}$$

A non-trivial solution exists only if the secular determinant vanishes.

$$\det \begin{vmatrix} 14 - \lambda & 4\sqrt{3} \\ 4\sqrt{3} & 12 - \lambda \end{vmatrix} = 0 \tag{9.53}$$

which has the solutions

$$\lambda = \begin{cases} 6 = 2(2 + 1) \\ 20 = 4(4 + 1) \end{cases} \tag{9.54}$$

If we pick the root $\lambda = 6$ and impose the normalization condition

$$|\langle P|R\rangle|^2 + |\langle Q|R\rangle|^2 = 1 \tag{9.55}$$

then the secular equations are satisfied by

$$\langle P|R\rangle = -\sqrt{\frac{3}{7}} \qquad \langle Q|R\rangle = \frac{2}{\sqrt{7}} \tag{9.56}$$

so that we finally obtain the Russel–Saunders eigenfunction

$$|d^2, \tfrac{1}{2}D, 2, 0\rangle = \frac{1}{\sqrt{7}}(-\sqrt{3}\,b_1^\dagger b_1^\dagger + \sqrt{2}\,b_2^\dagger b_0^\dagger + \sqrt{2}\,b_0^\dagger b_2^\dagger)|A\rangle \tag{9.57}$$

In a similar way, acting with L^2 on the trial function $b_0^\dagger b_1^\dagger|A\rangle$ gives

$$(6 - \lambda)b_0^\dagger b_1^\dagger|A\rangle + 2\sqrt{6}\,b_{-1}^\dagger b_2^\dagger|A\rangle = 0$$
$$2\sqrt{6}\,b_0^\dagger b_1^\dagger|A\rangle + (8 - \lambda)b_{-1}^\dagger b_2^\dagger|A\rangle = 0 \tag{9.58}$$

from which we obtain the Russel–Saunders eigenfunction

$$|d^2, \tfrac{3}{2}P, 1, 1\rangle = \frac{1}{\sqrt{5}}(\sqrt{3}\,b_0^\dagger b_1^\dagger - \sqrt{2}\,b_{-1}^\dagger b_2^\dagger)|A\rangle \tag{9.59}$$

Table 9.3 gives a complete list of the $(d)^1$, $(d)^2$, and $(d)^3$ multiplets, to which the $(d)^9$, $(d)^8$, and $(d)^7$ multiplets are related by repeated application of $B^\dagger$. Application of $B^\dagger$ also gives the $(d)^4$, $(d)^5$, and $(d)^6$ multiplets of seniority $v \leq 3$.

Table 9.3

N	v	L	M_L	S	M_S	Name	$(d)^N$ eigenfunction	$(2S+1)$ $\times (2L+1)$
0	0	0	0	0	0	^1_0S	$\lvert A\rangle$	1
1	1	2	2	$\frac{1}{2}$	$\frac{1}{2}$	^2_1D	$b^\dagger_2\lvert A\rangle$	10
2	0	0	0	0	0	^1_0S	$B^\dagger\lvert A\rangle \equiv 1/\sqrt{5}\,(b^\dagger_2 b^\dagger_{-2}$ $- b^\dagger_1 b^\dagger_{-1} + b^\dagger_0 b^\dagger_0$ $- b^\dagger_{-1}b^\dagger_1 + b^\dagger_{-2}b^\dagger_2)\lvert A\rangle$	1
		4	4	0	0	^1_2G	$b^\dagger_2 b^\dagger_2\lvert A\rangle$	9
		3	3	1	1	^3_2F	$b^\dagger_2 b^\dagger_1\lvert A\rangle$	21
	2	2	2	0	0	^1_2D	$1/\sqrt{7}\,(-\sqrt{3}\,b^\dagger_1 b^\dagger_1$ $+\sqrt{2}\,b^\dagger_2 b^\dagger_0$ $+\sqrt{2}\,b^\dagger_0 b^\dagger_2)\lvert A\rangle$	5
		1	1	1	1	^3_2P	$1/\sqrt{5}\,(\sqrt{3}\,b^\dagger_0 b^\dagger_1$ $-\sqrt{2}\,b^\dagger_{-1}b^\dagger_2)\lvert A\rangle$	9
3	1	2	2	$\frac{1}{2}$	$\frac{1}{2}$	^2_1D	$B^\dagger b^\dagger_2\lvert A\rangle$	10
		5	5	$\frac{1}{2}$	$\frac{1}{2}$	^2_3H	$b^\dagger_2 b^\dagger_1 b^\dagger_2\lvert A\rangle$	22
	3	4	4	$\frac{1}{2}$	$\frac{1}{2}$	^2_3G	$1/\sqrt{5}\,(\sqrt{3}\,b^\dagger_2 b^\dagger_1 b^\dagger_1$ $-\sqrt{2}\,b^\dagger_2 b^\dagger_0 b^\dagger_2)\lvert A\rangle$	18

Problem (9.3)   Show that the $(d)^3$ state

$$\frac{1}{\sqrt{5}}(\sqrt{3}\,b^\dagger_2 b^\dagger_1 b^\dagger_1 - \sqrt{2}\,b^\dagger_2 b^\dagger_0 b^\dagger_2)\lvert A\rangle$$

is a ^2G Russel–Saunders eigenfunction with the quantum numbers $L = 4$, $M_L = 4$, $S = \frac{1}{2}$, and $M_S = \frac{1}{2}$. Apply the spin-lowering operator and find the other member of the doublet.

The energy of multiplets in an unperturbed atom

Having found eigenfunctions of L^2, L_z, S^2, and S_z, the next step is to put them back into Eq. (9.2) and find the electrostatic energy of the corresponding

Table 9.3 *(continued)*

N	v	L	M_L	S	M_S	Name	$(d)^N$ eigenfunction	$(2S+1)$ $\times (2L+1)$
		3	3	$\frac{3}{2}$	$\frac{3}{2}$	^4_3F	$b_2^\dagger b_1^\dagger b_0^\dagger \lvert A\rangle$	28
		3	3	$\frac{1}{2}$	$\frac{1}{2}$	^2_3F	$1/\sqrt{12}\,(b_2^\dagger b_1^\dagger b_0^\ddagger - b_2^\dagger b_0^\dagger b_1^\ddagger$ $+ \sqrt{6}\,b_2^\dagger b_{-1}^\ddagger b_2^\dagger$ $- 2b_1^\dagger b_0^\dagger b_2^\ddagger)\,\lvert A\rangle$	14
3	3	2	2	$\frac{1}{2}$	$\frac{1}{2}$	^2_3D	$1/\sqrt{84}\,(3b_2^\dagger b_1^\dagger b_{-\bar 1}^\ddagger$ $- 3b_2^\dagger b_1^\dagger b_0^\ddagger - b_2^\dagger b_{-1}^\ddagger b_1^\dagger$ $+ 5b_2^\dagger b_{-2}^\ddagger b_2^\dagger$ $+ 2\sqrt{6}\,b_1^\dagger b_0^\dagger b_{-\bar 1}^\ddagger$ $- 4\,b_1^\dagger b_{-1}^\ddagger b_2^\dagger)\,\lvert A\rangle$	10
		1	1	$\frac{1}{2}$	$\frac{1}{2}$	^2_3P	$1/\sqrt{210}\,(4\sqrt{3}\,b_2^\dagger b_1^\dagger b_{-\bar 2}^\ddagger$ $- 4\sqrt{2}\,b_2^\dagger b_0^\dagger b_{-\bar 1}^\ddagger$ $+ \sqrt{2}\,b_2^\dagger b_{-1}^\ddagger b_0^\dagger$ $+ 2\sqrt{3}\,b_2^\dagger b_{-2}^\ddagger b_1^\dagger$ $+ 3\sqrt{3}\,b_1^\dagger b_0^\dagger b_0^\ddagger$ $- 3\sqrt{3}\,b_1^\dagger b_{-1}^\ddagger b_1^\dagger$ $- 2\sqrt{3}\,b_1^\dagger b_{-2}^\ddagger b_2^\dagger$ $+ 5\sqrt{2}\,b_0^\dagger b_{-1}^\ddagger b_2^\dagger)\,\lvert A\rangle$	6

free atom multiplets. For example, suppose that we want to evaluate the energy of the $(d)^2$ multiplet

$$\lvert d^2, \tfrac{3}{2}F, 3, 1\rangle = b_2^\dagger b_1^\dagger \lvert A\rangle \qquad (9.60)$$

We remember first that *in our notation, $b_m^\dagger$ is the creation operator associated with the spin-up orbital*

$$\Phi_{n, l, m, 1/2} = \varphi_{n, l, m}(\bar{x})\alpha = R_{n, l}(r)Y_{l, m}(\theta, \varphi)\alpha \qquad \textbf{(9.61)}$$

and $\lvert A\rangle$ is the closed-shell core of the atom. Then

$$b_2^\dagger b_1^\dagger \lvert A\rangle = A\,\big\lvert \Phi_{n, 2, 2, 1/2}\,\Phi_{n, 2, 1, 1/2}\cdots\Phi_{n'l'm'_l m'_s}\cdots\big\rvert \qquad (9.62)$$

287

The quantum theory of atoms, molecules, and photons

From Eq. (9.2) or Eq. (5.68) we have

$$\langle {}^3_2 F | H | {}^3_2 F \rangle$$

$$= \int d^3_x \, \varphi^*_{n,2,2} H^c \varphi_{n,2,2} + \int d^3_x \, \varphi^*_{n,2,1} H^c \varphi_{n,2,1}$$

$$+ \int d^3_{x_1} \int d^3_{x_2} \varphi^*_{n,2,2}(\vec{x}_1) \varphi_{n,2,1}(\vec{x}_2) \frac{e^2}{r_{12}} (1 - \mathscr{P}_{12}) \varphi_{n,2,2}(\vec{x}_1) \varphi_{n,2,1}(\vec{x}_2)$$

$$+ E_{\text{core-shell}} + E_{\text{core}} \tag{9.63}$$

where

$$E_{\text{core-shell}} = \int d\tau \Phi^*_{n,2,2,1/2} (J_{\text{core}} - K_{\text{core}}) \Phi_{n,2,2,1/2}$$

$$+ \int d\tau \Phi^*_{n,2,1,1/2} (J_{\text{core}} - K_{\text{core}}) \Phi_{n,2,1,1/2} \tag{9.64}$$

J_{core} and K_{core} being the coulomb and exchange operators associated with the core orbitals, Eqs. (5.84) and (5.85). Since the core is spherically symmetric, the core-shell interaction energy is independent of the m_l and m_s of the orbitals involved in the $(d)^2$ multiplet and hence it is the same for all the $(d)^2$ multiplets of an atom. Similarly, since the operator H^c is spherically symmetric we can write

$$\int d^3_{x_1} \varphi^*_{n,2,2} H^c \varphi_{n,2,2} = \int d^3_{x_2} \varphi^*_{n,2,1} H^c \varphi_{n,2,1} \tag{9.65}$$

Again the contribution is independent of which one-electron orbitals are involved in the multiplet. This example shows (and it is also true in general) that if we are only interested in the energy differences between multiplets, we need only consider the inter-electron interaction terms. From Eq. (9.63) we can see that we will need to evaluate integrals of the form

$$\int d^3_{x_1} \int d^3_{x_2} |\varphi_{n,l,m}(\vec{x}_1)|^2 \frac{1}{r_{12}} |\varphi_{n,l,m'}(\vec{x}_2)|^2 \equiv \langle m, m' | \frac{1}{r_{12}} | m, m' \rangle \quad \textbf{(9.66)}$$

or else the form

$$\int d^3_{x_1} \int d^3_{x_2} \varphi^*_{n,l,m}(\vec{x}_1) \varphi^*_{n,l,m'}(\vec{x}_2) \frac{1}{r_{12}} \varphi_{n,l,m'}(\vec{x}_1) \varphi_{n,l,m}(\vec{x}_2)$$

$$= \langle m, m' | \frac{1}{r_{12}} | m', m \rangle \quad \textbf{(9.67)}$$

Expansion of $1/r_{12}$; Condon–Shortley coefficients; Slater–Condon parameters; Wigner's Clebsch–Gordan coefficients

It is convenient to expand $1/r_{12}$ in the series.

$$\frac{1}{r_{12}} = \sum_{k=0}^{\infty} \sum_{\mu=-k}^{k} \frac{4\pi}{2k+1} \frac{r_<^k}{r_>^{k+1}} Y_{k,\mu}^*(\theta_1, \varphi_1) Y_{k,\mu}(\theta_2, \varphi_2) \qquad \textbf{(9.68)}$$

where

$$\frac{r_<^k}{r_>^{k+1}} = \begin{cases} \dfrac{r_1^k}{r_2^{k+1}} & \text{if } r_1 < r_2 \\[2ex] \dfrac{r_2^k}{r_1^{k+1}} & \text{if } r_1 > r_2 \end{cases} \qquad \textbf{(9.69)}$$

(For a proof of Eqs. (9.68)–(9.69) see J. S. Griffeth, *The Theory of Transition Metal Ions*, Cambridge (1961) pp. 73–75.) Use of this series allows us to evaluate the integrations over solid angles $d\Omega_1$ and $d\Omega_2$ separately and, as we shall see, all but a few terms in the series vanish. Substituting Eq. (9.68) into Eq. (9.66) we have

$$\langle m, m' | \frac{e^2}{r_{12}} | m, m' \rangle$$

$$= \sum_{k=0}^{\infty} \frac{e^2 4\pi}{2k+1} \int_0^\infty r_1^2 \, dr_1 \int_0^\infty r_2^2 \, dr_2 \, |R_{n,l}(r_1)|^2$$

$$\times |R_{n,l}(r_2)|^2 \frac{r_<^k}{r_>^{k+1}} \int d\Omega_1 \, Y_{l,m}^* Y_{k,0}^* Y_{l,m} \int d\Omega_2 Y_{l,m'}^* Y_{k,0} Y_{l,m'} \quad \textbf{(9.70)}$$

It is convenient to define the 'Condon–Shortley coefficients'

$$C^k(l, m; l', m') \equiv \sqrt{\frac{4\pi}{2k+1}} \int d\Omega Y_{l,m}^* Y_{k,m-m'} Y_{l',m'} \qquad \textbf{(9.71)}$$

and the 'Slater–Condon parameters':

$$F^k \equiv e^2 \int_0^\infty r_1{}^2 dr_1 \int_0^\infty r_2{}^2 dr_2 \frac{r_<^k}{r_>^{k+1}} |R_{n,l}(r_1)|^2 |R_{n,l}(r_2)|^2 \qquad \textbf{(9.72)}$$

Then we can rewrite Eq. (9.70) in the form

$$\langle m, m' | \frac{e^2}{r_{12}} | m, m' \rangle = \sum_k F^k C^k(l, m; l, m) C^k(l, m'; l, m') \qquad \textbf{(9.73)}$$

and similarly

$$\langle m, m' | \frac{e^2}{r_{12}} | m', m \rangle = \sum_k F^k |C^k(l, m; l, m')|^2 \qquad \textbf{(9.74)}$$

The Condon–Shortley coefficients $C^k(l, m; l', m')$ can be expressed in terms of Wigner's Clebsch–Gordan coefficients, Eq. (4.89)

$$C^k(l', m'; l, m) = \sqrt{\frac{2l + 1}{2l' + 1}} \; \langle 0, 0 \overset{lk}{\mid} l', 0 \rangle$$
$$\times \langle m, m' - m \overset{lk}{\mid} l', m' \rangle \tag{9.75}$$

where, according to a formula derived by Wigner,

$$\langle m_1, m_2 \overset{j_1 j_2}{\mid} j, m \rangle$$
$$= \sqrt{\frac{(j + m)!(j - m)!(j_1 - m_1)!(j_2 - m_2)!(j_1 + j_2 - j)!(2j + 1)}{(j_1 + m_1)!(j_2 + m_2)!(j_1 - j_2 + j)!(j_2 - j_1 + j)!(j_1 + j_2 + j + 1)!}}$$
$$\times \delta_{m, m_1 + m_2} \sum_r \frac{(-1)^{j_1 + r - m_1}(j_1 + m_1 + r)!(j_2 + j - r - m_1)!}{r!(j - m - r)!(j_1 - m_1 - r)!(j_2 - j + m_1 + r)!} \tag{9.76}$$

the sum being taken over all non-negative factorials (for a discussion of Eq. (9.75) and Eq. (9.76) see J. M. Blatt and V. Weisskopf *Theoretical Nuclear Physics*, Wiley (1952), p. 793 and J. S. Griffeth, *The Theory of Transition Metal Ions*, Cambridge (1961), pp. 19–21). Wigner's Clebsch–Gordan coefficients vanish unless $k + l' \geq l \geq k - l'$, and also the integral $\int d\Omega Y^*_{L, M} Y_{l, m} Y_{l', m'}$ must vanish unless the argument is even under the coordinate inversion $\vec{x} \to -\vec{x}$. Since the inversion symmetry of the spherical harmonics goes as $(-1)^l$, this means that the integral will vanish unless $k + l + l'$ is even. Thus the number of terms appearing in the series of Eqs. (9.73)–(9.74) is quite limited. Table (9.4) shows the non-zero values of $C^k(l, m; l, m')$ for the p-shell and d-shell.

Table 9.4

$C^k(l, m; l', m') \equiv \sqrt{\dfrac{4\pi}{2k + 1}} \int d\Omega \, Y^*_{l, m} \, Y_{k, m - m'} \, Y_{l', m'}$ $l = l' = 1$			
m	m'	C^0	$5C^2$
± 1	± 1	1	-1
± 1	0	0	$\sqrt{3}$
0	0	1	2
± 1	∓ 1	0	$-\sqrt{6}$

Table 9.4 *(continued)*

		$l = l' = 2$		
m	m'	C^0	$7C^2$	$21C^4$
± 2	± 2	1	-2	1
± 2	± 1	0	$\sqrt{6}$	$-\sqrt{5}$
± 2	0	0	-2	$\sqrt{15}$
± 1	± 1	1	1	-4
± 1	0	0	1	$\sqrt{30}$
0	0	1	2	6
± 2	∓ 2	0	0	$\sqrt{70}$
± 2	∓ 1	0	0	$-\sqrt{35}$
± 1	∓ 1	0	$-\sqrt{6}$	$-\sqrt{40}$

Problem (9.4) Use Wigner's formula, Eq. (9.76), together with Eq. (9.71) to evaluate the Condon–Shortley coefficient, $C^2(1, -1; 1, 1)$, and compare the answer with Table 9.4. Try to repeat the calculation by integrating the spherical harmonics directly.

The energy of the $\frac{3}{2}F$ multiplet in the d^2 configuration

Returning to our example of Eq. (9.63) we have for the energy of the $\frac{3}{2}F$ multiplet:

$$\langle \tfrac{3}{2}F | H_0 | \tfrac{3}{2}F \rangle - E_{(d)^2}$$

$$= \int d_{x_1}^3 \int d_{x_2}^3 \, \varphi_{n,2,2}^*(\vec{x}_1)\varphi_{n,2,1}^*(\vec{x}_2) \frac{e^2}{r_{12}} (1 - \mathscr{P}_{12})\varphi_{n,2,2}(\vec{x}_1)\varphi_{n,2,1}(\vec{x}_2)$$

$$\equiv \langle 2, 1| \frac{e^2}{r_{12}} |2, 1\rangle - \langle 1, 2| \frac{e^2}{r_{12}} |2, 1\rangle$$

$$\sum_{k=0,2,4} F^k C^k(2, 2; 2, 2) C^k(2, 1; 2, 1) - \sum_{k=0,2,4} F^k |C^k(2, 2; 2, 1)|^2$$

$$= F^0 + F^2 \left(-\frac{2}{7}\right)\left(\frac{1}{7}\right) + F^4 \left(\frac{1}{21}\right)\left(\frac{-4}{21}\right) - F^2 \left(\frac{\sqrt{6}}{7}\right)^2 - F^4 \left(\frac{-\sqrt{5}}{21}\right)^2$$

$$= F^0 - \frac{8F^2}{49} - \frac{9F^4}{441} \tag{9.77}$$

Where we have used Eqs. (9.73), (9.74) and Table 9.4. It is convenient to define a new set of Slater–Condon parameters $F_k = F^k/D_k$, so as to include the denominators without continually writing them. In the d-shell we let

$$F_0 \equiv F^0, \qquad F_2 \equiv \frac{F^2}{49} \quad \text{and} \quad F_4 \equiv \frac{F^4}{441} \tag{9.78}$$

Thus the energy of the $(d)^2$ $_2^3F$ multiplet can finally be written in the form

$$\langle _2^3F | H_0 | _2^3F \rangle - E_{(d)^2} = F_0 - 8F_2 - 9F_4 \tag{9.79}$$

where

$$E_{(d)^2} = 2\langle H^c \rangle + E_{\text{core–shell}} + E_{\text{core}} \tag{9.80}$$

is a term common to all the $(d)^2$ multiplets.

Racah parameters; energies of the p-shell multiplets

One sometimes sees the d-shell multiplet energies expressed in terms of the so-called Racah parameters A, B, and C which are related to the Slater–Condon parameters by

$$A \equiv F_0 - 49F_4 \qquad F_0 = A + \frac{49C}{35}$$

$$B \equiv F_2 - 5F_4 \qquad F_2 = B + \frac{C}{7}$$

$$C \equiv 35F_4 \qquad F_4 = \frac{C}{35} \tag{9.81}$$

In terms of the Racah parameters, we would write

$$\langle _2^3F | H_0 | _2^3F \rangle - E_{(d)^2} = A - 8B \tag{9.82}$$

Continuing in this way we can find the energies of the other Russel–Saunders multiplets, and these are shown in Table 9.5 for the $(d)^2$ and $(d)^3$ configurations. (Tables of the $(d)^4$ and $(d)^5$ energies are given in the books of Ballhausen, Griffeth, and Watanabe, cited on p. 282 above.) Van Vleck[28] was able to derive the following general formula for the energies of the $(p)^n$ multiplets

$$\langle p^N, {}^{2S+1}_vL | H | p^N, {}^{2S+1}_vL \rangle - E_{(p)^N}$$

$$= \tfrac{1}{2}N(N-1)F_0 - \tfrac{1}{2}\{5N^2 - 20N + 3L(L+1) + 12S(S+1)\}F_2 \tag{9.83}$$

where (in the p-shell)

$$F_0 \equiv F^0, \qquad F_2 \equiv \frac{F^2}{25} \qquad\qquad (9.84)$$

with F^0 and F^2 defined by Eq. (9.72).

Problem (9.5) Show that the energy of the $(d)^3$, ^2_3H eigenfunction $b_2^\dagger b_1^\dagger b_2^\dagger |A\rangle$, (Table 9.3), is $3F_0 - 6F_2 - 12F_4$, (Table 9.5).

Table 9.5 Multiplet energies

N	Name	Slater–Condon notation	Racah notation
$(d)^2$	^3_2F	$F_0 - 8F_2 - 9F_4$	$A - 8B$
	^3_2P	$F_0 + 7F_2 - 84F_4$	$A + 7B$
	^1_2G	$F_0 + 4F_2 + F_4$	$A + 4B + 2C$
	^1_2D	$F_0 - 3F_2 + 36F_4$	$A - 3B + 2C$
	^1_0S	$F_0 + 14F_2 + 126F_4$	$A + 14B + 7C$
$(d)^3$	^4_3F	$3F_0 - 15F_2 - 72F_4$	$3A - 15B$
	^4_3P	$3F_0 - 147F_4$	$3A$
	$^2_3H, ^2_3P$	$3F_0 - 6F_2 - 12F_4$	$3A - 6B + 3C$
	^2_3G	$3F_0 - 11F_2 + 13F_4$	$3A - 11B + 3C$
	^2_3F	$3F_0 + 9F_2 - 87F_4$	$3A + 9B + 3C$
	$^2_3D, ^2_1D$ $(+)(-)$	$3F_0 + 5F_2 + 3F_4$ $\pm\sqrt{(193F_2^2 - 1650F_2F_4 + 8325F_4^2)}$	$3A + 5B + 5C$ $\pm\sqrt{(193B^2 + 8BC + 4C^2)}$

Spin-orbit coupling; the relativistic Hamiltonian expanded in powers of v/c

We have until now been using the approximate free-atom Hamiltonian given by Eq. (9.3). Let us now try to see what happens when we add on extra terms representing the effect of spin-orbit coupling, and the effect of the electrostatic field due to surrounding atoms. Let us consider first the spin-orbit coupling. In chapter 8 we mentioned that the term $(e/2m_0c)\vec{E}.\vec{\alpha}$ in Eq. (8.24) was responsible for spin-orbit coupling in atoms. Since we wish to use 2-component electron spin functions rather than 4-component

Dirac spin functions we have to solve for the two small components in terms of the two large components. When this is done, we obtain the following *Hamiltonian for an electron in an external electromagnetic field correct to order* $(v/c)^2$:

$$H = \frac{(\vec{p} - (e/c)\vec{A})^2}{2m} - \frac{p^4}{8m^3 c^2} + e\phi - \frac{eh}{2mc}\vec{\sigma}.\vec{H} + \frac{eh^2}{8m^2 c^2}\nabla^2\phi$$

$$- \frac{eh}{4m^2 c^2}\vec{\sigma}\left\{\vec{E} \wedge \left(\vec{p} - \frac{e}{c}\vec{A}\right)\right\} \quad (9.85)$$

(For a derivation of Eq. (9.85), see A. I. Akhiezer and V. B. Berestetskii, *Quantum Electrodynamics*, Interscience (1965), pp. 144–148.) The term $(e/4m^2 c^2)\vec{\sigma}(\vec{E} \wedge \vec{p})$ in Eq. (9.85) is responsible for the spin-orbit coupling. When $\partial\vec{A}/\partial t = 0$, the electric field $\vec{E}$ is the negative gradient of the electrostatic potential ϕ: $\vec{E} = -\vec{\nabla}\phi$. Let us also particularize to the case where ϕ is spherically symmetric. Then

$$\vec{\sigma}(\vec{E} \wedge \vec{p}) = -\det \begin{vmatrix} \sigma_x & \sigma_y & \sigma_z \\ \dfrac{\partial\phi}{\partial x} & \dfrac{\partial\phi}{\partial y} & \dfrac{\partial\phi}{\partial z} \\ p_x & p_y & p_z \end{vmatrix}$$

$$= -\frac{\partial\phi}{\partial r}\det \begin{vmatrix} \sigma_x & \sigma_y & \sigma_z \\ \dfrac{\partial r}{\partial x} & \dfrac{\partial r}{\partial y} & \dfrac{\partial r}{\partial z} \\ p_x & p_y & p_z \end{vmatrix}$$

$$= -\frac{1}{r}\frac{\partial\phi}{\partial r}\det \begin{vmatrix} \sigma_x & \sigma_y & \sigma_z \\ x & y & z \\ p_x & p_y & p_z \end{vmatrix}$$

$$= -\frac{1}{r}\frac{\partial\phi}{\partial r}\vec{\sigma}(\vec{x} \wedge \vec{p}) \quad (9.86)$$

Thus, *when the electrostatic potential ϕ is spherically symmetric, the spin-orbit coupling term becomes*

$$-\frac{eh}{4m^2 c^2}\vec{\sigma}(\vec{E} \wedge p) = \frac{eh}{2m^2 c^2 r}\frac{\partial\phi}{\partial r}\vec{L}_1.\vec{S}_1 \equiv \xi(r)\vec{L}_1.\vec{S}_1 \quad (9.87)$$

where

$$\vec{L}_1 \equiv \vec{r} \wedge \vec{p}, \qquad \vec{S}_1 = \tfrac{1}{2}\vec{\sigma}_1, \qquad \xi(r) = \frac{e\hbar}{2m^2c^2r}\frac{\partial\phi}{\partial r} \qquad (9.88)$$

We should notice that *when the electrostatic potential ϕ is not spherically symmetric (e.g., when the electrostatic field of the surrounding atoms is also included) then Eq. (9.87) does not hold and we must go back to Eq. (9.85).*

The spin-orbit coupling operator expressed in terms of creation and annihilation operators

The matrix elements of the one-electron operator $\vec{L}_1.\vec{S}_1$ based on the one-electron spin-orbitals Φ_{n,l,m,m_s} are given by

$$\langle m', m'_s|\,\vec{L}_1, \vec{S}_1\,|m, m_s\rangle$$
$$= \langle m', m'_s|\,(\tfrac{1}{2}L_+S_- + \tfrac{1}{2}L_-S_+ + L_zS_z)\,|m, m_s\rangle \qquad (9.89)$$

From Eq. (3.169) and Eq. (3.171) we have

$$\tfrac{1}{2}L_+S_-\,|m, m_s\rangle$$
$$= \tfrac{1}{2}\sqrt{\{l(l+1) - m(m+1)\}\{\tfrac{3}{4} - m_s(m_s - 1)\}}\,|m+1, m_s - 1\rangle$$

$$\tfrac{1}{2}L_-S_+\,|m, m_s\rangle$$
$$= \tfrac{1}{2}\sqrt{\{l(l+1) - m(m-1)\}\{\tfrac{3}{4} - m_s(m_s + 1)\}}\,|m-1, m_s + 1\rangle$$

$$L_zS_z\,|m, m_s\rangle = mm_s\,|m, m_s\rangle \qquad (9.90)$$

so that

$$\langle m', m'_s|\,\vec{L}_1.\vec{S}_1\,|m, m_s\rangle$$
$$= \tfrac{1}{2}\sqrt{\{l(l+1) - m(m+1)\}\{\tfrac{3}{4} - m_s(m_s - 1)\}}\,\delta_{m', m+1}\,\delta_{m'_s, m_s - 1}$$
$$+ \tfrac{1}{2}\sqrt{\{l(l+1) - m(m-1)\}\{\tfrac{3}{4} - m_s(m_s + 1)\}}\,\delta_{m', m-1}\,\delta_{m'_s, m_s + 1}$$
$$+ mm_s\,\delta_{m'm}\,\delta_{m'_sm_s} \qquad (9.91)$$

The many-electron spin-orbit interaction operator which has to be added to the Hamiltonian of Eq. (9.3) is an operator of 'type-F', and according to Eq. (9.9) and Eq. (9.91) it can be written in the form

$$\sum_i \xi(r_i)\vec{L}_i.\vec{S}_i \equiv H^{(1)}$$

$$= \tfrac{1}{2}\lambda \sum_m \Big[\sqrt{l(l+1) - m(m+1)}\,b^\dagger_{\bar{m}+\bar{1}}b_m$$

$$+ \sqrt{l(l+1) - m(m-1)}\,b^\dagger_{m-1}b_{\bar{m}}$$

$$+ m(b^\dagger_m b_m - b^\dagger_{\bar{m}} b_{\bar{m}})\Big] \qquad (9.92)$$

where

$$\lambda \equiv \frac{e\hbar}{2m^2c^2} \int_0^\infty r \, dr \, |R_{n,\,l}(r)|^2 \frac{\partial \phi}{\partial r} \tag{9.93}$$

Commutation rules for the spin-orbit interaction; mixing of multiplets; the Landé interval rule

From Eq. (9.92) we obtain the commutation relations

$$\left[\sum_i \xi(r_i)\vec{L}_i.\vec{S}_i, b_m^\dagger\right] \equiv \left[H^{(1)}, b_m^\dagger\right]$$
$$= \frac{\lambda}{2}\left[\sqrt{l(l+1)-m(m+1)}\, b_{\bar{m}+\bar{1}}^\dagger + mb_m^\dagger\right]$$

$$\left[\sum_i \xi(r_i)\vec{L}_i.\vec{S}_i, b_m^{\dagger}\right] \equiv \left[H^{(1)}, b_m^{\dagger}\right]$$
$$= \frac{\lambda}{2}\left[\sqrt{l(l+1)-m(m-1)}\, b_{m-1}^\dagger - mb_{\bar{m}}^\dagger\right] \tag{9.94}$$

where $H^{(1)} \equiv \sum_i \xi(r_i)\vec{L}_i.\vec{S}_i$ is the part of the Hamiltonian due to spin-orbit coupling. For example in the d-shell the commutation relations of Eq. (9.94) become

$$\frac{1}{\lambda}\left[H^{(1)}, b_2^\dagger\right] = b_2^\dagger$$

$$\frac{1}{\lambda}\left[H^{(1)}, b_1^\dagger\right] = b_2^{\dagger} + \tfrac{1}{2}b_1^\dagger$$

$$\frac{1}{\lambda}\left[H^{(1)}, b_0^\dagger\right] = \sqrt{\tfrac{3}{2}}b_{\bar{1}}^\dagger$$

$$\frac{1}{\lambda}\left[H^{(1)}, b_{-1}^\dagger\right] = \sqrt{\tfrac{3}{2}}b_0^{\dagger} - \tfrac{1}{2}b_{-1}^\dagger$$

$$\frac{1}{\lambda}\left[H^{(1)}, b_{-2}^\dagger\right] = b_{\bar{1}}^\dagger - b_{-2}^\dagger$$

$$\frac{1}{\lambda}\left[H^{(1)}, b_2^{\dagger}\right] = b_1^\dagger - b_2^{\dagger}$$

$$\frac{1}{\lambda}\left[H^{(1)}, b_{\bar{1}}^{\dagger}\right] = \sqrt{\tfrac{3}{2}}b_0^\dagger - \tfrac{1}{2}b_{\bar{1}}^{\dagger}$$

$$\frac{1}{\lambda}\left[H^{(1)}, b_0^{\dagger}\right] = \sqrt{\tfrac{3}{2}}b_{-1}^\dagger$$

$$\frac{1}{\lambda} [H^{(1)}, b^{\dagger}_{-\bar{1}}] = b^{\dagger}_{-2} + \tfrac{1}{2}b^{\dagger}_{-\bar{1}}$$

$$\frac{1}{\lambda} [H^{(1)}, b^{\dagger}_{-\bar{2}}] = b^{\dagger}_{-\bar{2}} \tag{9.95}$$

These commutation relations allow us to find the effect of the spin-orbit coupling operator on the Russel–Saunders eigenfunctions. For example, if we let $H^{(1)} \equiv \sum_i \xi(i)\vec{L}_i . \vec{S}_i$ act on the $(d)^2$ ${}^3_2 F$ function we obtain

$$
\begin{aligned}
H^{(1)} |2, \tfrac{3}{2}F, 3, 1\rangle &= H^{(1)} b^{\dagger}_2 b^{\dagger}_1 |A\rangle \\
&= ([H^{(1)}, b^{\dagger}_2]b^{\dagger}_1 + b^{\dagger}_2[H^{(1)}, b^{\dagger}_1]) |A\rangle \\
&= \lambda(\tfrac{3}{2}b^{\dagger}_2 b^{\dagger}_1 + b^{\dagger}_2 b^{\dagger}_2) |A\rangle \\
&= \lambda(\tfrac{3}{2} |d^2, \tfrac{3}{2}F, 3, 1\rangle + |d^2, \tfrac{1}{2}G, 4, 0\rangle) \tag{9.96}
\end{aligned}
$$

where we have used Eq. (9.95) and Table 9.2 together with the fact that $H^{(1)} |A\rangle = 0$. This demonstrates that the spin-orbit coupling operator can mix states with different values of L and S. However (except in atoms with very large values of Z), the value of the parameter λ is small compared with the Racah parameters A, B, and C, so that one often neglects the hybridization between different multiplets. It can be shown (see for example Griffeth, loc. cit., p. 108), that within a particular multiplet it is legitimate to replace the operator $H^{(1)} = \lambda \sum_i \vec{L}_i . \vec{S}_i$ with the operator

$$\lambda' \vec{L}.\vec{S} \equiv \lambda'(\sum_i \vec{L}_i) \cdot (\sum_j \vec{S}_j)$$

Then, within the multiplet we have

$$
\begin{aligned}
\langle L, S, M'_L, M'_S| &\, H^{(1)} |L, S, M_L, M_S\rangle \\
&= \frac{\lambda'}{2} [\sqrt{\{L(L+1) - M_L(M_L+1)\}\{S(S+1) - M_S(M_S-1)\}} \\
&\quad \times \delta_{M'_L, M_L+1} \, \delta_{M'_S, M_S-1} \\
&\quad + \sqrt{\{L(L+1) - M_L(M_L-1)\}\{S(S+1) - M_S(M_S+1)\}} \\
&\quad \times \delta_{M'_L, M_L-1} \, \delta_{M'_S, M_S+1} \\
&\quad + 2M_L M_S \delta_{M'_L, M_L} \, \delta_{M'_S, M_S}] \tag{9.97}
\end{aligned}
$$

Now we notice that the square of total angular momentum (orbital plus spin) is given by

$$J^2 \equiv (\vec{L} + \vec{S})^2 = L^2 + 2\vec{L}.\vec{S} + S^2 \tag{9.98}$$

so that

$$\lambda' \vec{L} . \vec{S} = \frac{\lambda'}{2} (J^2 - L^2 - S^2) \qquad (9.99)$$

We can make a unitary transformation among the members of the multiplet such that the members of the new basis set will be eigenfunctions of L^2, S^2, J^2, and J_z, instead of eigenfunctions of L^2, S^2, L_z, and S_z. As we mentioned in chapter 4, Eq. (4.89), the coefficients in such a transformation are Wigner's Clebsch–Gordan coefficients.

$$|L, S, J, M\rangle$$
$$= \sum_{M_L, M_S} |L, S, M_L, M_S\rangle\langle M_L, M_S \overset{LS}{|} J, M_J\rangle \qquad (9.100)$$

Since the functions $|L, S, J, M_J\rangle$ are eigenfunctions of J^2, L^2, and S^2, then, according to Eq. (9.99) they are also eigenfunctions of $\lambda' \vec{L} . \vec{S}$

$$\lambda' \vec{L} . \vec{S} |L, S, J, M_J\rangle$$
$$= \frac{\lambda'}{2} \{J(J + 1) - L(L + 1) - S(S + 1)\} |L, S, J, M_J\rangle \qquad (9.101)$$

Thus, in the approximation which neglects hybridization between different Russel–Saunders multiplets, the effect of the spin-orbit interaction is to split the $(2S + 1).(2L + 1)$ degenerate levels into submultiplets each of which is characterized by a value of J. The energy of each submultiplet (in this approximation) is the Russel–Saunders energy as given by Table 9.5 or Eq. (9.83) plus the spin-orbit coupling energy given by Eq. (9.101). According to the discussion following Eq. (4.87) J can take on the values $L + S, L + S - 1, \ldots, |L - S|$, and for each value of J, M_J can take on $2J + 1$ values, so that the submultiplet is $(2J + 1)$-fold degenerate.
Since

$$\frac{\lambda'}{2} J(J + 1) - \frac{\lambda'}{2} (J - 1)(J - J + 1) = \lambda' J \qquad (9.102)$$

the successive submultiplets differ from one another by an energy $\lambda' J$, J being the quantum number associated with the higher submultiplet. This rule was discovered empirically by Landé before the advent of quantum mechanics, and it is known as the Landé interval rule. It is usual to write the value of J as a subscript on the lower right-hand side of the multiplet name. Thus, for example $^3P_2$ would denote a submultiplet with $S = 1$, $L = 1$, and $J = 2$, while $^3P_0$ would denote a submultiplet with $S = 1$, $L = 1$, and $J = 0$. Spin-orbit coupling splits the $(2S + 1).(2L + 1) = 9$-fold degenerate ^3P level into a $2J + 1 = 2.2 + 1 = 5$-fold degenerate $^3P_2$ sublevel, a $2J + 1 = 2.1 + 1 = 3$-fold degenerate $^3P_1$ sublevel and a non-degenerate $(2J + 1 = 2.0 + 1 = 1)$ $^3P_0$ sublevel. As an exercise, the interested reader might try constructing the eigenfunction corresponding to the $p^2, \frac{3}{2}P_0$ sublevel using Table 9.1.

The effect of ligands; crystal field theory

We have until now been considering a free atom. Now we would like to find out what happens when the atom interacts with other atoms in a molecule or crystal. The surrounding atoms or groups of atoms are called 'ligands'. One is usually interested in a central metal atom surrounded in a symmetrical way by ligands. The orbitals of the metal atom and those of the ligands will combine to form molecular orbitals. However, if the metal atomic orbital has a very much higher energy than the ligand atomic orbital, then the bonding molecular orbital formed by combining the two will be localized mainly on the ligand. For example, in sodium chloride, the bonding has a largely ionic character; that is to say an electron is almost entirely transferred from sodium to chlorine. *In the approximation where we neglect mixing between the orbitals of the metal atoms and the ligands, we can represent the effect of the ligands on the metal by an electrostatic field.* This approximation, developed by Bethe,[1] Schlapp, Penney,[23] and others is called 'crystal field' approximation. The more rigorous treatment, which includes metal–ligand mixing, is called 'ligand field' theory. It is becoming increasingly apparent that in most transition metal complexes metal–ligand mixing is significant and that the ligand field methods developed by Gray, Ballhausen,[9] Dahl,[4] and others are to be preferred to the crystal field approximation. However, let us discuss the crystal field treatment first since it is more simple.

If ϕ represents the electrostatic field produced by the ligands, then, according to Poisson's equation, Eq. (1.153), $\nabla^2\phi = 4\pi\rho$ where ρ is the density of excess charge on the ligands. Since this charge is entirely outside the region of the central metal atom, it follows that in the region of the metal ion $\nabla^2\phi = 0$. If we represent the excess charge density on the ligands as a sum of point charges, Eq. (1.151), then

$$\phi(\bar{x}) = \sum_n \frac{e_n}{|\bar{x} - \bar{x}_n|} \qquad (9.103)$$

where $\bar{x}_n$ is the position of the point charge e_n. Then, expanding $1/|\bar{x} - \bar{x}_n|$ in terms of spherical harmonics by means of Eq. (9.68) we have

$$e\varphi(\bar{x}) = e\sum_n e_n \sum_{k=0}^{\infty} \sum_{\mu=-k}^{k} \frac{4\pi}{2k+1} \frac{r^k}{r_n^{k+1}} Y_{k,\mu}^*(\theta_n, \varphi_n) Y_{k,\mu}(\theta, \varphi) \qquad (9.104)$$

where r, θ, and φ are the spherical polar coordinates corresponding to $\bar{x}$, and r_n, θ_n, and φ_n are the spherical polar coordinates corresponding to $\bar{x}_n$.

299

Notice that in the region of interest (near the metal ion), $r < r_n$ so that we do not need to worry which should go in the numerator (Eq. (9.69)). Notice also that if we write the Laplacian operator in terms of spherical polar coordinates (Eqs. (2.24–2.25)), and let it act on ϕ we obtain $\nabla^2 \phi = 0$, letting

$$A_{k,\mu} \equiv \frac{4\pi e}{2k+1} \sum_n \frac{e_n Y^*_{k,\mu}(\theta_n, \varphi_n)}{r_n^{k+1}} \tag{9.105}$$

and we can rewrite Eq. (9.104) in the form

$$e\phi(\vec{x}) = \sum_{k=0}^{\infty} \sum_{\mu=-k}^{k} A_{k,\mu} r^k Y_{k,\mu}(\theta, \varphi) \tag{9.106}$$

If the excess charge on the ligands is expressed as a continuously distributed density ρ rather than as a superposition of point charges, then Eq. (9.103) and Eq. (9.105) become

$$\phi(\vec{x}) = \int dV' \frac{\rho(\vec{x}')}{|\vec{x} - \vec{x}'|} \tag{9.107}$$

and

$$A_{k,\mu} = \frac{4\pi e}{2k+1} \int dV \frac{Y^*_{k,\mu}(\theta, \varphi) \rho(r, \theta, \varphi)}{r^{k+1}} \tag{9.108}$$

It might seem at first that the integrand of Eq. (9.108) can be singular near $r_n = 0$ but since $\rho = 0$ in that region there is no danger.

Restrictions of symmetry; tetrahedral and octahedral crystal fields

Instead of determining the crystal field coefficients $A_{k,\mu}$ by means of Eq. (9.105) or Eq. (9.107), one sometimes leaves them as empirical parameters. The number of different independent coefficients $A_{k,\mu}$ entering the series of Eq. (9.106) is reduced by the requirement that the potential ϕ must have the symmetry of the ligands. For example, suppose that we know that the molecule is symmetrical with respect to the inversion $\vec{x} \rightarrow -\vec{x}$. Then it follows that the series of Eq. (9.106) cannot contain any odd values of k, because ϕ must be symmetrical with respect to inversion, and the inversion-symmetry of the spherical harmonics goes as $(-1)^k$. More generally, we can say that if R is an operator belonging to the group of symmetry operations which leave the environment of the metal atom unchanged, then we must have $R\phi = \phi$. The effect of the operator R on the spherical harmonics $Y_{k,\mu}$ can be found by expressing $r^k Y_{k,\mu}$ in terms of cartesian coordinates and then seeing how the cartesian coordinates

300

transform under the operation R. In this way one can show that for tetrahedral symmetry the crystal field perturbation must have the form

$$e\phi(T_d) = A_{3,2}r^3(Y_{3,2} - Y_{3,-2})$$
$$+ A_{4,0}r^4\{Y_{4,0} + \sqrt{\tfrac{5}{14}}(Y_{4,4} + Y_{4,-4})\} \quad (9.109)$$

and for octahedral symmetry,

$$e\phi(O_h) = A_{4,0}r^4\{Y_{4,0} + \sqrt{\tfrac{5}{14}}(Y_{4,4} + Y_{4,-4})\} \quad (9.110)$$

The x-, y-, and z-axes here are taken in the directions of the $(1, 0, 0)$, $(0, 1, 0)$, and $(0, 0, 1)$ crystallographic axes as shown in Fig. 9.2. 'T_d' and

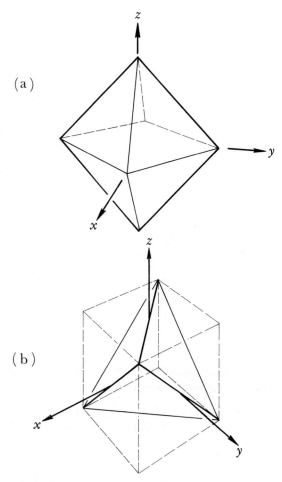

Figure 9.2 shows a regular octahedron (a) and a regular tetrahedron (b). The cube in which the tetrahedron is inscribed is indicated by a dotted line.

The quantum theory of atoms, molecules, and photons

'O_h' are the conventional symbols which stand for tetrahedral and octahedral symmetry. We have neglected terms proportional to $Y_{k,\mu}$ with $k > 4$ since we are primarily interested in the p and d shells, and, as we remarked above, the integral $\int d\Omega Y^*_{lm'} Y_{k,\mu} Y_{l,m}$ vanishes for $k > 2l$.

The crystal field perturbation $H^{(2)} \equiv e \sum_i \phi(\bar{x}_i)$ is an operator of type F and we can evaluate its matrix elements by means of the Slater–Condon rules. If Δ is a Slater determinant of the type shown in Eq. (9.1), then

$$\int d\tau \Delta^* H^{(2)}\Delta \equiv \int d\tau \Delta^* e \sum_i \phi(\bar{x}_i)\Delta$$

$$= e \sum_{m, m_s} \langle m, m_s| \phi(\bar{x}) |m, m_s\rangle$$

$$= \sum_{k, \mu} A_{k, \mu} \sum_{m, m_s} \langle m, m_s| r^k Y_{k, \mu} |m, m_s\rangle \quad (9.111)$$

while

$$\int d\tau \Delta^*_{m, m_s \to m', m'_s} H^{(2)}\Delta = \sum_{k, \mu} A_{k, \mu} \langle m', m'_s| r^k Y_{k, \mu} |m, m_s\rangle \quad (9.112)$$

The one-electron elements can be expressed in terms of the Slater–Condon parameters

$$\langle m', m'_s| r^k Y_{k, \mu} |m, m_s\rangle = \delta_{m'_s, m_s} \overline{r^k} \sqrt{\frac{2k+1}{4\pi}} C^k(l, m' + \mu; l, m) \quad (9.113)$$

where

$$\overline{r^k} \equiv \int_0^\infty dr\, r^{k+2} |R_{n, l}(r)|^2 \quad (9.114)$$

Problem (9.6) An atom is placed in the centre of a tetrahedron on the corners of which are four equal point charges q. Use Eq. (9.105) to evaluate the coefficients $A_{k, \mu}$ in the expansion of the potential experienced by the atom, Eq. (9.106). (Evaluate only the coefficients $A_{3, 2}$, $A_{3, -2}$, $A_{4, 0}$, $A_{4, 4}$, and $A_{4, -4}$.) Compare the result with Eq. (9.109).

The crystal field expressed in terms of creation and annihilation operators; commutation rules in the d-shell

We can also use Eqs. (9.9), (9.113), and (9.114) to express the crystal field perturbation in terms of creation and annihilation operators

$$H^{(2)} = \sum_{k, \mu} A_{k, \mu} \overline{r^k} \sqrt{\frac{2k+1}{4\pi}}$$

$$\times \sum_m C^k(l, m + \mu; l, m)(b^\dagger_{m+\mu} b_m + b^\dagger_{\bar{m}+\bar{\mu}} b_{\bar{m}}) \quad (9.115)$$

302

from which we find the commutation relation

$$[H^{(2)}, b_m^\dagger] = \sum_{k,\mu} A_{k,\mu} r^k \sqrt{\frac{2k+1}{4\pi}} \, C^k(l, m+\mu; l, m) b_{m+\mu}^\dagger \quad \textbf{(9.116)}$$

For example, we can use Eq. (9.116), Eq. (9.110), and Table 9.4 to show that both the tetrahedral and octahedral crystal field operators satisfy the following commutation relations with the d-shell creation operators.

$$[H^{(2)}_{\binom{O_h}{T_d}}, b_0^\dagger] = 6D_q b_0^\dagger$$

$$[H^{(2)}_{\binom{O_h}{T_d}}, b_{\pm1}^\dagger] = -4D_q b_{\pm1}^\dagger$$

$$[H^{(2)}_{\binom{O_h}{T_d}}, b_{\pm2}^\dagger] = D_q(b_{\pm2}^\dagger + 5b_{\pm2}^\dagger) \quad \textbf{(9.117)}$$

where $D_q \equiv A_{4,0} \, \overline{r^4}/(14\sqrt{\pi})$.

(The commutation relations for the spin-down d-shell creation operators are the same, except that there are bars everywhere.)

Using Eq. (9.116) we can find the effect of the crystal field on our determinantal wave functions. If the crystal field is very weak compared with the inter-electron interaction, then we can begin with the Russel–Saunders eigenfunctions and treat both the crystal field $H^{(2)}$ and the spin-orbit coupling $H^{(1)}$ as small perturbations. For example, suppose that we are considering a metal ion with a $(d)^3$ configuration in an octahedral crystal field, and suppose that we would like to know the effect of the crystal field on the ^4F state $b_2^\dagger b_1^\dagger b_0^\dagger |A\rangle$ (see Table 9.3). According to Eq. (9.117) we have

$$H^{(2)} b_2^\dagger b_1^\dagger b_0^\dagger |A\rangle$$

$$= \{[H^{(2)}, b_2^\dagger] b_1^\dagger b_0^\dagger + b_2^\dagger [H^{(2)}, b_1^\dagger] b_0^\dagger + b_2^\dagger b_1^\dagger [H^{(2)}, b_0^\dagger]\} |A\rangle$$

$$= D_q\{3b_2^\dagger b_1^\dagger b_0^\dagger + 5b_{-2}^\dagger b_1^\dagger b_0^\dagger\} |A\rangle\} \quad \textbf{(9.118)}$$

and similarly

$$H^{(2)} b_{-2}^\dagger b_1^\dagger b_0^\dagger |A\rangle = D_q\{3b_{-2}^\dagger b_1^\dagger b_0^\dagger + 5b_2^\dagger b_1^\dagger b_0^\dagger\} |A\rangle \quad \textbf{(9.119)}$$

From Table 9.3 we can see that the state $b_{-2}^\dagger b_1^\dagger b_0^\dagger |A\rangle$ must also belong to the ^4F multiplet since no other $(d)^3$ multiplets have $S = \frac{3}{2}$. Therefore $b_2^\dagger b_1^\dagger b_0^\dagger |A\rangle$ and $b_{-2}^\dagger b_1^\dagger b_0^\dagger |A\rangle$ are degenerate eigenfunctions of $H^{(0)}$ corresponding to the energy $3A - 15B$. The effect of the crystal field Hamiltonian $H^{(2)}$ is to remove this degeneracy and mix the two states. From Eqs. (9.118)–(9.119) it follows that the state $1/\sqrt{2} \, (b_2^\dagger b_1^\dagger b_0^\dagger + b_{-2}^\dagger b_1^\dagger b_0^\dagger) |A\rangle$ is an eigenfunction of $H^{(0)} + H^{(2)}$ corresponding to the energy $3A - 15B + 8D_q$ while the state $1/\sqrt{2} \, (b_2^\dagger b_1^\dagger b_0^\dagger - b_{-2}^\dagger b_1^\dagger b_0^\dagger) |A\rangle$ is an eigenfunction of $H^{(0)} + H^{(2)}$ corresponding to the energy $3A - 15B - 2D_q$.

The next step is to apply the spin-orbit coupling Hamiltonian $H^{(1)}$ as a small perturbation: from Eq. (9.94) we have

$$\tfrac{1}{2} \langle A| (b_0 b_1 b_2 \pm b_0 b_1 b_{-2})H^{(1)}(b_2^\dagger b_1^\dagger b_0^\dagger \pm b_{-2}^\dagger b_1^\dagger b_0^\dagger) |A\rangle = \frac{\lambda}{2} \quad (9.120)$$

so that the effect of spin-orbit coupling is to raise the energies of both states by an amount $\lambda/2$.

The approximation which begins with Russel–Saunders eigenfunctions and then adds the crystal field and the spin-orbit coupling is called the 'weak field approximation'. The opposite approximation which begins with eigenfunctions of the crystal field Hamiltonian and then treats the interelectron repulsion and the spin-orbit coupling as a small perturbation is called the 'strong-field approximation'. If we calculate matrix elements of the complete Hamiltonian, including interelectron repulsion, spin-orbit coupling and crystal field, using functions of the type shown in Eq. (9.1) as a basis, and if we diagonalize the resulting Hamiltonian matrix we shall then obtain a more exact solution called the 'complete crystal field theory'[12] containing both the weak-field approximation and the strong-field approximation as limits.

Problem (9.7)   Use the commutation relations, Eqs. (9.95) and (9.117), to calculate the splitting of the 10-fold degenerate $(d)^1$, $_1^2 D$ multiplet when it is acted on by a tetrahedral or octahedral crystal field together with a small perturbation due to spin-orbit coupling.

Appendix I. Small vibrations of a classical system about its equilibrium position

Consider a classical system whose kinetic energy T has the form

$$T = \tfrac{1}{2} \sum_{i,j=1}^{N} m(i)\, \delta_{ij} \frac{\mathrm{d}x^i}{\mathrm{d}t} \frac{\mathrm{d}x^j}{\mathrm{d}t} \tag{I.1}$$

and whose potential energy has the form

$$V = \tfrac{1}{2} \sum_{i,j=1}^{N} V_{ij} x^i x^j \tag{I.2}$$

The coordinates $x^1, x^2, \ldots, x^N$ are by no means the most convenient ones for solving the equation of motion of such a system.

Let us begin to improve matters by going over to 'mass-weighted' coordinates defined by

$$x^{i'} \equiv \sqrt{m(i)}\, x^i \tag{I.3}$$

In terms of $x^{1'}, \ldots, x^{N'}$ the kinetic energy T becomes

$$T = \tfrac{1}{2} \sum_{i,j} \delta_{ij} \frac{\mathrm{d}x^{i'}}{\mathrm{d}t} \frac{\mathrm{d}x^{j'}}{\mathrm{d}t} \tag{I.4}$$

while the potential energy is

$$V = \tfrac{1}{2} \sum_{i,j} V'_{ij} x^{i'} x^{j'} \tag{I.5}$$

$$V'_{ij} = \sum_{r,s} V_{rs} \frac{\partial x^r}{\partial x^{i'}} \frac{\partial x^s}{\partial x^{j'}} = V_{ij} \frac{1}{\sqrt{m(i)m(j)}} \tag{I.6}$$

The mass-weighted coordinates are still not very good ones to use because V'_{ij} is still not diagonal, and the cross terms linking $x^{i'}$ and $x^{j'}$, $i \neq j$, would be a nuisance. Fortunately we can get rid of them by another transformation. Let us try to find a set of constant transformation coefficients

The quantum theory of atoms, molecules, and photons

$U_{i\mu}$ such that if we express the potential energy in terms of the new coordinates

$$X^\mu = \sum_i x^{i'} U_{i\mu} = \sum_i x^i \sqrt{m(i)} \; U_{i\mu} \tag{I.7}$$

the cross-terms will disappear.

Writing V in terms of the capitalized coordinates we have

$$\begin{aligned} V &= \tfrac{1}{2} \sum_{\mu,\nu} V_{\mu\nu} X^\mu X^\nu \\ &= \tfrac{1}{2} \sum_{\mu,\nu} \sum_{i,j} V_{\mu\nu}(x^{i'} U_{i\mu})(x^{j'} U_{j\nu}) \\ &\equiv \tfrac{1}{2} \sum_{i,j} V'_{ij} x^{i'} x^{j'} \end{aligned} \tag{I.8}$$

From Eq. (I.8) we can see that the new coefficients $V_{\mu\nu}$ are related to the old ones V'_{ij} by

$$\sum_{\mu,\nu} U_{i\mu} V_{\mu\nu} U_{j\nu} \equiv V'_{ij} \equiv \frac{1}{\sqrt{m(i)m(j)}} V_{ij} \tag{I.9}$$

We would like the transformation from the primed coordinates $x^{1'}, \ldots, x^{N'}$ to the capitalized coordinates $X^1, \ldots, X^N$ to leave the kinetic energy term in its convenient mass-normalized form. In other words, we would like to have

$$\begin{aligned} T &= \tfrac{1}{2} \sum_{\mu,\nu} \delta_{\mu\nu} X^\mu X^\nu \\ &= \tfrac{1}{2} \sum_{\mu,\nu} \sum_{i,j} \delta_{\mu\nu}(x^i U_{i\mu})(x^j U_{j\nu}) = \tfrac{1}{2} \sum_{i,j} \delta_{ij} x^i x^j \end{aligned} \tag{I.10}$$

so that we need to have

$$\sum_{\mu,\nu} U_{i\mu} \delta_{\mu\nu} U_{j\nu} = \sum_\mu U_{i\mu} U_{j\mu} \equiv \sum_\mu U_{i\mu} U^T_{\mu j} = \delta_{ij} \tag{I.11}$$

Equation (I.11) states that the matrix $U_{i\mu}$ multiplied by its transpose $U^T_{\mu j} \equiv U_{j\mu}$ is equal to the unit matrix. This means that the transpose of the matrix U is its inverse,

$$U^T = U^{-1} \tag{I.12}$$

A matrix whose conjugate transpose is equal to its inverse is said to be 'unitary'. In our case, the matrix is real and taking the complex conjugate has no effect. This means that Eq. (I.12) is equivalent to the unitarity condition. We can use the unitarity property to rewrite Eq. (I.9)

$$\sum_{\mu,\nu} U_{i\mu} V_{\mu\nu} U_{j\nu} = \sum_{\mu,\nu} U_{i\mu} V_{\mu\nu} U^{-1}_{\nu j} = V'_{ij} \tag{I.13}$$

306

Then multiplying from the right by $U_{j\tau}$ we have

$$\sum_{\mu, \nu, j} U_{i\mu} V_{\mu\nu} U_{\nu j}^{-1} U_{j\tau} = \sum_{\mu, \nu} U_{i\mu} V_{\mu\nu} \delta_{\nu\tau} = \sum_{\mu} U_{i\mu} V_{\mu\tau} = \sum_{j} V'_{ij} U_{j\tau} \quad \text{(I.14)}$$

We now remember that the purpose of the transformation was to diagonalize $V_{\mu\tau}$. This means that we would like $V_{\mu\tau}$ to have the form

$$V_{\mu\tau} = V(\tau) \delta_{\mu\tau} \quad \text{(I.15)}$$

Substituting Eq. (I.15) into Eq. (I.14) we have

$$\sum_{\mu} U_{i\mu} V_{\mu\tau} = V(\tau) \sum_{\mu} U_{i\mu} \delta_{\mu\tau} = V(\tau) U_{i\tau} = \sum_{j} \delta_{ij} V(\tau) U_{j\tau} \quad \text{(I.16)}$$

and finally

$$\sum_{j} \{V'_{ij} - \delta_{ij} V(\tau)\} U_{j\tau} = 0, \qquad i = 1, 2, 3, \ldots, N \quad \textbf{(I.17)}$$

This set of N simultaneous algebraic equations for the unknown coefficients $U_{j\tau}$ is called the set of 'secular equations'. These equations will have a non-trivial solution only if the 'secular determinant' vanishes:

$$\det |V'_{ij} - \delta_{ij} V(\tau)| = 0 \quad \textbf{(I.18)}$$

Equation (I.18) leads to an Nth order algebraic equation with N roots $V(1), V(2), \ldots, V(N)$. Having found a root $V(\tau)$ we can put it back into the secular equations and solve for the N coefficients $C_{i\tau}, C_{2\tau}, \ldots, C_{N,\tau}$.

Summarizing the procedure, we can give the following prescription for calculating the small vibrations of a classical system about its equilibrium position:

(1) *Write down the kinetic and potential energy of the system as in Eq. (I.1) and Eq. (I.2).*

(2) *From the set of potential energy coefficients V_{ij} form the 'mass-weighted' coefficients*

$$V'_{ij} \equiv \frac{1}{\sqrt{m(i)m(j)}} V_{ij}$$

(3) *Find the unitary transformation $U_{i\mu}$ which diagonalizes V'_{ij}. When the Lagrangian of the system is expressed in terms of the 'normal coordinates' $X^{\mu} = \sum_{i} x^{i} \sqrt{m(i)} U_{i\mu}$ the cross terms will disappear.*

Appendix II. Tensor analysis

Let us consider a coordinate system $x^1, x^2, \ldots, x^N$ labelling the points in an N-dimensional space. We can label the points in a different way by going to a new coordinate system $X^1, X^2, \ldots, X^N$ where the new coordinates are expressed as functions of the old ones

$$X^1 = X^1(x^1, x^2, \ldots, x^N)$$

$$X^2 = X^2(x^1, x^2, \ldots, x^N)$$

$$\cdot \quad \cdot \quad \cdot \quad \cdot \quad \cdot \quad \cdot \quad \cdot \quad \cdot \quad \cdot$$

$$X^N = X^N(x^1, x^2, \ldots, x^N) \tag{II.1}$$

For example, Eq. (II.1) might represent a transformation from cartesian coordinates to spherical polar coordinates. If we have an equation written in terms of the old coordinates, we can ask how to rewrite it in terms of the new ones. More generally, we can try to write physical equations in such a way that they will look the same in every coordinate system. Suppose for example that the space is Euclidean (flat) so that in terms of cartesian coordinates $x^1, x^2 \ldots, x^N$ the infinitesimal element of length ds separating two neighbouring points is given by the Pythagorean rule

$$\mathrm{d}s^2 = (\mathrm{d}x^1)^2 + (\mathrm{d}x^2)^2 + \cdots + (\mathrm{d}x^N)^2$$

$$= \delta_{ij}\, \mathrm{d}x^i\, \mathrm{d}x^j \equiv g_{ij}\, \mathrm{d}x^i\, \mathrm{d}x^j \tag{II.2}$$

(In Eq. (II.2) and in the remainder of this section we use the convention of summing over repeated indices.) Using the identity

$$\mathrm{d}x^i = \frac{\partial x^i}{\partial X^n}\, \mathrm{d}X^n \tag{II.3}$$

we can rewrite Eq. (II.2) as

$$\mathrm{d}s^2 = \delta_{ij} \frac{\partial x^i}{\partial X^\mu} \frac{\partial x^j}{\partial X^\nu}\, \mathrm{d}X^\mu\, \mathrm{d}X^\nu$$

$$\equiv G_{\mu\nu}\, \mathrm{d}X^\mu\, \mathrm{d}X^\nu \tag{II.4}$$

where

$$G_{\mu v} \equiv g_{ij} \frac{\partial x^i}{\partial X^\mu} \frac{\partial x^j}{\partial X^v}, \qquad g_{ij} = \delta_{ij} \qquad \text{(II.5)}$$

The quantity $G_{\mu v}$ defined by Eqs. (II.4) and (II.5) is called the 'covariant metric tensor'. The word 'tensor' refers to the way that a quantity transforms under a change of coordinate system. The 'rank' of a tensor is the number of indices. The covariant metric tensor is the prototype of a covariant tensor of second rank. Any physical quantity which must be transformed according to the rule

$$A_{\mu v} = a_{ij} \frac{\partial x^i}{\partial X^\mu} \frac{\partial x^j}{\partial X^v} \qquad \text{(II.6)}$$

under the coordinate transformation $x^1, \ldots, x^N \to X^1, \ldots, X^N$ is said to be a covariant tensor of second rank. The N-component entity

$$\mathrm{d}X^\mu = \frac{\partial X^\mu}{\partial x^i} \mathrm{d}x^i \qquad \text{(II.7)}$$

is the prototype of contravariant tensor of first rank. Any quantity which transforms according to the rule

$$A^\mu = \frac{\partial X^\mu}{\partial x^i} a^i \qquad \text{(II.8)}$$

is said to be a contravariant tensor of first rank. (These are also called contravariant vectors.) The distance element $\mathrm{d}s$ is the prototype of an invariant or scalar. Any quantity Φ which is invariant under coordinate transformations is said to be a scalar. The gradient of a scalar

$$\frac{\partial \phi}{\partial X^\mu} = \frac{\partial x^i}{\partial X^\mu} \frac{\partial \phi}{\partial x^i} \qquad \text{(II.9)}$$

is the prototype of a covariant tensor of first rank. (These are also called covariant vectors.) Any quantity which transforms according to the rule

$$A_\mu = \frac{\partial x^i}{\partial X^\mu} a_i \qquad \text{(II.10)}$$

is said to be a covariant vector. We can also define tensors of higher rank. For example, a quantity which transforms according to the rule

$$A^{\mu v \sigma} = \frac{\partial X^\mu}{\partial x^i} \frac{\partial X^v}{\partial x^j} \frac{\partial X^\sigma}{\partial x^k} a^{ijk} \qquad \text{(II.11)}$$

is said to be a contravariant tensor of third rank. A covariant vector and a contravariant vector can be 'contracted' into a scalar: We can see that if A_μ

The quantum theory of atoms, molecules, and photons

transforms according to Eq. (II.10) while B^μ transforms according to Eq. (II.8), then $A_\mu B^\mu$ is invariant:

$$A_\mu B^\mu = \frac{\partial x^i}{\partial X^\mu} \frac{\partial X^\mu}{\partial x^j} a_i b^j$$

$$= \delta_j^i a_i b^j = a_i b^i \tag{II.12}$$

where we have used the identity

$$\frac{\partial x^i}{\partial X^\mu} \frac{\partial X^\mu}{\partial x^j} = \delta_j^i \equiv \begin{cases} 0 & i \neq j \\ 1 & i = j \end{cases} \tag{II.13}$$

If we contract a contravariant vector with the covariant metric tensor, we obtain a covariant vector:

$$G_{\mu\nu} A^\nu = g_{ij} \frac{\partial x^i}{\partial X^\mu} \frac{\partial x^j}{\partial X^\nu} \frac{\partial X^\nu}{\partial x^k} a^k$$

$$= g_{ij} \frac{\partial x^i}{\partial X^\mu} \delta_k^j a^k$$

$$= \frac{\partial x^i}{\partial X^\mu} (g_{ij} a^j) \tag{II.14}$$

Comparing Eq. (II.14) with Eq. (II.10) we can write

$$G_{\mu\nu} A^\nu = A_\mu$$

$$g_{ij} a^j = a_i \tag{II.15}$$

It is useful to define a quantity called the contravariant metric tensor, which gives the Kroneker δ-function when it is contracted with the covariant metric tensor

$$G^{\mu\nu} G_{\nu\sigma} = \delta_\sigma^\mu$$

$$g^{ij} g_{jk} = \delta_k^i$$

$$G^{\mu\nu} = \frac{\partial X^\mu}{\partial x^i} \frac{\partial X^\nu}{\partial x^j} g^{ij} \tag{II.16}$$

If we contract a covariant vector with the contravariant metric tensor we obtain a contravariant vector

$$G^{\mu\nu} A_\nu = g^{ij} \frac{\partial X^\mu}{\partial x^i} \frac{\partial X^\nu}{\partial x^j} \frac{\partial x^k}{\partial X^\nu} a_k$$

$$= g^{ij} \frac{\partial X^\mu}{\partial x^i} \delta_j^k a_k$$

$$= \frac{\partial X^\mu}{\partial x^i} (g^{ij} a_j) \tag{II.17}$$

Comparing Eq. (II.17) with Eq. (II.7) we can see that the entity which we write as $g^{ij}a_j$ (in terms of the old coordinates) or as $G^{\mu\nu}A_\nu$ (in terms of the new coordinates) is a contravariant vector

$$G^{\mu\nu}A_\nu = A^\mu$$

$$g^{ij}a_j = a^i \tag{II.18}$$

In a similar way we can raise or lower the indices of a tensor of higher rank. For example it is easy to show that

$$G_{\mu\nu}A^{\nu\sigma\rho} = A_\mu^{\sigma\rho} \tag{II.19}$$

transforms according to the rule

$$A_\mu^{\sigma\rho} = \frac{\partial x^i}{\partial X^\mu} \frac{\partial X^\sigma}{\partial x^j} \frac{\partial X^\rho}{\partial x^k} a_i^{jk} \tag{II.20}$$

$A_\mu^{\sigma\rho}$ is said to be a 'mixed' tensor of third rank, i.e., some of the indices are covariant and others are contravariant. The distinction between covariant and contravariant indices needs to be maintained if we are dealing with a general curvilinear coordinate transformation such as the transformation from Cartesian coordinates to spherical polar coordinates. On the other hand, if we are dealing with pure rotation translation or reflection of a Cartesian coordinate system, then we can forget the distinction between covariant and contravariant indices, because in that case the metric tensor is a unit matrix in both the old and the new coordinate systems.

In a coordinate system with unit metric we would write the volume element as

$$dV = dx^1 dx^2 \dots dx^N \tag{II.21}$$

It is easy to see that from the standpoint of tensor analysis, this way of writing the volume element is unsatisfactory, since the right-hand side of Eq. (II.21) appears to be a contravariant tensor of rank N (or rather a particular component of such a tensor) while the left-hand side has no indices at all. In order to write the volume element in an invariant way Levi–Cività has introduced a totally antisymmetric covariant unit tensor of rank N, $e_{ijk\dots l}$, defined in such a way that in a coordinate system where $g_{ij} = \delta_{ij}$, $e_{ijk\dots l}$ is zero unless the N indices $ijk \dots l$ are some permutation of $1, 2, 3, \dots, N$. If they are such a permutation then $e_{ijk\dots l}$ is defined as being equal to ± 1 the sign being chosen as positive when the permutation is even and negative when the permutation is odd.

Thus if $g_{ij} = \delta_{ij}$

$$e_{ijk\dots l} = \begin{cases} (-1)^P & \text{if } ijk \dots l = P(1, 2, 3, \dots, N) \\ 0 & \text{otherwise} \end{cases} \tag{II.22}$$

Now suppose that we define the volume element as

$$dV = \frac{1}{N!} e_{ijk \cdots l} \, dx^i \, dx^j \, dx^k \, \ldots \, dx^l \tag{II.23}$$

Then in our original cartesian coordinate system, where $g_{ij} = \delta_{ij}$, the definition of dV reduces to the usual one, Eq. (II.21). However, in Eq. (II.23) we have eliminated the loose indices on the right-hand side so that from the standpoint of tensor analysis, we have a correct equation. In a general curvilinear coordinate system the volume element becomes

$$dV = \frac{1}{N!} E_{\mu\nu\sigma \cdots \rho} \, dX^\mu \, dX^\nu \, dX^\sigma \, \ldots \, dX^\rho \tag{II.24}$$

where

$$E_{\mu\nu\sigma \cdots \rho} = e_{ijk \cdots l} \frac{\partial x^i}{\partial X^\mu} \frac{\partial x^j}{\partial X^\nu} \frac{\partial x^k}{\partial X^\sigma} \cdots \frac{\partial x^l}{\partial X^\rho} \tag{II.25}$$

Combining Eqs. (II.22), (II.24), and (II.25) with a definition of a determinant we have

$$dV = \det \left| \frac{\partial x^i}{\partial X^\mu} \right| dX^1 dX^2 \ldots dX^N \tag{II.26}$$

The quantity $\det |\partial x^i / \partial X^\mu|$ is called the 'Jacobian' of the transformation $x^1 \ldots x^N \rightarrow X^1 \ldots X^N$. It can be shown that the Jacobian associated with a transformation from a system with unit metric $g_{ij} = \delta_{ij}$ to system with metric $G_{\mu\nu}$ is just the square root of the determinant of the covariant metric tensor:

$$\det |G_{\mu\nu}| = \det \left| \frac{\partial x^i}{\partial X^\mu} \delta_{ij} \frac{\partial x^j}{\partial X^\nu} \right|$$

$$= \det \left| \frac{\partial x^i}{\partial X^\mu} \right| \det \left| \frac{\partial x^j}{\partial X^\nu} \right|$$

$$= \left(\det \left| \frac{\partial x^i}{\partial X^\mu} \right| \right)^2 \equiv G \tag{II.27}$$

The Jacobian $\det |\partial x^i / \partial X^\mu| = \sqrt{G}$ is the prototype of a scalar density. Any quantity which transforms in the same way as $\sqrt{G}$ is said to be a scalar density. We can also construct tensor densities of higher rank by multiplying an ordinary tensor by $\sqrt{G}$. It is interesting to notice that the Levi–Civitá tensor $E_{\mu\nu\sigma \ldots \rho}$ has only one independent component and that this component transforms like a scalar density.

$$E_{123\cdots N} = \frac{\partial x^i}{\partial X^1}\frac{\partial x^j}{\partial X^2}\frac{\partial x^k}{\partial X^3}\cdots\frac{\partial x^l}{\partial X^N}\,e_{ijk\cdots l}$$

$$= \det\left|\frac{\partial x^i}{\partial X^\mu}\right| = \det\left|\frac{\partial x^i}{\partial X^\mu}\right|e_{123\cdots N}$$

$$= \sqrt{G}\,e_{123\cdots N} \tag{II.28}$$

The quantity $dX^1\,dX^2\,\ldots\,dX^N$ transforms in the opposite way: since $\sqrt{G}\,dX^1\,dX^2\,\ldots\,dX^N$ is a scalar, it follows that $dX^1\,dX^2\,\ldots\,dX^N$ transforms like $1/\sqrt{G}$ and it is the prototype of a scalar capacity. We can construct tensor capacities of higher rank by dividing ordinary tensors by $\sqrt{G}$. The product of a capacity and a density is an ordinary tensor.

Now consider a scalar function ψ. The gradient $\partial\psi/\partial X^\mu$ will be a covariant vector and $(\partial\psi/\partial X^\mu)(\partial\psi/\partial X^\nu)$ will be a covariant tensor of second rank. If we contract it with a contravariant metric tensor we will obtain a scalar

$$G^{\mu\nu}\frac{\partial\psi}{\partial X^\mu}\frac{\partial\psi}{\partial X^\nu} = \text{scalar} \tag{II.29}$$

Since $k^2\psi^2$ is a scalar (where k is a constant) and since $\sqrt{G}\,dX^1\,dX^2\,\ldots\,dX^N$ is a scalar, we also have

$$\mathscr{L}\,dX^1\,dX^2\,\ldots\,dX^N = \text{scalar}$$

if

$$\mathscr{L} = \sqrt{G}\left\{G^{\mu\nu}\frac{\partial\psi}{\partial X^\mu}\frac{\partial\psi}{\partial X^\nu} + k^2\psi^2\right\} \tag{II.30}$$

The variational principle

$$\delta\int\int\cdots\int\mathscr{L}\,dX^1\,dX^2\,\ldots\,dX^N = 0 \tag{II.31}$$

will be invariant under curvilinear coordinate transformations because the integrand is a scalar. If we change ψ by a small amount $\delta\psi$, the resulting change in the Lagrangian density will be

$$\delta\mathscr{L} = \frac{\partial\mathscr{L}}{\partial\left(\frac{\partial\psi}{\partial X^\mu}\right)}\,\delta\left(\frac{\partial\psi}{\partial X^\mu}\right) + \frac{\partial\mathscr{L}}{\partial\psi}\,\delta\psi \tag{II.32}$$

Integrating by parts, we have

$$0 = \delta \int\int \cdots \int \mathcal{L} \, dX^1 \, dX^2 \ldots dX^N$$

$$= \int\int \cdots \int \delta\mathcal{L} \, dX^1 \, dX^2 \ldots dX^N$$

$$= \left[\int\int \cdots \int \frac{\partial\mathcal{L}}{\partial\left(\dfrac{\partial\psi}{\partial X^1}\right)} \, d\psi \, dX^2 \, dX^3 \ldots dX^N \right]_{X_a^1}^{X_b^1}$$

$$+ \left[\int\int \cdots \int \frac{\partial\mathcal{L}}{\partial\left(\dfrac{\partial\psi}{\partial X^2}\right)} \, \delta\psi \, dX^1 \, dX^3 \ldots dX^N \right]_{X_a^2}^{X_b^2}$$

$$+ \cdots$$

$$+ \int\int \cdots \int \delta\psi \left\{ \frac{\partial\mathcal{L}}{\partial\psi} - \frac{\partial}{\partial X^\mu} \frac{\partial\mathcal{L}}{\partial\left(\dfrac{\partial\psi}{\partial X^\mu}\right)} \right\} dX^1 \, dX^2 \ldots dX^N \tag{II.33}$$

With the boundary conditions $\delta\psi = 0$ at X_a^μ and X_b^μ, the surface integrals vanish and we are left with

$$\int\int \cdots \int \delta\psi \left\{ \frac{\partial\mathcal{L}}{\partial\psi} - \frac{\partial}{\partial X^\mu} \frac{\partial\mathcal{L}}{\partial\left(\dfrac{\partial\psi}{\partial X^\mu}\right)} \right\} dX^1 \, dX^2 \ldots dX^N = 0 \tag{II.34}$$

Since the variation $\delta\psi$ is arbitrary, the only way we can ensure the vanishing of the integral is for the factor multiplying $\delta\psi$ in Eq. (II.34) to vanish everywhere

$$\frac{\partial}{\partial X^\mu} \frac{\partial\mathcal{L}}{\partial\left(\dfrac{\partial\psi}{\partial X^\mu}\right)} - \frac{\partial\mathcal{L}}{\partial\psi} = 0 \tag{II.35}$$

With the Lagrangian density of Eq. (II.30) this becomes

$$\frac{1}{\sqrt{G}} \frac{\partial}{\partial X^\mu} \sqrt{G} \, G^{\mu\nu} \frac{\partial\psi}{\partial X^\nu} = k^2\psi \tag{II.36}$$

In a three-dimensional cartesian coordinate system the differential operator of Eq. (II.36) reduces to the Laplacian operator, i.e., if

$$N = 3 \qquad g_{ij} = \delta_{ij}$$
$$\sqrt{g} = 1 \qquad g^{ij} = \delta^{ij} \tag{II.37}$$

then

$$\frac{1}{\sqrt{g}} \frac{\partial}{\partial x^i} \sqrt{g}\, g^{ij} \frac{\partial}{\partial x^j} = \frac{\partial}{\partial x^i} \delta^{ij} \frac{\partial}{\partial x^j} = \nabla^2 \qquad \text{(II.38)}$$

Since the variational principle from which Eq. (II.36) was derived is invariant under curvilinear coordinate transformations it follows that for any coordinate system at all in three-dimensional Euclidean space, the Laplacian can be written as

$$\nabla^2 = \frac{1}{\sqrt{G}} \frac{\partial}{\partial X^\mu} \sqrt{G}\, G^{\mu\nu} \frac{\partial}{\partial X^\nu} \qquad \textbf{(II.39)}$$

For example, in spherical polar coordinates

$$X^1 = r \qquad X^2 = \theta \qquad X^3 = \varphi$$
$$x^1 = r \sin\theta \cos\varphi \qquad x^2 = r \sin\theta \sin\varphi \qquad x^3 = r \cos\theta \quad \text{(II.40)}$$

the covariant metric tensor, Eq. (II.5), becomes

$$G_{\mu\nu} = \frac{\partial x^i}{\partial X^\mu} \delta_{ij} \frac{\partial x^j}{\partial X^\nu} = \begin{pmatrix} 1 & 0 & 0 \\ 0 & r^2 & 0 \\ 0 & 0 & r^2 \sin^2\theta \end{pmatrix}$$

and

$$\sqrt{G} = \sqrt{\det|G_{\mu\nu}|} = r^2 \sin\theta \qquad \text{(II.41)}$$

so that the elements of volume and length are

$$dV = \sqrt{G}\, dX^1\, dX^2\, dX^3$$
$$= r^2 \sin\theta\, dr\, d\theta\, d\varphi \qquad \text{(II.42)}$$

and

$$ds^2 = G_{\mu\nu}\, dX^\mu\, dX^\nu$$
$$= dr^2 + r^2\, d\theta^2 + r^2 \sin^2\theta\, d\varphi^2 \qquad \text{(II.43)}$$

The contravariant metric tensor $G^{\mu\nu}$ is the reciprocal of $G_{\mu\nu}$

$$G^{\mu\nu} = \begin{pmatrix} 1 & 0 & 0 \\ 0 & \dfrac{1}{r^2} & 0 \\ 0 & 0 & \dfrac{1}{r^2 \sin^2\theta} \end{pmatrix} \qquad \text{(II.44)}$$

Substituting this into the expression for the Laplacian, Eq. (II.39), we obtain

$$\nabla^2 = \frac{1}{\sqrt{G}} \frac{\partial}{\partial X^\mu} \sqrt{G}\, G^{\mu\nu} \frac{\partial}{\partial X^\nu}$$

$$= \frac{1}{r^2 \sin\theta} \left(\frac{\partial}{\partial r} r^2 \sin\theta \frac{\partial}{\partial r} + \frac{\partial}{\partial\theta} \frac{r^2 \sin\theta}{r^2} \frac{\partial}{\partial\theta} + \frac{\partial}{\partial\varphi} \frac{r^2 \sin\theta}{r^2 \sin\theta} \frac{\partial}{\partial\varphi} \right)$$

$$= \frac{1}{r^2} \frac{\partial}{\partial r} r^2 \frac{\partial}{\partial r} + \frac{1}{r^2 \sin\theta} \frac{\partial}{\partial\theta} \sin\theta \frac{\partial}{\partial\theta} + \frac{1}{r^2 \sin^2\theta} \frac{\partial^2}{\partial\varphi^2} \tag{II.45}$$

As a second example, we can try to write the volume element and the element of length in terms of the spheroidal coordinates shown in Fig. (II.1)

$$X^1 = \xi, \qquad X^2 = \eta, \qquad X^3 = \varphi$$

$$x^1 = C\xi\eta$$

$$x^2 = C\sqrt{(\xi^2 - 1)(1 - \eta^2)} \cos\varphi$$

$$x^3 = C\sqrt{(\xi^2 - 1)(1 - \eta^2)} \sin\varphi \tag{II.46}$$

From Eq. (II.46) we have

$$G_{\mu\nu} = \frac{\partial x^i}{\partial X^\mu} \delta_{ij} \frac{\partial x^j}{\partial X^\nu}$$

$$= \begin{pmatrix} c^2 \left(\dfrac{\xi^2 - \eta^2}{\xi^2 - 1} \right) & 0 & 0 \\ 0 & c^2 \left(\dfrac{\xi^2 - \eta^2}{1 - \eta^2} \right) & 0 \\ 0 & 0 & c^2(\xi^2 - 1)(1 - \eta^2) \end{pmatrix} \tag{II.47}$$

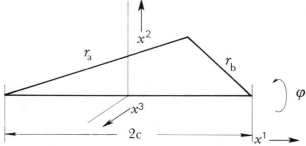

Figure II.1 shows the spheroidal coordinate system discussed in Eqs. (II.46)–(II.48). This coordinate system is sometimes used in evaluating overlap integrals. The variables ξ and η are related to cartesian coordinates by Eq. (II.46). At the same time they are related to r_a and r_b by $\xi = (r_a + r_b)/2c$ and $\eta = (r_a - r_b)/2c$.

so that

$$\sqrt{G} = c^3(\xi^2 - \eta^2)$$

$$dV = c^3(\xi^2 - \eta^2) \, d\xi \, d\eta \, d\varphi$$

$$\frac{ds^2}{c^2} = \frac{\xi^2 - \eta^2}{\xi^2 - 1} \, d\xi^2 + \left(\frac{\xi^2 - \eta^2}{1 - \eta^2}\right) d\eta^2 + (\xi^2 - 1)(1 - \eta^2) \, d\varphi^2$$

$$(\text{II.48})$$

Both the spherical polar coordinate system and the spheroidal coordinate system are examples of 'orthogonal' coordinates, i.e., in both these examples the metric tensors are diagonal. A non-orthogonal coordinate system would have a non-diagonal metric tensor. For example, the coordinates

$$X^1 = \frac{1}{2} x^1 - \frac{\sqrt{3}}{2} x^2$$

$$X^2 = \frac{1}{2} x^1 + \frac{\sqrt{3}}{2} x^2$$

$$X^3 = x^3 \qquad (\text{II.49})$$

(which are appropriate for discussing hexagonal crystal lattices) are non-orthogonal since the metric tensor has off-diagonal elements

$$G_{\mu\nu} = \frac{\partial x^i}{\partial X^\mu} \delta_{ij} \frac{\partial x^j}{\partial X^\nu} = \begin{pmatrix} \frac{4}{3} & \frac{2}{3} & 0 \\ \frac{2}{3} & \frac{4}{3} & 0 \\ 0 & 0 & 1 \end{pmatrix} \qquad (\text{II.50})$$

and

$$G^{\mu\nu} = \frac{\partial X^\mu}{\partial x^i} \delta^{ij} \frac{\partial X^\nu}{\partial x^j} = \begin{pmatrix} 1 & -\frac{1}{2} & 0 \\ -\frac{1}{2} & 1 & 0 \\ 0 & 0 & 1 \end{pmatrix} \qquad (\text{II.51})$$

so that the element of length and the Laplacian operator contain cross terms mixing X^1 and X^2

$$\sqrt{G} = \sqrt{\tfrac{4}{3}}$$

$$dV = \sqrt{\tfrac{4}{3}} \, dX^1 \, dX^2 \, dX^3$$

$$ds^2 = \tfrac{4}{3} \, dX^1 \, dX^1 + \tfrac{4}{3} \, dX^1 \, dX^2 + \tfrac{4}{3} \, dX^2 \, dX^2 + dX^3 \, dX^3$$

$$(\text{II.52})$$

and

$$\nabla^2 = \frac{1}{\sqrt{G}} \frac{\partial}{\partial X^\mu} \sqrt{G} \, G^{\mu\nu} \frac{\partial}{\partial X^\nu}$$

$$= \frac{\partial^2}{\partial X^1 \, \partial X^1} - \frac{\partial^2}{\partial X^1 \, \partial X^2} + \frac{\partial^2}{\partial X^2 \, \partial X^2} + \frac{\partial^2}{\partial X^3 \, \partial X^3} \qquad (\text{II.53})$$

Since Eq. (II.36) was derived from an invariant variational principle and since the right-hand side is a scalar, it follows that the left-hand side is also a scalar.

$$\frac{1}{\sqrt{G}} \frac{\partial}{\partial X^\mu} \sqrt{G}\, G^{\mu\nu} \frac{\partial \psi}{\partial X^\nu} = \text{scalar} \tag{II.54}$$

We can replace $\partial \psi / \partial X^\nu$ by an arbitrary covariant vector A_ν without affecting the transformation properties of Eq. (II.54)

$$\frac{1}{\sqrt{G}} \frac{\partial}{\partial X^\mu} \sqrt{G}\, G^{\mu\nu} A_\nu = \text{scalar} \tag{II.55}$$

Now we can notice that for a coordinate system with unit metric, $g_{ij} = \delta_{ij}$, Eq. (II.55) reduces to

$$\frac{1}{\sqrt{g}} \frac{\partial}{\partial x^i} \sqrt{g}\, g^{ij} a_j = \frac{\partial}{\partial x^i} \delta^{ij} a_j \equiv \text{div}\, \vec{a} \tag{II.56}$$

Thus Eq. (II.55) gives us an invariant prescription for calculating the divergence of a covariant vector. Similarly,

$$\frac{1}{\sqrt{G}} \frac{\partial}{\partial X^\mu} \sqrt{G}\, A^\mu = \text{scalar} \tag{II.57}$$

gives us an invariant prescription for calculating the divergence of a contravariant vector.

Appendix III. The Heisenberg representation

In 1926, Werner Heisenberg, Max Born, and Pascaul Jordan, working at the University of Göttingen, developed a form of quantum theory which they called 'matrix mechanics'. They based their theory on a formalism of classical Newtonian mechanics called the 'Poisson bracket' formalism. Hamilton's equations of motion, Eqs. (1.118) and (1.119), state that if the Hamiltonian function of a mechanical system is constructed from the coordinates x^μ and the momenta p_μ according to the prescription given in Eq. (1.117), then

$$\frac{\mathrm{d}p_\mu}{\mathrm{d}t} = -\frac{\partial H}{\partial x^\mu} \tag{III.1}$$

and

$$\frac{\mathrm{d}x^\mu}{\mathrm{d}t} = \frac{\partial H}{\partial p_\mu} \tag{III.2}$$

Now suppose that $F(x^1, \ldots, x^N, p_1, \ldots, p_N)$ is some function of the coordinates and the momenta. Then

$$\frac{\mathrm{d}F}{\mathrm{d}t} = \sum_{\mu=1}^{N} \left(\frac{\partial F}{\partial x^\mu} \frac{\mathrm{d}x^\mu}{\mathrm{d}t} + \frac{\partial F}{\partial p_\mu} \frac{\mathrm{d}p_\mu}{\mathrm{d}t} \right) = \sum_{\mu=1}^{N} \left(\frac{\partial F}{\partial x^\mu} \frac{\partial H}{\partial p_\mu} - \frac{\partial H}{\partial x^\mu} \frac{\partial F}{\partial p_\mu} \right) \tag{III.3}$$

If we introduce the notation,

$$\{A, B\} \equiv \sum_\mu \left(\frac{\partial A}{\partial x^\mu} \frac{\partial B}{\partial p_\mu} - \frac{\partial B}{\partial x^\mu} \frac{\partial A}{\partial p_\mu} \right) \tag{III.4}$$

then Eq. (III.3) can be written in the form

$$\frac{\mathrm{d}F}{\mathrm{d}t} = \{F, H\} \tag{III.5}$$

The curly brackets defined by Eq. (III.4) are called 'Poisson's brackets'. If we take the Poisson's bracket of x^μ and p_μ we have

$$\{x^\mu, p_\nu\} = \sum_\sigma \left(\frac{\partial x^\mu}{\partial x^\sigma} \frac{\partial p_\nu}{\partial p_\sigma} - \frac{\partial p_\nu}{\partial x^\sigma} \frac{\partial x^\mu}{\partial p_\sigma} \right) = \delta^\mu_\nu \qquad \text{(III.6)}$$

With Eq. (III.6) (and a little work) one can evaluate the Poisson bracket of any two operators. Heisenberg, Born, and Jordan had the idea of trying to *pass from classical mechanics to quantum mechanics by replacing the Poisson's brackets everywhere by the commutator brackets of Eq.* (3.67) *divided by* $i\hbar$,

$$\{A, B\} \to \frac{1}{i\hbar} [A, B] \qquad \text{(III.7)}$$

With this substitution, Eq. (III.5) and Eq. (III.6) go over into

$$i\hbar \frac{dF}{dt} = [F, H] \qquad \text{(III.8)}$$

and

$$[x^\mu, p_\nu] = i\hbar\, \delta^\mu_\nu \qquad \text{(III.9)}$$

Using the commutation relations of Eq. (III.9), Heisenberg, Born, and Jordan were able to construct matrix representations of the various dynamical quantities in which they were interested. The evolution of these matrices in time could be calculated from Eq. (III.8).

It was soon obvious to the Göttingen mathematicians that the matrix formulation of quantum theory was completely equivalent to Schrödinger's differential formulation. The famous Norwegian quantum chemist E. A. Hylleraas who was working with Max Born at the time, writes:

'. . . Another deeper question was the completeness of the functional system from which the wave function had to be built up. . . . In connection with these mathematical aspects of the theory . . . valuable support was given by the two famous Göttingen mathematicians Richard Courant and David Hilbert, and occasionally also by Hermann Weyl, a visitor from Zurich. . . . Hilbert . . . was extremely popular, and it was a real pleasure to listen to his mild voice and look into his white-bearded gentle face. To him, the inventor of Hilbert Space, the pathways leading from matrix to wave mechanics and vice versa were, of course, no secret.' (*Rev. Mod. Phys.* (1963) **35**, 421.)

In the Heisenberg formulation, dynamical variables are represented by time-dependent matrices, and eigenfunctions by time-independent many-component vectors. We can see the connection with the Schrödinger formulation in the following way. Suppose that the state of the system is represented in the Schrödinger formulation by the wave function $\Psi(x^1, \ldots, x^N, t)$ and that this can be expanded in a series of eigenfunctions of some operator. For example, Ψ might be expanded in eigenfunctions of the Hamiltonian

$$\Psi(x^1, \ldots, x^N, t) = \sum_n |n\rangle \, e^{-iE_n t/\hbar} \langle n|\psi\rangle \qquad \text{(III.10)}$$

where

$$H|n\rangle \, e^{-iE_n t/\hbar} = i\hbar \frac{\partial}{\partial t} |n\rangle \, e^{-iE_n t/\hbar} = E_n |n\rangle \, e^{-iE_n t/\hbar} \qquad \text{(III.11)}$$

The expansion coefficients $\langle n \mid \psi \rangle$ are independent of time. We could specify the state of the system by listing all of the expansion coefficients in a long column, and this is exactly what one does in the Heisenberg representation.

$$\Psi \Rightarrow \begin{pmatrix} \langle 1 \mid \psi \rangle \\ \langle 2 \mid \psi \rangle \\ \langle 3 \mid \psi \rangle \\ \vdots \end{pmatrix} \qquad \text{(III.12)}$$

The time-dependence is included in the matrix representation of an operator

$$F \Rightarrow \langle n'|F|n\rangle \, e^{-i(E_n - E_{n'})t/\hbar} \qquad \text{(III.13)}$$

From this it follows that

$$i\hbar \frac{\partial}{\partial t} \langle n'|F|n\rangle \, e^{-i(E_n - E_{n'})t/\hbar} = (E_{n'} - E_n)\langle n'|F|n\rangle \, e^{-i(E_n - E_{n'})t/\hbar}$$
$$= \langle n'|[F, H]|n\rangle \, e^{-i(E_n - E_{n'})t/\hbar} \qquad \text{(III.14)}$$

which is to be compared with Eq. (III.8).

Appendix IV. Projection operators

Consider an operator Ω whose eigenfunctions form a complete ortho-normal set

$$(\Omega - \lambda_n)|n\rangle = 0$$

$$\langle n \mid n'\rangle = \delta_{nn'}$$

$$\sum_n |n\rangle\langle n| = 1 \tag{IV.1}$$

From the orthonormality relation $\langle n \mid n'\rangle = \delta_{nn'}$ it follows that

$$P_n \equiv |n\rangle\langle n| \tag{IV.2}$$

is an operator which will annihilate the eigenfunction $|n'\rangle$, $n' \neq n$, while it leaves $|n\rangle$ unharmed.

$$P_n|n'\rangle = |n\rangle\langle n \mid n'\rangle = |n\rangle \delta_{nn'} \tag{IV.3}$$

Now consider the operator $(\Omega - \lambda_{n'})$. From Eq. (IV.1) it follows that this operator will annihilate the eigenfunction $|n'\rangle$. If we take the product $\Pi_{n' \neq n} (\Omega - \lambda_{n'})$ we will have an operator which annihilates $|n'\rangle$ if $n' \neq n$. If we divide this by the normalizing factor $\Pi_{n' \neq n} (\lambda_n - \lambda_{n'})$, the resulting operator will also leave $|n\rangle$ unharmed, and we can identify it with P_n

$$\prod_{n' \neq n} \left(\frac{\Omega - \lambda_{n'}}{\lambda_n - \lambda_{n'}}\right) |n''\rangle = \prod_{n' \neq n} \left(\frac{\lambda_{n''} - \lambda_{n'}}{\lambda_n - \lambda_{n'}}\right) |n''\rangle = |n''\rangle \delta_{n'',n} \tag{IV.4}$$

Comparing this with Eq. (IV.3) we can make the identification

$$P_n = |n\rangle \langle n| = \prod_{n' \neq n} \left(\frac{\Omega - \lambda_{n'}}{\lambda_n - \lambda_{n'}}\right) \tag{IV.5}$$

The product $\Pi_{n' \neq n}$ is taken over the whole set of eigenvalues of Ω except λ_n. When P_n acts on an arbitrary function $|f\rangle$ it 'projects out' the component of $|f\rangle$ which is an eigenfunction of Ω belonging to the eigenvalue λ_n. Expanding $|f\rangle$ as a superposition of eigenfunctions we have

$$|f\rangle = \sum_{n'} |n'\rangle\langle n' \mid f\rangle \tag{IV.6}$$

and

$$P_n|f\rangle = |n\rangle\langle n| \sum_{n'} |n'\rangle\langle n' | f\rangle$$

$$= \sum_{n'} |n\rangle \, \delta_{nn'}\langle n' | f\rangle = |n\rangle\langle n | f\rangle \qquad \text{(IV.7)}$$

This is analogous to projecting out the component of a vector in the direction of one of the coordinate axes in geometrical space, and for this reason P_n is called a projection operator. From the completeness relation it follows that the projection operators sum up to unity

$$\sum_n P_n \equiv \sum_n |n\rangle\langle n| = 1 \qquad \textbf{(IV.8)}$$

Also P_n is an 'idempotent', i.e., $P_n^2 = P_n$. This is easy to see, since

$$P_n P_{n'} \equiv |n\rangle\langle n | n'\rangle\langle n'|$$

$$= |n\rangle \, \delta_{nn'}\langle n'| = \delta_{nn'} P_n \qquad \text{(IV.9)}$$

from which

$$P_n^N = P_n \qquad \text{(IV.10)}$$

The sum of several projection operators is also an idempotent (and is also called a projection operator) for example:

$$(P_1 + P_2)^2 = P_1^2 + P_1 P_2 + P_2 P_1 + P_2^2$$

$$= P_1^2 + P_2^2 = P_1 + P_2 \qquad \text{(IV.11)}$$

or more generally

$$(P_n + P_{n'} + P_{n''} + \cdots)^N = P_n + P_{n'} + P_{n''} + \cdots \qquad \text{(IV.12)}$$

In calculating polarizabilities, and in other applications, one frequently wishes to evaluate sums of the form,

$$S = \sum_{q=1}^m \langle 0|A|q\rangle f(E_q)\langle q|B|0\rangle \qquad \text{(IV.13)}$$

where A and B are operators, and the functions $|q\rangle$ are eigenfunctions of the Hamiltonian

$$(H - E_q)|q\rangle = 0 \qquad \text{(IV.14)}$$

In Eq. (IV.13), $f(E_q)$ is an arbitrary well-behaved function of the energy eigenvalues. We can use the projection operators to derive a theorem which may be useful in evaluating sums of this type. Suppose that the eigenfunctions $|q\rangle$ of the Hamiltonian can be represented as a superposition of a set of basis functions $|n\rangle$

$$|q\rangle = \sum_{n=1}^{m} |n\rangle C_{nq}$$

$$q = 1, 2, \ldots, m \tag{IV.15}$$

In other words, the basis functions $|n\rangle$ span the same part of Hilbert space as the set of eigenfunctions $|q\rangle$. It follows that the projection operator corresponding to this part of Hilbert space can be expressed either in terms of the set $|q\rangle$ or the set $|n\rangle$.

$$P_b \equiv \sum_{q=1}^{m} |q\rangle\langle q| = \sum_{n=1}^{m} |n\rangle\langle n| \tag{IV.16}$$

From Eq. (IV.16) and Eq. (IV.14) we have

$$P_b f(H) P_b = \sum_{q,q'=1}^{m} |q'\rangle\langle q'|f(H)|q\rangle\langle q|$$

$$= \sum_{q,q'=1}^{m} |q'\rangle f(E_q)\langle q' \mid q\rangle\langle q|$$

$$= \sum_{q=1}^{m} |q\rangle f(E_q)\langle q| \tag{IV.17}$$

so that

$$\sum_{q=1}^{m} |q\rangle f(E_q)\langle q| = P_b f(H) P_b$$

$$= \sum_{n',n=1}^{m} |n'\rangle\langle n'|f(H)|n\rangle\langle n| \tag{\textbf{IV.18}}$$

If we have a matrix representation of the operators A, B and H in terms of the basis set $|n\rangle$ then we can use the identity (IV.18) to evaluate the sum S without solving for the eigenfunctions $|q\rangle$ and the corresponding energies, since we can write,

$$S = \langle 0|A P_b f(H) P_b B|0\rangle$$

$$= \sum_{n',n=1}^{m} \langle 0|A|n'\rangle\langle n'|f(H)|n\rangle\langle n|B|0\rangle \tag{IV.19}$$

Group-theoretical projection operators, which project out functions with a certain transformation property, will be discussed in Appendix VII.

Appendix V. Perturbation theory

Let us consider first the time-independent equation

$$H|\psi_n\rangle = E_n|\psi_n\rangle \tag{V.1}$$

Suppose that the operator H can be divided into a main part H_0, whose eigenfunctions and eigenvalues are known, and a small perturbation $\lambda H'$

$$H = H_0 + \lambda H' \tag{V.2}$$

In Eq. (V.2) H' is an operator while λ is a numerical parameter which we have factored out from the perturbation. The wave function $|\psi_n\rangle$ will be a function of the parameter λ and we can expand it in a Taylor series

$$|\psi_n\rangle = |\psi_n^{(0)}\rangle + \lambda|\psi_n^{(1)}\rangle + \lambda^2|\psi_n^{(2)}\rangle + \cdots \tag{V.3}$$

$|\psi_n^{(0)}\rangle$ is called the 'zeroth-order' wave function, $|\psi_n^{(1)}\rangle$ the 'first-order correction', $|\psi_n^{(2)}\rangle$ the 'second-order correction', and so on. If we could turn off the perturbation by letting $\lambda = 0$ and $H = H_0$ then the wave function $|\psi\rangle$ would reduce to the zeroth-order wave function $|\psi^{(0)}\rangle$. The eigenvalue E_n will also be a function of λ which can be expressed as a Taylor series,

$$E_n = E_n^{(0)} + \lambda E_n^{(1)} + \lambda^2 E_n^{(2)} + \cdots \tag{V.4}$$

the wave function and energy must satisfy Eq. (V.1) so we must have

$$(H_0 + \lambda H')(|\psi_n^{(0)}\rangle + \lambda|\psi_n^{(1)}\rangle + \lambda^2|\psi_n^{(2)}\rangle + \cdots)$$
$$= (E_n^{(0)} + \lambda E_n^{(1)} + \lambda^2 E_n^{(2)} + \cdots)(|\psi_n^{(0)}\rangle + \lambda|\psi_n^{(1)}\rangle + \lambda^2|\psi_n^{(2)}\rangle + \cdots) \tag{V.5}$$

Since Eq. (V.5) must hold for any value of λ the terms proportional to each power of λ on the left-hand side must be equal to those proportional to the same power of λ on the right.

$$H_0|\psi_n^{(0)}\rangle = E_n^{(0)}|\psi_n^{(0)}\rangle \tag{V.6a}$$

$$H_0|\psi_n^{(1)}\rangle + H'|\psi_n^{(0)}\rangle = E_n^{(0)}|\psi_n^{(1)}\rangle + E_n^{(1)}|\psi_n^{(0)}\rangle \tag{V.6b}$$

$$H_0|\psi_n^{(2)}\rangle + H'|\psi_n^{(1)}\rangle = E_n^{(0)}|\psi_n^{(2)}\rangle + E_n^{(1)}|\psi_n^{(1)}\rangle + E_n^{(2)}|\psi^{(0)}\rangle \tag{V.6c}$$

325

The quantum theory of atoms, molecules, and photons

Now suppose that we know the eigenfunctions and eigenvalues of H_0. In other words, suppose that we already have in our possession a set of zeroth-order wave functions $|\psi_n^{(0)}\rangle \equiv |n\rangle$ which satisfy Eq. (V.6a). We can express the first-order correction $|\psi_n^{(1)}\rangle$ as a linear combination of the zeroth-order functions

$$|\psi_n^{(1)}\rangle = \sum_{m \neq n} |m\rangle\langle m \mid \psi_n^{(1)}\rangle \qquad (V.7)$$

Substituting this into Eq. (V.6b) and taking the scalar product with the conjugate function $\langle k|$ we obtain

$$\sum_{m \neq n} \langle k|(H_0 - E_n^{(0)})|m\rangle\langle m \mid \psi_n^{(1)}\rangle + \langle k|H'|n\rangle = E_n^{(1)}\langle k \mid n\rangle \quad (V.8)$$

Because of the orthonormality of the zeroth-order functions,

$$\langle k \mid n\rangle = \delta_{k,n} \qquad (V.9)$$

and

$$\sum_{m \neq n} \langle k|(H_0 - E_n^{(0)})|m\rangle\langle m \mid \psi_n^{(1)}\rangle = \sum_{n' \neq n} (E_m^{(0)} - E_n^{(0)})\, \delta_{k,m}$$

$$\times \langle m \mid \psi_n^{(0)}\rangle = (E_k^{(0)} - E_n^{(0)})\langle k \mid \psi_n^{(1)}\rangle \qquad (V.10)$$

If $k \neq n$ the right-hand side of Eq. (V.8) vanishes and we obtain an equation for the first-order correction to the wave function

$$(E_k^{(0)} - E_n^{(0)})\langle k \mid \psi_n^{(1)}\rangle + \langle k|H'|n\rangle = 0 \qquad (V.11)$$

then from Eqs. (V.7) and (V.11)

$$|\psi_n^{(1)}\rangle = \sum_{m \neq n} |m\rangle \frac{\langle m|H'|n\rangle}{E_n^{(0)} - E_m^{(0)}} \qquad (V.12)$$

If $k = n$ then Eq. (V.8) becomes an equation for the first-order correction to the eigenvalue:

$$E_n^{(1)} = \langle n|H'|n\rangle \qquad (V.13)$$

Equation (V.6c) can now be solved for the second-order corrections. Substituting the zeroth-order and first-order corrections into Eq. (V.6c) and letting

$$|\psi^{(2)}\rangle = \sum_m |m\rangle\langle m \mid \psi^{(2)}\rangle \qquad (V.14)$$

we have

$$(H_0 - E_n^{(0)}) \sum_m |m\rangle\langle m \mid \psi_n^{(2)}\rangle$$

$$+ (H' - \langle n|H'|n\rangle) \sum_{m \neq n} \frac{|m\rangle\langle m|H'|n\rangle}{E_n^{(0)} - E_m^{(0)}} = E_n^{(2)}|n\rangle \quad (V.15)$$

We now take the scalar product of Eq. (V.15) with the conjugate function $\langle k|$ and make use of the orthonormality relation, Eq. (V.9). When $k \neq n$, Eq. (V.15) yields the second-order correction to the wave function

$$\langle k \mid \psi_n^{(2)} \rangle = \sum_{m \neq n} \frac{\langle k|H'|m\rangle\langle m|H'|n\rangle}{(E_n^{(0)} - E_m^{(0)})(E_n^{(0)} - E_k^{(0)})} - \frac{\langle n|H'|n\rangle\langle k|H'|n\rangle}{(E_n^{(0)} - E_k^{(0)})^2} \quad \text{(V.16)}$$

When $k = n$ we obtain the second-order correction to the eigenvalue

$$E_n^{(2)} = \sum_{m \neq n} \frac{\langle n|H'|m\rangle\langle m|H'|n\rangle}{E_n^{(0)} - E_m^{(0)}} \quad \text{(V.17)}$$

(We have been calling E_n the 'eigenvalue' rather than the 'energy' because the operator H in Eq. (V.1) need not be the Hamiltonian. The time-independent perturbation theory described here could equally well be applied to the problem of finding the changes in the eigenfunctions and eigenvalues of any operator when a small perturbation is applied.)

In deriving Eq. (V.6) we factored a numerical constant λ out of the perturbation. The set of equations Eqs. (V.6a), (V.6b), (V.6c), etc., must hold regardless of the value of λ and *we can now let $\lambda = 1$ without any loss of generality. Then*

$$|\psi_n\rangle = |\psi_n^{(0)}\rangle + |\psi_n^{(1)}\rangle + \cdots$$

$$= |n\rangle + \sum_{m \neq n} |m\rangle \frac{\langle m|H'|n\rangle}{E_n^{(0)} - E_m^{(0)}} + \cdots \quad \textbf{(V.18)}$$

and

$$E_n = E_n^{(0)} + E_n^{(1)} + E_n^{(2)} + \cdots$$

$$= E_n^{(0)} + \langle n|H'|n\rangle + \sum_{m \neq n} \frac{\langle n|H'|m\rangle\langle m|H'|n\rangle}{E_n^{(0)} - E_m^{(0)}} + \cdots \quad \textbf{(V.19)}$$

In order for the perturbation series, Eqs. (V.18) and (V.19), to converge the successive terms must become smaller and smaller. The second-order corrections must be smaller than the first-order corrections, and so on. Generally speaking, a perturbation series will converge if the matrix elements of the perturbing operator are small compared with differences in the zeroth-order eigenvalues. In other words, we require that

$$|\langle n|H'|m\rangle| \ll |E_n^{(0)} - E_m^{(0)}| \quad \text{(V.20)}$$

Obviously the method goes to pieces if two of the zeroth-order eigenfunctions are degenerate. In that case it is necessary to attack the degeneracy before beginning to apply perturbation theory. Suppose that we add a minute amount of the perturbation into the unperturbed part of the Hamiltonian so that $H_0 \rightarrow H_0 + \varepsilon H'$ where $\varepsilon \ll 1$. We can ask what the new zeroth-order wave functions will be. Because the amount of the perturbation operator H' contained in the new H_0 is so extremely small the non-degenerate eigenfunctions will be almost unaffected. However even the very small amount of H' contained in the new H_0 will cause hybridization among the set of degenerate levels. The hybrid orbitals will be such that the matrix elements of H' between two of them will be zero. Thus the new zeroth-order eigenfunctions will fulfil the convergence condition, Eq. (V.20), and perturbation theory can safely be applied.

Let us now consider effect of a time-dependent perturbation. We would like to find solutions of the time-dependent wave equation

$$i\hbar \frac{\partial}{\partial t} |\psi\rangle = H|\psi\rangle \qquad (V.21)$$

Suppose that the Hamiltonian operator H can be divided into two parts

$$H = H_0 + \lambda H' \qquad (V.22)$$

(where H' may be a function of t) and suppose that we know the solutions of the unperturbed equation

$$i\hbar \frac{\partial}{\partial t} |n\rangle = H_0|n\rangle = E_n|n\rangle \qquad (V.23)$$

We can expand the time-dependent wave function $|\psi\rangle$ as a series of the unperturbed functions with time-dependent coefficients.

$$|\psi\rangle = \sum_n |n\rangle a_n(t) \qquad (V.24)$$

Substituting this expansion into Eq. (V.21) we have

$$i\hbar \frac{\partial}{\partial t} \sum_n |n\rangle a_n = \sum_n \left(E_n|n\rangle a_n + i\hbar \frac{\partial a_n}{\partial t} |n\rangle \right)$$

$$= (H_0 + \lambda H') \sum_n |n\rangle a_n$$

$$= \sum_n (E_n|n\rangle a_n + \lambda H'|n\rangle a_n) \qquad (V.25)$$

so that

$$i\hbar \sum_m \frac{\partial a_m}{\partial t} |m\rangle = \lambda \sum_k H'|k\rangle a_k \qquad (V.26)$$

Taking the scalar product of Eq. (V.26) with the conjugate function $\langle n|$ and using the orthonormality condition we have

$$i\hbar \frac{\partial a_n}{\partial t} = \lambda \sum \langle n|H'|k\rangle a_k \qquad (V.27)$$

Let us expand the coefficients a_n as a Taylor series in powers of λ

$$a_n = a_n^{(0)} + \lambda a_n^{(1)} + \lambda^2 a_n^{(2)} + \cdots \qquad \text{(V.28)}$$

If we put this back into Eq. (V.27) and collect the terms in successive powers of λ we get a set of equations relating the higher-order corrections to the lower-order ones.

$$i\hbar \frac{\partial a_n^{(0)}}{\partial t} = 0 \qquad \text{(V.29a)}$$

$$i\hbar \frac{\partial a_n^{(1)}}{\partial t} = \sum_k \langle n|H'|k\rangle a_k^{(0)} \qquad \text{(V.29b)}$$

$$i\hbar \frac{\partial a_n^{(2)}}{\partial t} = \sum_k \langle n|H'|k\rangle a_k^{(1)}, \text{ etc.} \qquad \text{(V.29c)}$$

Having got these equations we can set $\lambda = 1$ without any loss of generality. From Eq. (V.29a) it can be seen that the zeroth-order coefficient is just a constant. Suppose that the system is initially in the state $|m\rangle$. Then

$$a_n^{(0)} = \delta_{n,m} \qquad \text{(V.30)}$$

Putting this into Eq. (V.29b) and integrating with respect to time, we have

$$a_n^{(1)} = \frac{1}{i\hbar} \int_0^t dt' \langle n|H'|m\rangle \qquad \text{(V.31)}$$

This can in turn be substituted into Eq. (V.29c) which can then be integrated to give $a_n^{(2)}$, and so on. An important special case occurs when the perturbation has harmonic dependence on time.

$$H'(x, t) = H'(x)\, e^{i\omega t} \qquad \text{(V.32)}$$

In that case because of Eq. (V.23) we can write the matrix element of H' in the form

$$\langle n|H'|m\rangle = H'_{n,m}\, e^{i(\omega - \omega_{n,m})t} \qquad \text{(V.33)}$$

where $H'_{n,m}$ is independent of time and

$$\omega_{n,m} \equiv \omega_n - \omega_m \equiv \frac{E_n - E_m}{\hbar} \qquad \text{(V.34)}$$

In the case of an harmonic perturbation it is easy to integrate with respect to time and to find the first-order coefficient

$$a_n^{(1)}(t) = \frac{H'_{n,m}}{i\hbar} \int_0^t dt'\, e^{i(\omega - \omega_{n,m})t'} = \frac{H'_{n,m}}{\hbar} \left\{ \frac{1 - e^{i(\omega - \omega_{n,m})t}}{\omega - \omega_{n,m}} \right\} \qquad \text{(V.35)}$$

According to the Copenhagen interpretation of the wave function (see Eq. (3.15)), the probability that the perturbation H' will cause a system initially in the state $|m\rangle$ to go over into the state $|n\rangle$ by time t is given by

$$a_n^{(1)*}a_n^{(1)} = |a_n^{(1)}|^2$$

$$= \frac{(H'_{n,m})^2}{\hbar^2(\omega - \omega_{n,m})^2}\{1 - e^{-i(\omega - \omega_{n,m})t}\}\{1 - e^{i(\omega - \omega_{n,m})t}\}$$

$$= \frac{|H'_{n,m}|^2}{\hbar^2}\frac{4\sin^2\{(\omega - \omega_{n,m})(t/2)\}}{(\omega - \omega_{n,m})^2} \qquad \text{(V.36)}$$

If we consider $|a_n^{(1)}|^2$ as a function of ω, we can see from Eq. (V.36) that the larger the value of t, the more sharply it is centred on the frequency $\omega_{n,m}$. This means that the harmonic perturbation is ineffective in causing a transition between the state $|k\rangle$ and the state $|n\rangle$ unless

$$\hbar\omega = \hbar\omega_{n,m} = E_n - E_m \qquad \text{(V.37)}$$

This is the explanation of Planck's hypothesis. The harmonic perturbation due to a light wave will cause a transition between two stationary states of a system only if Planck's condition, Eq. (V.37), is fulfilled. Using the relation

$$\int_{-\infty}^{\infty} d\omega \, \frac{2\sin^2\{\omega(t/2)\}}{\pi\omega^2 t} = 1 \qquad \text{(V.38)}$$

(which can be derived by means of 'contour integration') we can see that as t becomes very large the function $2\sin^2\{\omega(t/2)\}/(\pi\omega^2 t)$ becomes more and more nearly a representation of the Dirac δ-function, $\delta(\omega)$. Therefore for large values of t we can write

$$|a_n^{(1)}|^2 = \frac{|H'_{n,m}|^2}{\hbar^2} 2\pi \, \delta(\omega - \omega_{n,m})t \qquad \text{(V.39)}$$

In practice we are always interested in transitions where the final state belongs to a continuum. If a system of finite size were completely isolated from the outside world, the energy eigenvalues of the system would form a spectrum of completely sharp lines. However, in practice there is always a small coupling with the outside world which has the effect of giving each level a finite 'line width'. For example, the excited states of an atom have a line-width $\Delta E = \hbar\Gamma$ where $1/\Gamma = \Delta t$ is the average lifetime of the excited state before coupling with the outside world causes the excitation energy to be lost. Thus, in practice, the final state of a system will always belong to a continuum. We can introduce a function $\rho(\omega_n)$ such that $\rho(\omega_n)\,d\omega_n$ represents the number of final states with energy between $\hbar\omega_n$ and $\hbar(\omega_n + d\omega_n)$. Then the probability per unit time that the perturbation H'

will cause the system to make a transition from the initial state $|m\rangle$ to one or another of the continuum of final state $|n\rangle$ is given by

$$W = \frac{1}{t} \int d\omega_n \rho(\omega_n) \left| a_n^{(1)} \right|^2 = 2\pi \frac{\left| H'_{n,m} \right|^2}{\hbar^2} \int d\omega_n \rho(\omega_n)\, \delta(\omega - \omega_n + \omega_m)$$

$$= \frac{2\pi \left| H'_{n,m} \right|^2}{\hbar^2}\, \rho(\omega_m + \omega) \qquad \text{(V.40)}$$

Equation (V.40) is sometimes called the 'Golden Rule Number 2', a name given to it by Enrico Fermi.

Appendix VI. The Löwdin method for symmetrical orthogonalization

Let us represent the original non-orthogonal atomic orbitals by the symbol $|a\rangle$ and the desired mutually orthogonal orbitals by the symbol $|l\rangle$. Now suppose that $|l\rangle$ can be represented by a linear superposition of the functions $|a\rangle$

$$|l\rangle = \sum_a |a\rangle T_{al} \qquad \text{(VI.1)}$$

Then a conjugate function $\langle l'|$ in the orthogonal set will be given by

$$\langle l'| = \sum_{a'} T_{l'a'}^* \langle a'| \qquad \text{(VI.2)}$$

The orthonormality condition thus becomes

$$\langle l' \mid l \rangle = \sum_{a',a} T_{l'a'}^* \langle a' \mid a \rangle T_{al} = \sum_{a',a} T_{l'a'}^* S_{a'a} T_{al} = \delta_{l'l} \qquad \text{(VI.3)}$$

where we have represented the matrix of overlap integrals by

$$\langle a' \mid a \rangle \equiv S_{a'a} \qquad \text{(VI.4)}$$

According to the definition of matrix multiplication, a matrix C is equal to the matrix product AB if

$$C_{ij} = \sum_k A_{ik} B_{kj} \qquad \text{(VI.5)}$$

In an abbreviated notation, Eq. (VI.5) can be written as

$$C = AB \qquad \text{(VI.6)}$$

If we denote the conjugate transpose of the matrix T by $T^\dagger$, and the identity matrix $\delta_{l'l}$ by I, then we can rewrite Eq. (VI.3) in the abbreviated notation of Eq. (VI.6) as

$$T^\dagger S T = I \qquad \text{(VI.7)}$$

Equation (VI.7) holds for any transformation matrix T which takes us from a non-orthogonal set of basis functions whose scalar product matrix is S to an orthonormal set whose scalar product matrix is I. Following the method of Wannier and Löwdin[13] we choose from the many possible solutions of Eq. (VI.7) the particular transformation for which

$$T^\dagger = T \tag{VI.8}$$

Using Eq. (VI.8) and multiplying Eq. (VI.7) from both sides by T^{-1} we have

$$S = (TT)^{-1} \tag{VI.9}$$

so that

$$T = S^{-1/2} \tag{VI.10}$$

The only question now is how to find the reciprocal square root of the scalar product matrix S. This would be easy if S were diagonal. In that case, $S^{-1/2}$ would also be diagonal and each element of $S^{-1/2}$ would be the reciprocal square root of the corresponding diagonal element of S. This is, in fact, a practical method for finding $S^{-1/2}$. *We first diagonalize S by means of a unitary transformation* (see Eqs. (3.97)–(3.133)).

$$U^{-1}SU = S' \tag{VI.11}$$

then we find $S'^{-1/2}$ by taking the reciprocal square root of each diagonal element. Finally we transform $S'^{-1/2}$ back to the original representation.

$$S^{-1/2} = U(S'^{-1/2})U^{-1} \tag{VI.12}$$

Appendix VII. Group theory

The set of coordinate transformations which leave the Hamiltonian of a molecule invariant fulfils the mathematical definition of a 'group'. *If any two elements belonging to the group are multiplied together, the product is another element belonging to the group. There is an identity element, and each element has an inverse. Multiplication of the elements is associative* ($A(BC) = (AB)C$) *but not necessarily commutative.* As a simple example, we might think of a molecule which is symmetric under rotations through an angle of $2\pi/3$ about some axis but which has no other symmetry. Then the symmetry group of the molecule has three elements: the identity operation, a rotation through an angle $2\pi/3$ and a rotation through an angle $4\pi/3$ about the same axis. Let us denote these operations respectively by the symbols E, C_3, and C_3^{-1}, and denote the whole group by the symbol C_3. We can easily construct a multiplication table for the group as shown in Table (VII.1). *Each element of the group will appear once and only once in any row or column of the multiplication table.* This follows from the fact that every equation of the form $AX = B$ has one and only one solution among the group elements. Since A^{-1} and B belong to the group and since the product of any two elements belongs to the group $X = A^{-1}B$ is also a uniquely defined element. Now suppose that an element B appears more than once in the Ath row of the multiplication table. Then $AX = B$ will have more than one solution which is impossible. Since no element can appear more than once, each element must appear once because there are g elements and g places in the row, all of which have to be filled.

The elements of a geometrical symmetry group are linear coordinate transformations. Such a transformation has the form:

$$X^\mu = \sum_{v=1}^{3} \frac{\partial X^\mu}{\partial x^v} x^v + b^\mu \tag{VII.1}$$

where the $\partial X^\mu/\partial x^v$'s and b^μ's are constant coefficients.

Now consider a complete set of functions $\Phi_1, \Phi_2, \ldots, \Phi_N$. We can use Eq. (VII.1) to express $\Phi_n(\bar{x})$ as a function of $\bar{X}$. If we then expand the

Table VII.1

(a) Multiplication table of C_3

	E	C_3	C_3^{-1}
E	E	C_3	C_3^{-1}
C_3	C_3	C_3^{-1}	E
C_3^{-1}	C_3^{-1}	E	C_3

(b) Character table of C_3

	E	C_3	C_3^{-1}
A	1	1	-1
Γ_c	1	$e^{+i(2\pi/3)}$	$e^{-i(2\pi/3)}$
Γ_c^*	1	$e^{-i(2\pi/3)}$	$e^{+i(2\pi/3)}$

resulting function of $\vec{X}$ in terms of the other Φ's we shall obtain a relation of the form

$$\Phi_n(\vec{x}) = \sum_{n'} \Phi_{n'}(\vec{X})D_{n'n} \tag{VII.2}$$

If we denote the coordinate transformation by the symbol R we can rewrite Eqs. (VII.1) and (VII.2) in the form

$$\vec{X} = R\vec{x}$$

$$\Phi_n(\vec{x}) \equiv \Phi_n(R^{-1}\vec{X}) \equiv R\Phi_n(\vec{X})$$

$$= \sum_{n'} \Phi_{n'}(\vec{X})D_{n',n}(R) \tag{VII.3}$$

In this sense, the coordinate transformation defines an operator R and $D_{n'n}(R)$ is a matrix representing R. In chapter 2 we saw that the matrices which represent a set of operators $R_1, R_2, \ldots, R_g$ obey the same multiplication table as the operators themselves. For example if we know that

$$C_3 C_3^{-1} = E \tag{VII.4}$$

335

(see Table (VII.1)), and that:

$$C_3\Phi_n = \sum_{n'} \Phi_{n'} D_{n'n}(C_3)$$

$$C_3^{-1}\Phi_n = \sum_{n'} \Phi_{n'} D_{n'n}(C_3^{-1})$$

$$E\Phi_n = \sum_{n'} \Phi_{n'} D_{n'n}(E) \qquad \text{(VII.5)}$$

Then it follows that:

$$C_3 C_3^{-1}\Phi_n = \sum_{n'} C_3\Phi_{n'} D_{n'n}(C_3^{-1})$$

$$= \sum_{n''} \Phi_{n''} \left\{ \sum_{n'} D_{n''n'}(C_3) D_{n'n}(C_3^{-1}) \right\}$$

$$= E\Phi_n = \sum_{n''} \Phi_{n''} D_{n''n}(E) \qquad \text{(VII.6)}$$

so that we must have

$$D_{n'',n}(E) = \sum_{n'} D_{n'',n'}(C_3) D_{n',n}(C_3^{-1}) \qquad \text{(VII.7)}$$

Thus, *given any set of basis functions* $\Phi_1, \Phi_2, \ldots, \Phi_N$ *which mix together under the elements of a group* $R_1, R_2, \ldots, R_g$ *we can obtain a set of matrices* $D_{n'n}(R_j)$ *defined by the relationship*

$$R_j\Phi_n = \sum_{n'} \Phi_{n'} D_{n'n}(R_j), \quad j = 1, \ldots, g \qquad \textbf{(VII.8)}$$

These matrices will obey the same multiplication table as the operators $R_1, R_2, \ldots, R_g$ *and they are said to form a representation of the group.*

Now let us consider another representation $D'_{m'm}(R)$ based on a set of functions $\Phi'_1, \Phi'_2, \ldots, \Phi'_N$ which are related to our original set $\Phi_1, \Phi_2, \ldots, \Phi_N$ by the transformation

$$\Phi'_m = \sum_n \Phi_n S_{nm}$$

$$\Phi_n = \sum_m \Phi'_m S_{mn}^{-1} \qquad \textbf{(VII.9)}$$

The primed representation is defined by the relationship

$$R_j\Phi'_m = \sum_m \Phi'_{m'} D'_{m'm}(R_j), \quad j = 1, 2, \ldots, g \qquad \text{(VII.10)}$$

Then from Eqs. (VII.8)–(VII.10) we have

$$R_j\Phi'_m = \sum_m \Phi'_{m'}D'_{m'm}(R_j)$$

$$= R_j\sum_n \Phi_n S_{nm} = \sum_{n,n'} \Phi_{n'}D_{n'n}(R_j)S_{nm}$$

$$= \sum_{m',n,n'} \Phi'_{m'}S^{-1}_{m'n'}D_{n'n}(R_j)S_{nm} \qquad \text{(VII.11)}$$

so that we must have

$$D'_{m'm}(R_j) = \sum_{n',n} S^{-1}_{m'n'}D_{n'n}(R_j)S_{nm}$$

or

$$D' = S^{-1}DS \qquad \text{(VII.12)}$$

A transformation of this type, where the matrix S need not be unitary is called a 'similarity transformation'. The 'character' $\chi(R_j)$ of the matrix $D_{n'n}(R_j)$ is defined as the sum of the diagonal elements

$$\chi(R_j) = \sum_n D_{nn}(R_j) \qquad \text{(VII.13)}$$

We would like to show that the character of each element in a representation is invariant under a similarity transformation. From Eq. (VII.12) we have

$$\chi'(R_j) \equiv \sum_m D'_{mm}(R_j)$$

$$= \sum_{m,n,n'} S^{-1}_{mn'}D_{n'n}(R_j)S_{nm}$$

$$= \sum_{n,n'} \left(\sum_m S_{nm}S^{-1}_{mn'}\right) D_{n'n}(R_j)$$

$$= \sum_{n,n'} \delta_{nn'}D_{n'n}(R_j)$$

$$= \sum_n D_{nn}(R_j) \equiv \chi(R_j) \qquad \text{(VII.14)}$$

q.e.d.

If two representations are connected by a similarity transformation, then they are said to be 'equivalent'. From Eq. (VII.14) it follows that *when two representations are equivalent*, $\chi'(R_j) = \chi(R_j), j = 1, 2, \ldots, g$.

Sometimes it is possible, by means of a similarity transformation, to bring each element of a representation into a block-diagonal form such that $D'_{mm'}(R_j) = 0$ if $M < m \leq N$ and $1 \leq m' \leq M$ or if $1 \leq m \leq M$ and $M < m' \leq N$ for all $j = 1, 2, \ldots, g$.

In other words it is sometimes possible by means of a similarity transformation, Eq. (VII.9) to go over from the original basis functions $\Phi_1, \Phi_2, \ldots, \Phi_N$ to a new set of basis functions $\Phi'_1, \Phi'_2, \ldots, \Phi'_N$ which separates into two subsets $\Phi'_1, \Phi'_2, \ldots, \Phi'_M$ and $\Phi'_{M+1}, \ldots, \Phi'_N$ in such a way that the elements of the group $R_1, R_2, \ldots, R_g$ acting on the functions in one subset produce linear combinations of functions belonging to the same subset. *A representation based on two subsets of functions each of which mixes only with itself under the elements of the group is said to be 'reduced'. When it is possible to bring a representation into the reduced form by means of a similarity transformation, then it is said to be 'reducible'. When this is not possible, the representation is said to be 'irreducible'.*

Schur's lemma states that if $D^\alpha_{n'n}(R_j)$ and $D^\beta_{m'm}(R_j)$ are two irreducible representations of a group and if

$$\sum_{m'} S_{n'm'} D^\beta_{m'm}(R_j) = \sum_n D^\alpha_{n'n}(R_j) S_{nm}, \quad j = 1, 2, \ldots, g \quad \text{(VII.15)}$$

then either $S_{nm} = 0$ or else S_{nm} is square, has an inverse, and

$$D^\beta_{m'm}(R_j) = \sum_{n, n'} S^{-1}_{m'n'} D^\alpha_{n'n}(R_j) S_{nm} \quad \text{(VII.16)}$$

In other words if Eq. (VII.15) holds, then either S_{nm} is the null matrix or else D^α and D^β are equivalent representations, i.e., connected by a similarity transformation as in Eq. (VII.12). From Schur's lemma we can establish the very important orthogonality relation

$$\sum_{j=1}^g D^\alpha_{m'm}(R_j) D^\beta_{n'n}(R_j^{-1}) = \frac{g}{d_\alpha} \varepsilon_{\alpha\beta} S_{m'n'} S^{-1}_{nm}$$

where

$$\varepsilon_{\alpha\beta} \equiv \begin{cases} 0 & \text{if } D^\alpha \text{ and } D^\beta \text{ are not equivalent} \\ 1 & \text{if } D^\alpha \text{ and } D^\beta \text{ are equivalent} \end{cases} \quad \textbf{(VII.17)}$$

and $S_{m'n'}$ is given by Eq. (VII.16).

The proof is as follows: Let d_α and d_β be the dimension of the matrices $D^\alpha_{m'm}$ and $D^\beta_{nn'}$ and let X_{mn}, $m = 1, \ldots, d_\alpha$; $n = 1, \ldots, d_\beta$ be an arbitrary matrix. We now define the matrix S by the relation

$$S_{m'n'} = \sum_{j=1}^g \sum_{m=1}^{d_\alpha} \sum_{n=1}^{d_\beta} D^\alpha_{m'm}(R_j) X_{mn} D^\beta_{nn'}(R_j^{-1}) \quad \text{(VII.18)}$$

or in the abbreviated notation of matrix multiplication,

$$S = \sum_{j=1}^{g} D^{\alpha}(R_j) X D^{\beta}(R_j^{-1}) \qquad \text{(VII.19)}$$

Multiplying Eq. (VII.19) from the left by $D^{\alpha}(R_k)$ and from the right by $D^{\beta}(R_k^{-1})$ we obtain

$$D^{\alpha}(R_k) S D^{\beta}(R_k^{-1}) = \sum_{j=1}^{g} D^{\alpha}(R_k) D^{\alpha}(R_j) X D^{\beta}(R_j^{-1}) D^{\beta}(R_k^{-1})$$

$$= \sum_{l=1}^{g} D^{\alpha}(R_l) S D^{\beta}(R_l^{-1}) = S \qquad \text{(VII.20)}$$

In Eq. (VII.20) we have used the fact that if $R_k R_j = R_l$ then $D^{\alpha}(R_k) D^{\alpha}(R_j) = D^{\alpha}(R_l)$.

Summing over all the elements R_l has the same effect as keeping R_k fixed and summing over all the elements R_j because each element appears once and only once in each row of the multiplication table.

From Eq. (VII.20) it follows that

$$D^{\alpha}(R_k) S = S D^{\beta}(R_k), \quad k = 1, \ldots, g \qquad \text{(VII.21)}$$

Then according to Schur's lemma we have only two possibilities: Either S is the null matrix or else $D^{\alpha}(R_k)$ and $D^{\beta}(R_k)$ are equivalent representations related by the similarity transformation

$$S^{-1} D^{\alpha}(R_k) S = D^{\beta}(R_k) \qquad \text{(VII.22)}$$

Let us consider the first possibility: Suppose that D^{α} and D^{β} are inequivalent and S is the null matrix. Then from Eq. (VII.19) we have that for an arbitrary matrix X_{mn}

$$\sum_{j=1}^{g} \sum_{m=1}^{d_{\alpha}} \sum_{n=1}^{d_{\beta}} D^{\alpha}_{m'm}(R_j) X_{mn} D^{\beta}_{nn'}(R_j^{-1}) = 0 \qquad \text{(VII.23)}$$

But X_{mn} is arbitrary, and therefore

$$\sum_{j=1}^{g} D^{\alpha}_{m'm}(R_j) D^{\beta}_{nn'}(R_j^{-1}) = 0 \qquad \text{(VII.24)}$$

Now let us consider the second possibility: Suppose that D^{α} and D^{β} are equivalent representations connected by a similarity transformation. Then, combining Eq. (VII.22) with Eq. (VII.18) and multiplying on the left by S^{-1} we have

$$S^{-1}S = I$$

$$= \sum_{j=1}^{g} S^{-1}D^{\alpha}(R_j)XD^{\beta}(R_j^{-1})$$

$$= \sum_{j=1}^{g} S^{-1}D^{\alpha}(R_j)SS^{-1}XD^{\beta}(R_j^{-1})$$

$$= \sum_{j=1}^{g} D^{\beta}(R_j)S^{-1}XD^{\beta}(R_j^{-1})$$

$$\equiv \sum_{j=1}^{g} \sum_{l,m,n=1}^{d_{\beta}} D_{kl}^{\beta}(R_j)S_{lm}^{-1}X_{mn}D_{nn'}^{\beta}(R_j^{-1})$$

$$= \delta_{kn'} \qquad\qquad\qquad \text{(VII.25)}$$

Dividing Eq. (VII.25) by $d_{\alpha} = d_{\beta}$ and taking the trace of both sides, we have

$$\frac{1}{d_{\beta}} \sum_{j=1}^{g} \sum_{k,l,m,n=1}^{d_{\beta}} \{D_{nk}^{\beta}(R_j^{-1})D_{kl}^{\beta}(R_j)\}S_{lm}^{-1}X_{mn}$$

$$= \frac{1}{d_{\beta}} \sum_{j=1}^{g} \sum_{lmn=1}^{d_{\beta}} \delta_{nl}S_{lm}^{-1}X_{mn}$$

$$= \frac{1}{d_{\beta}} \sum_{j=1}^{g} \sum_{m,n=1}^{d_{\beta}} S_{nm}^{-1}X_{mn}$$

$$= \frac{g}{d_{\beta}} \sum_{m,n=1}^{d_{\beta}} S_{nm}^{-1}X_{mn} = \frac{1}{d_{\beta}} \sum_{k=1}^{d_{\beta}} \delta_{kk} = 1 \qquad \text{(VII.26)}$$

Multiplying Eq. (VII.18) by Eq. (VII.26) gives

$$\frac{g}{d_{\beta}} S_{m'n'} \sum_{m,n=1}^{d_{\beta}} S_{nm}^{-1}X_{mn} = \sum_{j=1}^{g} \sum_{m,n=1}^{d_{\beta}} D_{m'm}^{\alpha}(R_j)X_{mn}D_{nn'}^{\beta}(R_j^{-1}) \quad \text{(VII.27)}$$

Since X_{mn} is arbitrary, Eq. (VII.27) will hold only if

$$\sum_{j=1}^{g} D_{m'm}^{\alpha}(R_j)D_{nn'}^{\beta}(R_j^{-1}) = \frac{g}{d_{\beta}} S_{m'n'}S_{nm}^{-1} \qquad \text{(VII.28)}$$

Combining Eq. (VII.28) and Eq. (VII.24) we obtain the orthogonality relation Eq. (VII.17), q.e.d. If the representation consists of unitary matrices, so that the inverse of each matrix is equal to its conjugate transpose, then the orthogonality relation can be written in the form

$$\sum_{j=1}^{g} D_{mm'}^{\alpha*}(R_j)D_{nn'}^{\beta}(R_j) = \frac{g}{d_{\alpha}} \varepsilon_{\alpha\beta}S_{m'n'}S_{nm}^{-1} \qquad \text{(VII.29)}$$

In the special case where D^α and D^β are not only equivalent but also identical $S_{m'n'} = C\,\delta_{m'n'}$ where C is a constant so that

$$\sum_{j=1}^{g} D_{mm'}^{\alpha *}(R_j)D_{nn'}^{\beta}(R_j) = \frac{g}{d_\alpha}\,\varepsilon_{\alpha\beta}\,\delta_{m'n'}\,\delta_{nm} \qquad \textbf{(VII.30)}$$

The orthogonality relation is very central and almost all of the results of group theory depend upon it. For example combining Eq. (VII.29) with the definition $\chi^\alpha(R_j) \equiv \sum_n D_{nn}^\alpha(R_j)$ we obtain for unitary representations

$$\sum_{j=1}^{g}\left\{\sum_m D_{mm}^{\alpha *}(R_j)\right\}\left\{\sum_n D_{nn}^{\beta}(R_j)\right\} \equiv \sum_{j=1}^{g} \chi^{\alpha *}(R_j)\chi^{\beta}(R_j)$$

$$= \frac{g\varepsilon_{\alpha\beta}}{d_\alpha}\sum_n\sum_m S_{mn}S_{mn}^{-1} = g\varepsilon_{\alpha\beta}$$
$$(VII.31)$$

Equation (VII.29) only holds for unitary representations, but every representation is equivalent to a unitary representation since it is always possible to perform a similarity transformation which orthonormalizes the basis functions. Therefore since $\chi^\alpha(R_j)$ is invariant under similarity transformations the orthogonality of characters

$$\frac{1}{g}\sum_{j=1}^{g} \chi^{\alpha *}(R_j)\chi^{\beta}(R_j) = \varepsilon_{\alpha\beta} \equiv \begin{cases} 0 & \text{if } D^\alpha \text{ and } D^\beta \text{ are inequivalent} \\ 1 & \text{if } D^\alpha \text{ and } D^\beta \text{ are equivalent} \end{cases} \qquad \textbf{(VII.32)}$$

holds even for non-unitary irreducible representations.

Now consider a representation $D_{n'n}(R_j)$ which may be reducible. If we reduce it by means of a similarity transformation, then in its reduced form it will be block-diagonal, each block being irreducible. Taking the trace we find that the character of an element in the reduced representation $D_{n'n}'(R_j)$ is the sum of the characters of the irreducible elements of which it consists. If $D_{n'n}'(R_j)$ has the form

$$D_{n'n}'(R_j) = \begin{array}{|c|c|} \hline D^1(R_j) & 0 \\ \hline 0 & D^2(R_j) \\ \hline & \text{etc.} \\ \hline \end{array} \quad \text{etc.} \qquad (VII.33)$$

then

$$\chi'(R_j) \equiv \sum_{n=1}^{d} D_{nn}'(R_j)$$

$$= \sum_{n=1}^{d_1} D_{nn}^1(R_j) + \sum_{n=d_1+1}^{d_1+d_2} D_{nn}^2(R_j) + \cdots$$

$$\equiv \chi^1(R_j) + \chi^2(R_j) + \cdots$$

$$= \sum_\beta n_\beta \chi^\beta(R_j) \qquad (VII.34)$$

where n_β is the number of times that the irreducible representation D^β occurs among the diagonal blocks of D'. Since characters are invariant under a similarity transformation the character $\chi(R_j)$ of an element $D_{n'n}(R_j)$ in our original reducible representation D will be equal to $\chi'(R_j)$ and

$$\chi(R_j) \equiv \sum_\beta n_\beta \chi^\beta(R_j) \qquad \text{(VII.35)}$$

Then from Eq. (VII.32) we have

$$\frac{1}{g} \sum_{j=1}^g \chi^{\alpha*}(R_j)\chi(R_j) = \sum_\beta n_\beta \sum_{j=1}^g \chi^{\alpha*}(R_j)\chi^\beta(R_j)$$

$$= \sum_\beta n_\beta \varepsilon_{\alpha\beta} = n_\alpha \qquad \textbf{(VII.36)}$$

This gives us a way of finding out how many times a particular irreducible representation D^α 'occurs' in a reducible representation D. According to Eq. (VII.36) we just have to take the scalar product of the characters and divide by the order of the group. *When we say that D^α 'occurs' n_α times in D we mean that it is possible by means of a similarity transformation to bring D in to block diagonal form where D^α occurs n_α times along the diagonal blocks.* The relationship is sometimes written in the form

$$D = n_1 D^1 + n_2 D^2 + \cdots \qquad \text{(VII.37)}$$

Obviously in Eqs. (VII.34)–(VI.37) we do not need to distinguish between the different equivalent forms of an irreducible representation D^α, since all of them have the same character and it is possible to go from one to another by means of a similarity transformation.

Two elements of the group, R_i and R_j, are said to belong to the same 'class' if there exists another element R_l in the group such that

$$R_i = R_l^{-1} R_j R_l \qquad \textbf{(VII.38)}$$

Thus, if we start with a particular element R_j, we can generate the set of elements belonging to the same class by keeping j fixed and letting R_l run through the whole group in Eq. (VII.38). It also follows from Eq. (VII.38) that *we can construct an operator M_k which commutes with all of the elements of the group by summing the elements of a particular class.*

$$M_k \equiv \sum_{\text{class } k} R_j \qquad \textbf{(VII.39)}$$

Then for an arbitrary group element R_l we have

$$R_l^{-1}[M_k, R_l] = R_l^{-1} \sum_{\text{class } k} [R_j, R_l]$$

$$= \sum_{\text{class } k} (R_l^{-1} R_j R_l - R_j) = \sum_{\text{class } k} (R_i - R_j) = 0 \qquad \text{(VII.40)}$$

Equation (VII.40) can hold only if $[M_k, R_l] = 0$. *An operator such as M_k which commutes with every element of the group is called an 'invariant'. If there are r classes in the group, there will be r linearly independent invariants which can be constructed in this way.*

For any representation of two elements R_i and R_j in the same class it follows from Eq. (VII.38) that

$$D(R_i) = D(R_l^{-1})D(R_j)D(R_l) = D(R_l)^{-1}D(R_j)D(R_l) \quad \text{(VII.41)}$$

Since the form of Eq. (VII.41) is the same as the form of Eq. (VII.12) it follows from Eq. (VII.14) that $\chi(R_i) = \chi(R_j)$. In other words, *all elements in the same class have the same character.* This means that in applying Eq. (VII.36) we do not need to go through quite so much work. Instead of summing over all of the elements in the group we can take the product of characters for a representative element in each class, multiply by the number of elements in the class, and then sum over the different classes. If g_k represents the number of elements in the class k then the orthogonality relation for characters, Eq. (VII.32) can be written in the form

$$\sum_{k=1}^{r} \frac{\sqrt{g_k}}{g} \chi_k^{\alpha*} \frac{\sqrt{g_k}}{g} \chi_k^{\beta} = \delta_{\alpha\beta} \quad \textbf{(VII.42)}$$

where χ_k^{α} is the character of a representative element of the class k in the irreducible representation α. In Eq. (VII.42) we let the index $\alpha = 1, 2, \ldots, r'$ label the r' non-equivalent irreducible representations and the $\varepsilon_{\alpha\beta}$ of Eq. (VII.32) can be replaced by $\delta_{\alpha\beta}$.

The orthogonality relationship, Eq. (VII.29), can be used to reduce a representation. Suppose that the set of functions $\Phi_1^1, \Phi_2^1, \ldots, \Phi_{d_1}^1$, $\Phi_1^2, \Phi_2^2, \ldots, \Phi_{d_2}^2, \ldots$, etc., forms the basis for r' non-equivalent unitary irreducible representations of a group so that

$$R_j \Phi_n^{\beta} = \sum_{n'=1}^{d_\beta} \Phi_{n'}^{\beta} D_{n'n}^{\beta}(R_j) \quad \text{(VII.43)}$$

Then from Eqs. (VII.29) and (VII.30) we have

$$\sum_{j=1}^{g} D_{mm'}^{\alpha}(R_j^{-1}) R_j \Phi_{n'}^{\beta} = \sum_{n=1}^{d_\beta} \sum_{j=1}^{g} D_{mm'}^{\alpha}(R_j^{-1}) D_{nn'}^{\beta}(R_j) \Phi_n^{\beta}$$

$$= \frac{g}{d_\beta} \delta_{\alpha\beta} \sum_{n=1}^{d_\beta} \delta_{m'n'} \delta_{mn} \Phi_n^{\beta} = \frac{g}{d_\beta} \delta_{\alpha\beta} \delta_{m'n'} \Phi_m^{\beta} \quad \text{(VII.44)}$$

If we let

$$P_m^{\alpha} \equiv \frac{d_\alpha}{g} \sum_{j=1}^{g} D_{mm}^{\alpha}(R_j^{-1}) R_j \quad \textbf{(VII.45)}$$

then from Eq. (VII.44) *it follows that*

$$P^\alpha_m \Phi_n{}^\beta = \delta_{\alpha\beta}\,\delta_{mn}\Phi^\beta_m \qquad \text{(VII.46)}$$

In other words, when the operator P^α_m defined by Eq. (VII.46) acts on a function Φ^β_n in the set $\Phi^1_1,\ \Phi^1_2,\cdots,\ \Phi^1_{d_1},\ \Phi^2_1,\ \Phi^2_2,\cdots,\ \Phi^r_{d_r}$, the function is given back unharmed provided that $m = n$ and $\alpha = \beta$. Otherwise the function is annihilated. *Thus P^α_m is a projection operator corresponding to the mth basis function of the irreducible unitary representation D^α.* If P^α_m acts on an arbitrary function it will annihilate all of it except the component which transforms like the mth basis function of D^α. If we sum over m we obtain a 'weak' projection operator

$$P^\alpha \equiv \sum_{m=1}^{d_\alpha} P^\alpha_m = \frac{d_\alpha}{g}\sum_{j=1}^{g}\sum_{m=1}^{d_\alpha} D^{\alpha*}_{mm}(R_j)R_j \equiv \frac{d_\alpha}{g}\sum_{j=1}^{g}\chi^{\alpha*}(R_j)R_j \ \text{(VII.47)}$$

Remembering that when two elements are in the same class their characters must be equal we can also express P^α in the form

$$P^\alpha = \frac{d_\alpha}{g}\sum_{k=1}^{r}\chi^{\alpha*}_k M_k \qquad \text{(VII.48)}$$

where $M_k \equiv \sum_{\text{class }k} R_j$, (Eq. (VII.39)). From Eq. (VII.46) it follows that

$$P^\alpha\Phi^\beta_n \equiv \sum_{m=1}^{d_\alpha} P^\alpha_m\Phi^\beta_n = \delta_{\alpha\beta}\sum_{m=1}^{d_\alpha}\delta_{mn}\Phi^\beta_n = \delta_{\alpha\beta}\Phi^\beta_n \qquad \text{(VII.49)}$$

In other words, when the weak projection operator P^α acts on a function in the set $\Phi^1_1,\ \Phi^1_2,\ \ldots,\ \Phi^r_{d_r}$, it annihilates it if $\alpha \neq \beta$, but if $\alpha = \beta$ it leaves the function unharmed. *When P^α acts on an arbitrary function it annihilates everything except for a component which can be expressed as a linear combination of the basis functions of the irreducible representation D^α.* Finally, if we sum Eq. (VII.49) over all of the irreducible representations of the group we obtain

$$\sum_{\alpha=1}^{r'} P^\alpha\Phi^\beta_n = \sum_{\alpha=1}^{r'}\delta_{\alpha\beta}\Phi^\beta_n = \Phi^\beta_n \qquad \text{(VII.50)}$$

The operator $\sum_{\alpha=1}^{r'} P^\alpha$ leaves Φ^β_n unharmed no matter what the values of β and n. Therefore it must be the identity operator

$$\sum_{\alpha=1}^{r'} P^\alpha = E \qquad \text{(VII.51)}$$

Then combining Eqs. (VII.47) and (VII.51) we have

$$\sum_{j=1}^{g}\sum_{\alpha=1}^{r'}\frac{d_\alpha}{g}\chi^{\alpha*}(R_j)R_j = E \equiv R_1 \qquad \text{(VII.52)}$$

Since the group elements $R_1, \ldots, R_g$ are linearly independent, Eq. (VII.52) can hold only if

$$\sum_{\alpha=1}^{r'} \frac{d_\alpha}{g} \chi^{\alpha*}(R_j) = \delta_{j1} \qquad \text{(VII.53)}$$

The character of the identity element in any representation is equal to the dimension of that representation

$$\chi^{\alpha*}(E) = \chi^\alpha(E) = d_\alpha \qquad \text{(VII.54)}$$

Therefore, when $j = 1$, Eq. (VII.53) becomes

$$\sum_{\alpha=1}^{r'} d_\alpha^2 = g \qquad \textbf{(VII.55)}$$

i.e., *the sum of the squares of the dimensions of the irreducible representations is equal to the order of the group.* Also we can see from Eq. (VII.54) that Eq. (VII.53) can be rewritten in the form

$$\sum_{\alpha=1}^{r'} \frac{1}{g} \chi^{\alpha*}(R_j) \chi^\alpha(E) = \delta_{j1} \qquad \text{(VII.56)}$$

or

$$\sum_{\alpha=1}^{r'} \sqrt{\frac{g_k}{g}} \chi_k^{\alpha*} \sqrt{\frac{g_1}{g}} \chi_1^\alpha = \sqrt{g_k g_1} \, \delta_{k1} = \delta_{k1} \qquad \text{(VII.57)}$$

where g_k is the number of elements in the class k and χ_k^α is the character of a representative element. In Eq. (VII.57) we have used the fact that the identity element is in a class by itself so that $g_1 = 1$ and $\sqrt{g_k g_1} \, \delta_{k1} = \delta_{k1}$. Since $P^\alpha = (d_\alpha/g) \sum_k \chi_k^{\alpha*} M_k$ it is clear that a projection operator of the type P^α can be represented as a linear superposition of the r invariants M_k. Because the projection operators P^α are linearly independent and because there are r' of them (where r' is the number of irreducible representations), this shows that $r' \leq r$. We can also show that the invariants M_k of Eq. (VII.39) can be represented as linear superpositions of the projection operators P^α. In fact, we can show that any invariant whatever can be represented in the form $M = \sum_{\alpha=1}^{r} a_\alpha P^\alpha$ where the a_α's are constants. The proof is as follows:

An invariant must commute with every element of the group, so that if M is an invariant, then

$$MR_j = R_j M$$

and

$$MR_j M^{-1} = R_j, \quad j = 1, \ldots, g \qquad \text{(VII.58)}$$

345

The quantum theory of atoms, molecules, and photons

In the irreducible representation D^α, Eq. (VII.58) becomes

$$D^\alpha(M)D^\alpha(R_j)D^\alpha(M)^{-1} = D^\alpha(R_j), \quad j = 1, \ldots, g \quad \text{(VII.59)}$$

Since the similarity transformation shown in Eq. (VII.59) leaves all of the elements $D^\alpha(R_j), j = 1, \ldots, g$ unchanged, $D^\alpha(M)$ must be a multiple of the unit matrix.

$$D^\alpha(M) = a_\alpha D^\alpha(E) \quad \text{(VII.60)}$$

The projection operator P^α leaves the basis functions $\Phi_1^\alpha, \ldots, \Phi_{d_\alpha}^\alpha$ unchanged, so as far as these functions are concerned P^α acts as though it were the identity operator, and

$$D^\alpha(M) = a_\alpha D^\alpha(E) = D^\alpha(a_\alpha P^\alpha) = D^\alpha \left(\sum_{\beta=1}^{r'} a_\beta P^\beta \right) \quad \text{(VII.61)}$$

Thus in any irreducible representation D^α, an arbitrary invariant can be represented in the form $\sum_{\beta=1}^{r'} a_\beta P^\beta$ and this must be true in any representation, q.e.d. Therefore, there can only be r' linearly independent invariants. But we have already shown that there are r linearly independent invariants M_k, $k = 1, \ldots, r$ and that $r' \leq r$. Hence $r' = r$, i.e., *the number of inequivalent irreducible representations is equal to the number of classes.* Now let us define the matrix U as

$$U_{k\beta} \equiv \sqrt{\frac{g_k}{g}} \chi_k^\beta$$

$$k = 1, \ldots, r, \quad \beta = 1, \ldots, r' \quad \text{(VII.62)}$$

Since $r = r'$ this matrix must be square, and Eq. (VII.42) tells us that it is unitary, i.e., $U^\dagger = U^{-1}$. Not only the rows, but also the columns of a unitary matrix are mutually orthogonal so that we have the 'orthogonality relationships of the second kind'

$$\sum_{\alpha=1}^{r} \sqrt{\frac{g_{k'}}{g}} \chi_{k'}^{\alpha*} \sqrt{\frac{g_k}{g}} \chi_k^\alpha = \delta_{k'k} \quad \textbf{(VII.63)}$$

of which Eq. (VII.57) is a particular example. Substituting Eq. (VII.63) into Eq. (VII.48) we obtain an expression for the invariants M_k in terms of the projection operators P^α

$$M_k = \sum_{\alpha=1}^{r} \frac{g_k}{d_\alpha} \chi_k^\alpha P^\alpha \quad \textbf{(VII.64)}$$

of which $E = \sum_{\alpha=1}^{r} P^\alpha$ is a particular example. In a reduced representation the projection operator P^α is represented by a matrix containing the identity matrix E in the blocks corresponding to D^α and zeros everywhere else. From

346

Eq. (VII.64) we can see that in a reduced representation a class-invariant M_k is represented by a matrix with a multiple of the unit matrix in each block, and that the factor multiplying the $d_\alpha \times d_\alpha$ unit matrix in the blocks corresponding to D^α is $(g_k/d_\alpha)\chi_k^\alpha$. We can see from this that in a reduced representation the class-invariants M_k are all simultaneously diagonal and that their eigenvalues are $(g_k/d_\alpha)\chi_k^\alpha$. The operators M_k are not necessarily Hermitian, since their eigenvalues, $(1/d_\alpha)\chi_k^\alpha$, are not necessarily real. On the other hand, the projection operators P^α and P_n^α are certainly Hermitian, since their eigenvalues, (0 and 1) are real. We can define an adjoint operator $M_k^\dagger$ as the sum over all the elements R_j in a class k of the reciprocal element R_j^{-1}

$$M_k^\dagger \equiv \sum_{\text{class } k} R_j^{-1} \qquad \text{(VII.65)}$$

In any unitary representation, R_j^{-1} is represented by the conjugate transpose of the matrix representing R_j. Therefore, if we confine ourselves to unitary representations, $M_k^\dagger$ will be represented by the conjugate transpose of the matrix which represents M_k. However, we know that P^α is self-adjoint and therefore,

$$M_k^\dagger = \sum_{\alpha=1}^r \frac{g_k}{d_\alpha} \chi_k^{\alpha*} P^\alpha \qquad \text{(VII.66)}$$

It follows that the adjoint operators $M_k^\dagger$ are also invariants of the group, since they can be represented by a linear combination of the projection operators P^α. The operators

$$N_k \equiv \tfrac{1}{2}(M_k + M_k^\dagger) = \sum_{\text{class } k} \tfrac{1}{2}(R_j + R_j^{-1}) = \sum_{\alpha=1}^r \frac{g_k}{2d_\alpha}(\chi_k^\alpha + \chi_k^{\alpha*})P^\alpha \qquad \text{(VII.67)}$$

and

$$\bar{N}_k \equiv \frac{1}{2i}(M_k - M_k^\dagger) = \sum_{\text{class } k} \frac{1}{2i}(R_j - R_j^{-1}) = \sum_{\alpha=1}^r \frac{g_k}{2id_\alpha}(\chi_k^\alpha - \chi_k^{\alpha*})P^\alpha \qquad \text{(VII.68)}$$

are Hermitian since their eigenvalues are necessarily real. Now suppose that we have a group about which we know nothing at all except the multiplication table and suppose that we would like to calculate the characters of the irreducible representations. *We can use the multiplication table to obtain a special representation (called the 'regular representation') based on the group elements themselves.* In other words, we let the group elements

347

$R_1, R_2, \ldots, R_g$ take the place of the basis functions $\Phi_1, \ldots, \Phi_N$ in Eq. (VII.8) so that we obtain a relation of the form

$$R_i R_n \equiv \sum_{n'=1}^{g} R_{n'} D^{\text{reg}}_{n'n}(R_i) \qquad \text{(VII.69)}$$

The matrices of the regular representation as defined by Eq. (VII.69) are of course determined by the multiplication table. In the regular representation the identity element is represented by a $g \times g$ unit matrix so that $\chi^{\text{reg}}(E) = g$. Since $R_i R_i \neq R_i$ for $R_i \neq E$, $\chi^{\text{reg}}(R_i) = 0$ for $R_i \neq E$. Then from Eq. (VII.36) we can see that the number of times that the irreducible representation D^{α} is contained in the regular representation is given by

$$n_\alpha = \frac{1}{g} \sum_{j=1}^{g} \chi^{\alpha *}(R_j)\chi^{\text{reg}}(R_j) = \frac{1}{g} \chi^{\alpha *}(E)\chi^{\text{reg}}(E) = d_\alpha \qquad \text{(VII.70)}$$

Now *suppose that we diagonalize the Hermitian class-invariants* $D^{\text{reg}}(N_k)$ *and* $D^{\text{reg}}(\bar{N}_k)$. *Then, according to Eqs.* (VII.67)–(VII.70) *we shall find the eigenvalues* $(g_k/2d_\alpha)(\chi_k^\alpha + \chi_k^{\alpha *})$ *and* $(g_k/2id_\alpha)(\chi_k^\alpha - \chi_k^{\alpha *})$ *each appearing* d_α^2 *times along the diagonal. In order to find* d_α *we just need to count up the number of times which each eigenvalue appears and take the square root.* Since g_k (the number of elements in the class k) is determined from the multiplication table, the real and imaginary parts of χ_k^α can be found by multiplying the eigenvalues by d_α/g_k. *Since the set of Hermitian class-invariants* N_k *and* $\bar{N}_k$, $k = 1, \ldots, r$, *defined by Eqs.* (VII.67) *and* (VII.68) *commute with each other, we can find a single unitary transformation which makes all of them simultaneously diagonal.* One way of finding such a transformation would be as follows. We first diagonalize $N_2(N_1 = E$ is already diagonal) by solving the secular equation

$$\sum_n \{D^{\text{reg}}(N_2)_{n'n} - \delta_{n'n}\lambda_m\}S_{nm}^{(2)} = 0 \qquad \text{(VII.71)}$$

If we find $S_{nm}^{(2)}$ by means of a computer program which arranges the eigenvalues and eigenvectors in order according to their size, then the eigenvectors corresponding to the $n_\alpha d_\alpha$ degenerate eigenvalues $\lambda_m = (g_2/2d_\alpha) \times (\chi_2^\alpha + \chi_2^{\alpha *})$ will be collected in consecutive columns of $S_{n,m}^{(2)}$. Next, we calculate $(S^{(2)})^{-1} N_3 S^{(2)}$.

This matrix will be block-diagonal, since N_3 commutes with N_2 and therefore it can only mix degenerate eigenfunctions of N_2. We then find $S^{(3)}$, a matrix which diagonalizes each block of $(S^{(2)})^{-1} N_3 S^{(2)}$ without mixing eigenvectors corresponding to different blocks. Next we calculate $(S^{(2)}S^{(3)})^{-1} N_4 (S^{(2)}S^{(3)})$. This will be a block-diagonal matrix, and we find a transformation matrix $S^{(4)}$ which diagonalizes each block without mixing the eigenfunctions corresponding to different blocks. Next we calculate $(S^{(2)}S^{(3)}S^{(4)})^{-1}N_5(S^{(2)}S^{(3)}S^{(4)})$ and so on until we have run through all the N_k's and $\bar{N}_k$'s. The result will be a transformation $S = S^{(2)}S^{(3)} \dots S^{(r)} \times \bar{S}^{(2)} \dots \bar{S}^{(r)}$ which makes all of the Hermitian class-invariants $N_1, \dots, N_r$, $\bar{N}_1, \dots, \bar{N}_r$ simultaneously diagonal and completely reduces the representation. By reducing the regular representation in this way we can obtain a set of matrices $D^\alpha(R_j)_{n'n}, \alpha = 1, \dots, r, j = 1, \dots, g$ which are irreducible representations of the group. These in turn can be used to construct the 'strong' projection operators $P_n^\alpha = (d_\alpha/g)\sum_{j=1}^g D_{nn}^\alpha(R_j^{-1})R_j$ of Eq. (VII.45), and these projection operators, acting on an arbitrary set of functions, can generate sets of basis functions of the irreducible representations.

For example, looking back at Table (VII.1) we can see from the multiplication table of the group C_3 that each of the $g = 3$ elements, E, C_3, and C_3^{-1}, is in a class by itself. Thus, $r = 3$, i.e., there are three classes each with $g_k = 1$, and three irreducible representations. We can also use the multiplication table to find the regular representation of the Hermitian class invariants of Eqs. (VII.67) and (VII.68).

$$D^{\text{reg}}(N_1) = D^{\text{reg}}(E) = \begin{pmatrix} 1 & 0 & 0 \\ 0 & 1 & 0 \\ 0 & 0 & 1 \end{pmatrix}$$

$$D^{\text{reg}}(N_2) = \tfrac{1}{2}\{D^{\text{reg}}(C_3) + D^{\text{reg}}(C_3^{-1})\} = D^{\text{reg}}(N_3)$$

$$= \tfrac{1}{2}\begin{pmatrix} 0 & 1 & 1 \\ 1 & 0 & 1 \\ 1 & 1 & 0 \end{pmatrix}$$

$$D^{\text{reg}}(\bar{N}_2) = \frac{1}{2i}(D^{\text{reg}}(C_3) - D^{\text{reg}}(C_3^{-1})) = -D^{\text{reg}}(\bar{N}_3)$$

$$= \tfrac{1}{2}\begin{pmatrix} 0 & -i & i \\ i & 0 & -i \\ -i & i & 0 \end{pmatrix} \tag{VII.72}$$

Solving the secular equation, Eq. (VII.71), we find a unitary transformation matrix $S^{(2)}$ which diagonalizes N_2.

$$S^{(2)} = \frac{1}{\sqrt{3}}\begin{pmatrix} 1 & 1 & 1 \\ 1 & e^{i2\pi/3} & e^{-i2\pi/3} \\ 1 & e^{-i2\pi/3} & e^{i2\pi/3} \end{pmatrix} \tag{VII.73}$$

349

The quantum theory of atoms, molecules, and photons

(In this example we don't need a computer to diagonalize N_2. We just think of benzene!) Then in the diagonal representation we find

$$(S^{(2)})^{-1}D^{\text{reg}}(N_2)S^{(2)} = \begin{pmatrix} 1 & 0 & 0 \\ 0 & -\frac{1}{2} & 0 \\ 0 & 0 & -\frac{1}{2} \end{pmatrix}$$

$$(S^{(2)})^{-1}D^{\text{reg}}(\bar{N}_2)S^{(2)} = \begin{pmatrix} 0 & 0 & 0 \\ 0 & \frac{\sqrt{3}}{2} & 0 \\ 0 & 0 & -\frac{\sqrt{3}}{2} \end{pmatrix} \quad \text{(VII.74)}$$

Here by a coincidence, the unitary transformation $S^{(2)}$ which diagonalizes $D^{\text{reg}}(N_2)$ also diagonalizes $D^{\text{reg}}(\bar{N}_2)$. Also in this example $N_3 = N_2$ and $\bar{N}_3 = -\bar{N}_2$, so that $S^{(2)}$ diagonalizes all of the class-invariants and completely reduces the representation. Looking at Eq. (VII.74) we can see that $\bar{N}_2$ has three different eigenvalues each of which appears once. Therefore $d_1^2 = d_2^2 = d_3^2 = 1$. Multiplying the αth eigenvalue of N_k and $\bar{N}_k$ by $d_\alpha/g_k = 1$, we obtain the real and imaginary parts of χ_k^α. Thus we find that

$$\chi_k^1 = (1, 1, 1)$$

$$\chi_k^2 = \left(1, \frac{-1 + i\sqrt{3}}{2}, \frac{-1 - i\sqrt{3}}{2}\right) = (1, e^{i2\pi/3}, e^{-i2\pi/3})$$

$$\chi_k^3 = \left(1, \frac{-1 - i\sqrt{3}}{2}, \frac{-1 + i\sqrt{3}}{2}\right) = (1, e^{-i2\pi/3}, e^{i2\pi/3}) \quad \text{(VII.75)}$$

and this is the character table of the group C_3 as summarized in Table (VII.1). In the case of C_3, all of the irreducible representations are one-dimensional, so there is no difference between the strong projection operators P_n^α of Eq. (VII.45) and the weak projection operators P^α of Eq. (VII.47). In a case where $d_\alpha > 1$ we would need to calculate $D_{n'n}^\alpha(R_j), j = 1, \ldots, g$, by transforming each element of the regular representation to its reduced form, $S^{-1}D^{\text{reg}}(R_j)S$. Here we see directly from the characters that

$$D^1(R_j) = (1, 1, 1)$$

$$D^2(R_j) = (1, e^{i2\pi/3}, e^{-i2\pi/3})$$

$$D^3(R_j) = (1, e^{-i2\pi/3}, e^{i2\pi/3}) \quad \text{(VII.76)}$$

and

$$P^1 = \tfrac{1}{3}(E + C_3 + C_3^{-1})$$

$$P^2 = \tfrac{1}{3}(E + e^{-i2\pi/3}C_3 + e^{i2\pi/3}C_3^{-1})$$

$$P^3 = \tfrac{1}{3}(E + e^{i2\pi/3}C_3 + e^{-i2\pi/3}C_3^{-1}) \quad \text{(VII.77)}$$

(Notice that $P^1 + P^2 + P^3 = E$ in agreement with Eq. (VII.51) and that $P^\alpha P^\beta = \delta_{\alpha\beta} P^\alpha$.) Having found the projection operators P_n^α or P^α we can produce symmetry-adapted functions by acting on an arbitrary basis set. For example suppose that our basis set consists of atomic orbitals

$$\Phi_{nlm} = R_{nl}(r) Y_{lm}(\theta, \varphi) = f(r, \theta)\, e^{im\varphi} \qquad \text{(VII.78)}$$

where φ is the angle of rotation about the three-fold symmetry axis. Looking back at Eq. (VII.3) we can see that

$$E\, e^{im\varphi} = e^{im\varphi}$$

$$C_3\, e^{im\varphi} = e^{im\{\varphi - (2\pi/3)\}}$$

$$C_3^{-1}\, e^{im\varphi} = e^{im\{\varphi + (2\pi/3)\}} \qquad \text{(VII.79)}$$

so that

$$P^1\, e^{im\varphi} = \tfrac{1}{3}\{e^{im\varphi} + e^{im\{\varphi - (2\pi/3)\}} + e^{im\{\varphi + (2\pi/3)\}}\}$$

$$= \tfrac{1}{3} e^{im\varphi}\{1 + 2\cos 2\pi m/3\}$$

$$= \begin{cases} 0 & \text{if } m = \pm 1, \pm 2, \pm 4, \pm 5, \ldots \\ e^{im\varphi} & \text{if } m = 0, \pm 3, \pm 6, \pm 6, \ldots \end{cases} \qquad \text{(VII.80)}$$

$$P^2\, e^{im\varphi} = \begin{cases} 0 & \text{if } m + 1 = \pm 1, \pm 2, \pm 4, \ldots \\ e^{im\varphi} & \text{if } m + 1 = 0, \pm 3, \pm 6, \ldots \end{cases} \qquad \text{(VII.81)}$$

$$P^3\, e^{im\varphi} = \begin{cases} 0 & \text{if } m - 1 = \pm 1, \pm 2, \pm 4, \pm 5, \ldots \\ e^{im\varphi} & \text{if } m - 1 = 0, \pm 3, \pm 6, \pm 9, \ldots \end{cases} \qquad \text{(VII.82)}$$

Thus we obtain symmetry-adapted basis functions, classified according to their transformation properties under the group C_3. The projection operators P^1, P^2, and P^3 separate the Hilbert space spanned by the functions $\Phi_{n,l,m}$ into three subspaces. The functions $\Phi_{n,l,0}$, $\Phi_{n,l,\pm 3}$, $\Phi_{n,l,\pm 6}$, etc., are basis functions of the irreducible representation D^1, the functions $\Phi_{n,l,-5}$, $\Phi_{n,l,-2}$, $\Phi_{n,l,1}$, $\Phi_{n,l,4}$, ..., etc., are basis functions of D^2 and the functions $\Phi_{n,l,-4}$, $\Phi_{n,l,-1}$, $\Phi_{n,l,2}$, $\Phi_{n,l,5}$, ..., etc., are basis functions of D^3.

Now *suppose that we have divided the Hilbert space spanned by a set of basis functions into a number of subspaces by means of the strong projection operators P_n^α so that the functions $\Phi_1, \ldots, \Phi_N$ are eigenfunctions of P_n^α*

$$P_n^\alpha \Phi_j = \lambda_j \Phi_j$$

$$\lambda_j = 0 \text{ or } 1 \qquad \text{(VII.83)}$$

We can show that if an operator H commutes with every element of the group, then the matrix elements of H linking functions belonging to different subspaces must necessarily vanish. The proof is as follows: Since H commutes

The quantum theory of atoms, molecules, and photons

with every element of the group, and since the projection operators P_n^α are constructed from group elements, it follows that $[P_n^\alpha, H] = 0$ and from Eq. (VII.83) we have

$$\int d\tau \Phi_j^* [P_n^\alpha, H]\Phi_k = (\lambda_j - \lambda_k) \int d\tau \Phi_j^* H\Phi_k = 0 \qquad \text{(VII.84)}$$

If $\lambda_j - \lambda_k \neq 0$, i.e., if Φ_j and Φ_k belong to different subspaces, then Eq. (VII.84) implies that $\int d\tau \Phi_j^* H\Phi_k = 0$, q.e.d. Now suppose that besides being eigenfunctions of P_n^α, the functions $\Phi_1, \ldots, \Phi_n$ are also eigenfunctions of the operator H. For example, suppose that H is the Hamiltonian of a molecule and that $R_1, \ldots, R_g$ is the group of symmetry operators which commute with H. If we wish to construct eigenfunctions of H, then we can begin by partitioning the Hilbert space spanned by the basis functions into $\sum_{\alpha=1}^{r} d_\alpha$ subspaces by means of the strong projection operators P_n^α. According to Eqs. (VII.83) and (VII.84) the matrix representation of the Hamiltonian based on such a set of symmetry-adapted functions will be a block-diagonal. We do not need to calculate the matrix elements of H linking different subspaces, because we know in advance that these will be zero. Thus, *if the functions* $\Phi_n^{1\alpha}, \Phi_n^{2\alpha}, \ldots$, *etc., all satisfy the relation*

$$P_n^\alpha \Phi_n^{u\alpha} = \Phi_n^{u\alpha} \qquad \textbf{(VII.85)}$$

then the eigenfunctions of H,

$$H\psi_n^{b\alpha} = E^{b\alpha}\psi_n^{b\alpha} \qquad \textbf{(VII.86)}$$

can be expressed in the form

$$\psi_n^{b\alpha} = \sum_u \Phi_n^{u\alpha} C_{ub} \qquad \textbf{(VII.87)}$$

In other words *a set of basis functions all of which transform like the nth basis function of the αth standard irreducible representation of the group $R_1, \ldots, R_g$, combine to form an eigenfunction of an operator H which commutes with all the group elements.* (We choose a standard representation from among the many equivalent forms of an irreducible representation when we define the projection operators P_n^α, Eq. (VII.45).) The extra indices u and b in Eq. (VII.87) are needed to distinguish between different functions all of which have the same transformation properties. You might ask why we have omitted the index n from the eigenvalue $E^{b\alpha}$. This is because *the d_α eigenfunctions $\psi_1^{b\alpha}, \psi_2^{b\alpha}, \ldots, \psi_{d_\alpha}^{b\alpha}$ must be degenerate:* From Eq. (VII.44) we can see that the operator

$$P_{mm'}^\alpha \equiv \frac{d_\alpha}{g} \sum_{j=1}^{g} D_{mm'}^\alpha(R_j^{-1}) R_j \qquad \text{(VII.88)}$$

will annihilate the function $\psi_{m'}^{b\alpha}$ and create the function $\psi_m^{b\alpha}$:

$$P_{mm'}^\alpha \psi_{m'}^{b\alpha} = \psi_m^{b\alpha} \qquad \text{(VII.89)}$$

But since $P_{mm'}^\alpha$ is constructed from group elements, it must commute with H. Therefore it cannot mix states of different energies, i.e.,

$$\int d\tau \psi_m^{b\alpha*} [P_{mm'}^\alpha, H] \psi_{m'}^{b\alpha} = (E_{m'}^{b\alpha} - E_m^{b\alpha}) \int d\tau \psi_m^{b\alpha*} P_{mm'}^\alpha \psi_{m'}^{b\alpha}$$

$$= (E_{m'}^{b\alpha} - E_m^{b\alpha}) = 0 \qquad \text{(VII.90)}$$

so that the set of d_α eigenfunctions $\psi_1^{b\alpha}, \ldots, \psi_{d_\alpha}^{b\alpha}$ must be degenerate,

$$E_{m'}^{b\alpha} = E_m^{b\alpha} \equiv E^{b\alpha}$$

A degeneracy which follows from symmetry in this way is called a 'due degeneracy'. Very rarely, as in the case of the hydrogen atom and the three-dimensional harmonic oscillator, one encounters a degeneracy which does not follow from geometrical symmetry. Such a degeneracy is called an 'accidental degeneracy'. (However, it is usually possible to show that the degeneracy is not really accidental but follows in fact from dynamical symmetry.)

We have been discussing the matrix representation of an operator H which commutes with all of the elements of a group. One might also ask if group theory can supply any rules for calculating the matrix elements of operators which do not commute with all the group elements. In order to answer this question let us first introduce the concept of a 'classified operator'. *A classified operator is defined as an operator which transforms according to the relation*

$$R_j \Omega_n^{u\alpha} R_j^{-1} = \sum_{n'} \Omega_{n'}^{u\alpha} D_{n'n}^\alpha(R_j) \qquad \textbf{(VII.91)}$$

where $D_{n'n}^\alpha$ is irreducible. When a classified operator acts on the basis function of another irreducible representation we obtain an entity which transforms according to the relation

$$R_j \Omega_n^{u\alpha} \Phi_m^{v\beta} = (R_j \Omega_n^{u\alpha} R_j^{-1})(R_j \Phi_m^{v\beta})$$

$$= \sum_{n'} \sum_{m'} \Omega_{n'}^{u\alpha} \Phi_{m'}^{v\beta} D_{n'n}^\alpha(R_j) D_{m'm}^\beta(R_j) \qquad \text{(VII.92)}$$

From Eq. (VII.92) we can see that *the set of functions $\Omega_n^{u\alpha} \Phi_m^{v\beta}$, $n = 1, \ldots, d_\alpha$, $m = 1, \ldots, d_\beta$, forms the basis for a representation of the group*

$$D_{(n'm'),(nm)}^{\alpha \times \beta}(R_j) \equiv D_{n'n}^\alpha(R_j) D_{m'm}^\beta(R_j) \qquad \textbf{(VII.93)}$$

The quantum theory of atoms, molecules, and photons

This is called the 'direct product' or 'Kroneker product' of the two irreducible representations D^α and D^β. The direct product of two irreducible representations is in general reducible. We can ask how many times each of the irreducible representations of the group is contained in it. In order to answer this question we need to find the character of a typical element in each class. If the element R_j is in the class k we have

$$\chi_k^{\alpha \times \beta} = \text{Tr}\left\{D^{\alpha \times \beta}(R_j)\right\}$$

$$= \sum_{n=1}^{d_\alpha} \sum_{m=1}^{d_\beta} D_{nn}^\alpha(R_j) D_{mm}^\beta(R_j) = \chi_k^\alpha \chi_k^\beta \qquad \text{(VII.94)}$$

Then, according to Eq. (VII.36), *we can calculate the number of times that the irreducible representation D^γ occurs in $D^{\alpha \times \beta}$ by multiplying $\chi_k^{\alpha \times \beta}$ by $\chi_k^{\gamma *}$ and summing over k.*

$$n_\gamma = \frac{g_k}{g} \sum_{k=1}^{r} \chi_k^{\gamma *} \chi_k^\alpha \chi_k^\beta \qquad \textbf{(VII.95)}$$

One usually expresses the fact that D^γ is contained n_γ times in $D^{\alpha \times \beta}$ by writing

$$D^\alpha \times D^\beta = n_1 D^1 + n_2 D^2 + \cdots \qquad \text{(VII.96)}$$

as we did in Eq. (VII.37). *The transformation matrix which reduces $D^{\alpha \times \beta}$ is called the matrix of Clebsch–Gordan coefficients.* For example, Wigner's Clebsch–Gordan coefficients, (Eq. 9.76) and Tables (4.1)–(4.3), form a unitary transformation matrix which reduces the direct product of two irreducible representations of the three-dimensional rotation group. However, as we see here, Wigner's Clebsch–Gordan coefficients are only a special case of a more general concept. In general the name is used to denote the transformation which reduces the direct product of two irreducible representations of any group. We said above that a classified operator $\Omega_n^{u\alpha}$, Eq. (VII.91), acting on the basis function $\Phi_m^{v\beta}$ of an irreducible representation gives a basis function of the direct product representation $D^{\alpha \times \beta}$. The transformation which reduces $D^{\alpha \times \beta}$ expresses $\Omega_n^{u\alpha}\Phi_m^{v\beta}$ as a linear combination of basis functions of the reduced representation;

$$\Omega_n^{u\alpha}\Phi_m^{v\beta} = \sum_{\gamma=1}^{r} \sum_{l=1}^{d_\gamma} C_{nm,l}^{\alpha\beta,\gamma} \Phi_l^{w\gamma} \qquad \text{(VII.97)}$$

In Eq. (VII.97) we have assumed that D^γ does not occur more than once in $D^{\alpha \times \beta}$. This is always the case in ordinary molecular point groups but in the so-called double groups (e.g., half-integral angular momentum) D^γ can occur twice in $D^{\alpha \times \beta}$. Therefore the discussion which follows does not cover the case of double groups. The function $\Phi_l^{w\gamma}$ which occurs on the right-hand side of Eq. (VII.97) is some function (not necessarily normalized) which

354

transforms like lth basis function of the γth standard irreducible representation. What sort of functions $\Phi_l^{w\gamma}$ we have on the right-hand side of Eq. (VII.97) depends, of course, on what sort of classified operator $\Omega_n^{u\alpha}$ and basis function $\Phi_m^{v\beta}$ we have on the left-hand side. However, if we insist that the representation $D_{n'n}^{\alpha}(R_j)$ which occurs in the definition of the classified operator $\Omega_n^{u\alpha}$, Eq. (VII.91), shall be a *standard* representation of D^{α} and if $\Phi_m^{v\beta}$ is the basis function of a *standard* representation of D^{β} then the matrix $D_{(n'm'),\,(nm)}^{\alpha\times\beta}(R_j)$ of Eq. (VII.93) will be independent of u and v. It follows that this standard form of $D^{\alpha\times\beta}$ can be reduced by a standard Clebsch–Gordan transformation $C_{nm,\,l}^{\alpha\beta,\,\gamma}$ which is independent of u and v.

Now, let us take the scalar product of $\Phi_p^{t\rho}$ with Eq. (VII.97), this gives

$$\int d\tau \Phi_p^{*t\rho}\Omega_n^{u\alpha}\Phi_m^{v\beta}$$

$$= \sum_{\gamma=1}^{r}\sum_{l=1}^{d_\gamma} C_{nm,\,l}^{\alpha\beta,\,\gamma}\int d\tau \Phi_p^{*t\rho}\Phi_l^{w\gamma}$$

$$= C_{nm,\,p}^{\alpha\beta,\,\rho}\int d\tau \Phi_p^{*t\rho}\Phi_p^{w\rho} \qquad\qquad \text{(VII.98)}$$

Now from Eq. (VII.88) we obtain the relation

$$\sum_{\sigma,\,m} P_{mq}^{\sigma}P_{qm}^{\sigma} = 1 \qquad\qquad \text{(VII.99)}$$

and

$$\int d\tau \Phi_p^{*t\rho}\Phi_p^{w\rho} = \sum_{\sigma,\,m}\int d\tau \Phi_p^{*t\rho}P_{mq}^{\sigma}P_{qm}^{\sigma}\Phi_p^{w\rho}$$

$$= \int d\tau \Phi_q^{*t\rho}\Phi_q^{w\rho} \qquad\qquad \text{(VII.100)}$$

so that the integral $\int d\tau \Phi_p^{*t\rho}\Phi_p^{w\rho}$ must be independent of p. Thus we have finally that

$$\int d\tau \Phi_p^{*t\rho}\Omega_n^{u\alpha}\Phi_m^{v\beta} = C_{nm,\,p}^{\alpha\beta,\,\rho}\,f(t\rho,\,u\alpha,\,v\beta) \qquad\qquad \textbf{(VII.101)}$$

where f is independent of n, m, and p. Equation (VII.101) is known as the Wigner–Eckart replacement theorem. It states that *the matrix element of a classified operator taken between basis functions of irreducible representations is proportional to the appropriate Clebsch–Gordan coefficient, the constant of proportionality being independent of the indices labelling the basis functions.* If D^{γ} does not occur in $D^{\alpha\times\beta}$ then $C_{nm,\,p}^{\alpha\beta,\,\gamma} = 0$ and a selection rule follows as a special case of Eq. (VII.101). In applying the Wigner–Eckart replacement theorem, two important provisions must be remembered, (and let us state them again for emphasis): First, *we must select from among the various equivalent forms of the irreducible representations a particular standard set and stick to it.* Otherwise the matrix element of Eq. (VII.101) will not be proportional to a standard Clebsch–Gordan coefficient! Secondly, the Wigner–Eckart theorem as it stands in Eq. (VII.101) cannot be applied to cases where D^γ occurs more than once in $D^{\alpha \times \beta}$.

References and notes

(1) H. Bethe, *Ann. d. Phys.*, **3**, 133 (1929).
(2) E. U. Condon, *Rev. Mod. Phys.*, **9**, 432 (1937).
(3) C. A. Coulson, *Nature*, **154**, 797 (1944).
(4) J. P. Dahl and C. J. Ballhausen, *Adv. Quan. Chem.*, **4**, 170 (1968).
(5) A. S. Davydov, *Zhur. Exsperim. i Teor. Fiz.*, **18**, 210 (1948).
(6) P. A. M. Dirac, *Proc. Roy. Soc.*, **A117**, 610 (1928).
(7) E. U. Condon, *Phys. Rev.*, **28**, 1182 (1926).
(8) J. Frenkel, *Phys. Rev.*, **37**, 1276 (1931).
(9) H. B. Gray and C. J. Ballhausen, *J. Am. Chem. Soc.*, **85**, 260 (1963).
(10) D. R. Hartree, *Proc. Camb. Phil. Soc.*, **24**, 89 (1927); V. Fock, *Z. Phys.*, **61**, (1930).
(11) E. Hückel, *Z. Phys.*, **70**, 204 (1931).
(12) A. D. Liehr and C. J. Ballhausen, *Ann. Phys.*, **6**, 134 (1959).
(13) P. O. Löwdin, *J. Chem. Phys.*, **18**, 365 (1950).
(14) P. O. Löwdin and O. Goscinski, *Int. J. Quant. Chem.*, **3**, 533 (1970). In the case of the hydrogen negative ion, independent Hartree–Fock variation followed by symmetry projection leads, as it should, to a bound-state orbital, ϕ_{15}, and a free-state orbital, $\phi_{15'}$. On the other hand, Kaplan and Kleiner (*Phys. Rev.* **156**, 1, (1967)), have shown that this procedure, applied to helium, leads to $\phi_{15} = \phi_{15'}$. In order to obtain different orbitals for different spins in the case of helium, we would need to perform the variational calculation *after* the symmetry projection. The procedure in which one applies the symmetry projection operators first and performs the variational calculation afterwards leads to Löwdin's extended Hartree–Fock scheme.
(15) N. Mataga and K. Nishimoto, *Z. Phys. Chem.*, **13**, 140 (1957).
(16) K. Ohno, *Notes on Molecular Orbital Calculation of π-Electron Systems*, Quantum Chemistry Group, Uppsala (1963).
(17) R. Peierls, *Ann. Phys.*, **13**, 905 (1932).
(18) J. A. Pople, *Trans Faraday Soc.*, **49**, 1375 (1953); R. Pariser and R. Parr, *J. Chem. Phys.*, **21**, 466, 767 (1953).
(19) J. A. Pople and G. A. Segal, *J. Chem. Phys.*, **44**, 3289 (1966).
(20) R. Sibley, J. Jortner, M. T. Vala, Jr., and S. A. Rice, *J. Chem. Phys.*, **42**, 2948 (1965).
(21) C. C. J. Roothaan, *Rev. Mod. Phys.*, **23**, 69 (1951).
(22) R. Schlapp and W. G. Penney, *Phys. Rev.*, **42**, 666 (1932).
(23) M. J. Stephen, *Proc. Camb. Phil. Soc.*, **54**, 81 (1958).
(24) G. E. Uhlenbeck and S. Goudschmidt, *Nature*, **117**, 264 (1926). The account of the discovery of spin, given in chapter 2, is somewhat oversimplified. The

interested reader can find a much more complete history of this event in *Sources of Quantum Mechanics*, edited by B. L. van der Waerden, North Holland (1967), Dover (1968).

(25) M. H. Cohen and F. Keffer, *Phys. Rev.*, **99**, 1128 (1955).

(26) P. P. Ewald, *Ann. Phys. Lpz.*, **64**, 253 (1921); M. Born and M. Bradburn, *Proc. Camb. Phil. Soc.*, **39**, 104 (1943).

(27) G. Wannier, *Phys. Rev.*, **52**, 191 (1937).

(28) J. H. Van Vleck, *Phys. Rev.*, **45**, 416 (1934).

(29) M. G. Mayer and A. L. Sklar, *J. Chem. Phys.*, **6**, 645 (1938).

(30) Prof. J. P. Dahl has pointed out to me that in the filling of subshells, an $n + l$ rule holds: Subshells are filled after increasing $n + l$ values. Whenever $n + l$ values are equal, the subshell with the lowest n value is filled first.

Bibliography

History of science

E. T. Bell, *Men of Mathematics*, Simon and Shuster (1937).
F. K. Richtmyer, *Introduction to Modern Physics*, McGraw-Hill (1928).
S. Rosenthal, editor, *Niels Bohr, His Life and Work*, North Holland (1967).
E. T. Whittaker, *A History of Theories of the Aether and Electricity*, Cambridge (1953).

Mathematical methods

L. Brillouin, *Les Tenseurs en Mécanique et en Elasticité*, Dover (1946).
R. Courant, *Differential and Integral Calculus*, Blackie and Son, London (1936).
J. N. Franklin, *Matrix Theory*, Prentice Hall (1968).
B. Friedman, *Principles and Techniques of Applied Mathematics*, Wiley (1956).
F. B. Hildebrand, *Advanced Calculus for Engineers*, Prentice Hall (1949).
F. E. Horn, *Elementary Matrix Algebra*, Macmillan (1964).
J. D. Jackson, *Mathematics for Quantum Mechanics*, Benjamin (1962).
J. Mathews and R. L. Walker, *Mathematical Methods of Physics*, Benjamin (1965).
P. Moon and D. E. Spencer, *Field Theory Handbook, Including Coordinate Systems, Differential Equations, and Their Solutions*, Springer-Verlag (1961).
P. M. Morse and H. Feshbach, *Methods of Theoretical Physics*, McGraw-Hill (1953).
I. S. Sokolnikoff and R. M. Redheffer, *Mathematics of Physics and Modern Engineering*, McGraw-Hill (1966).
R. Stuart, *Introduction to Fourier Analysis*, Chapman and Hall (1969).

Classical mechanics

H. Goldstein, *Classical Mechanics*, Addison Wesley (1959).
J. C. Slater and N. H. Frank, *Mechanics*, McGraw-Hill (1947).
A. Sommerfeld, *Mechanics*, Academic Press (1964).

General quantum theory

D. R. Bates, editor, *Quantum Theory*, Vol. 1, *Elements*, Academic Press (1961).
D. R. Bates, editor, *Quantum Theory*, Vol. 2, *Aggregates of Particles*, Academic Press (1962).

359

The quantum theory of atoms, molecules, and photons

H. A. Bethe and R. W. Jackiw, *Intermediate Quantum Mechanics*, Benjamin (1968).

D. Bohm, *Quantum Theory*, Prentice Hall (1951).

P. A. M. Dirac, *The Principles of Quantum Mechanics*, Clarendon, Oxford, 3rd edition (1947).

F. R. Halpern, *Special Relativity and Quantum Mechanics*, Prentice Hall (1968).

W. Heitler, *Elementary Wave Mechanics*, Oxford (1956).

H. A. Kramers, *Quantum Mechanics*, Dover (1964); North Holland (1957).

L. D. Landau and E. M. Lifshitz, *Quantum Mechanics*, Pergamon (1959).

P. O. Löwdin, editor, *Advances in Quantum Chemistry*, Academic Press (1964–).

P. O. Löwdin, editor, *Quantum Theory of Atoms, Molecules and the Solid State*, Academic Press (1966).

A. March, *Quantum Mechanics of Particles and Wave Fields*, Wiley (1951).

N. H. March, W. H. Young, and S. Sampanthar, *The Many-Body Problem in Quantum Mechanics*, Cambridge University Press (1967).

P. T. Mathews, *Introduction to Quantum Mechanics*, McGraw-Hill (1968).

R. D. Mattuck, *A Guide to Feyman Diagrams in the Many-Body Problem*, McGraw-Hill (1967).

A. Messiah, *Quantum Mechanics*, North Holland (1964).

P. Nozieres, *Theory of Interacting Fermi Systems*, Benjamin (1964).

L. Pauling and E. B. Wilson, *Introduction to Quantum Mechanics*, McGraw-Hill (1936).

Proceedings of the International Symposium on Atomic and Molecular Quantum Mechanics, *Rev. Mod. Phys.*, **35**, 415–733 (1963).

V. Rojansky, *Introductory Quantum Mechanics*, Prentice Hall (1938).

P. Roman, *Advanced Quantum Theory*, Addison Wesley (1965).

L. I. Schiff, *Quantum Mechanics*, McGraw-Hill (1955).

J. C. Slater, *Quantum Theory of Molecules and Solids*, Vols. **1** and **2**, McGraw-Hill (1963).

J. C. Slater, *Quantum Theory of Matter*, McGraw-Hill (1968).

D. Ter Haar, *Introduction to the Physics of Many-Body Systems*, Interscience (1958).

S. I. Tomonaga, *Quantum Mechanics*, North Holland (1965).

D. J. Thouless, *The Quantum Mechanics of Many-Body Systems*, Academic Press (1961).

J. M. Ziman, *Elements of Advanced Quantum Theory*, Cambridge (1969).

General molecular orbital theory

J. M. Anderson, *Introduction to Quantum Chemistry*, Benjamin (1969).

P. W. Atkins, *Molecular Quantum Mechanics*, Clarendon, Oxford (1970).

Borge Bak, *Elementary Introduction to Molecular Spectra*, North Holland (1954).

W. A. Bingel, *Theory of Molecular Spectra*, Wiley (1969).

E. Cartmell, *Valency and Molecular Structure*, Butterworth (1970).

C. A. Coulson, *Valence*, Oxford (1952).

H. Eyring, D. Henderson, and W. Jost, editors, *Physical Chemistry, an Advanced Treatise, Vol. 3, Electronic Structure of Atoms and Molecules, Vol. 4, Molecular Properties, Vol. 5, Valency*, Academic Press (1970).

H. Eyring, J. Walter, and G. E. Kemball, *Quantum Chemistry*, Wiley (1944).

Faraday Society Symposium, *Molecular Wave Functions*, Butterworth (1969).

S. Flügge, editor, *Handbuch der Physik*, Vol. 37, *Molecules*, Springer-Verlag (1961).

M. W. Hanna, *Quantum Mechanics in Chemistry*, Benjamin (1966).

R. de L. Kronig, *Band Spectra and Molecular Structure*, Cambridge (1930).

I. N. Levine, *Quantum Chemistry*, Allyn and Bacon (1970).

R. D. Levine, *Quantum Mechanics of Molecular Rate Processes*, Oxford University Press (1969).

J. W. Linnet, *Wave Mechanics and Valency*, Methuen (1960).

J. W. Linnet, *The Electronic Structure of Molecules*, Wiley (1964).

P. O. Löwdin and B. Pullman, editors, *Molecular Orbitals in Chemistry, Physics and Biology*, Academic Press (1964).

R. McWeeny and B. T. Sutcliffe, *Methods of Molecular Quantum Mechanics*, Academic Press (1969).

J. N. Murrell and A. J. Harget, *Semi-empirical Self-consistent-field Molecular-orbital Theory of Molecules*, Wiley-Interscience (1972).

J. N. Murrel, S. F. A. Kettel, and J. M. Tedder, *Valence Theory*, Wiley (1965).

L. Pauling, *The Nature of the Chemical Bond*, Cornell University Press, 2nd edition (1945).

T. E. Peacock, *Foundations of Quantum Chemistry*, Wiley (1968).

F. L. Pilar, *Elementary Quantum Chemistry*, McGraw-Hill (1968).

K. S. Pitzer, *Quantum Chemistry*, Prentice Hall (1953).

F. O. Rice and F. Teller, *The Structure of Matter*, Wiley (1949).

W. G. Richards and J. A. Horsley, *Ab Initio Molecular Orbital Calculations for Chemists*, Oxford University Press (1970).

W. G. Richards, T. E. H. Walker, and R. K. Hinkley, *A Bibliography of Ab Initio Molecular Wave Functions*, Oxford (1971).

N. V. Riggs, *Quantum Chemistry*, Macmillan (1969).

C. J. H. Schutte, *The Wave Mechanics of Atoms, Molecules and Ions*, Arnold (1968).

O. Sinanoglu, editor, *Modern Quantum Chemistry*, Academic Press (1965).

O. Sinanoglu and K. B. Wiberg, *Sigma Molecular Orbital Theory*, Yale University Press (1970).

M. G. Veselov, *et al.*, *Methods of Quantum Chemistry*, Academic Press (1965).

π-electrons in flat organic molecules

R. Daudel, R. Lefevre, and C. Moser, *Quantum Chemistry, Methods and Applications*, Interscience (1959).

M. J. S. Dewar, *The Molecular Orbital Theory of Organic Chemistry*, McGraw-Hill (1969).

J. N. Murrell, *The Theory of the Electronic Spectra of Organic Molecules*, Wiley (1963).

R. G. Parr, *The Quantum Theory of Molecular Electronic Structure*, Benjamin (1963).

T. E. Peacock, *Electronic Properties of Heterocyclic Molecules*, Academic Press (1965).

J. R. Platt, *Systematics of Electronic Spectra of Conjugated Molecules*, Wiley (1964).

J. R. Platt, *et al.*, *Free-Electron Theory of Conjugated Molecules*, Wiley (1964).

J. A. Pople, D. P. Santry, and G. A. Segal, *Approximate Self-Consistent Molecular Orbital Theory. I: Invariant Procedures*, *J. Chem. Phys.*, **43**, S 129 (1965).

The quantum theory of atoms, molecules, and photons

J. D. Roberts, *Molecular Orbital Calculations*, Benjamin (1961).
L. Salem, *The Molecular Orbital Theory of Conjugated Systems*, Benjamin (1966).
C. Sandorfy, *Electronic Spectra and Quantum Chemistry*, Prentice Hall (1964).
W. T. Simpson, *Theories of Electrons in Molecules*, Prentice Hall (1962).
A. Streitwieser, Jr., *Molecular Orbital Theory*, Wiley (1961).

Quantum biochemistry

L. Augenstein, editor, *Bioenergetics*, Academic Press (1960).
L. Augenstein, R. Mason, and B. Rosenberg, editors, *Physical Processes in Radiation Biology*, Academic Press (1964).
M. Florkin and H. S. Mason, editors, *Comparative Biochemistry*, Vol. 1, *Sources of Free Energy*, Academic Press (1960).
T. W. Goodwin, editor, *Biochemistry of Chloroplasts*, Academic Press, Vol. 1 (1966), Vol. 2 (1967).
M. Kasha and B. Pullman, editors, *Horizons of Biochemistry*, Academic Press (1962).
I. M. Klotz, *Some Principles of Energetics in Biochemical Reactions*, Academic Press (1957).
B. Pullman and A. Pullman, *Quantum Biochemistry*, Wiley (1963).
B. Pullman, editor, *Electronic Aspects of Biochemistry*, Academic Press (1964).
Albert Szent-Györgyi, *Bioenergetics*, Academic Press (1957).
Albert Szent-Györgyi, *Introduction to a Submolecular Biology*, Academic Press (1960).
M. Weisbluth, editor, *Quantum Aspects of Polypeptides and Polynucleotides*, *Biopolymers Symposia* 1, Interscience (1965).

Solid state theory

L. Brillouin, *Wave Propagation in Periodic Structures*, Dover (1953); McGraw-Hill (1946).
J. Calloway, *Energy Band Theory*, Academic Press (1964).
D. P. Craig and S. H. Walmsley, *Excitons in Molecular Crystals*, Benjamin (1968).
A. S. Davydov, *Theory of Molecular Excitons* (translated by M. Kasha and M. Oppenheimer Jr.), McGraw-Hill (1962).
D. L. Dexter and R. S. Knox, *Excitons*, Interscience (1965).
Charles Kittel, *Introduction to Solid State Physics*, Wiley (1956).
R. S. Knox, *Theory of Excitons*, *Solid State Physics*, Supplement 3, Academic Press (1963).
D. S. McClure, *Electronic Spectra of Molecules and Ions in Crystals*, Academic Press (1959).
N. F. Mott and H. Jones, *The Theory of the Properties of Metals and Alloys*, Dover (1958); Clarendon, Oxford (1936).
R. E. Peierls, *Quantum Theory of Solids*, Oxford (1956).
F. Seitz, *The Modern Theory of Solids*, McGraw-Hill (1940).
W. Shockley, *Electrons and Holes in Semiconductors*, Van Nostrand (1950).
J. C. Slater, *Quantum Theory of Molecules and Solids*, Vol. 2, *Symmetry and Energy Bands in Crystals*, McGraw-Hill (1965).

J. C. Slater, *Insulators, Semiconductors and Metals*, McGraw-Hill (1967).
A. H. Wilson, *The Theory of Metals*, Cambridge (1954).
J. M. Ziman, *Principles of the Theory of Solids*, Cambridge (1971).

The interaction between matter and radiation

A. I. Akheizer and V. B. Berestetskii, *Quantum Electrodynamics*, Interscience (1965).
H. C. Allen, Jr. and P. C. Cross, *Molecular Vib-Rotors*, Wiley (1963).
P. Crabbe, *Optical Rotatory Dispersion and Circular Dichroism in Organic Chemistry*, (1965).
D. J. Caldwell and H. Eyring, *Theory of Optical Activity*, Wiley (1971).
C. Djerassi, *Optical Rotatory Dispersion*, McGraw-Hill (1960).
Ya. G. Dorfman, *Diamagnetism and the Chemical Bond*, Edward Arnold (1965).
Faraday Society Symposium, *Magneto Optical Effects*, Butterworth (1970).
R. P. Feynman, *Quantum Electrodynamics*, Benjamin (1961).
L. L. Foldy, *Relativistic Wave Equations*, in *Quantum Theory*, Vol. **3**, edited by D. R. Bates, Academic Press (1962).
G. N. Fowler, *Noncovariant Quantum Theory of Radiation* and *Covariant Theory of Radiation*, in *Quantum Theory*, Vol. **3**, edited by D. R. Bates, Academic Press (1962).
W. Heitler, *The Quantum Theory of Radiation*, Oxford University Press, 3rd edition (1954).
G. Herzberg, *Spectra of Diatomic Molecules*, van Nostrand (1950).
L. Landau and E. Lifshitz, *The Classical Theory of Fields*, Addison Wesley (1951).
T. M. Lowry, *Optical Rotatory Power*, Dover (1964); Longmans, Green and Co. (1935).
F. Mandl, *Introduction to Quantum Field Theory*, Interscience (1959).
J. D. Memory, *Quantum Theory of Magnetic Resonance Parameters*, McGraw-Hill (1968).
W. K. H. Panosky and M. Phillips, *Classical Electricity and Magnetism*, Addison-Wesley (1955).
J. R. Partington, *An Advanced Treatise on Physical Chemistry Vol. IV, Physico-Chemical Optics, Vol. V, Molecular Spectra and Structure*, Longmans (1954).
E. A. Power, *Introduction to Quantum Electrodynamics*, Longmans (1964).
G. T. Rado and H. Suhl, editors, *Magnetism*, Academic Press (1965).
L. Rosenfeld, *Theory of Electrons*, Dover (1965); North Holland (1951).
G. Snatzke, editor, *Optical Rotatory Dispersion and Circular Dichroism in Organic Chemistry*, Heydon and Son (1967).
J. A. Stratton, *Electromagnetic Theory*, McGraw-Hill (1941).
J. H. Van Vleck, *The Theory of Electric and Magnetic Susceptibilities*, Clarendon, Oxford (1932).
J. S. Waugh, *Advances in Magnetic Resonance*, Academic Press (1966).
R. M. White, *Quantum Theory of Magnetism*, McGraw-Hill (1970).
E. B. Wilson, Jr., J. C. Decius, and P. C. Cross, *Molecular Vibrations*, McGraw-Hill (1955).
A. B. Zahlan, editor, *The Triplet State*, Cambridge (1967).

Ligand field theory and the theory of atomic spectra

A. Abragam and B. Bleaney, *Electron Paramagnetic Resonance of Transition Ions*, Clarendon (1970).

C. J. Ballhausen, *Introduction to Ligand Field Theory*, McGraw-Hill (1962).

C. J. Ballhausen and H. B. Gray, *Molecular Orbital Theory*, Benjamin (1964).

D. M. Brink and D. R. Satchler, *Angular Momentum*, Clarendon, Oxford (1968).

E. U. Condon and G. H. Shortley, *The Theory of Atomic Spectra*, Cambridge (1953).

T. M. Dunn, D. S. McClure, and R. G. Peterson, *Some Aspects of Crystal Field Theory*, Harper and Row (1965).

B. N. Figgis, *Introduction to Ligand Fields*, Interscience (1966).

H. B. Gray, *Electrons and Chemical Bonding*, Benjamin (1964).

J. S. Griffeth, *The Theory of Transition Metal Ions*, Cambridge (1964).

B. R. Judd, *Operator Techniques in Atomic Spectroscopy*, McGraw-Hill (1963).

Brian Judd, *Second Quantization and Atomic Spectroscopy*, Johns Hopkins Press (1967).

I. B. Levinson and A. A. Nikitin, *Handbook for Theoretical Computation of Line Intensities in Atomic Spectra*, Israel Program for Scientific Translations, Jerusalem (1965).

L. E. Orgel, *An Introduction to Transition Metal Chemistry Ligand-Field Theory*, Methuen (1960).

M. E. Rose, *Elementary Theory of Angular Momentum*, Wiley (1957).

H. L. Schläfer and G. Gliemann, *Basic Principles of Ligand Field Theory*, Wiley-Interscience (1969).

O. Sinanoglu and K. Brueckner, *Three Approaches to Electron Correlation in Atoms*, Yale University Press (1970).

J. C. Slater, *Quantum Theory of Atomic Structure*, McGraw-Hill (1960).

S. Sugano, Y. Tanabe and H. Kamimura, *Multiplets of Transition-Metal Ions in Crystals*, Academic Press (1970).

H. Watanabe, *Operator Methods in Ligand Field Theory*, Prentice Hall (1966).

Group theory

P. W. Atkins, M. S. Child, and C. S. G. Phillips, *Tables for Group Theory*, Oxford (1970).

F. Albert Cotton, *Chemical Applications of Group Theory*, Interscience (1963).

G. G. Hall, *Applied Group Theory*, Longmans (1967).

Morten Hammermesh, *Group Theory*, Addison-Wesley (1962).

V. Heine, *Group Theory in Quantum Mechanics*, Pergamon (1960).

R. M. Hochstrasser, *Molecular Aspects of Symmetry*, Benjamin (1966).

J. M. Hollas, *Symmetry in Molecules*, Chapman (1972).

H. H. Jaffé and M. Orchin, *Symmetry in Chemistry*, Wiley (1965).

R. S. Knox and A. Gold, *Symmetry in the Solid State*, Benjamin (1964).

J. W. Leech and D. J. Newman, *How to Use Groups*, Methuen (1969).

E. M. Loebl, editor, *Group Theory and its Applications*, Academic Press (1968).

J. S. Lomont, *Applications of Finite Group Theory*, Academic Press (1959).

R. McWeeny, *Symmetry*, Pergamon (1963).

Bibliography

P. H. E. Meijer and E. Bauer, *Group Theory*, North Holland (1962).

M. Motenberg, R. Bivins, N. Metropolis, and J. K. Wooten, Jr., *The 3-j and 6-j Symbols*, Technology Press, M.I.T., Cambridge, Mass., and Crosby Lockwood and Son Ltd., London (1959).

F. D. Murnaghan, *The Theory of Group Representations*, Johns Hopkins Press, Baltimore (1938).

M. Orchin and H. H. Jaffe, *Symmetry, Orbitals and Spectra*, Wiley (1971).

M. I. Petrashen and E. D. Trifonov, *Group Theory in Quantum Mechanics*, Iliffe (1969).

D. S. Schönland, *Molecular Symmetry*, Van Nostrand (1965).

H. Suzuki, *Electronic Absorption Spectra and Geometry of Organic Molecules*, Academic Press (1967).

M. Tinkham, *Group Theory and Quantum Mechanics*, McGraw-Hill (1964).

D. S. Urch, *Orbitals and Symmetry*, Penguin (1970).

Hermann Weyl, *The Theory of Groups in Quantum Mechanics*, Dover (1931).

E. P. Wigner, *Group Theory and its Applications to the Quantum Mechanics of Atomic Spectra*, Academic Press (1959).

Index

Index

Descartes, René, 3, 15
Determinental wave Function, 160
Diagonalization of a matrix, 112, 113–5, 307, 333
Diagonal matrix, 111
Diatomic molecule, vibration of nuclei, 215
Diatomic molecules, heteronuclear, 145, 146
Dichroism,
circular, 248–9
linear, 248–9
Differentiation, 6, 7, 8
partial, 18, 19
second derivative, 19
Different orbitals for different spins method, 117
Diffraction, in mechanics, 44, 45
in optics, 41, 44, 45, 60, 209
of electrons, 209–13
of neutrons, 212
of X-rays, 209–13
Dipole–dipole interaction, 199
Dipole–Quadrupole interaction, 200
Dirac, P.A.M., 62, 69, 82, 237–43, 258
Dirac bra and ket notation, 109
Dirac delta function, 102, 104, 109, 110, 330
definition of, 101
Dirac's equation, non-relativistic limit, 241–2
Dirac's relativistic wave equation, 69, 82, 131, 237–71
Direct lattice, 188–96, 205
Direct product of representations, in group theory, 353–6
Discrete spectrum, 105
Displacement from equilibrium, 17, 18, 21, 22
Dispersion of light, 256–71
Dispersion of sound, 233–6
Divergence of a vector, 318
DODS method, 177, 178
Doubly excited configurations, 170–1, 174, 178
d-shell multiplets, 283–304
energies of, 293
Dyson, F. J., 258

Effective charge, 146
Effective nuclear charge, 159

Effective potential, 73, 74
for nuclear motion, 214–5
Ehrenfest's theorem, 96
Eigenfunctions, 94, 95, 98, 99, 111, 148
Eigenvalues, 94, 95, 98, 99
Einstein, Albert, 50, 52, 53, 61, 62, 64, 67, 68, 95
Electric dipole approximation, 244, 255, 269
Electric quadrupole terms in radiation theory, 270–1
Electrodynamics, 50
Electromagnetic field, 56
Electromagnetic potential, 55, 56, 59
Electromagnetic waves, 51, 60
Electron affinities of the elements, table of, 89–91
Electron affinity, 174, 177
Electron configuration of the elements, 86, 87, 88
table of, 89, 90, 91
Electron creation and annihilation operators, 259–304
Electron,
discovery of, 61, 63
mass of an, 65
theory of metals, 63
volts, 65
Electron-hole bound state, 203
Electron-photon system, Hamiltonian of an, 261–2
Electrostatic potential, 54
Ellis, C. D., 67
Emission of a photon, 244, 252, 265-6
Empirical parameters, calibration of, 174
Energies of molecular orbitals, 143–45, 151–3
Energy,
in wave mechanics, 69
kinetic, 27, 64
of a many electron system, 166, 167, 261, 262
of an harmonic oscillator, 226
of excitation, 166
of multiplets, 286–93
potential, 27, 48, 53, 64
total, 38, 39, 65
units, 65
Equations of motion of a charged particle, 56

370

Index

THIS BOOK HAS BEEN SET IN MONOPHOTO TIMES NEW ROMAN
AND PRINTED AND BOUND IN GREAT BRITAIN BY
WILLIAM CLOWES & SONS, LIMITED, LONDON, BECCLES AND COLCHESTER